The Collected Oz

Volume Five

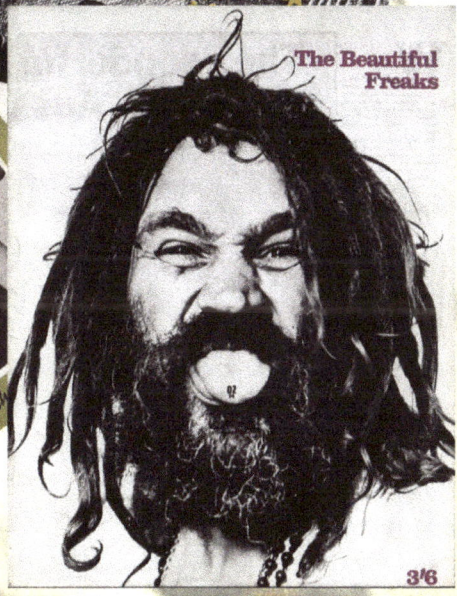

Richard Neville et. al.

Edited by Jonathan Downes
Typeset by Jonathan Downes
Cover and Internal Layout by Jon Downes for Gonzo Multimedia
Using Microsoft Word 2000, Microsoft , Publisher 2000, Adobe Photoshop.

First edition published 2016 by Gonzo Multimedia

c/o Brooks City,
6th Floor New Baltic House
65 Fenchurch Street,
London EC3M 4BE
Fax: +44 (0)191 5121104
Tel: +44 (0) 191 5849144
International Numbers:
Germany: Freephone 08000 825 699
USA: Freephone 18666 747 289

ISBN: 978-1-908728-62-3

For Richard, Felix and Jim

OZ Obscenity Trial — Old Bailey London 1971

Trial begins 22 June
Any information contact Friends of Oz,
39a Pottery Lane, London W11. 01-229 5887.

Introduction

Back in the day, and this particular day was about twenty years ago, I was friendly with a notorious Irish Republican musical ensemble known as *Athenrye*, and particularly with their guitarist, a guy called Terry Manton. I was very angry about a lot of things at the time, and quite how drinking with various groups of slightly dodgy Hibernians actually made me feel any better I am not sure, but it seemed to have the desired effect.

09

On one of their albums there is a song about Éamon de Valera. For those of you not in the know, over to those jolly nice people at Wikipedia.

"Éamon de Valera first registered as George de Valero; changed some time before 1901 to Edward de Valera; 14 October 1882 – 29 August 1975) was a prominent politician and statesman in twentieth-century Ireland. His political career spanned over half a century, from 1917 to 1973; he served several terms as head of government and head of state. He also led the introduction of the Constitution of Ireland.

De Valera was a leader in the War of Independence and of the anti-Treaty opposition in the ensuing Irish Civil War (1922–1923). After leaving Sinn Féin in 1926 due to its policy of abstentionism, he founded Fianna Fáil, and was head of government (President of the Executive Council, later Taoiseach) from 1932 to 1948, 1951 to 1954, and 1957 to 1959, when he resigned after being elected as President of Ireland. His political creed evolved from militant republicanism to social and cultural conservatism.

Assessments of de Valera's career have varied; he has often been characterised as

Lucky man of our times

Chorus
He was loved he was hated he was cherished despised
There were rivers of tears when the chieftain he died
But love him or hate him I cannot decide
What to make of old Dev this man of our times."

And it ended up:

"Now Spain had it's Franco and France it's De Gaulle
We had our Dev and god rest his soul"

It has been many years since I bounced up and down in a weird Gaelic moshpit shouting "Tiocfaidh ár lá" and I strongly doubt whether I shall ever do so again. My foray into such things had more to do with my reaction to the way that I perceived that I had been treated by my family over my particularly scabrous divorce, than any genuine political fervour, although I thought then (and think now) that the British history in Ireland has not been our greatest or most honourable hour. However, today I have had that song going round and around my head, ever since I read an email from Tony Palmer telling me that Richard Neville had died at the age of 74, in Byron Bay, New South Wales, the Australian hippy enclave where Gilli Smyth breathed her last only a few days before.

Now I never met Neville. Our acquaintanceship was confined to two emails about five years ago when I was working on the new edition of Tony Palmer's *The Trials of Oz*. I exchanged a few more emails with Jim Anderson, and had no contact whatsoever with Felix Dennis, so I cannot really be called an insider of the *Oz* scene. But Neville came out with one of my favourite quotes from the counterculture: "There is some corner of a foreign field that is forever Woodstock", and was an undeniably major figure in that much maligned social movement.

He seemed to be someone who brought out strong reactions in people. Whilst I was working on *The Trials of Oz* I discovered that people were either terribly fond of the man or disliked him intensely. I never found anyone who was ambivalent towards him. Even after his death, as I sent emails around the usual suspects asking for their memories of him, most people refused to be drawn one way or the other, with those who had been friends with him at various periods of their lives being totally devastated that they had woken up this morning to a planet on which Richard Neville was no longer alive.

Me? I am no better than any of the others. I have no knowledge of him personally, and whereas I found large chunks of *Oz* unreadable, I was impressed by his book *Playpower* and in the passages about him in Tony Palmer's book he struck an undeniably heroic figure against the same sort of establishment malice which had (as alluded to above) turned me against my parents twenty years back.

His book *Hippy Hippy Shake* was entertaining, even though its hedonism left a slightly bitter taste in one's mouth, but I remember being told that the movie that was made from it was so bad that several of the major figures portrayed refused to let it come out. In July 2007, in a piece for *The Guardian*, feminist author Germaine Greer vehemently expressed her displeasure at being depicted, writing, "You used to have to die before assorted hacks started munching your remains and modelling a new version of you out of their own excreta." Greer refused to be involved with the film, just as she declined to read Neville's memoir before it was published (he had offered to change anything she found offensive). She did not want to meet with Emma Booth, who portrays her in the film, and concluded her article with her only advice for the actress: "Get an honest job."

So where is this taking me? I truly don't know, but if there had not been a Richard Neville, there might well not have been a *Gonzo Weekly* magazine. I first read *The Trials of Oz* whilst on holiday with my patients back when I was a Registered Nurse for the Mentally Subnormal [RNMS] nearly thirty years ago, and it was one of the sacred texts, together with *A Series of Shock Slogans and Mindless Token Tantrums* by Penny Rimbaud et al, that set me on the path that I am on now. But when I finally read the *Schoolkid's Oz*, I thought it was puerile bollocks, and was massively underwhelmed.

And I too find it hard to adjust to the fact that I have woken up this morning to a planet on which Richard Neville was no longer alive.

So, if I may:

"He was loved he was hated he was cherished despised
There were rivers of tears when the Oz editor died
But love him or hate him I cannot decide
What to make of old Nev this man of our times."

Hare Bol Mr Neville

OUTCRY AS OZ EDITORS ARE JAILED

Labour MPs attack 'act of revenge'   *Daily Telegraph*

FURY OVER OZ JAILINGS

OZ: OBSCENE! BUT WHY THE FEROCIOUS SENTENCES?

Angry MPs join the wave of protest   *The Sun*

Oz sentences — Labour MPs sign protest

Daily Express

COMMENT

MPs condemn OZ gaolings as 'Establishment revenge'   *The Guardian*

Demonstrations and protests against 'Oz' jail sentences

'Shocked MPs protest: It looks like revenge'

Fury as three editors are jailed   *Daily Mirror*

STORM OVER OZ SENTENCES

Daily Mail

Apple are donating royalties on this record to the Oz Obscenity Fund

In Mitigation

So what was *Oz?* And why was it so important?

OZ was an underground alternative magazine. First published in Sydney, Australia, in 1963, a second version appeared in London, England from 1967 and is better known.

The original Australian *OZ* took the form of a satirical magazine published between 1963 and 1969, while the British incarnation was a "psychedelic hippy" magazine which appeared from 1967 to 1973. Strongly identified as part of the underground press, it was the subject of two celebrated obscenity trials, one in Australia in 1964 and the other in the United Kingdom in 1971. On both occasions the magazine's editors were acquitted on appeal after initially being found guilty and sentenced to harsh jail terms. An earlier, 1963 obscenity charge was dealt with expeditiously when, upon the advice of a solicitor, the three editors pleaded guilty.

The central editor throughout the magazine's life in both Australia and Britain was Richard Neville. Co-editors of the Sydney version were Richard Walsh and Martin Sharp. Co-editors of the London version were Jim Anderson and, later, Felix Dennis.

In early 1966 Neville and Sharp travelled to the UK and in early 1967, with fellow Australian Jim Anderson, they founded the London *OZ*. Contributors included Germaine Greer, artist and filmmaker Philippe Mora, illustrator Stewart Mackinnon, photographer Robert Whitaker, journalist Lillian Roxon, cartoonist Michael Leunig, Angelo Quattrocchi, Barney Bubbles and David Widgery.

With access to new print stocks, including metallic foils, new fluorescent inks and the freedom of layout offered by the offset printing system, Sharp's artistic skills came to the fore and *OZ* quickly won renown as one of the most visually exciting publications of its day. Several editions of *Oz* included dazzling psychedelic wrap-around or pull-out posters by Sharp, London design duo Hapshash and the Coloured Coat and others; these instantly became sought-after collectors' items and now command high prices. Another innovation was the cover of *Oz* No.11, which included a collection of detachable adhesive labels, printed in either red, yellow or green. The all-graphic "Magic Theatre" edition (*OZ* No.16, November 1968), overseen by Sharp and Mora, has been described by British author Jonathon Green as "arguably the greatest achievement of the entire British underground press". During this period Sharp also created the two famous psychedelic album covers for the group Cream, Disraeli Gears and Wheels Of Fire.

Sharp's involvement gradually decreased during 1968-69 and the "Magic Theatre" edition was one of his last major contributions to the magazine. In his place, young Londoner Felix Dennis, who had been selling issues on the street, was eventually brought in as Neville and Anderson's new partner. The magazine regularly enraged the British Establishment with a range of left-field stories including heavy critical coverage of the Vietnam War and the anti-war movement, discussions of drugs, sex and alternative lifestyles, and contentious political stories, such as the magazine's revelations about the torture of citizens under the rule of the military junta in Greece.

In 1970, reacting to criticism that *OZ* had lost touch with youth, the editors put a notice in the magazine inviting "school kids" to edit an issue. The opportunity was taken up by around 20 secondary school students (including Charles Shaar Murray and Deyan Sudjic), who were responsible for *OZ* No.28 (May 1970), generally known as "Schoolkids OZ". This term was widely misunderstood to mean that it was intended for schoolchildren, whereas it was an issue that had been created by them. As Richard Neville said in his opening statement, other issues had been assembled by gay people and members of the Female Liberation Movement. One of the resulting articles was a highly sexualised Rupert Bear parody. It was created by 15-year-old schoolboy Vivian Berger by pasting the head of Rupert onto the lead character of an X-rated satirical cartoon by Robert Crumb.

OZ was one of several 'underground' publications targeted by the Obscene Publications Squad, and their offices had already been raided on several occasions, but the conjunction of schoolchildren, and what some viewed as obscene material, set the scene for the *Oz* obscenity trial of 1971.

The trial was, at the time, the longest obscenity trial in British legal history, and it was the first time that an obscenity charge was combined with the charge of conspiring to corrupt public morals. Defence witnesses included artist Feliks Topolski, comedian Marty Feldman, artist and drugs activist Caroline Coon, DJ John Peel, musician and writer George Melly, legal philosopher Ronald Dworkin and academic Edward de Bono.

At the conclusion of the trial the "OZ Three" were found not guilty on the conspiracy charge, but they were convicted of two lesser offences and sentenced to imprisonment; although Dennis was given a lesser sentence because the judge, Justice Michael Argyle, considered that Dennis was "very much less intelligent" than the others. Shortly after the verdicts were handed down, they were taken to prison and their long hair forcibly cut, an act which caused an even greater stir on top of the already considerable outcry surrounding the trial and verdict.

The best known images of the trial come from the committal hearing, at which Neville, Dennis and Anderson all appeared, wearing rented schoolgirl costumes.

At the appeal trial (where the defendants appeared wearing long wigs) it was found that Justice Argyle had grossly misdirected the jury on numerous occasions and the defence also alleged that Berger, who was called as a prosecution witness, had been harassed and assaulted by police. The convictions were overturned. Years later, Felix Dennis told author Jonathon Green that on the night before the appeal was heard, the *OZ* editors were taken to a secret meeting with the Chief Justice, Lord Widgery, who reportedly said that Argyle had made a "fat mess" of the trial, and informed them that they would be acquitted, but insisted that they had to agree to give up work on *OZ*. Dennis also stated that, in his opinion, MPs Tony Benn and Michael Foot had interceded with Widgery on their behalf.

Despite their supposed undertaking to Lord Widgery, *OZ* continued after the trial, and thanks to the intense public interest the trial generated, its circulation briefly rose to 80,000. However its popularity faded over the next two years and by the time the last issue (*OZ* No.48) was published in November 1973 Oz Publications was £20,000 in debt and the magazine had "no readership worth the name".

We are publishing these magazines in these collected editions, partly as a tribute to the late Richard Neville (1943-2016) and partly because we believe that they constitute a valuable socio-political document reflecting the counterculture of 1967-74. This collection has been made available due to its historical and research importance. It contains explicit language and images that reflect attitudes of the era in which the material was originally published, and that some viewers may find confronting. However, we have taken the decision to blank out a very few images which would be seen as unacceptable in today's society.

Times have changed a lot in the past half century. The magazine's obsession with pornography, for example, has not stood the test of time very well, and some of the typography is so muddy as to be unreadable. Every effort has been made by the present publishers to clean up the typography, but in most cases it proved to be impossible, so we have left it as it was. The *Oz* readers of the late 1960s were unable to read it. Why should the present generation be any different?

Some of the pictures in the original magazine, especially artwork by Martin Sharp, was printed so it could fold out into a poster. We have therefore included these twice - as per the original pages so they can be read easily, and as extrapolations of the original artwork. Richard Neville stipulated in the extract from the notorious *Schoolkid's Oz* reproduced below that the material in these magazines could be used for any purpose, and we are taking him at his word.

Peace and Love

Ronnie Rooster
September 2016

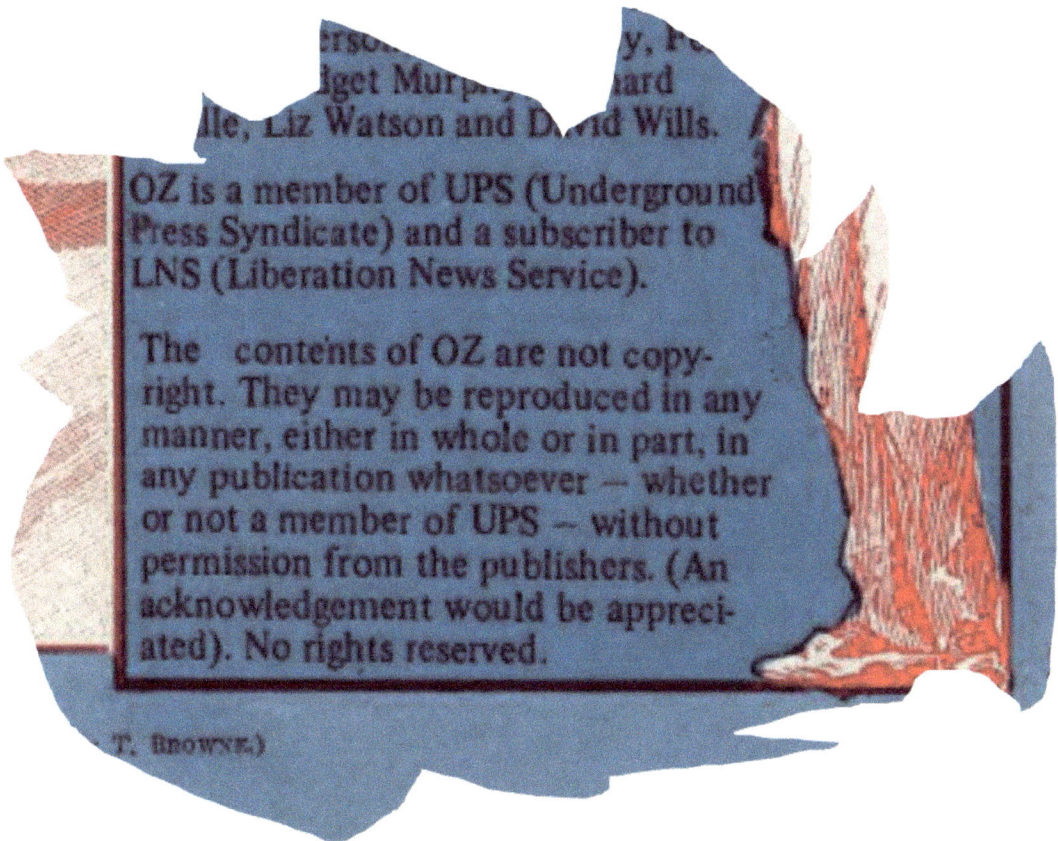

erso... y, ...
...get Murp..., ...ard
...lle, Liz Watson and D...id Wills.

OZ is a member of UPS (Underground Press Syndicate) and a subscriber to LNS (Liberation News Service).

The contents of OZ are not copyright. They may be reproduced in any manner, either in whole or in part, in any publication whatsoever — whether or not a member of UPS — without permission from the publishers. (An acknowledgement would be appreciated). No rights reserved.

T. Brown...)

OZ

8 PAGE COMIC SPLURGE
Pete Townsnend Speaks
Living Theatre Shrieks
Bernadette Devlin Freaks Out
CHE's Consentual Sodomy
Murray Roman BURNS
Plant Your Own Pot
John Gerassi Lives the Revol-
ution.
PLUS famous
regular features:
Hip-pocrates,
Poverty Cooking,
Magnaphall Ad.

No 21 3s

elektra

Records present for your

AMAZEMENT

AMUSEMENT

TITILLATION

DIVERSION

&

SUBVERSION

OUTRAGEOUS

z:

OZ is published monthly by OZ Publications Ink Ltd., 52 Princedale Road, London, W 11. Phone 229·7841. Directors: Richard Neville, Andrew Fisher.

OZ appears with the help of: Jon Goodchild, Felix Dennis, Louise Ferrier, Brigid Harrison, Keith Morris, Lyn Richards, Ken Petty, Miss Murphy, Phillipe von Mora, Jim Anderson & Martin Sharp.

Typesetting: Papyrotype. *Distribution: Britain* (overground) Moore-Harness Ltd., 11 Lever Street, London, EC1. Phone: CLE 4882 *(Underground)* ECAL, 22 Betterton Street, London, WC2. Phone TEM 8606. Transmutation. Guildford 65694. *California:* Rattner Distributors, 2428 McGee St, Berkley, Calif. 94703. *Holland:* Thomas Rap, Regulierdwarsstraat 91, Amsterdam, Tel: 020-227065 *Denmark:* George Streeton, The Underground, Larshjorn straede 13, Copenhagen K. *Printed by:* OZ Publications Ink Ltd, 52 Princedale Rd; London W11

Advertising: Felix Dennis, 44, Wandsworth Bridge Road, London, S W 6. 01-736 1330

REX ORGAN, M. D.

POT IS AS DANGEROUS AS MASTURBATION! IT CAN MAKE YOU CRAZY! THESE DAMN HIPPIES ARE CRAZY! THEY DON'T KNOW SIMPLE FACTS--

IT'S A MEDICAL FACT THAT TOADS CAUSE WARTS! AND YOU GET THE CLAP FROM TOILET SEATS!

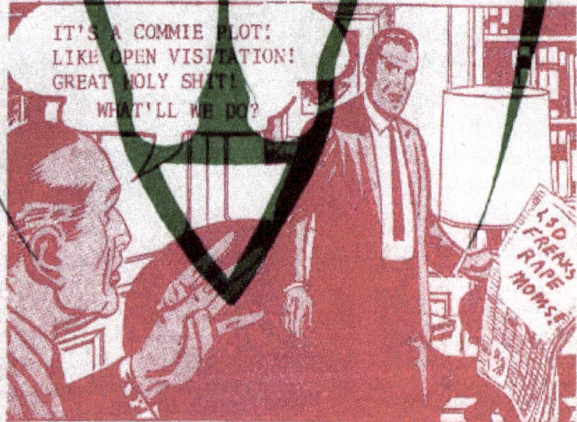

IT'S A COMMIE PLOT! LIKE OPEN VISITATION! GREAT HOLY SHIT! WHAT'LL WE DO?

2

Dear Sir
I am living in Bulgaria. I am eighteen years old and I live with my mamma and pappa and I think this idea might interest you . . . Do you know what 'an absolutely dull life' It is for me and for my friends. We've tried many things but they are not so much. Can you give me some advice or help me in some way.
Generation of 'The Sorrow Eyes'
Luchezar Manolov
Tsar Asen N24
Burgas, Bulgaria

Dear Editor,
my names ronald — so whats cool in a name eh — and I was walking out this afternoon round about — have you dope fiends actually seen stuff like a good april sky? — I mean, don't come on to me about beautiful people because most of you guys have got faces like collapsed lungs — and I saw a copy of your mag (the one with the peeky chick coming on coy about fishing out that poor guys whang-dang — some chance with him looking so pooped and useless — on the cover. It was sticking out of a dustbin — the mag I mean — ok there are lots of things sticking out of lots of dustbines and ive learnt not to be choosy so I snuck off to the park and had a good old read and when I finished my world was pretty cloudy and I say its just not healthy!
and I mean healthy healthy, if all you guys got out in the open air and did some physical action, that is work with your bodies — I don't mean for bread either — just a lot of football and walking or even climbing up scaffolding — dont tell me theres not much of that in the smoke — for a kick off, all that kind of stuff and youd stop shoving all this shit down the throats of kids like myself (accept the ones who dont keep their bodies fresh) who are so bored they'd cut off the old iron Dan if you told them there was a good thrash in it some where. I know kids who drank brasso because they thought it was a cool thing to do. And who are all these guys coming on about freedom for this and that and legalising pot — ugh — and wierd sexual details and all this 'come to jesus' bit about hunger (poverty natural for weak creeps) and all that piss in my bowler malarky. What I say is if guys get busted in north africa and land up in there shitty prisons they got to be dumb in the first place. I know because I been there and the beaches are a knockout — I was putting in twelve miles swimming a day and blocking in this yankee pee h.d. soon brought her off pot, the silly mouthy cow. She had a big ginger pussy and well reamed out I can tell you. This wog offered me bread for her and I took it — last I heard he was beating the piss out of her.
I went to greece after that and I don't see its such a bad scene there either, ok so the armys pushing the old snitch in everywhere but thats honest the way I see it and once you get to know the ordinary blokes you can play soccer with them. They don't speaghen much of the english bit from what I could gather they think english beatnik chicks are a big joke — there was one called pearla who was about

as sexy as a pigs trotter but she thought she was some kind of goddess because they were all lamming it into her.
She's the sort who thinks oz is like the bible man — and full of pox what's more. I played soccer instead in greece. And I had a game of soccer this afternoon and afterwards popped a bit into my salt — she don't take none of your tablets either, nor my desecrating myself with artificial objects, desecrate is the right word. What I mean is I feel real good and I don't need none of your hernandos hidyway so: on your faggoty bums.
ps. to get the lion on the tub you got to crack the whip — right?

From an Ex Public School Boy:
I have recently been thrown out of St Pauls public school in London for smoking, (after great interrogation and bluff on the part of the headmaster). I am fifteen, and am due to sit my 'O' level exams this June. I have been lucky in finding somewhere to carry on with my studies (on the condition that I mention nothing in school about St. Pauls), but that does not happen to everyone. A witch-hunt is starting throughout the country for school-boy heads, and before it does, let's try and get teacher's sense of proportions right.
Hash smoking is now a widespread social habit, almost in the same class as whisky and soda. Without arguing the pros and cons of it, the fact remains that people are turning on at 13, 14 or 15 years old. The school leaving age stands at fifteen by law. If people are being expelled from schools throughout the country, with a good chance of their careers being ruined, for a misdemeanour for which by law they would probably receive a penalty comparable to that for pulling the alarm cord on a train, it has to stop somewhere. I do not advocate legalisation of pot, merely because I dread the inevitable hassle of commercialism that would fall upon the magic weed; I just know that everything would work out much better if those in "responsible" positions would keep their cool.
Anonymous.

Dear Poverty Cooking,
I was absolutely horrified to read your recipe for roast Trafalgar Squan Pigeon. The gourmet in charge of this column cannot be aware of the nasty things that the Trafalgar Squan Pigeons are in fact fed on. Not only do they eat pigeon-repellant from the National Gallery, but they are full of contraceptive pills (an experiment to reduce their numbers)

OZ darling,
Didn't they tell your gastronome about parasites? Anybody who eats one of your Trafalgar birds is liable to do themselves a decided NASTY. Pigeons from towns are poisonous. As most of your readers follow the OZ cookery column avidly, I forsee a sudden drop in your subscription numbers. Suggest you print a bit saying catch 'em in the country. Then you will only die of pesticides. Much nicer. Ask Hippocrates or someone.
Yours till the cows come home
Peter Samuelson.
Old Grove House,
Hampstead NW3.

and other mean, nasty and horrible things.
The net effect of eating one of these pigeons would probably cause sterility, blindness etc, etc. Otherwise it's a good way of freaking out tourists in London.
Love,
Nelson
c/o Admiralty, London, S.W.1.

PS. It is not even illegal to kill them, as the author of the column pointed out.

Dear OZ,
Please stop nucking about.
Love,
Honest John.

Dear OZ,
Thanks for a look at the London Oz. I think the relative liberalism of the UK might have gone to your head a little. Your chances of getting Oz through customs — and believe me, we'd like to take a crack at distributing it — are so remote as to make the experiment virtually a waste of time, unless you're particularly flush at the moment. Things in this country have got worse instead of better since the early days of Oz. Queensland is banning things outright as usual, Tasmania is doing likewise — two of our magazines last year — and Victoria has started persecuting poor old 'Man', 'Girls and Gags' etc. Nipples do not exist in Victoria. The kids are fed by osmosis or something. Even NSW has passed legislation empowering Chief Secretary Willis (the bloke who banned Motel without even reading the script) to 'restrict' ie knock it off the newstands, any publication he feels like — and without formal redress through theCourts. So far he's banned half a dozen or so. Same thing, bare tit. Not even box. Just tit. And lately the customs people have really become tough. Their score last year — all but two copies of Playboy, Gareth Powell's Chance (a nup-to-dated super-slick Man, quite harmless); Squire (both these latter were printed in Hong Kong and shipped back, so there might be more to it than just Customs) and Christ knows what-all else we didn't ever hear about. Furthermore, the Judge, in describing Chance as erotic and perverted, was particularly upset by an imported French comic strip called Barbarella. The lesbian tendencies, bare bosoms and erotica were all bad news, said his worship. Yet around the corner from the Supreme Court, the movie version of Barbarella, with Jane Fonda's tits hanging all over the place, symbolic gang bungs and enough lesbianism to turn on a rabbit, was playing to packed houses. Same department —

Customs — places its tawdry stamp of approval on movies about which, while we're on the subject, an alarming new tendency has developed, overseas distributors, realising the new freedom in cinema overseas will be frowned upon by the mutton-floggers in our Customs department, now submit a version for censoring, hack out what Customs people don't like and strip in pre-filmed replacements, meaning, of course, that we only see what the government wants us to see, luvly stuff.
All of which is to bring you mildly up to date on the state of retrogression in your fair homeland. The population is still in the hands of dirty-minded cretins, and that's being polite. When I think of the political potential latent in the Australian censorship system, I go creepy all over. In brief, yes, we'd love to distribute Oz if you can get it through customs. But I wouldn't spend too much money on trying to get it through.
Regards to all, and best of luck to London Oz from all at Whisper.
Terry Blake.
Group Publications Pty. Ltd.
263 Oxford Street
Darlinghurst, Box 3021,
Sydney 2001, Australia.

LETTERS CONTINUED P.14

3

THEATRE: The LIVING THEATRE will be in London the month of June performing Frankenstein, Mysteries, Antigone, and Paradise Now at the Roundhouse (tel: 485-8073); plus late-night intimate things at the Arts Lab.

Late at night and over the weekend Oz has a robot answering the phone. (229 7541). If you have news or information that Oz can use ring up and tell the robot. Or, as an alternative to writing a letter to the editor, record a 15 second message. We'll publish the least boring messages in the next Oz.

THIS IS A CHAIN LETTER. WITHIN THE NEXT FIFTY-FIVE DAYS YOU WILL RECEIVE THIRTY-ELEVEN-HUNDRED POUNDS OF CHAINS.

In the meantime, plant your seeds.

If a lot of people who receive this letter plant a few seeds and a lot of people receive this letter then a lot of seeds will get planted.

to four inches apart with inter-spacing rows. In an apple box up to 35 plants may be planted.

Plant your sprouts with the seed above the ground and the sprout in the soil. Tamp the soil firmly, but not packed, around each plant as you insert the sprouts.
NUMBER TWO:

The second method is to use small flower pots made up the same way as the first method and plant one

usually taller. Some people smoke the male plant also, but it has no-where near the strength of the fe-male. Of the female plant, the top leaves and the flowers are the best, but the whole plant, root and all, have the quality we are looking for.
HARVESTING.

When your plants are ready to harvest, (you'll know by the flowers and seed pods) wet the soil and pull the whole plants out, root and all.

PLANT YOUR SEEDS

Make a few copies of this letter (5 would be nice) and send them and this copy to friends of yours. Try to mail to different cities and states, even different countries. If you would rather not, then please pass this copy on to someone and perhaps they would like to

THERE IS NO TRUTH to the legend that if you throw away a chain letter then all sorts of catastrophic abom-inable and outrageous disasters will happen. Except, of course, from your seeds point of view.

****
GROWING AND CULTIVATING POT

This should help you grow better quality plants in less time.

The first thing in growing a better plant, naturally, would be to start with seeds of good quality. If your some of your friends have had access to good grass, use those seeds. After all, not all the grass we smoke does the same thing for us.

Select the largest seeds and place them between two napkins, blotting paper, etc. and add enough water to cover the napkins. Then cover the top or put them in a dark closet for two or three days, until the seeds have sprouted at least a half inch or longer.

In the time it takes to sprout the seeds, you can prepare your gar-den. To do this, you can use one of two methods.
NUMBER ONE:

Use a flat wooden box like an apple box, tomato flat, etc. and add about one inch of gravel to the bottom. Fill the rest of the box with a good grade of soil or add a commercial fertilizer per manu-facturers instructions. Remember, too much fertilizer will burn the plants and retard or kill your charges.

Moisten the soil thoroughly, then level the top. Using a pencil or similar article punch holes two

sprout to each pot—a kind of a "potted pot." This method saves transplanting later. Though with adequate nourishment and light the first method is the easiest for both space and time. From here on, both methods are the same.

If you have a closet you can use, fine. A garage or any place where you can set your plants without them being trampled on will do also.

One word of caution on any trans-planting to the outside. The little "beasties" of the wild love young, tender plants and unless some method of protecting them is taken, more than likely you will only tend stalks and stubble to harvest.
LIGHTING.

Now as to the lighting—grass grows from three to fifteen feet high so lighting is important. If you use artificial light you can keep the unwanted stalk down in size, without sacrificing the lovely foliage simply by using a blue light for the first 30 days. You can leave the light on for 24 hours a day though 17 hours is as good. Plants don't need to sleep; the more light, the faster they mature.

Blue light keeps the stem from growing in height but will make a sturdier stem to hold our head factory. Set your lights (as many as needed to give good illumination) so they are 12 to 14 inches away from the top of your plants. If the temperature at plant level rises above 100 degrees use ventilation or less light. At the end of 30 days you will have quite a garden.

At the end of 30 days, change to red bulbs and start the gradual cut down on the time you have the lights on, from 24 to 18 hours. After a week cut to 14 hours, at the end of that week, to 12 hours. Leave at 12 hours until the plants begin to flower. When the plants flower you will be able to tell the worthless male plant from the sweetness of the female, as the female will have larger and heavier flower structure while the male will be skimpier and

Remove the flowers and top leaves (this is the best and is referred to as "supergrass"). Dry these, whole, in the sun for two weeks or until they are crumbly—this is grass at its best. If you like, after drying, sprinkle wine or rum lightly on the dried leaves and put in a "baggie" or a covered bottle and it will en-hance the flavor of your grass immensely. For the rest of the plant, remove the leaves from the stem and dry the same way or hang the whole plant upside down for two weeks and pick all the leaves as you want, saving the stem and root for the last as it is much harder to smoke. Or you can remove the leaves and place a small quantity in the oven under low, low heat for 20 to 30 minutes, or until crumbly, and run them through a strainer. A word of caution on the oven: Too much heat will burn the leaves—need I say more?

Chain letter originated in Los An-geles at Christmas time 1968 as a joint effort of the Paratheo-Ana-metamystikhood of Eris Esoteric and the Bavarian Illuminati of Chi-cago and the Tampa Society for the Laughing Buddha-Jesus. Re-ceived and passed on by the Ex-press Times along with growing tips from "Growing Marijuana", a pamphlet by Langdon Enterprizes.

PLANT YOUR SEEDS.

4

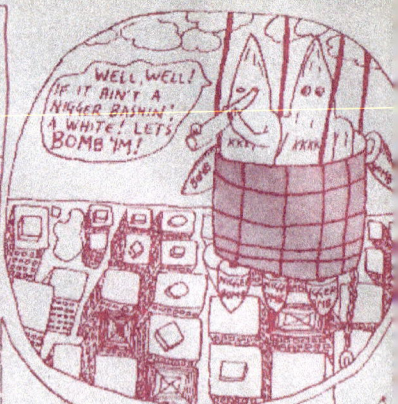

THE MAGIC THEATRE

PSSST LET THERE BE LIGHT

Fig. 673 — These two spiral nebulae (type Sc) — one seen in plan and the other edge-on — give some idea of the probable general appearance of our galaxy as seen by an observer in extragalactic space.

......MEANWHILE......

...AND SO!

SUDDENLY !!

PLATE 60. Second photo of North Pacific UFO.

WHEN THE VESSEL REACHED OUR PLANET THE CHILD WAS FOUND BY AN ELDERLY COUPLE THE RENTS

LOOK, MARY! — IT'S A CHILD!

THE POOR THING! — IT'S BEEN ABANDONED!

The entities

We come now to the most astonishing part of the lady's story. For she claims that, standing in front of the landed UFO, there were three men about 2 metres in height. "They were wearing skin - tight shining black clothes, and black boots that were also shiny. Their suits also covered their heads, leaving only the faces bare." (See Fig. 4.)

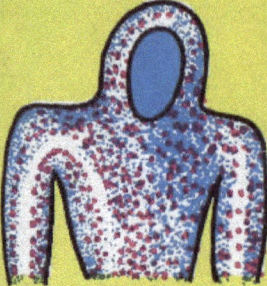

Fig. 4

MEANWHILE

Fig. 1. Witness's own sketch.

Fig. 2. A. Antenna with red light. B. Dome, in segments. C. Skirt, seemed to be spinning clockwise. D. Patch of violet light beneath.

8

and sam laughed

-12

SMALLS

4th-28th JUNE '69
THE LIVING THEATRE

Frankenstein JUNE 4,5,13,14,16,17.
Mysteries JUNE 6 & 7.
Paradise Now JUNE 9 & 10.
Antigone JUNE 11 & 12

All Performances start at 8pm.

THERE WILL BE APPROXIMATELY SIX PERFOR-
MANCES OF EACH PRODUCTION. WE HAVE
SCHEDULED THE FIRST TWO WEEKS; THE 2ND
TWO WEEKS WILL BE SCHEDULED SHORTLY

Box Office: ROUND HOUSE
Chalk Farm Road, LONDON NW1.
Tel: 01-485 8073

PRICES:
MONDAY - THURSDAY: 5s. 10s. 20s .40s.
FRIDAY & SATURDAY: 10s .15s. 25s. 60s.

PLEASE SEND ME	TICKETS AT	/s EACH
FOR PERFORMANCE OF :	ON:	JUNE '69
I ENCLOSE CHEQUE/PO FOR : £ : s: d.		
(PAYABLE TO THE ROUNDHOUSE)		
NAME:		
ADDRESS:		

Dear OZ,
Pete's letter (OZ 19) couldn't have
come at a better time, when the whole
scene is becoming fucked up with
cynicism & violence. Whatever happened
to 'freedom & hope?
Like, what do we get at the average
demonstration? A load of bums, armed
with cockneyeyed slogans & abuse for
the police (some of them have stones
instead of abuse). The police are sick,
they need acid & hope, not stones. By
adopting violent methods, one is
lowering oneself to the level of the
establishment one is trying to overthrow.
Flowers up their noses will worry the
fuzz much more than petrol-bombs;
they're used to them.
Let's get ourselves straight: 'hippies'
(you are hippies, aren't you) are
essentially non-violent. The blokes
who organise these demonstrations are
'communists' of the greyest, most
conventional type. At a recent demo
(March 9th) many of the demonstrators
were chanting 'Lenin, STALIN, Mao-Tse-
Tung.' Shit. What have we got to do with
people like this.
Many of the militant underground are
getting mightly confused, & you're not
helping by publishing crap like AGIT.
OZ! There seems no other way of
showing one's feelings than going to
these shitted-up demos. What we need
is hope-ins, be-ins, & smoke-ins on a vast
scale, like the free concerts, except bigger
& better.
This summer will probably be a fine
one — why not turn it into one long
demonstration? The streets are for free,
the parks are for free. USE THEM. Be
in them, fuck in them, smoke in them,
if you're brave enough, they can't arrest
50,000 people. Get out your bells &
beads. Do anything beautiful
Sorry this is all a bit incoherent, but I
have strong feelings on this subject. My
apologies to Pete, if you publish this shit,
for saying it much worse than he did.
Good Luck with OZ.

Your Friend NICK.

"No, I don't want a blow job
— I'm a girl."

OZ

The Editor,
The Shorter Oxford English
Dictionary,
Oxford University Press,
Ely House, London W1.
Dear Sir,
We recently paid £7.5.0. for The
Shorter Oxford English Dictionary
The 1967 edition
for use in our office. We note that
in the Preface it is stated, "It is
hoped that both the student and
the general reader will find in this
work what they might reasonably
expect to find in a historical
dictionary of English compressed
within 2,500 quarto pages, which
covers not only the history of the
general English vocabulary from
the days of King Alfred down to
the present time but includes also a
large number of obsolete,
provincial, and foreign words and
phrases, and a multitude of terms
of art and science."
It does not contain the word 'fuck'.
We would be interested to know
the reason for this curious omission.
yours sincerely,
OZ Magazine

Dear Sir,
Thank you for your letter of 14
April. At the time the Shorter
Oxford English Dictionary was
first published (1933) no dictionary
for general use — as distinct from
dictionaries of slang — contained
the word of whose omission you
complain. Nor does it appear now in
any of the serious dictionaries,
including the main American
dictionaries, immediately accessible
to us. So far as we know it is to be
found so far only in the recent
Penguin Dictionary.
The reasons for its long omission
from the serious dictionaries are
complex and you will hardly expect
me to go into these in an answer
that must be brief. In the main, I
should guess that the permissive
attitudes that now prevail are of
such recent date that they have not
yet had time to become reflected
in large dictionaries that can only
be revised and reset at fairly long
intervals for reasons of cost. And to
have included the four-letter words,
until recently, in dictionaries meant
for general use might have meant
their being banned in this country
and elsewhere. Even now their
inclusion might still have this effect
in some countries and, failing this,
might mean that their market
became restricted in, for example,
schools. For a publishing house to
be affected by such considerations
does not necessarily imply that its
motives are wholly commercial: it
might well find that it would be a
pity to restrict, by the inclusion of
such sensitive words, the use of the
scholarship and useful knowledge
which a dictionary may otherwise
contain.
In short, then, the question is a
vexed one to which no easy answer
(other than the historical and
pragmatic one given here) can be
given. It will be under close
consideration in our own future
planning for a new edition of the
Shorter Oxford English Dictionary.
You may be interested to know that
this and similar words will be dealt
with in the new edition of the
Supplement to the large Oxford
English Dictionary now in
preparation.
Yours truly,
DM Davin
The Clarendon Press
Walton Street Oxford.

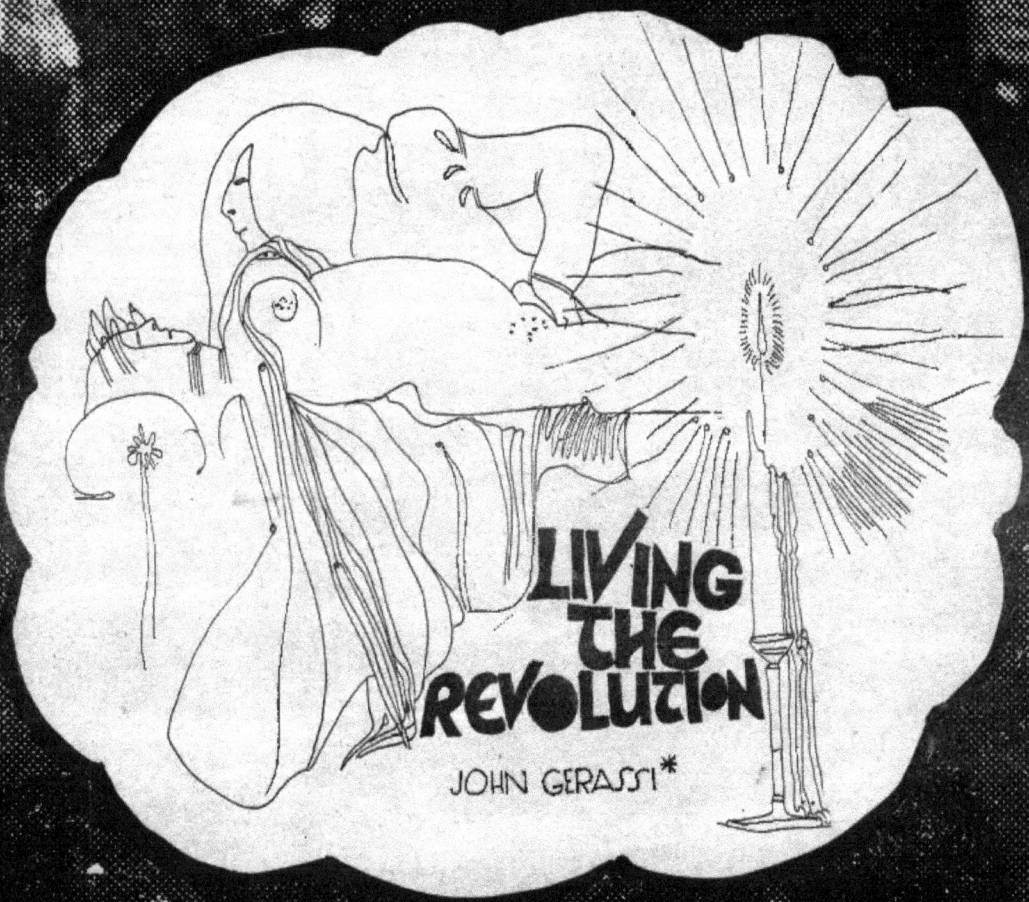

LIVING THE REVOLUTION

JOHN GERASSI*

So we call ourselves revolutionaries! Yet we — at least most of us white, middle-class, educated dreamers and drop-outs — have all the basic necessities we need to live more comfortably than ever before. We have more physical freedom, more sexual freedom, even more verbal freedom than ever before. At least in the rich capitalist world which we consider the real enemy and want to destroy. So, why *do* we want a revolution? And what kind?

Ask these questions to any 'traditional' revolutionary, one who thinks he is a 'Marxist-Leninist', and you'll get the traditional economic-political answers: the capitalist exploits the working class by blah-blah. But we're not working class!

Yes but we're intellectuals and the role of the intellectual revolutionary elite, conscious of the tida-tidum, is to papim papam. Why? Because that elite, realizing that it profits from the greed . . . Ho Hum.

I don't know about you, but that's not why I'm a revolutionary. Sure, I can make those tedious analyses. Sure, I even think such analyses have to be made, as fuel to bring about revolutionary situations. In order to thrive in my kind of society, I know I've got to convince others to view it as groovy. And, in order to keep them receptive to my future, I've got to make them conscious of our present. So I guess I'll keep trying to explain why we live in a dehumanizing society, the direct and necessary consequence of capitalism, and its mode of operation, capitalist bureaucracy.

But that's for the squares. We know we're being dehumanized, and we know why: they need us to do their dirty work. And not just in Vietnam, either. For how will they get the gadgets and experts they need for our materialistic society? And who will rationalize their necessity? Who will explain their political value? You and me. They need us more than we need them. We're the ones who must think up these things in their labs, the ones who must explain their value in their books, the ones who must show their appeal on their television, the ones who must defend

them in their courts. That's why we've got to go to their universities, join their factories, and institutions. Otherwise? Well, just imagine, as Abbie Hoffman (*Revolution for the Hell of It*) put it recently:

What would happen if large numbers of people in the country started getting together, forming communities, hustling free fish on Fulton Street, and passing out brass washers to use in laundromats and phones? What if people in slums started moving into abandoned buildings and refusing to move even to the point of defending them with guns? What if this movement grew and busy salesmen sweating under the collar on a hot summer day decided to say fuck the system and headed for welfare? What if secretaries got tired of typing memos to the boss's girlfriend and took to panhandling in the streets? What if when they called a war, no-one went? people who wanted to get educated just *went to a college classroom and sat-in without paying and without caring about a degree? Well, you know what? We'd have ourselves one hell of a revolution, that's what.*

Obviously, if the modern world's universities came to a standstill — or if we all refused to get educated *their* way — the whole capitalist-bureaucratic world would collapse. And it would do so faster than with guns and barricades. (The corollary, which I won't try to defend here but is, to me, a simplistic truism, is that the dehumanizing society's most important and necessary weapon is the university.) This is true

not only because of what they teach us but of why as well. In order to make us "experts" they have to dehumanize us, separate us, compartmentalize us. We have to be segregated, pigeon-holed, divorced from one another so totally that we cannot relate to one another (outside our own in-group) except through *their* institutions. What would happen to our society if a worker actually liked to sit and talk with intellectuals? If children were allowed to masturbate together instead of watching television? But that still isn't all. What our education system necessarily does is force us to enter and propagate the vicious circle which dehumanizes us — which teaches us that material achievements are the only valuable things in life. To make us "good" experts, we must prove our merit. How? By passing tests better than anyone else. By competing. In other words by considering our fellow men as our personal enemies. This is true in Russia as well as in America. We've got to "prove" ourselves — first in class, then in the army, then in the factory. Every value we have is based on individual achievement, on some rags-to-riches tale, on some poor bloke finding his god in the desert, overcoming his obstacles *alone*, struggling with *his* soul.

The so-called Communists are just the same. All Power to the Soviets! Yes, but later. First, let's be as good as the capitalist world. So Lenin rules. Then Stalin. Then what's-his-name. The Soviets can wait. They're made up of ordinary people, and some ordinary people are stupid and everybody knows stupid people don't count. Because they don't want to get to the moon first. And niggers don't count either because they love sex too much and are lazy. But they'll be okay when they get our values, when they understand that the meaning of life is to get ahead. Until then society can tell them how to live — with the police.

I'll tell you why I'm a revolutionary. It's very simple:

I just don't want that kind of a life. I want to live in a world where I don't have to stand while my boss or the commissar sits, where I can talk to a black man as an equal; where I don't get asphyxiated by fumes or killed by shoddy cars; where no-one wants to shoot me and I don't want to shoot anyone; where I can enjoy a painting without caring about who did it, just as I don't care who made the sun-set. I want to know what my neighbor thinks about the school where we both send our kids even though he likes music written by some guy named Beethoven while I groove to Jimi Hendrix. I want to be free to ask a girl to go to bed with me knowing that if she doesn't she'll feel free enough to say 'no thanks' and then we can still rap about a book we both read — and vice versa. I want to smoke pot if I like it. I don't want cops telling me where I can sit, but I do want to be able to listen to my neighbors, all kinds of people, and if they all feel that it's good for us all for me *not* to sit there, I won't and I won't feel my manhood is bitten off for going along with them. I know I can't participate in every decision, that I can't be everywhere at the same time and I don't want to — I'm lazy — so I want to be able to have some guy represent me there and another guy over yonder. But I want to be able to recall him anytime. I don't want to worry about food or clothing or a roof — I know the world is rich enough to give me all that — me and everybody else — and I'm willing to do my share of the work, but not for somebody else's profit. I don't want to accumulate property, I want free education, as I and the people I rap with think it important or pleasurable.

I'm no masochist; I don't believe I have to sacrifice myself in order to have a vacation or enjoy myself. I don't believe pleasure and work are antithetic; every man ought to enjoy what he does. I want free medicine, free transportation, free rent, free leisure, free theatre, free eye-glasses, free pot. I'll work, sure, I'll do my best, I can write — sometimes. I can teach. I'll do it, with pleasure. Or, if you all think it's a waste of time, well, I can make pretty good tables and dressers, with sliding doors that really slide. Maybe I can hoe potatoes. Why not? If a bunch of us do it together, singing, laughing. Well, not everyday maybe. So we'll take Mondays, you take Tuesdays.

Most important, I guess, I want to know what you think and feel, and why. And I want you to care about me. I don't care if you have an IQ of 20 and me 120 — that's luck. You have blond hair, I got brown. That's your human condition. If you have an IQ of 20, you're just as much a man as I am, me with my potato nose and you with that straight delicate one. Your experiences are worth mine and mine yours. Let's rap, brother. Let's see what we want from each other, what we have to do in private, what we agree on and can do together. And our schools together. And our factories. And, if after a while, there's no Spiro Agnew to pick up the garbage, and we agree that we want it out of our community, maybe I'll pick it up on Tuesdays if you can do it on Wednesdays.

I don't want customs, or passports, or work-permits, or foreign exchange. Of course, since we'll all be equals, we won't need any of that. True, there's always that guy, the one who invents a new way to fly and won't tell us unless he gets two cars to our one. Well, the hell with him and his invention. Suppose, though, what he invents is a pill that prolongs life for 50 years. We'd all like to live until we're 130. But then, what can he do with his invention? Together, you and I, we'll have fun. We'll laugh and enjoy ourselves and we won't have any reason to distrust each other, even if you do have a prettier nose and I envy you for it, and I have a higher IQ (which you won't envy since it won't get me more things). (I might have a prettier wife, though.) Still we'll relate. He'll be an outcast. Let him live till he's 130 — lonely and bitter. We'll die when we're 80. But it was fun.

That's what I want. That's what a lot of people I know want. I got taught by

having it. That's right, I'm a product of capitalist society. I've had the fancy home, the maid, the car, the expense account, the titles and the Bigelows on the floor. What I didn't have was happiness. I was bossed, cajoled, coerced, manipulated, pigeon-holed. I lived by the values of this society and they taught me to drive, drive for more, rush and rush some more. I was told not to think of happiness as a feeling only as a thing, a possession, a warm blanket like Linus always has.

It didn't work. I hadn't suffered from the Depression or World War II. I just couldn't be fooled. And there are thousands, perhaps millions of kids today who can't be fooled either. Brought up under the material incentives of capitalism, we are the product of capitalism's greatest contradiction — that it simply doesn't satisfy. And so we can no longer be manipulated by capitalism, at least not for very long.

But we can be repressed by it. That's why we need a revolution. We are being repressed by it, by its police, its universities, its televisions, its 'democracy', its parliament - - arianism, its secret services, its apologists and especially by its myths, most importantly, the myth that change must be peaceful and that only we revolutionaries are violent (though even the National Commission on the Causes and Prevention of Violence can't stomach that myth. It says: 'Like most ideologies, the myth of peaceful progress is intended at bottom to legitimize existing

political arrangements and to authorize the suppression of protest. It also serves to conceal the role of official violence in the maintenance of these arrangements.')

Let's settle a few things first. We want to throw out those in power to establish a new society.

Now if you think that elections can change anything, you just aren't with it. Those who have power are not those who are elected but those who set up elections. What we must overthrow is capitalist (State or Private) parliamentarianism, not the Democratic or Republican, Labour or Conservative parties. We have as much right to do so as the Americans who overthrew the English, the French bourgeoisie who overthrew their aristocrats. As Abe Lincoln put it: 'This country with its constitution belongs to us who live in it. Whenever they shall grow weary of the existing government they shall exercise their constitutional rights of amending it or their revolutionary right to dismember or overthrow it.' But then, influenced by a life-time of debates between 'majority' and 'minority', you might say that we're the minority, and that there are a lot of innocent bystanders, too. For one thing, every revolution, the English and American included, was started by a minority, a tiny one at that. It became a majority only as it proved it meant what it said. For another, we're the young. Among the young, we're probably the majority. In any case, the argument of numbers is irrelevant. if you feel strongly

50% SAY 'BAN PRIVATE CARS IN PEAK HOUR

about saving your capitalist regime, defend it. But don't call yourself an innocent bystander. There is no such thing. An innocent bystander in the American Revolution? To Hitler's occupations? Or, as Abbie Hoffman puts it: 'If you are a bystander, you are not innocent.'

So, we agree, it's a fight to the finish. Well then, why doesn't the Establishment hound us, arrest us, kill us? Because that is not what modern Capitalism is all about. It is not George Wallace, the KKK and Minutemen, the four colonels of the green beret calypso. No. The Establishment is IBM, Xerox, the Kennedys, the London and New York Times, Harvard University, LSE, the Courts – the liberal corporatists who, to survive, must maintain the semblance of fair play and reform-mindedness. It is no accident that no modern, developed capitalist state has ever resorted to dictatorship, not even in times of trouble. For as long as the liberocorporatists can maintain such a semblance, protesters tend to remain isolated and un-polarized. Destroy the verbal meaning of corporate liberalism – silence the Times, arrest the Eugene McCarthys – and the whole structure becomes threatened overnight. It can then be maintained only by an armed phalanx who are just as apt to bump off the Kennedys and the chairman of Xerox, IBM and the universities (who are often the same) as they are to cut my head off. In fact, more apt to do so – for the colonels (or police chiefs, as would be more likely in America) have more to gain from liquidating the former – the loot.

Thus, it is no accident that in the French revolution of May-June 1968, the power elite did not bring in the troops to open fire on students and workers, even on May 29 when it could fear total collapse of the corporative state apparatus.

The enemy is not going to kill us all. Some, here and there, by assassination, but not all, and not systematically. It will repress us (and is doing it) by massive individual arrests, tying us and our resources up in their courts while, simultaneously trying to buy off some of us here and there by paper reforms, changes in degree but not in kind. (For, suppose that they did let us run our universities, what would happen to their counter-insurgency, biochemical and ghetto-control research? What would happen to their moon-projects, their executive training and recruiting operations, their future civil servants, media-men, computer experts?). But let's not kid ourselves their form of repression is the most efficient yet devised. It is far better than guns or clubs. Useless car-safety legislation or an amendment to lower the voting age to 18 is far, far wiser than HUAC intimidations. Indeed, the best thing that happened for the Second American Revolution is Mayor Daley.

Well, then, what can we do against this monolithic liberal corporativism which bathes itself from head to toe in a pluralistic myth? Lenin once gave this answer: 'Give us an organization of revolutionaries, and we will overturn Russia!' And he did. But with what results? Never mind what he said, what did he do? He got his organization -- the

revolutionary party – and with it the elite corps that went on to rule Russia, creating Stalinism, Czechoslovakia and the trials of Daniel and Siniavski. History has judged Lenin right. His methods were the only ones capable of overturning the Czarist State. And ever since, I like scholastics mimicking St Thomas, 'Marxist-Leninists' have insisted that every revolution must be carried out in the same way. Yet Lenin wouldn't agree. He would say, as he did, that conditions determine tactics and that tactics are subservient to the reasons for the revolution. His reasons were land, bread, freedom. His revolution never got the third, but two out of three is a pretty good batting average in any league.

Almost. Not in ours. We're ambitious. We want a perfect score – or else forget it. But don't, because we'll get it. There are certain laws about revolutions. Not many, but a few. One is that a revolution is made by people, ie: a movement. The other is that it must (and does) function within two awarenesses:
1) the nature of the adversary;
2) the kind of structure, at least in general, which the movement wants to set up.

The first is easy: liberal corporativism, which we all know, or should. The second is harder. I've described my structure above. Other revolutionaries have other descriptions. But we all agree on one basic characteristic: that it be a humanizing society. That means that Lenin's elitist organization is out. Also, then, is his 'party' as defined by modern day 'Marxist-Leninists'. I put that in

REACTIONARY!

quotes because Marx never talked about a ruling party hierarchy such as Lenin put into motion. Marx, for example, spoke of 'the party arising spontaneously from the soil of modern society.' And Engels, in his best work, *Anti-Duhring*, said that the role of a revolutionary party is to destroy the State; not only the old state but all future states. After seizing power he wrote 'State interference in social relations becomes, in one domain after another, superfluous, and then withers away of itself; the government of persons is replaced by the administration of things. The State is not abolished. It withers away.' Even Lenin insisted that once the revolution is victorious ' *a special force* for suppression is *no longer necessary*. In this sense the State begins to wither away.'

Where Lenin went wrong was to believe in short cuts. There are none – neither to justice nor truth. Just as a revolution from above is bound to fail (since they do not participate in it, the masses do not consider it theirs and will not work for its post-victory success), so is one that forgets its principles in order to strengthen itself (once the value of man is relegated to second place it stays there). No matter how 'good' and just a cop's intentions may be, no matter how much he believes in the rationalization that he is being efficient in order to become chief whence he can have the power to humanize the whole force, by the time he is the chief he will have institutionalized his actions: every cop on the force will act as if man is an object, to be treated as such. Once manipulation is a way of life, human lives become manipulatable. The Russia of today is not the fault of a Stalin gone mad; it is the necessary consequence of a revolution that did not trust the people for whom it

fought. Because it was under attack from both a reactionary within and a capitalist without, it may have had no other historical choice. But that does not change the fact that today Daniel and Siniavski are in jail because Lenin believed in discipline and that Russians are stratofied and compartmentalized because Lenin reintroduced material incentives with his 'temporary' New Economic Policy.

Our revolution, then, must not cherish the principle of efficiency. It must not build followers. It must not sacrifice participation for effectiveness. It must not judge what is relevant according to doctrine. Nothing that is relevant to you or me can be considered irrelevant by the revolution. The only way we will ever see a New Man is by valuing all men. Men not theories. Men not programs. Is this heresy, as the 'Marxist-Leninists' yell? To their scholarly dogmatism, perhaps. Marx himself however, was no dogmatist. 'Every step of real movement' he wrote, 'is more important than a dozen programmes.' By real movement, of course, he meant *people*.

No party? No ideology? No program? How in hell then, do we make this 'humanizing' revolution?

By living it. By fighting for what's relevant to you, not to some theoretist. You want to turn on, turn on. You want to drop out, drop out. Groove to the MC5 singing John Lee Hooker's Motor City Is Burning ('All the cities will burn... You are the people who will build up the ashes') or the Lovin' Spoonful's Revelation: Revolution '69 ('I'm afraid to die but I'm a man inside and I need the revolution'). Live in a commune. Be faithful to your values, not your parents' (Remember Bob Dylan's The Times, They

are A-Changin': 'Your sons and your daughters are beyond your command; Your old road is rapidly aging.')? Don't be afraid to be happy. As Abbie Hoffman wrote: 'Look, you want to have more fun, you want to get laid more, you want to turn on with friends, you want an outlet for your creativity, then get out of school, quit your job. Come on out and help build and defend the society you want. Stop trying to organize everybody but yourself. Begin to live your vision.'

If we do, there's a great pay-off: once we win we won't have to worry about somebody having perverted the Revolution. Because the Revolution will be us.

✱

John Gerassi, an American, is the author of Venceremos, a definitive study of Che Guevara. He has been the Latin American editor of *Time* and *Newsweek*, and prior to coming to London where he is now resident, he was Professor of Political Science at San Francisco State College. He was sacked from this post for supporting the students in their demands for administrative reforms.

hip pocrates

Eugene Schoenfeld
M.D.

WARNING: The use of "reds" or barbiturates for highs (lows would be more descriptive) seems to be increasing again. Seconal (secobarbital) and Nembutal (pentobarbital) are two commonly prescribed medications often used in suicide attempts. Barbiturates are also physically addicting & kicking a barbiturate habit is more difficult & dangerous than kicking narcotics.

Mixing 'reds' & alcohol can lead to a one way trip because the two drugs potentiate each other, i.e. 1+1=more than 2. In the case of barbiturates & alcohol the whole equals more than the sum of the parts. A girl in San Fransisco died recently because she mixed booze with 'reds'.

QUESTION: I've recently heard that smoking catnip is very similar to smoking marijuana. Could you tell me if there is any truth in this or is it a big put-on by the catnip industry to get you to buy their product?

ANSWER: A recent story in the WALL STREET JOURNAL reported a surge in catnip sales around the country as well as an article in the JOURNAL of the AMA about catnip use by humans. A different kind of cat is using catnip these days & the WALL STREET JOURNAL notes that the price of the tabby turn-on is only 60¢ a lid. The JAMA informants claim that catnip is nearly as potent as marijuana but the research division of the Telegraph Avenue Irregulars disputes this finding. My informants claim that a catnip high is somewhere between banana peel timing and poor marijuana. Maybe there are grades of catnip like Calico Gold or Siamese Green. Is milk consumption on the increase?

Stalking further information I telephoned Alexander 'Sasha' Shulgin, the brilliant chemist who is best known to the public for his synthesis of STP (which was later illegally distributed in a dose form twice that "recommended").

'Sasha' I purred, 'what can you tel' me about catnip?'

He promised to send me some information in a few days and yesterday his letter arrived. Portions of it follow:

'The plant is called catnip or catmint (Nepeta cataria). Steam distillation of the plant yields a volatile oil (about 0.3%) that is mostly acidic (inactive).

'The volatiles seem to turn on members of the cat family only. McElvain screened his fractions using the lion as a test animal. There is some reputation of the use of catnip in humans, as a tea for nervous headache.'

'There is a report from Puerto Rico (1945) that catnip was detected as an adulterant in marijuana!'

'A number of other, chemicals have been established as being present in catnip (as citral, geraniol, nerol, camphor, citronellol) but of some interest is the content of ascorbic acid.' '...the active ingredient, nepetalactone.' 'An extremely similar substance... is isolated from the Argentine ant, Iridomyrmex humilis.' '...similar compounds are found in yet another, insect the stick insect Anisomorpha buprestoides.'

'The chemical...is completely unrelated to any known family of hallucinogens.'

...if catnip smoking seems to lose its charm, one can always turn to cigarettes made of Argentine ants.'

'. 'Maybe the person who coined the word 'Roach' knew something that we don't.'

Ground catnip closely resembles ground marijuana leaves. Nothing is known about possible harmful effects from short or long term use of the drug.

A recent drug conference in Buffalo, N.Y. featured as participants Drs. Joel Fort, Tim Leary, Ralph Metzner, and Tod Mikiyura as well as Allen Ginsberg & Paul Krasner. Also at the conference were a group of the Up Against the Wall Motherfuckers. The Motherfuckers, who carried chains, whips, knives & other weapons, continually harassed the speakers. Ginsberg tried to incorporate their screamed obscenities into his poems — with little success. Paul Krassner ended his talk with a few futile minutes of trying to banter with them.

Joel Fort gave an astute psychiatric diagnosis when he said to one of them, 'You're not only Motherfuckers but assholes as well.'

HIPPOCRATES is a collection of letters and answers published by Grove Press. $5.00. Dr Schoenfeld welcomes your questions. Write to him c/o PO Box 9002, Berkeley, California, 94709. Mark your letters OZ.

"Which side are you on, baby?"

22

MIKE ENGLISH

YES! MEN IT CAN BE DONE

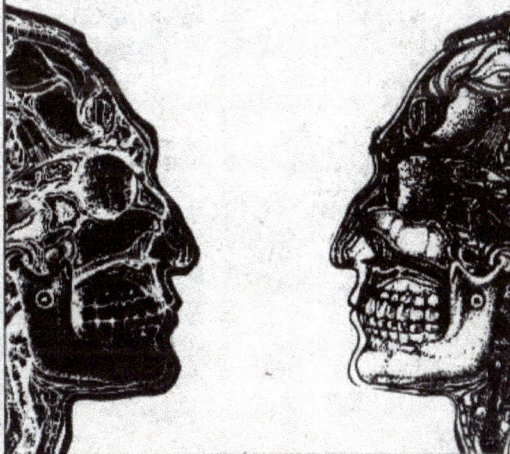

2

24

John
Hurford '69

26

Mōzic

BORN UNDER A BAD SIGN

Peter Townshend:

I'm today's powerful young man. I'm today's superstar, young man. I'm not saying that in any egotistic way at all, but you have to face it. It is us and people like us who dictate the musical formula; we dictate changing hair styles, the way people dress. This is what art is — this is what our music is. It involves people, completely. It does something to their whole way of existence, the way they dance, the way they express themselves socially, the way they think — everything. The world of pop and what it is achieving is unbelievable. I can't see that someone like Benjamin Britten, sitting in his little studio doing his thing, which I very much admire, getting through to the same kind of audience and having the same kind of effect. For this reason alone, pop music and its effect is crucial to an understanding of today's art. It's crucial that pop should be considered as art. It's crucial that it should progress as art, and not as much as it seems to be so desperately trying to do, to the kind of factory made, big agency controlled rubbish that it was before the Beatles came along.

It's very difficult to talk about pop music since to start with there isn't such a thing as pop music. There are many different kinds of music all called 'pop'. You can say that the sounds I produce are the same as those of Donald Peers. They're totally different — but they're both called 'pop'. For me, my kind of pop is the leader of youth. It's being in the present. But the more you talk about it, the more codified you become. The best thing is not to be talking but to pick up a guitar and be playing it. Because that's what pop music is about. Pop music isn't me sitting reasoning out its role; it's me picking up a guitar and playing you a song.

If you look at my form of art, you can find something in the best of pop which completely eliminates the old form. Completely eliminates it. If you think Beethoven's Ninth Symphony is overwhelming, I can play you a tape which I made in my studio at home which is more overwhelming. If you tell me that Italian opera is unsurpassable, then you're talking rubbish. If people dig Italian opera then let them dig it. I think we can do better in today's terms. Italian opera doesn't say anything for today. Benjamin Britten, for example, is hung up on Purcell. So am I, and I think I was getting nearer to what Purcell was getting at musically in my song 'I'm a Boy' than Benjamin Britten was in the whole of his work. I can read music, and I can arrange it. I know all about counterpoint — but as soon as I learned it completely, I realised that it was utterly useless to me. All it allowed me to do was to understand what other composers were trying to do. And once you've understood, you've got to go on and use today's terms to produce new music, not yesterday's.

I think the most important musical development we've made is in free form music. Complete abandon in music, completely uncontrolled music which does exactly what it wants. We don't allow our instruments to stop us doing what we want; we don't even allow our physical health to stop us doing what we want. We smash our instruments, tear our clothes and wreck everything. The expense doesn't worry us because that would be something which would get between us and our music. If I stood on stage worrying about the price of the guitar then I'm not really playing music. I'm getting involved in material values. I don't have a love affair with a guitar. I don't polish it after every performance. I play the fucking thing. Our actual intention is to play out all the adrenalin and all the aggression and all the things that are in us. We communicate aggression and frustration to the audience — musically and visually. We want to show the audience that we are frustrated characters, that we do what...

There will be a benefit concert for the Fairport Convention on Sunday 25th May 1969 at 6 pm at the RoundHouse Chalk Farm. Family, Pretty Things, Deviants, have agreed to play at the time of going to press, and many other musicians have intimated that they will be there for a blow, all being well.

---

to get something out of our system and we do wanna do it in front of them. I've written a thesis for Gustav Metzner — an auto destructive lecturer. I said that our audience is numbed by seeing violence in the same way that they're numbed by seeing a car crash. It's a traumatic experience. But it does release basic tensions — people flying off the handle. Lack of control and basic abandon which is something which people don't particularly admire or respect in other people but which everybody has put up inside them. So our performance and music has got much more to do with art than people imagine. Much, much more to do with pop music than anything else. Outside of football, there's been very little real expression of how we feel since the days when people ran around with no clothes on banging drums. It's all been — sophistication and glore.

We're not out to blow people's minds, however. We're out to get through to them. It's too easy to blow someone's mind. All we have to do is to go on either stark naked or explode — blow our toes off or something; you can always blow people's minds. You know, these guys that come up and say: wouldn't it be a mind-blower if we got 6,000 million kids all dressed in red unicorns and had a big freak out in the middle of Ealing Common. Sure it'll be mind-blowing, but what would it prove?

At the moment, I'm very interested in getting complete control over my music; in other words, I would write a piece of music, arrange it, play every instrument myself, record it all myself, in my own studio, sing any part that needed singing, produce it myself and also distribute it myself. Complete control. The more control you've got over what you're involved in, the nearer the finished product is to what you intended. It will be good when every individual can make music in the same way that every individual can paint a picture. Think how huge it could be; instead of the drab music classes that you have in school now, you could have something similar to an art class where everyone actually makes music themselves. This could be huge.

This interview with Peter Townshend is taken from a book, 'Born Under a Bad Sign' by Tony Palmer, to be published by William Kimber & Co Ltd in September 1969.

'Z' is for Zapple.

Introducing Zapple, a new label from Apple Records.

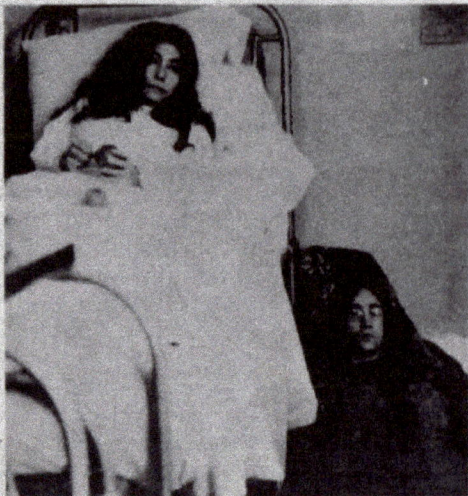

John Lennon/Yoko Ono: 'Life with the Lions:
(Zapple 01)   Unfinished Music No.2.'

George Harrison: 'Electronic Sound.'
(Zapple 02)

LP REVIEWS

TOMMY. The Who. *Track 613 014*

'Tommy', the Who's saga of "that deaf dumb and blind kid", is a fantasy for our times. It's not didactic at all ... there is no overall message. The final track 'We're Not Gonna Take It!' fades out into unresolved ambiguity ... Who isn't going to take what? Is the cry a revolutionary or a reactionary one? Is Tommy, by this time transformed into a seer and prophet, fighting his disciples or leading them? Or maybe trying to escape from them, back into the realm of pure sensation he knew as a child? The answers aren't important. The open-ending keeps the fantasy alive, gives free rein to its charm.

John Peel, that otherwise sensible fellow, has already been trapped into making "better than" comparisons between 'Tommy' and Sergeant Pepper. A pity, since while 'Tommy' is probably an equally important LP and an equally important "event" in the pop music world, the two are really incomparable in terms of the quality of what they attempt and achieve as music. Part of Sergeant Pepper's impact was the way it stood so obviously outside the existing pop tradition ... so obviously apart, for that matter, from anything the Beatles had tried before. It was truly revolutionary music. It was so *unexpected* it made your head sing. At the same time it had an integrity which ensured its success not only as an event but as music in its own right. 'Tommy' has that same integrity, but in a sense it is nothing new. There is really nothing here that the Who haven't done before and there are, literally, echoes ... a certain chord sequence, bass riff or melody line ... that link the present songs with previous ones. On the other hand one can honestly say there is nothing that they've ever done so well, 'Tommy' is a natural and, moreover, a triumphant progression from their earlier LPs.

Of course, the triumph is Pete Townshend's as much as anyone's. To produce an opera using the language, music and values of his own generation has been a personal ambition of his for many years now. The opera label then, Townshend's own, is as appropriate as any for 'Tommy'. The work has the formal strength and rigidity that the term implies (and which presumably first prompted Peel to make comparisons with Pepper). At the same time, however, the music is far from being studied. It's amazing, in fact, that within such a formal framework the Who could have produced songs of such rawness and violence, with such momentum and with such emotional impact as the ones we find here.

'Tommy' opens with an instrumental 'Overture', a bow to tradition which is wryly put in perspective as more of a thumbing-of-the-nose when it is followed up later with 'Undertune'. This impressive nine-minute instrumental trip is strongly rhythmic. By turns it pounds along like blood in the veins and then slips into gentler, broader soaring sequences, while Townshend's guitar works a pattern of complex chord inversions over everything. 'Undertune' is also interesting in that it is really a distillation of the instrumental spirit of the whole album. Tightly controlled and yet at times disruptive, it's the spirit of calculated violence we've come to expect from the Who, a violence of opposing and contrasting elements, of sudden, unexpected switches of mood. Again, the Who have never managed it so successfully as here. The musical production on this album as a whole would be hard to fault on any score. One particularly nice point is that although there is extensive over-dubbing it is always used, as where Townshend mixes accoustic and electric guitars, to intensify and augment the group's characteristic sound rather than transform it into something else. It shouldn't be too difficult, in short, for the Who to perform the entire opera live and one looks forward to them doing just that.

The songs themselves are concerned not so much with Tommy as with the people who surround him, the opportunists and the quacks, the people who use him and, in the case of his celebrated Uncle Ernie, who abuse him. Some of the songs have been called sick. They're not, of course, but it's interesting that the two which will probably be the most controversial in this respect, 'Cousin Kevin' and 'Fiddle About', are both John Entwhistle's creations. Townshend's songs, of course, constitute the solid backbone of the opera and his flair for the down-to-earth, almost colloquial lyric ('My Generation', 'I'm a Boy' etc.) is still in evidence. His lyrics always were perceptive, now they are consistently and brilliantly so. Once more it's a case of the songs achieving a superior level of quality rather than presenting us with anything drastically new in structure.

Finally a word about the cover and Mike McInnerney's graphics which really have to be seen to be believed. Every last thing adds up to make this album an experience you should try and take in.

Graham Charnock

THE AMAZING ADVENTURES OF ... The Liverpool Scene *RCA Victor*

What is great poetry? Is it the eternal pieces from poets such as Milton and T S Eliot, dealing with thoughts and problems which have always been, and always will be, a part of man's existence, or those passages of verse which have purely a contemporary relevance and soon fade into past days, past thoughts, at present being written by the so-called 'Liverpool Poets'? The first provides one with material with which one can delve into and explore, the second one can hear and enjoy; the first is the poetry of the intellectual, the second the poetry of the people (Prevert's poetry, for example, was often found scrawled by the people on walls, tablecloths, etc); the first is to be read, the second to be read out. The current popularity of the Liverpool Poets is due solely to their relevance to the life of the people plus the fact that their poems are read out rather than read, while it can hardly be a coincidence that the better-known of today's crop of young poets all seem to originate from Liverpool, when people all over the country are writing in the same style and language and often just as well (thank

you Beatles). Their poetry- is usually purely ephemeral and superficial, limited in time by catch-phrase or name (how long before we forget H P Lovecraft or SHELTER?): it carries an immediate impact only, ideal for readings; a second perusal or hearing affords nothing new. After a time the verse usually becomes uninteresting and boring.

But, for the most part, The Amazing Adventures of ... does not seem to drag with time. This is probably because of the presence of Adrian Henri, possibly the most promising from this rash of contemporary poets, and also because of the group's high musical ability. The most outstanding tracks on the LP are the songs or

instrumental pieces — the sweet-memoried Gliders and Parks, the Charlie Parker-type sax on Universes, Andy Robert's guitar in Burdock River Run, the pleasant Percy Parslow's Hamster Farm, the Love Story raga. The Liverpool Scene seem so versatile — on this record alone they present rock, folk, jazz, and blues, all of an equally high standard. Usually the words are pleasant, the musical effects brilliant. It is only the four-part The Amazing Adventures of Che Guevara which falls into the ephemeral trap of a great deal of today's poetry — this is simply a monologue which becomes rather tiring after a few plays, helped on its way by the inclusion of 'live' laughter which makes it all sound like one big mutual admiration society. But other contemporary pieces, like Henri's Batpoem, are helped by the music and dó not meet the same fate. It's really rather an outstanding record.

C. Cousin.

NASHVILLE SKYLINE Bob Dylan CBS KCS 9825

Somebody once said that when Bob Dylan first started his career he wanted to be Elvis Presley much more than he wanted to be Woody Guthrie, the trouble was that there was an opening for a Guthrie so he took the gig. Analysing Dylan's motive is a common and generally fruitless pastime, and indeed, everytime one particular section of the audience began to believe that Dylan had committed himself to their trip, he promptly turned about, and accompanied by cries of 'Traitor' and 'sell-out' began to explore another music form.

In St. Augustine on John Wesley Harding Dylan sings — 'No martyr is among you, for you to call your own', and with this sentiment he has shrugged off, in turn, the patronage of the ethnic folksters, the peace marchers, the pop fans and the acid freaks. None of these changes are really so surprising when one takes the time to examine Dylan's musical background. Sure he got into Woody and Leadbelly and Big Joe Williams at an early age, but at the same time he was almost certainly getting drunk for the first time, and pulling his first chicks to the

sound of Buddy Holly, Elvis, The Everly Brothers, Chuck Berry and Gene Vincent.

All through his first albums there is this manifest desire to put down some rock and roll: the Wake Up Little Susie riff on Highway 51 on his first album: The thumping Jerry Lee Lewis style Mixed Up Confusion that was recorded on the Freewheeling session but not included on the album, Black Crow Blues and even Jack O'Diamonds that he wrote for Ben Carruthers all led up to Subterranean Homesick Blues, itself an adaptation of Chuck Berry's Too Much Monkey Business, and the subsequent three albums in which he fully worked out the rock thing.

Nashville Skyline in someways seems almost to be the working out of the other half of his rock influences, even to the extent that many of the tracks sound very like Presley or Jerry Lee Lewis B-sides and album tracks. I Threw It All Away is very like Presley's I Was The One while One More Night is reminiscent of a slowed down version of Blue Moon Of Kentucky, this similarity to the country rock of the middle fifties (what was known at the time as Western-Bop) is taken to such a length on Country Pie the guitar sound is practically identical to Cliff (Galloping) Gallup of the Bluecaps (Gene Vincents backing group).

Most of the music press in recent weeks have been shouting about 'Dylan Going C & W' and announcing the 'Great country music revival', but I think that in terms of a Hank Williams and Married By The Bible, Divorced By The Law type of country music, this revival will be as major a non-event as the rock revival of last year. I really don't see white Stetsons and banjoes turning up at the freakout, although I can see a lot of country on the lines of the band getting through to groups like, say, Fairport Convention. As Joe MacDonald said in IT, country music is music in E.

I am very tempted to think of Nashville Skyline as a pleasant and relaxed intermission in Dylans progress as an artist. It is produced with studied carelessness, he and Johnny Cash goof the words on Girl From The North Country, but nobody bothers with another take. On To Be Alone With You you hear Dylan asking 'is it (the tape) rolling Bob', while on Country Pie nobody bothers to do proper fade-out, they just shut down the faders.

Nashville Skyline may not exactly be Bob Dylans Ruben And The Jets but at times it comes close.

Mick Farren

Dr Byrds & Mr Hyde Byrds CBS 6345
Retrospective: Buffalo Springfield Atco 228012

When in their early days, the Byrds were compared to the Beatles by many American rock critics and fans, one of the factors they must have had in mind was the eclecticism common to both groups; and the Byrds, like the Beatles always had a strong enough sense of form and style so that whatever influences they drew on, the groups identity was firmly stamped on the material.

The Sweetheart of the Rodeo was a surprise in the context of the Byrds development on record. While each album prior to that had seemed a logical development and progression from the previous albums, Sweetheart of the Rodeo showed a different approach. For once the material, in this case country in origin and influence, was more dominant than the Byrds style, excepting in the vocals.

The new Byrds LP is also basically country, but it does show more of a reaffirmation of the basic Byrds style. Most of the tracks have more in common with the country influenced tracks such as Old John Robertson on the Notorious Byrds Brothers than with the Sweetheart of the Rodeo.

But while there was more of an attempt to achieve a synthesis of the two forms, electric rock and country music, the result is the least organic of the last four Byrds albums. Nevertheless, individual tracks are superb. The old country song, Old Blue, sheer corn, but a case of the Byrds style transmuting the original corniness of the song, and in fact making that

corniness one of the song's strengths. Their country instrumental, Nashville West, is like Dylan's, Nashville Skyline, pure fun. To show the Byrds are still masters of electric rock with taste and still the best interpreters of Dylan, is what is probably the best version yet of Wheels on Fire.

One of the problems facing groups like the Byrds and the Flying Burrito Brothers is in how to conciliate their liking for C & W styles with some of the attitudes and values to be found inherent in the music at its grass roots level. A problem that manifests itself in Drug Store Truck Driving Man a beautifully countrified number by Roger McGuinn, that is my favourite track on the album, and a track that shows McGuinn, (who wrote 5D and Eight Miles High, the prototypes of electric acid rock), has fully mastered the country music form.

Country music's influence on rock didn't of course begin with John Wesley Harding though one might think so reading some of the musical papers in this country, but has been an integral part of rock since the beginning. Presley had his roots in C & W as well as blues; Buddy Holly and the Everly Brothers even more so; while even a negro R & B/rock performer like Chuck Berry wrote songs such as Memphis which have a country feel to them; and Jerry Lee Lewis works now almost entirely in the C & W field. But most of the current interest in the form is due to Dylan and the country influenced rock albums that have been released since John Wesley Harding: The Bands' 'music From Big Pink, The Fantastic Expedition of Dillard and Clark, The Byrds' Sweetheart of the Rodeo, and the Flying Burrito Brothers Gilded Palace of Sin.

Another modern group who successfully formed a synthesis between rock and country was Buffalo Springfield. Their latest album is, as the title implies, a backward look over their career, and contains some of the best tracks from their previous albums.

The Springfield belong to the same genre as Moby Grape, The Spoonful, Byrds etc — white, country and folk influenced, friendly good time music, even if the Springfield were at times a little frightening or sad. If you haven't any of their previous LPs this is a good buy and almost essential as the Springfield was among the alltime great American Rock Bands.

Both Steve Stills and Neil Young were important songwriters and should continue to be so — Stills with the Crosby-Stills-Nash team and Young as a solo artist. Beautiful rolling rhythms on Stills compositions and sad, moving, sometimes almost frightening melodies and themes on Youngs'. Like The Band's LP this record presents a true synthesis of styles rather than a conscious attempt by a rock group to simply assimilate C & W styles.

Peter Dalton

music for the mind and body

POVERTY COOKING

Leg of Long Pig *
(Cuissot d'Enfant) Serves six.

Total cost: Nil. Perhaps 6d for a bag of sweets from Woolworths for use as a lure.

Ingredients: One plump school boy between the age of five and nine. Younger the flesh is too bland and lacks character, later the disappearance of pre-pubertal juices makes it tough and sinewy.

Method: Keep the boy (or girl) without food for at least a day. Then slit the throat and remove head, feet and hands. Allow the body to hang until the blood has stopped dripping. Remove one of the legs with a cut along the line of the groin, and saw it into six pieces, leaving the meat on the bone. Insert a clove of garlic into each piece of meat, season well with salt and pepper and sprinkle with thyme and marjoram. Put in a moderate pre-heated oven for approximately three hours. From time to time baste it with its own juices or with olive oil. The remainder of the carcass should be put in a deep freeze or left to pickle in a strong solution of salt and water, flavoured with herbs and spices, vinegar or wine and so on. It will keep a large family for at least a week.

The beautifully flavoured fat from this dish can be spread on slices of toasted French bread and makes a treat for the children at tea time.

* 'Do not forget that human flesh is edible, and of all animals, the human is the easiest to catch. Cook it well.'
Instructions in U.S. Army Survival Manual, quoted in Berkeley Barb, April 5-11 1968.

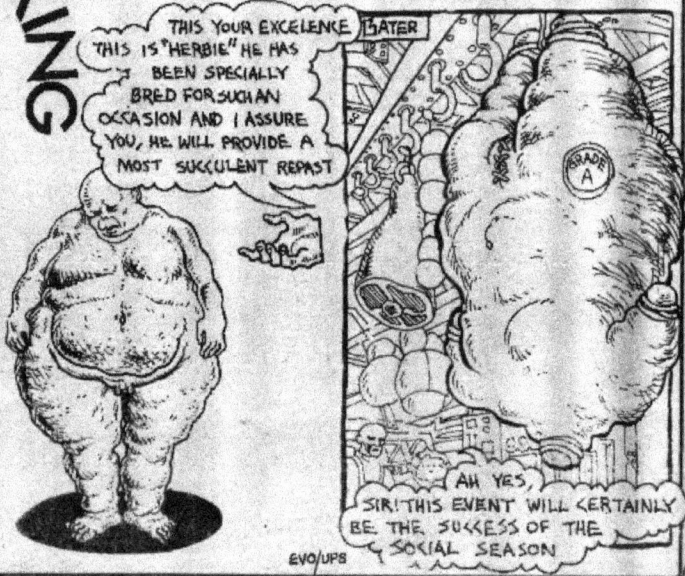

THIS YOUR EXCELENCE THIS IS "HERBIE" HE HAS BEEN SPECIALLY BRED FOR SUCH AN OCCASION AND I ASSURE YOU, HE WILL PROVIDE A MOST SUCCULENT REPAST

LATER

GRADE A

AH YES, SIR! THIS EVENT WILL CERTAINLY BE THE SUCCESS OF THE SOCIAL SEASON

EVO/UPS

3

Tommy

WRITTEN BY PETE TOWNSHEND

by
THE WHO

double album   triptych cover
12 page book in colour

Track Record

613 013/014

DISTRIBUTED BY
POLYDOR RECORDS LTD

34

It was the real thing that made my ring-a-ling ding...

Summertime Blues

Words and Music by Eddie Cochran and Jerry Capehart

I'm a-gonna raise a fuss, I'm a-gonna raise a holler,
About a-workin' all summer just to try to earn a dollar,
Ev'rytime I call my Baby, try to get a date,
My Boss says, "No dice, Son, you gotta work late"
Sometimes I wonder what I'm a-gonna do,
But there ain't no cure for the Summertime Blues.

Ah, well, my Mom 'n' Pa-pa told me, "Son, you gotta make some money,
If you want-ta use the car to go a-ridin' next Sunday,"
Well, I didn't go to work, told the Boss I was sick,
"Now you can't use the car 'cause you didn't work a lick."
Sometimes I wonder what I'm a-gonna do,
But there ain't no cure for the Summertime Blues.

I'm gonna take two weeks, gonna have a fine vacation,
I'm gonna take my problem to the United Nations!
Well, I called my Congress-man and he said (quote),
"I'd like to help you, Son, but you're too young to vote."
Sometimes I wonder what I'm a-gonna do,
But there ain't no cure for the Summertime Blues.

Recorded on Liberty by **EDDIE COCHRAN**
Music of all Music Dealers and of the Copyright Owners—Cinephonic Music Co. Ltd., 8 Denmark Street, London WC2

the CHIFFONS

My Boyfriend's Back

Words and Music by Robert Feldman, Gerald Goldstein and Richard Gotteherer

My boyfriend's back, and you're gonna be in trouble,
When you see him comin', better cut on the double,
You've been spreadin' lies that I was untrue,
So look out now 'cause he's comin' after you,
And he knows that you've been tryin',
And he knows that you've been lyin'.

He's been gone for such a long time,
Now he's back and things will be fine,
You're gonna be sorry you ever were born,
'Cause he's kind of big and he's awful strong,
And he knows about your cheatin',
Now you're gonna get a beatin'.

What made you think he'd believe all your lies?
You're a big man now but he'll cut you down to size! Wait and see!
My boyfriend's back, he's gonna save my reputation,
If I were you I'd take a permanent vacation.
La di la, my boyfriend's back! La di la, my boyfriend's back!

Recorded on Stateside by **THE CHIFFONS**
Music of all Music Dealers and of the Copyright Owners—KPM Music Ltd., 21 Denmark Street, WC2

Shakin' All Over

Words and Music by Johnny Kidd.

When you move in right up close to me,
That's when I get the shakes all over me,
Quivers down my backbone,
I've got the shakes down the kneebone,
Yeh! the tremors in the thighbone.
Shakin' all over.

Just the way you say goodnight to me,
Brings that feeling on inside of me,
Quivers down my backbone,
I've got the shakes down the kneebone,
Yeh! the tremors in the thighbone.
Shakin' all over.
Well, you make me shake and I like it.
Baby, well, you make me shake and I like it,
Baby, well, you make me shake and I like it.

Jenny Take A Ride

Words and Music by E. Johnson, R. Tenninan and Bob Crewe.

C—C—C—Rider see what you have done now,
C—C—C—Rider see what you have done now.
You made me love you,
Now, now, now, now—your man has come.
I'm goin' with my baby, won't be back for four years,
I'm goin' with my baby, and I won't be back for four years.
If I find me a new love, I won't be back at all!
Jenny, Jenny, Jenny, won't you come along with me,
Jenny, Jenny, Jenny, won't you come along with me,
Don't worry 'bout tomorrow, won't you come along with me!
Spinnin' spinnin' spinnin', spinnin' like a spinnin' top,
Spinnin' spinnin' spinnin', spinnin' like a spinnin' top,
So come along, babe, we're gonna reach the top!

C'mon Everybody

Words and Music by Eddie Cochran and Jerry Capehart

Well, c'mon, ev'rybody, and let's get together tonight!
I got some money in my jeans and I'm really gonna spend it right!
Been a-doin' my homework all week long,
Now the house is empty, the folks are gone.
Oo, oo! C'mon, ev'rybody!

Well, my baby's number one, but I'm gonna dance with three or four,
And the house'll be shakin' from my bare feet slappin' the floor
When you hear that music your feet won't sit still.
If your brother won't, then your sister will.
Oo, oo! C'mon, ev'rybody!

Well, we'll really have a party, but we gotta put a car outside,
If the folks come home I'm afraid they gonna have my hide.
There'll be no more movies for a week or two;
No more runnin' around with the usual crew.
Who cares. C'mon, ev'rybody!

Recorded on Liberty by **EDDIE COCHRAN**

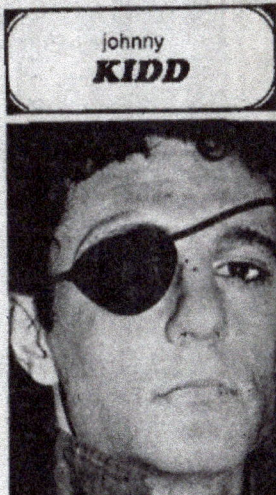

johnny KIDD

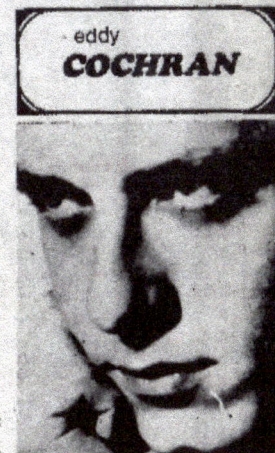

eddy COCHRAN

little RICHARD

35

THE GROOVY THING IS - YOU'RE NOT ALONE...

'The groovy thing is, you're not alone and there are more of us every day' All the time he's talking to you, Murray Roman reaffirms his connection with hip society. He employs the generation gap to win your sympathy – I'm with you man – and he's careful to stress the number, and the names, of the rock musicians he's friendly with.
'In the paper today it said that Jimmy Hendrix got busted for smack. I don't think Jimmy Hendrix was on smack 'cos I was with him last Saturday night and I know when a man's on smack and he wasn't.'
– that's professional name-dropping. Perhaps that's being overly critical. It's not until you've recovered from his amazing fluency and volume that the techniques by which he engages and retains your sympathy become more apparent.
That doesn't mean that he's not worth listening to. Murray Roman, one-time manager of the Righteous Brothers, head writer for the Smothers Brothers TV show and comedian in his own right, is one of the funniest and most perceptive guys ever. As a comedian he's more formidable than anyone in this country – he's no Ted Rogers; rapping with the mums and dads; no mothers-in-law and Mick Jagger impersonations for him.
'I wanted to relate to things that were making me laugh, making my friends laugh'
If you've heard his first album 'You Can't Beat People Up and Have Them Say I Love You', released on Track over here, you'll know that all those things relate to five subjects – drugs, sex, rock, authority and revolution. Our kind of subjects, right?
The strange thing is, although his approach, and the content of his comedy, seem cynically calculated to appeal to the market he's trying to reach – which is, for want of a better definition, the underground – when you talk to him you realise.... that, by a happy coincidence, he believes in 90% of what he says. In this interview he talked solidly for nearly forty-five minutes – he'd said it all before, many times, to all the underground papers in the States. When he came into the Track office, and saw a copy of OZ, he pressed the Underground Press Interview button.

MURRAY ROMAN

'(OZ) is a filthy paper published by filthy people. Drugs, orgies, police, loot, rape, gang-bang – fantastic! You could stand for Parliament on this platform and I know about 100,000 people who would vote for you.'
'The world is becoming a divided place divided between pro – and anti-life people. Pro-life people are pro – being alive – anti-life people make cigarettes.'
'They tell you that your mother is filthy – not above the neck or below the knees, but everything else is filth!
'Yes, but I came out of her ..... ;
'No you didn't – she didn't look.'
'Let them promote – let them take all the capitalistic approaches to selling our life-style. Beautiful! They gonna have to hire us to do it. Nobody's going to sell a rock-and roll record in this town without the underground press, because nobody is going to read the EMI press bulletin about what 'really good' music there is. I hope they open 5,000 FM stations in London. They're going to have to have somebody to rap to the kids and it can't be somebody who's gonna do numbers like 'Here's a really groovy JUDY GARLAND record, and here it is – OVER THE RAINBOW – let's hear it ...' – it's going to have to be some guy who can say 'Hey, here's a record that I played last night and I really dug it and I'm going to play it for you today, and I hope you like it – it could be a good trip.''
'English music made L B J resign – it's true! The kids were listening to the music – one day they appeared in the streets. And one of the great opportunists – a brilliant man, but an opportunist – Bobby Kennedy – said 'That many people really believe in Peace' – I'm gonna run for President.''
'We have a mayor in Los Angeles who has the I Q of a plant – his name is Sam Yorty. After Sirhan Sirhan killed Kennedy he went on National Television and gave the address of Sirhan's family in Pasadena in case you were a maniac and wanted to kill them.'

President Nixon makes these statements – 'As I've said before, as I'll say again, what I've said many times before is that I stand today where I have always stood', and you sit there and if you're a little smashed you say 'It's a put-on man – I tell you someone put acid in the water of the city and it's a hype.'
'The fantastic adventure of Anguilla – thousands of British troops conquering one snotty-nosed black kid with a goat. Officers standing on hills, glasses peering to see if they could find a frozen, rusted, double-barrelled shot gun to send to the Queen – 'They were armed Your Majesty.' – with skin.'
'Our Pueblo incident is just as heavy as your Anguilla – it's hysterical. The US navy sent the ship within 12 miles of the North Korean coast when they had been warned that they were liable to be attacked. On board they had 4000lbs of classified material – information about N A T O The captain did'nt want it –, what did he want information about N A T O for? – but the Navy forced him to accept it. When the ship was attacked, somebody said 'What are we going to do now?' they didn't even have an alternative plan, they didn't know what they were going to do and to destroy the classified equipment they had one paper-shredder and a pair of pliers and the guns were frozen and didn't work... It's one of the great sagas of American Naval History.'
'The United States is a country dedicated to saying 'Well, we made a terrible mistake in Vietnam but we'll keep killing them until they admit we weren't that wrong.'
'The Press in this country distorted the whole Cornell University trip. The filthy, foul Manchester Guardian – it's supposed to be a fair paper. Alistair Cooke wrote an article from the 21 club about what was happening in Ithaca, New York, 460 miles away. Nobody reported that the black kids never went into the building with those rifles – that they didn't collect the guns until 12 hours after they had been in there, and the reason that they got rifles was because they heard that 200 white men were coming in cars to kill them. The University officials didn't capitulate at gun-point and, what's worse, none of the ammunition the black kids had fitted the guns they

37

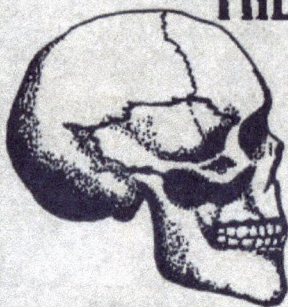

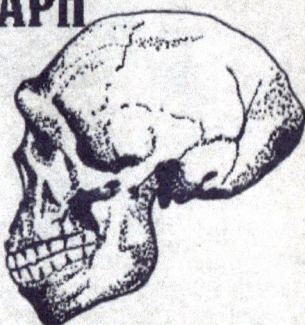

carried. They were scared — how old were they? — they averaged between 17 and 18½ years old. Scared, dead scared in a big, empty, draughty fucking building and the night before, in front of the Fraternity House, the Sorority House, where there were twelve black women, somebody burned the Cross. What were the kids supposed to believe — that they were beloved? I want to tell you that if I were at Cornell, and I were black, and somebody told me that there were 200 white men coming to shoot my ass I'd get me a double-barrelled shot-gun myself and say —. 'OK Whiteface, you come and get me and I'll take your ass with me' The Manchester Guardian reported it as 'Armed Black Militant Students Force University Authorities to Capitulate'. For six months those kids had tried every legal recourse to get a black studies programme and when there was nothing left they occupied the building — twelve of them.'

'If it wasn't for papers like OZ nobody would ever read the truth, and maybe nobody ever reads the truth anyway. The America that Alistair Cooke writes about from the 21 Club is the America he saw once in a movie with Betty Grable — who is a star here and nowhere else. Noel Redding's a star — if Betty Grable went into Madison Square Garden she wouldn't even draw my mother if you gave her a free ticket and Noel Redding will draw 21,000 people and jam it to the rafters — so who's the star? Donovan will fill the Hollywood Bowl — Betty Grable couldn't even get the usher to remain. But what I'm really talking about is what Mr. Cooke thinks is a star and what Mr. Cooke thinks is America.'

'We worship Bob Hope. Bob Hope himself has never had a funny thought in his life — which is already funny. His script-writers have... Every year Bob Hope goes to Vietnam and entertains the troops and all of America falls to its knees and sucks Bob off. We as tax-payers pay for his trip as he takes along 50 broads and other entertainers and they fly over first-class with Army camera men shooting film of the whole thing. I don't mind that — Bob's a big star — but then six weeks later N.B.C. has a show called 'Bob Hope In Vietnam' and it was sold for half a million dollars. Now for half a million dollars I would be willing to go away every year and entertain the boys anywhere they wanted me to — to the fucking South Pole. And yet we pay for everything — the hotels, the expenses, and a detachment of

our finest troops to make sure the Vietcong don't shoot Bob's balls off.
'Let's stop talking about drugs — we're helping them. Timothy Leary should have shut up 'Give it to kids...' — Oh 'Shut Up. There were no laws against it in the States until that loud-mouth got on the tube. What with Timothy Leary and Jerry Rubin we got enough trouble to last for years.'

'If you make a statement you make a statement that helps us all, you don't act so that every uncommited American says 'They're all filthy — they're crazy — they run around in their underwear.' I'm going to start to wear a suit, but I'm going to be who I am because I know who I am, and that's the difference between us — I can sit and look at myself in a mirror and I like Me.'

'I've never heard anybody who smoked dope to say 'I can lick any man in the house.' cos if somebody says it at any party I've ever been at they say 'Go ahead and lick me man — I'll sit back and unzip myself. Fred, he wants to lick you first.'

'Maybe we shouldn't wear uniforms — maybe that's where we're going wrong, like if the Vietcong wore signs around their necks saying 'I'm a Vietcong' they

wouldn't have any trouble figuring out who was who in the villages. Like, if we walked along the street together, and a policeman saw us, do you think the thought would ever cross his mind that we smoked dope? All you have to do is to get into a category and then they know who you are. You'll only upset them if they don't know who you are.'

'I'm cool all the time — I wouldn't let them have that shot at me. I'm too smart, why should I help them? Let's go and give ourselves up and we'll see who comes with us. Man, don't you see that they're taking us one by one? — and that's how we'll fall. We're all ashamed — 'Did you hear so-and-so got busted?' — 'No where, when?'. Just like in Munich — 'Did you hear Bergstein got taken by the Gestapo?'; 'You're kidding — when?'. And everybody said after the war 'How come the Jews never fought back?'. Will they say that about us? Among Jews anyway, the burning question is —.. 'How did they do it? — load them into cattle cars, pile them into ovens, stuff hot lead up their asses?' The answer is — they did it ONE BY ONE.'

'If we're going to fall let's all fall together — at least if they put us in jail we'd know everybody.'

Harvest will be in
June this year —

HARVEST

Danny Hughes

CHE
BODY POLITIC

In New York today, some actors and actresses are lobbying their union to ban nudity from the stage. This is an 'inevitable reaction where sex, rock and drugs are part of the movement, & where black & white don't just denote skin but symbolise polar areas of thought. There are bridges everywhere in Manhattan except between lifestyles & the way its inhabitants think, feel & act.

Not surprising, then, that on 24 March *Che*, the play that took the puritanism which still grips most Americans to its opposite and logical extreme by having actors fuck on stage, was busted; & its entire cast, author, director & 16 year-old stage hand, were charged with public lewdness, consentual sodomy, impairing the morals of a minor, & conspiring to commit the same.

On Saturday 25 April, *Che* illegally re-opened where it had started -- the Free Store Theatre on Cooper Square – thus giving a few more avid readers of Screw, Pleasure, Rat, Other Scenes, Nyrs, etc, to say nothing of the Morals Squad, another chance to see it.

After an evening of organised boredom with the Performance Group's *Dionysus in 69*, I had apprehensions about *Che*.

Written over a period of two years by Lennox Raphael, a West Indian from Trinidad (who, to quote him, is 'the product of a good fuck'), *Che* is an explicit and coherently extended sexual metaphor of the body politic and its convulsions. A complicated series of sexual games develops between Che, who is a general symbol of revolutionary energy; the President of the United States, naked except for a star-spangled Uncle Sam topper & a red-white-and-blue cord tied round his waist; Mayfang, the lesbian 'angelspy', representing variously the new technology, the Military and the CIA; the 'viciously delicious' Sister of Mercy, who is a composite of the real Che Guevara's Tania & the Catholic nun who was photographed washing Che's wounds & smiling over his dead body; & Chili Billy, son of King Kong.

'King Kong was the first sign of sanity in America after that freak Thomas Paine,' Raphael thinks, 'I wanted to use King Kong just to provoke us to dig the ape in all of us, the beauty of the Ape.'

Neither the President (played by Paul Georgiou, whose body carried rather more conviction than the rest of his acting) who tries constantly & unsuccessfully to seduce Che (Larry Bercowitz), nor Mayfang (Jeanne Baretich, sinister in silver lamé with a clear plastic dildo slung round her neck, Mattel submachinegun under arm, plastic nipples & steel wool crutch, who has a go at everyone) – ever have orgasms.

Che makes it with 'the chosen clit', Sister Mary Anne (Mary Anne Shelley, with the best tits off-off Broadway), who comes with everyone, even whilst being beaten by Mayfang, & again – very violent – when ravished by the fur-suited and priapic Chili Billy (David Zaslow).

The fucking scene between Che & Sister Mary Anne is inevitably the most notorious moment of the play, but it is also the best. They screw in various positions on the Star-Spangled Bedcover, beneath a slow strobe which increases its tempo with the lovers. This was mime: Bercowitz didn't have an erection. But my reservation about the sexual mime in Dionysus didn't apply here. Why? Because, the scene was not so obviously choreographed, because it was not 'removed' from the audience and, being so skilfully and *realistically* performed, the symbolic functioning of its reality was not impaired.

The end comes fast & savagely. The President declares, 'On my Dickery-Dick is Capitalista', and Che, disregarding the warning never to bite 'the cock that feeds you', bites it while blowing the President. Whereupon the anguished and outraged embodiment of Western capitalism grabs Mayfang's handy machine-gun epigrammatically bellows 'Fuck you . . . motherfucker!', shoots Che & his bride of Christ, & collapses sobbing on the prime object of his lust, the body of Che. 'I worked on the premise,' said Raphael, 'that Che was killed because he bit on America's pride' & expansionist ecstasies.'

This, of course, is a simplification of the action, even in sexual terms. There was much group-groping, blowing & invitation to buggery. There are some hilarious moments, as when the President, in a desperate and contorted attempt to locate 'the real me' by orgasm, tries to suck himself off; although in the first half-hour or so the constant bombardment of snap-lines ('Mudpack my passion'; 'I seek the real me in the debris of your lust'; 'Semen surrounds my teardrops'; 'We are the nature of our games'; 'Pain has its own reflection') is lightened only by tentative fingerings between Che & the President & a bit of half-hearted dildo-sucking from Mayfang, as Lolita with her popsicle, threatens to overbalance the play by making it too wordbound. Raphael has packed so much into it that the temptation is to get hung up at this or that point, deciphering the significance of a single detail instead of flowing with the action. It is a 100-minute one-acter without any breathing-spaces.

A source of confusion on the night I saw it was that no-one at all got a hard-on (though the cast had made it five times before, according to Bercowitz and Raphael – whose paternal advice to his actors went, 'Do it if you can & if you can't it doesn't matter'; and the critic of Screw reports seeing the Presidential prick semi-erect after leaving Mayfang's lips). Thus it was often uncertain whether limpness had political implications or not. In the end, this ambiguity didn't matter. The metaphor worked & in a single viewing it is possible to extract the implication that established power always tries to assimilate to itself subversive forces, & if it fails, has those energies crushed by the occasional servant of both – modern technology, which, being simply a tool, wants to be used by (or come with) either.

The Foreplay note to *Che* indicates Lennox Raphael's motives & sympathies: "*Writing is revolution when done in the interests of revolution;* . . . *the revolution is being revolutionised because it is also an ecstasy of who lays whom.*"

&even though Raphael sta..ted in an EVO interview with DA Latimer that . . .

'*The play is intended to displease Left & Right, & provoke people to dig what's happened to themselves. The way we destroy ourselves with our power games, the way a big powerful congestive country like America could gang up against Cuba, for example. The way we could consider that morally right. The way we rationalise, moralize, the violence in Vietnam, North & South, very functional.*'

Che works both as revolutionary event & as revolutionary theatre. (Assuming Abbie Hoffman is right when he claims that confusing your enemies is the primary act of revolt.) It is a play where all action takes place in terms of the functions of the human body, & the breaking of social & theatrical taboos which has confused the straight press, at least, is not gratuitous. The obscenity is structural. Though there's nothing technically new in Ed Wode's production, *Che* is one of the first convincing images, in art, of the counter-culture's belief that sex, politics & violence cannot be disassociated in revolutionary contexts. 'Revolution is a wolf howling in the vestibules of your passion.'

The night before I left New York, *Che* was busted again, for being performed in an unlicensed theatre – a legal point which applies to almost every off-off Broadway production. A pity; but the enforced rest may give the cast bigger & better horns in future matiness. The script is to be issued by Raphael's own newly-formed publishing company, Hotwax.

robert Bauman NYRS

Peter Buckman

There's some corner of a foreign field, that is
for ever England, where only those who have
houses may vote in local elections, & such
houses are in the personal gift of local
councillors who don't give them to people
likely to vote against them. The government of
this same field, that is for ever England,
encourages foreign investment, so Entre
Preneurs from all over move in & start up
factories, thus doing their mite to relieve a
chronic unemployment situation. However, as
soon as these factories have started making a
profit, the owners make a quick sale & move
out, leaving their workers worse off than
before. There is an act that has been on the
statute books of this field, that is for ever
England, since 1922. Called the Special Powers
Act, it enables the police to arrest without
warrant, imprison without charge, forcibly
enter houses to make a search, flog prisoners &
deny an inquest if they die, forbid anyone,
whether lawyer or relation, to meet with the
prisoner, prohibit the circulation of any
newspaper & the possession of any film or
gramophone record, & arrest anyone who does
anything 'calculated to be prejudicial to the
preservation or maintenance of order in
Northern Ireland & not specifically provided
for in the regulations'. You may wonder why
any British government would permit a corner
of her field to have such arrangements. That is
the question Bernadette Devlin asked in
Westminster.
The civil rights movement in Ulster, like any
radical movement anywhere in the world, is
trying to organize support on class lines. It
takes a lot of bloodied heads before people
realize that there are those who exploit and
those who are exploited. In Ulster the problem
is complicated by the religious factor; people
are denied houses & jobs because they may be
Catholic & the council who represents them is
100% Protestant. But the movement for which
Bernadette Devlin is just one spokeswoman is
not after justice for Catholics, but justice for all
the exploited. Seen from England itself the
notion sounds absurdly old-fashioned &
doctrinaire. But it's way ahead of the separatist
demands made by, say, Black Power groups. It's
at the same advanced stage as the American
radical movement, where at least – & under the
tremendous threat of immediate extinction –
black & white radicals are giving each other
support in the name of justice for all the
_____. Sounds terrible unless you are
_____ you don't have to be out of a job
_____ that. Just go on any peaceful
_____ march outside the range of television
_____ras.
_____adette Devlin has the knack of making
_____estminster seem ridiculous, in a far more
_____btle way than Jerry Rubin made the House of
_____-American Activities Committee seem absurd
_____y appearing in full guerillero rig. She did
_____ need to dress up. Bernadette spent her maiden
speech in telling the Commons just what it
could do with itself.

People's Democracy is trying to do what the
black-white radical coalition in America is
doing: build a movement on lines of class rather
than colour or religion. What kind of success
have you had, & how long do you think it will
last? How do you avoid problems between
students & workers?
Bernadette Devlin: U_____ _____ _____ p_____
we don't have th_____ _____ _____ _____ feel
themselves to be a _____ _____ _____ _____
themselves in terms _____ _____ _____
background _____ _____ _____
been no fric_____ _____ _____ _____
working-class people in U_____ _____ _____
very open _____ _____ _____ _____
come to its meetings. We _____ going _____ _____
tied up in rigid b_____ cratic procedures. As to
the success of the movement in building along
class lines, we've only just begun. It's very
difficult to make people see that we don't stand
for an IRA or a 'Pan_____ _____ iot. Our aim is
to smash the Unio_____ _____ _____ is to blame
for the present _____ _____ _____ Prime
Minister, M_____ _____ James Daw_____

Chichester-Clark, isn't going to make any
difference: he's just another squire. But we
don't want union with Eire either: we want
them to organize and demand their social
justice. And in England too – it was very
encouraging when I went down to a building
site & talked to the Irish workers. They were
ready to go & do something.

Has your movement learnt anything from
American experience?
I don't think directly, because you're dealing
with political backwoodsmen. Vietnam doesn't
mean anything there. But indirectly, yes. The
Irish student too realized he was just part of a
sausage-factory: the campaign for the elect_____
let him see that it was possible to organi_____ _____
_____ radical acti_____ _____ _____ king class.

_____ about the _____ _____ _____ ssociation?
People's Democ_____ _____ _____ is _____ _____ _____ as
becomes mor_____ _____
The CRA_____ _____ _____ _____ _____ _____, you
know, it's _____ _____ _____ _____ _____ _____ who
are getting _____ _____ _____ _____ _____ in A_____ _____ _____
up a con_____ _____ _____ _____ _____ to put together
all the _____ _____ _____ _____ up until the
electio_____ _____ _____ _____ _____ start organizing
befo_____ _____ _____ _____ _____ _____: up to now
we'_____ only _____ _____ _____ _____ _____ start
initiating – thin_____ like _____ _____ _____ strikes,
squatting, workers' co_____ _____ of _____ _____ _____

_____ll you form a politica_____ _____? Is _____ _____ you
want possible without it?
Not a political party as it is normally
understood. We must retain our spontaneity,
but we must also have a programme & be ready
to meet the challenge of repression. Our
programme – which we've said we'll stop all
our activities for – it's granted – is in the
points made during the election. But the
government can't grant them, because they're
revolutionary. We have to organize, & we have
to build up from the roots. How you do that
without becoming structure-bound we don't
yet know. But we ought to begin talking about
it before it's too late.

Do you foresee extended street action?
Yes, because what the government is offering is
only tokenism. Chichester-Clark'll be out soon,
& Faulkner (the ex-Deputy Prime Minister) will
come in like a blinding light, & he'll give us one
man-one vote. But god help anyone who wants
anything more. We shall get "strong
government". Faulkner is a fascist, but an
extremely clever one. Westminster will just look
on & make noises. My function there is just to
make sure they don't forget they have the
ultimate responsibility.

Can you organize to prevent this? You've
talked of a Citizen's Army.
It's still a spontaneous movement, you see. We
don't control it: something has started which
has to be given its head. I don't think a
Citizen's Army such a bad idea: it worked in
Bogside, in Derry.

Won't you then have the problem of being
isolated – depending on the surrounding areas
for sustenance?
Bogside wasn't isolated. Workers were allowed
to come & go, to do their jobs. Anyone was
allowed out: we were just careful about who we
allowed in. The police were kept out, but it
wasn't a siege. The ghettoes are there, like in
America, but we've proved we can defend
them.

What about Westminster?
I suppose I compromised myself by standing,
but I don't expect anything from them. It airs
the principles of the cause. The English workers
should bring pressure on Westminster if we
can't at Stormont. I know I can't do much,
except remind them of their responsibilities.

Then was your campaign a waste of time?
It helped us to consolidate our organization, &
the publicity's useful, I don't think it's going to
affect me. What matters is that the true
conditions be exposed so that a united
movement – a socialist movement – can be
built up. There has to be civil rights activities in
the South as well as in the North, & in England
too. That's the only way we'll get through to
the Protestant working class & convince them it
isn't all a Popish plot. But first we have to solve
our own problems in Ulster – get a just society
for Protestants and Catholics.

What's going to happen?
We'll have a three-sided civil war – the
Protestant bigots, the Papist bigots, & us in the
middle. We should really get our best men out
_____ Ireland's tragedy has always been that they
_____ot. As for me, I keep getting letters saying
_____ a gun and learn how to use it". I don't
thin_____ coul bring myself to shoot anyone. I
can _____ ct _____ way.
_____ we have to do is to sit down & talk about
_____ next moves. So far there hasn't been time:
_____ _____ _____ ly defending ourselves against the
_____ _____ _____ _____ _____ _____ by the government
_____ _____ _____ _____ _____ ambush. 90 of the people in
_____ _____ _____ _____ _____ _____ Specials: we took
_____ their pictures _____ _____ _____. We have to be
_____ganized to protect ours_____, but also we
_____ _____ _____ _____ _____ people think things will
die d_____ n _____ _____ _____. But we're getting
small g_____ _____ _____ _____ the country, in twos
& threes, _____ _____ to people, finding out what
they want. That was what the election helped
us to achieve – the participation of people who
had nothing to hope for from politics.

If your aims of a socialist Ireland are achieved,
won't it immediately become the victim of
economic isolation?
It could, but that's a long way off. We hoped
for a lot from the British Labour Party, but
were quickly disillusioned. We wouldn't be able
to rely on them & now we don't. We no longer
have to act in order to get their sympathy:
we're not interested. We must build unity –
that is our only task. As the situation isn't
revolutionary, there can't be any talk of
'counter-revolutionary tactics'. We have to
answer all the questions that are raised in
America & elsewhere: how to bring socialist
freedom & justice without becoming
bureaucratized & unfree. We don't know the
answers, but now we have to find the time to
sit down & ask them.

43

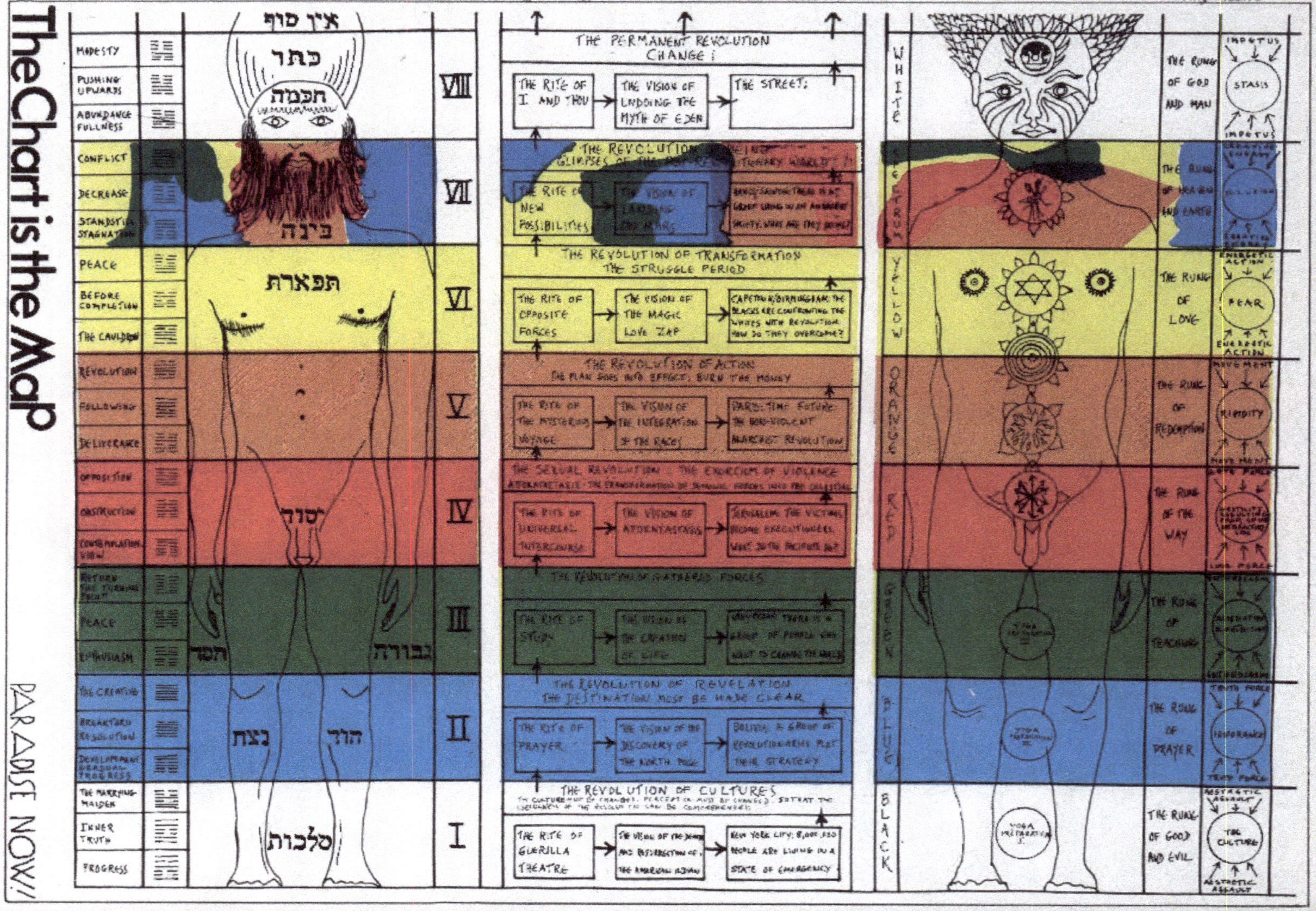
The Chart is the Map
PARADISE NOW!
אין סוף
כתר
חכמה
בינה
תפארת
יסוד
חסד
גבורה
נצח
הוד
מלכות
MODESTY
PUSHING UPWARDS
ABUNDANCE FULLNESS
CONFLICT
DECREASE
STANDSTILL STAGNATION
PEACE
BEFORE COMPLETION
THE CAULDRON
REVOLUTION
FOLLOWING
DELIVERANCE
OPPOSITION
OBSTRUCTION
CONTEMPLATION VIEW
THE CREATIVE
BREAKTHRU RESOLUTION
DEVELOPMENT GRADUAL PROGRESS
THE MARRYING MAIDEN
INNER TRUTH
PROGRESS
VIII
VII
VI
V
IV
III
II
I
THE PERMANENT REVOLUTION CHANGE:
THE RITE OF I AND THOU
THE VISION OF UNDOING THE MYTH OF EDEN
THE STREET:
THE REVOLUTION OF TRANSFORMATION THE STRUGGLE PERIOD
THE RITE OF OPPOSITE FORCES
THE VISION OF THE MAGIC LOVE ZAP
CAPETOWN/BIRMINGHAM: THE BLACKS ARE CONFRONTING THE WHITES WITH REVOLUTION. HOW DO THEY OVERCOME?
THE REVOLUTION OF ACTION
THE PLAN GOES INTO EFFECT: BURN THE MONEY
THE RITE OF THE MYSTERIOUS VOYAGE
THE VISION OF THE INTEGRATION OF THE RACES
PARIS: TIME FUTURE: THE NON-VIOLENT ANARCHIST REVOLUTION
THE SEXUAL REVOLUTION: THE EXORCISM OF VIOLENCE
THE RITE OF UNIVERSAL INTERCOURSE
THE VISION OF APOKATASTASIS
JERUSALEM: THE VICTIMS BECOME EXECUTIONERS. WHAT DO THE PACIFISTS DO?
THE REVOLUTION OF REVELATION
THE DESTINATION MUST BE MADE CLEAR
THE RITE OF PRAYER
THE VISION OF THE DISCOVERY OF THE NORTH POLE
BOLIVIA: A GROUP OF REVOLUTIONARIES PLAN THEIR STRATEGY
THE REVOLUTION OF CULTURES
THE RITE OF GUERILLA THEATRE
NEW YORK CITY: 8,000,000 PEOPLE ARE LIVING IN A STATE OF EMERGENCY
WHITE
SPECTRUM
YELLOW
ORANGE
RED
GREEN
BLUE
BLACK
THE RUNG OF GOD AND MAN
THE RUNG OF HEAVEN AND EARTH
THE RUNG OF LOVE
THE RUNG OF REDEMPTION
THE RUNG OF THE WAY
THE RUNG OF TEACHING
THE RUNG OF PRAYER
THE RUNG OF GOOD AND EVIL
IMPETUS
STASIS
FEAR
ENERGETIC ACTION
MOVEMENT
RIGIDITY
TRUTH FORCE
IGNORANCE
AESTHETIC ASSAULT
THE CULTURE

The Plot is the Revolution

The Ritual is the Vision

"It is impossible to muster functions of life well if one does not live them fully ... This is the meaning of work democracy".
William Reich. *People in Trouble*

WHO?

The Living Theatre community : 30 plus large people ages 20 - 45, eight children, dealers, missionaries, camp-followers, etc, a school for teachers, the absolute gathering together around something Holy.

LIVING WITH THE LIVING

by Gunter Pannewitz

Travelling for three years with the Living Theatre means changing from city to city, from one reality to another. We play with a different audience night by night. Everything is a matter of circumstance; so are the people; so are we thirty-three persons living together and working together. We do not make the choice of running away; instead we teach love for each other and respect for each other. We have developed a great need to find our truth, our beauty, ourselves, in order to be strong and clear at every moment in all our self-expression; that means that we must develop belief in ourselves and in our spiritual beauty, recognizing that every single person, every single life, is his own messenger. It means discovering certain techniques of life in order to stay high. Well, thirty-three different peoples mean thirty-three different techniques, just as one million monks have one million different religions. All of this leads to a more or less poetic way of life, depending on your development of self-discipline, love and the beauty which you discover in yourself, in the world, in people; the way you relate to the world is the way you treat yourself.

Standing Under Signals

First I Take A Deep Breath
Then I Receive Cautiously
Carefully I Project What I Read
Delicately I Examine It
Forgetting What There Was Before
I Understand What's Now:
First I Take A Deep Breath
Then I Invite What Now
I Cautiously Receive

That I Carefully Project
Delicately Examine
Forgetting It
I Throw Out The Image
To Understand:
Now
I Take A Deep Breath
To Be Vital And Responsible
Responding With Compassion
To The Present Signal
Emergency !
Caution-Emergency !
Careful-Emergency !
Delicate-Emergency-Emerge !!
Invitation For Vita Emerging Through
The Deep Breath That Awakens Me To .
Life The Responsibility
Life The Reability To Respond
In Compassion To The :
Presence
Presenting Pre-Sent Emergency
Emerge !!!
Echnaton

WHEN

Frankenstein: June 4,5,13,14,16, & 17
Mysteries: June 6 & 7
Paradise Now: June 9 & 10
Antigone: June 11 & 12
All performances start at 8 p.m. Approximately six performances of each production. First and second weeks schedules above. Second two weeks scheduled shortly. Also individual and special events at Arts Lab, 182 Drury Lane WC2 during month of June.

WHAT?

Performing:

Mysteries and Smaller Pieces
'This special performance is a public enactment of ritual games which are part of our work... If our work should succeed at any moment, it is because we on stage will reflect every man on the street; that is, we will have achieved Artaud's vision of the actor 'being like victims burnt at the stake, signalling through the flames'
Julian Beck.

Antigone
After Sophocles/ after Holderin/ after Brecht a new translation by Judith Malina.

Frankenstein
A meditation the purpose of which is to lead to levitation. If it succeeds the play is consummated. If it fails it becomes a victimisation.

Paradise Now
Voyage from the Many to the One, Guerilla Theatre Rite, through visions, orgies, trances to Rite of I and Thou, The Street and the Open-ended possibility of Change and Permanent Revolution, Vision of the Landing on Mars, the Rite of New Possibilities. Ritual tells us the Content of actions. Paradise Now goes from ritual to vision to action.

STUDENT: Well, what can I do? I'm just one man.
SBI: (with a lot of passion) That's what you've been made to think. You've been made to think that you're an amorphous, hybrid thing. Like in the cowboy movies, there's always this group of guys up at the ranch who have no names. They're just waiting there to be called to fight. And They're the abstract, hybrid form — the boys back at the ranch. And that's what the people are. (Screaming) And you've been made and trained to think that.
STUDENT: That's violence.
SBI: No, I'm getting hot, the blood is going through my body; my body is feeling; my face is red; my blood is going to my head; there's more air in my brain right now; my consciousness is expanding; and I'm alive.
Steve Ben Israel

APRIL 13, 1968
It's total crap: I don't wanna be a poet but rather a sonofabitch to be shot in Bolivia or Memphis or Berlin.
Gianfranco Mantegna

MEDITATIONS: ON THE LIFE OF THEATRE

The following are portions from THE LIFE OF THEATRE, a book by Julian Beck which will be published by City Lights later this year:

Who says we are mistreating the body with our drugs our opium our marijuana our lysurgic acid psylocybin heroin cocaine peyote mescaline mushrooms hasheesh kheef amphetamine. We are honoring it and its ability to change like the moon, like an embryo, like a poem, like a war.
Ferrara, May 1966
The Theatre is the Wooden Horse by which we can take the town.
Paris, October 1967
The creature who is formed at the end of the 1st and 3rd acts of Frankenstein not only means the public, it is the public, the creature simultaneously menaces civilization and is civilization. It is civilization menacing itself.
Lausanne, January 1968
To remain sane in this civilization process demands the criminalization of the self.
Paris, December 1967
Violent action, violent revolution, changes

things, but remain what they are.
Perne. January 1968
You can never tell an actor to move to the right or to take a step downstage. He has to be doing something. You cant give an actor a technical direction. There has to be a motivation that is more than getting out of the way or filling in the space. Whatever the actor does he has to be creating something or else he is wasting his life. Now this same knowledge must be applied to life. The State and Capital are always telling the people to move over there and to fill in the space, their directions are not creative to the degree that none of the actors in the great world drama are not wasting their lives. Continuing the metaphor, that is why we have to change all the mises en scene.
Paris, December 1967, Granville, Ohio December 1968

Really   (?   (III)   I
it takes a lot of courage
these   days to say

"what   is   that"   ....(The Fuc)
                                    (Really)
because I
hear that we are
moving in something
which I can
                        I   see:
with my own eyes

but ———————— so ———————— what
THE FU   S THAT

Petra Vogt.

WHERE?

Roundhouse, Chalk Farm Road, London NW1, Tel 01-485-8073
Prices: Monday-Thursday: 5/- 10/- 20/- 40/-
Friday-Saturday: 10/- 15/- 15/6 60/-
"... all the ways of earth are the ways to heaven/'
Eric Gutkind, The Absolute Collective

HOW?

How much a night in the theatre has changed us is perhaps the wrong question. Perhaps the right question is, What, if anything, do we know after this experience that we didn't know before in terms of what we're going to do from now on? That's change. I think really the only change is the change that leads to some kind of change in action or activity. Of course this includes the intellectual Process, but our theatre is no longer purely intellectual theatre.
But it mustn't get as lost there as it can on an intellectual level.
But if the audience is already radicalized, then we have our next question.
How can we as theatre now serve you as students or you as audience or you as people twenty-five years younger than me? In Paradise Now we try very very much to give the stage to the audience so that we can learn just that. But even Paradise Now is set up from problems we thought six months ago were the pertinent problems, problems we thought of in France in a very specific political milieu. Here we're surrounded by another political milieu.
If the question is, How have the Mysteries changed you? or, How have you felt moved? let me amend the question: How can the theatre serve the revolution? That's what I want to know from you. That means you have to be the revolution too, you know. We call upon you to be the revolution!
Judith Malina

46

WALK ON
GILDED
SPLINTERS

Hot Rod
Poppa
Track
604030

MARSHA
HUNT

DAVID BAILEY

47

Track Record

DISTRIBUTED BY POLYDOR RECORDS LTD.

OZ 22
July 1969

OZ is published by
OZ Publications Ink
52 Princedale Road, London W1
Telephone 229 7541.

Printed by OZ Publications Ink.

This issue appears with the help of
Richard Neville, Felix Dennis, Virginia.
Jon Goodchild, Louise Ferrier,
Ken Petty, Miss Murphy, Jim Anderson,
Martin Sharp, Keith Morris,
Andrew Fisher, Brigid Harrison.

Distribution.
UK: Moore Harness Ltd, 11 Lever Street,
London EC1. E CAL, 22 Betterton Street,
London WC2. TEM 8606. Transmutation,
Guildford 65694. California: Rattner
Distributors, 2428 McGee Street, Berkeley,
California 94703. Holland: Thomas Rap,
Regulierwarstraat 91, Amsterdam, Tel:
020-227065. Denmark: George Streeton,
The Underground, Larsbjorn Straede 13,
Copenhagen K.

Advertising: Contact Felix Dennis at 727-8456.

ZAP COMIX

For our border units we gratefully acknowledge the cover design by Dave Loxley of the new Third Ear Band L.P. 'Alchemy' on EMI's Harvest label.

Music is the natural high.
JUST . . . .
laugh,
cry,
sigh,
snarl,
scream,
lurch,
move,
be silent,
fall about,
love,
be alone,
drop out,
work,
turn on,
be a head,
groove,
grope,
grovel,
fly,
float,
swim,
sleep,
speed,
protest,
energise,
own up,
crap,
creep,
or just be yourself . . . .
don't go short
(by courtesy of Alan Skidmore)

do it to Marmalade Records

On July 4th Marmalade is releasing:–
'Streetnoise'
Julie Driscoll and the Brian Auger Trinity
'If only for a moment'
Blossom Toes
'Battersea Rain Dance'
Chris Barber Band
'3,000 years with Ottilie'
Ottilie Patterson
'Thinking Back'
Gordon Jackson
'Extrapolation'
John McLaughlin
'Oliv 1 and 2'
Spontaneous Music Ensemble
'100% Proof'
The Marmalade Sampler—priced 14/6d
MARMALADE BRINGS MUSIC TO A HEAD

'Rolling Stone is not,' cried Jane Nicholson, 'repeat *not* an Underground paper,' as OZ and IT were busted.

'Well,' the friendly policemen might have replied, 'you use four letter words like rock and fuck and dope, don't you?'

Poor baby. It's awful to be so misunderstood. You just want to talk about music and fucking and dope, that's all. We *know* you have no intention of overthrowing this Vichy government; nothing is clearer than that English Rolling Stone presents no threat to any political institution of any kind. Well, sister, events of the past weeks should prove even to you that Rolling Stone had better develop some political principle and subversive knowhow, because when the Man decides he wants you for saying fuck and all that, he isn't going to check with the underground whether they claim you, let alone whether you think you belong.

Recent publicity in the Melody Maker (yet) for the Lyceum, filled Mecca magnates with terror & disgust. When Mick Farren fronted down there with a chick shortly after Tony Wilson's mild rave (which was mainly about how much more comfortable it was than the Roundhouse) he was barred from entering because they didn't want any 'superfreaks', were not underground, didn't want to know. After some agro they were let in free, just as arbitrarily as they had been excluded.

The real reason why Miss Nicholson and Mecca Ballrooms want to disassociate themselves from the underground is that they have to make money. Both want to be allowed to keep on making it, and that means keeping in with the cops and with the users of dope, rock and sex. Society will permit a brothel but not a house full of happy fuckers: the kids will be allowed to have their fun at the Lyceum within limits and for a price. Lyceum means high school, I believe, and this one is a 4½ million pound shit-heap, with flesh-coloured lights and writhing stucco ornaments more obscene than anything the underground has ever spontaneously emitted. To see hippikins and hippettes milling miserably around among the Mecca gorillas, who hate them, almost blurs the memory of police collaboration at the Roundhouse, and UFO seems another part of Summer '67. The Midnight Court (once associated with John Peel's name without his consent — a trick more underground than above board) at the Lyceum is doomed, because the underground that they milk for a pound a head will keep using it as a rendezvous, to pick up dope, or sleep in or freak out in, despite the fevered protestations of the square management. The management will co-operate with the police to show their good faith, and the police to show theirs will close it down. Who the hell cares?

Despite the two English issues which were contemptible, it would be sad if Rolling Stone goofed, as they are sure to do if they try to serve the cause of rock and the

Establishment simultaneously. In America it is clear that this divided loyalty is a no-no, as Janis Joplin pointed out with her comment on the meaning of long hair there and here, because persecution is less subtle and resourceful than in England. In England Miss Nicholson is tempted to please everybody all the time if she can get away with it, but she's playing poker in the dark. Once a paper admits any principle of censorship for survival, the we-don't-want-to-do-it-but-we-don't-want-to-lose-the-printer kind of censorship, it jeopardises the integrity of its editorial principle.

It's better to print and be damned, because you'll be damned anyway.

It is actually impossible for any paper worth reading to satisfy all the Man's requirements for trouble-free journalism, so it's strategically better to give him as much trouble as possible. The bitterness of the situation may be gauged from an example. Some issues ago OZ deleted an article which would have given them, in a deliberately disgusting form, a scoop, a possible libel (unlikely) and a more possible reaction from the printer. While still bleeding from this self-imposed wound, OZ was busted for something no-one expected and lost the printer and 6000 copies after all. If Rolling Stone continues to print only what is acceptable to Woodrow Wyatt's Papers & Publications, you'd be better off giving your two-and-six to the old guy failing to play the recorder in Sloane Square.

The underground is not simply some sort of scruffy club that Jane Nicholson and Mecca Ballrooms have refused to join. It's where the life is, before the Establishment forms as the crust on the top, and changes vitality for money. It's humus, the matrix that the city fathers pin down with foundations, spread asphalt over and crush under piles of glass and steel and concrete. Where it reappears in the Overground it is known as dirt. It is used as a repository for waste, shit, offal, dead bodies. From circumference to circumference through this old terrestrial ball whereon we all in darkness crawl, it extends, the wormy, undermined, intermind Underground. Most things that live in it communicate by smell and feel. Some are so primitive that their systems of sexual distinction and forms of copulation are utterly confused. They crawl and grope in the humming darkness, their unmapped, unremembered paths intersecting occasionally and tunnelling on. No signposts because there are no strangers and nothing to point at. You may take refuge there from the catastrophes of the overground. No fallout in the alleys where the moles root their lives away.

Analogy between subversion and the behaviour of badgers led to the coining of the term to describe groups formed in secret to undermine tyranny, particularly groups with a large organisational network, which, like a mole's system of tunnels, is impossible to trace, even if intersected. The term was

used for the non-establishment newspapers, for UFO and Middle Earth, because they were set up by consumers to satisfy their own requirements, which were not the acceptable ones of profit by exploitation. The political content of these manifestations was at first negligible, and in some cases still is, but confrontation is political awareness, and by trying to do their own thing, the phenomena now described as underground pretty soon re-discovered the machinery of repression. The political character of the underground is still amorphous, because it is principally a clamour for freedom to move, to test alternative forms of existence to find if they were practicable, and if they are more gratifying, more creative, more positive than mere endurance under the system. This partly explains the lack of ideology which combines so oddly with the growing peevishness of the underground, peevishness now developing into belligerence, with the threat of violence.

It is commonplace to remark that a politically decided elite may use the force of this generalised discontent to establish a more repressive system still, but so far the difference between Bolshevik revolution, Maoist revolution, Trotskyite revolution and revolution for the hell of it, has only resulted in grotesquely confused skirmishing within the underground. The Establishment however will hope in vain that the underground will destroy itself: the signs of internal dissension are the signs of continuing life; complacency and inertia are qualities prized only by the Establishment.

It is in our interests to let the police and their employers go on believing that the underground is a conspiracy, because it increases their paranoia and their inability to deal with what is really happening. As long as they look for ringleaders and documents they will miss their mark, which is that proportion of every personality which belongs in the underground. That is what responds to the peculiar poetry of rock, and feeds on the insecurity of the unlimited possibility. To silence that, it would be necessary not just to kill all the prophets of the new thing, but to utterly eradicate the memory.

The people who belong to the underground all the time are very few, but almost everybody has spent a season there. The Establishment has to draw nourishment from it, and so plunders and is plundered by, the underground. Despite the venal patronage of Elektra, Transatlantic, Polydor, EMI, Track, Apple, the Inland Revenue and Radio I, the underground remains uncharted, unreliable, unrewarding, and irresponsible. If every head who clamours to be of it today were to deny it tomorrow it would exist still.

Miss Nicholson may tell the fuzz anything she pleases — her cunt knows better.

Germaine

4

CORRESPONDENCE

Dear OZ,
I have very sad news for you. The 20 copies of OZ 20 that you sent me — have burst open in the post. The South African security police have been on my track, and all is very grim.
Love and Peace,
Jerry Tussons,
PO Box 1652,
Durban.

Dear OZ,
Having read most of your editions I know the general standard of your articles.
But are you honestly trying to tell me that Hell's Angels (OZ 20) are for real??? Granted, I don't know all that much about them, but I laughed my cock off when I read your article!
Where the hell are they going?
A musician (who knows where he's going)

People at OZ,
Instead of geraniums I'm planting pretty pot flowers in my old and long established public school. It's so nice and cheerful even down to the corridors of coldness and the melancholy tolling of the bell to call you not only to Matins but also to Vespers and never to hope, always to prayer and hypocrisy, never to friendship.
W. Haileybury & Imperial Service College.

Dear OZ,
'The best of Pop completely eliminates the old form.' (Pete Townshend — OZ 21)
Although Pete Townshend is right when he goes on to say that no art (viz. Italian Opera) is "insurpassable", surely an attitude of mind that only the art of the present is relevant to our lives is self-defeating. A lot of the rest is really too good to miss.
At the moment I'm turning on de Bruckner's Seventh Symphony, which has 'a lot to say' to me even though it probably wouldn't to Pete Townshend. This doesn't mean that I can't get on with Dylan (or the Mothers or that I'm not interested in MC5 or Monteverdi for that matter).
One of the interesting paradoxes of modern music is that its newest offspring

Pop is, with certain important exceptions, the most 'reactionary' in the sense that it's the most tonally obsessed. Abbe Liszt, who died nearly 100 years ago, was tonally more adventurous than the Beatles. Pop has yet to free itself of tonal hang-ups, and I found it interesting that Pete Townshend confesses to 'very much admire' Benjamin Britten, a composer who in modern musical terms is positively neanderthal. At least Don Giovanni was relevant to its own times, even if Pete Townshend thinks it has 'nothing to say' for today. I find it still has more 'to say' than anything by the great Britten.
I am not holding any brief for a bourgeois concept of "culture" as something defused and dead. Fuck "Kulchur". But what is really good, and still dangerous in the art of the past is worth the effort of understanding if we're not to become totally cut off. The past is too important to be left as something for polished superficial "cultural" mandarins like Kenneth Clark to put us all in our place on Sunday nights in glorious BBC Eastman Colour, just as Pop is too important to be left in the hands of the moronic fascist-orientated disc jockeys on Radio Wonderful. One day, when perhaps we are all artists we can afford to forget what other people did 500 years ago — but until then the lives of the artists remain the only models for a sane existence in a crazy world.
Yours,
Michael Hirst,
134 Finchley Road,
London, NW3.

Dear OZ,
Re: Dr Schoenfeld in OZ 20
"Agreed no gentle man would want to give his woman cervical cancer, and evidence seems to show that the uncircumcised run a horrid risk of doing that. But before all good men rush to the nearest hospital to offer their foreskin in tribute to an envious Matron

Dear OZ,
The letter about WORM at Hull University in your last issue did not exaggerate the effects it had on the atmosphere here. It was, I think, a major contribution to the fact that at the end of last term a record poll put me in as President for next year on the slogan "Vote Academic Thug" and a manifesto which worried the grey rulers of the place distinctly. They got even more worried on Wednesday when a Union meeting overwhelmingly made the main idea of my manifesto Union policy. If you could put the stuff in it would be nice, as things are really beginning to hum up here, and to save me from going all bureaucratic and heavy as President I'd like to have as many OZ-reading types come up here as possible. As much as any University atmosphere can be breathed ours can, and with revolt headed by WORM and the Brynmor Jones Preservation Society (he's Vice-Chancellor) It's one where you can be happy while revolting. You can't be serious if you're solemn. It's not all happening here, but quite a lot of it is, and if we get an entry this year that's even more subversive than last, all kinds of things could happen.
All good things to you,
Tim Poston
65 Princess Ave
Hull, Yorks

"The old school's inspiring motto was: Mediocria Firma, and happily there is a middle way: retract it! Accustom yourself to wearing the foreskin retracted, and with ordinary hygiene the smegma will disappear completely. The first few days will be ticklish and priapic, and for a while longer your friends may wonder at the sudden grimace which indicates that the skin has popped back to its old position, trapping a pubic hair on the way . . . But it will soon settle down, and doffing is far less painful than docking.
"The usual commission, please, from the first firm to bring out a — RETRACT IT! badge
Love and peace
Alan Pitt Clark,
Wichelo, Ipsden,
Oxford, OX9 6AP.

Dear OZ,
Just a short note for your paranoid readers. Your telephone tapping test is NOT infallible. If the telephone does not ring back it MAY be tapped; however there is another possibility. If, after having waited for the phone to ring back and it has not, you lift the receiver again, you may hear a pre-recorded voice saying: SIFTER OUT OF ORDER (whatever that means).
Love and Peace,
Bob,
4, Brunswick Road,
Withington,
Manchester, 20.

Dear Editor,
I subscribed OZ on the grounds that it is not to be taken seriously — that the magazine is such and such and such to a certain kind of class/society etc . . . I myself stand aside and laugh at OZ and all the freaks that go along with it. Sometimes I need a change in my reading and OZ is not a bad substitute. Alright, alright, the instructions of the poverty cooking sections were taken from a U.S. army survival manual. During the war, starvation and death perhaps such an army survival manual is needed — to survive, if the child is already dead.
But surely even you must know (I hope) in a British society, any society, even your underground movement, society

and what
have you
that what
OZ.21
suggests is insane,
cold-blooded murder.
And only an insane
person could think of
such a thing, let alone
bloody well publish it.
Roast Trafalger pigeon alright.
But God, not your casual 'perhaps
8d for the use of a lure' — of a
child's life. And even more so your
bold, typed lettered word 'Method'.
You convert this quoted material from
the survival manual, and turn it, quite
deliberately, into a beyond mockery,
repulsive, sick humoured title 'Leg of
long pig'. A child of all things.
It's no joke, not even in such a magazine
as OZ. We are all human, no matter who
or what society each one of us fall into.
I am sorry to find this particular piece of
material, which has such ill and inhuman
taste to it in OZ. In fact it is quite
dangerous to the sick minded individual,
and to the heartless brutally murdered
child, which is so often heard of.
No — that recipe was not called for, not
by anyone in their right sane mind. And
not in the way OZ Magazine tries —
wants — does put itself to the public.
After all, it is publicity.
Yours
C F English,
25 Charnwood Road,
Loughborough, Leics.

At 4.45 on Wednesday morning 25 June, a brick came through the window of 6, Woolands Road, Ilford. A battle followed.

The house had been occupied by squatters the preceding Saturday, and was being repaired and decorated by them in preparation for moving in a homeless family. Number 6, like about 40 other houses in the vicinity had been purchased by the London Borough of Redbridge in preparation for the Ilford Town Centre Redevelopment Plan. This is an expensive and extravagant scheme involving the demolition of 900 houses in the area. It is to be implemented in two stages, the second stage which involved No. 6 and a number of other houses, does not commence until 1977. Which means that these houses will remain empty for 8 years. Not only are they empty, but since the recent revival of squatting, the council has spent £2,520 on wrecking these houses and making them uninhabitable. So while homeless families have to make do with sordid council accommodation (cooking meals while sitting on the toilet etc.) the council goes round smashing up perfect dwellings. Last Wednesday following the brick came Barrie Quartermain and his twelve men. They wore helmets, carried shields and various weapons, iron bars, clubs etc. and were organised into a small fighting unit. They charged the house screaming and hurling bricks. Carrying two ladders they attempted to take the house by storm, but the squatters occupying the upper floor returned the bricks and smashed the 'bailiffs' and their ladders as they appeared. The gang realised after twenty minutes fighting that they could not gain access, so lit two fires to try and burn the squatters out. It was at this point that the police decides to intervene though they had been standing by since the beginning, and all they did was to move on the gang. They moved on, alright, to 23 Audrey Road, Ilford where another battle commenced. Luckily for the Flemings, who squat here, they had time to move their three children out, though Quartermaine did not know this.

Under the Statute of Forcible Entry if a person has a rightful claim to land that is in the possession of another, he must not attempt to recover this land by force, he must use only the remedies provided by the courts. Every single legal authority supports this statement which was passed at a time when Barons were returning from the crusades to find other Barons had occupied and taken possession of their lands. The purpose of the act was to prevent Barons employing private armies (like Quartermain 's) to take back their lands, WHETHER OR NOT THEIR CLAIM TO LAND WAS RIGHTFUL OR WRONGFUL WAS IRRELEVANT.

When a council decides to make an eviction it must a) employ a certificated bailiff, ie. a man who has been granted a bailiffs certificate by a court. b) It must serve a court order for the eviction, ie. naming the persons to be evicted and the property. Redbridge council has done neither of these. It hires its 'bailiffs' from Southern Provincial Investigations. This is run by Barrie Quartermain and is not even a member of the British Association of Private Detective Agencies. Quartermain supplies and leads a private army that specialises in evictions. "Councils who employ me don't have a squatter problem any more".

In the three illegal but successful evictions, and various other unsuccessful ones that he has carried out, he has shown what sort of an animal he and his 'lads' are.

On 20 March 1969 during the attempted eviction of the Mercer family from 84, Courtlands Avenue, Ilford, he hit Mrs Olive Mercer in the stomach with an iron bar, she was visibly pregnant and lost her child as a result. Two days later he followed her to the doctors and on the way back, stopped and beat her saying "Next time you or any of you cunts in that house interfere with the job we're sent to do, and we'll be back to finish it, you won't get a chance to get anyone". There are pages and pages of sworn affidavits.

evidence of this man's brutal activities. He is NOT a certificated bailiff. His certificate was taken from him by a Kingston magistrate in 1967 for some dubious activity which we can't go into here. NOR did Quartermain or Redbridge council have court orders for any of the three successful evictions or the attempts last week. So in fact what we are witnessing in Ilford by Redbridge council is an illegal action. A senior member of Redbridge council has intimated that the squatters could probably quite successfully sue the council. They don't mind being 'told off' as they have achieved their aims.

It is difficult to see any sort of logic behind the action the council is taking. A few empty houses filled with homeless families. There would seem to be certain men on Redbridge council who are so desperate about the redevelopment scheme that they are prepared to push it through at all costs. Their deep involvement indicates just how much they stand to lose if the large property development is even vaguely threatened.

The squatters seem to have no qualms about another battle. They are well prepared. While I was at 23 Audrey Road, a white Zephyr drove slowly past with four hard looking guys staring out. Immediately there was a sort of organized panic. The Flemings and their three children were quickly moved into a neighbouring house. While in 23 everybody suddenly acquired weapons and helmets. Stacks of bricks and shovels were uncovered by the windows. The back garden was hosed down to make any use of a battering ram difficult, and all downstairs entrances were barricaded. This was a false alarm but illustrates adequately how strongly the squatters feel.

IT is morally wrong to have perfect empty houses while there are homeless families. Redbridge Council, by smashing houses which will be empty for years and taking extreme measures (including a special agreement with the London Electricity Board to have the cables disconnected at the mains) and above all their incredible blunder by employing the Quartermain organisation to do their dirty work for them, have revealed their absolute bankruptcy of any kind of a human housing policy or fitness to act as servants of the local electorate.

John Crowley

With a few exceptions, London's critical response to the Living Theatre revealed less about what went on at the Roundhouse than about the destitute aesthetics of those paid to evaluate our culture. From JW Lambert in the Sunday Times to Milton Shulman in the Evening Standard, the critics tumbled triumphantly over each other in their bid to demonstrate that Julian Beck & Co failed to conform to the classical requirements of legitimate theatre. They can't act, they can't dance, they can't sing, snorted Fleet Street, as they tied blinkers to their motor cars and galloped forth to measure the hurricane with a slide rule. The night I saw Paradise Now, Judith Malina didn't kick her legs as high as Ginger

Rogers in Mame, angry black Rufus didn't deliver blank verse with the taut aplomb of Nicol Williamson; but within ten minutes most people had abandoned their seats and were roaming the auditorium tense, confused, excited and involved. It is commonly judged miraculous if British audiences even hum along, like Butliners at a jamboree, yet Roundhouse guests were randomly engaging each other and the cast in belligerent debate; some stripping, others kissing, some in trance, others fleeing in a state of shock. This was not a cozy night at the Opera; a few laughs, a few tears, home to pay the baby-sitter, a witty post mortem over supper, then back to the grind in the morning and absolutely no alteration in lifestyle.

The man who was spat upon will never be quite the same. One member of the cast (Steve Ben Israel), outraged by the vociferous frigidity of the audience pranced threateningly about like a caged ape, shouting: 'You people scare me . . . you really scare me' . . . finally spitting at a gentleman in a brown suit and drooping moustache. This man lunged furiously forward, as we are trained to do, grabbing Israel, ready to strike. Suddenly half a dozen of the cast melted into view, immediately improvising on the situation, and began to spit on each other and on Israel. "Look at this, Spit! Spit! Does it hurt? Is it painful? It's just water. Did you want to kill him?" The spectacle of the caste of the Living Theatre bathing in each other's phelgm and brown suit's horrified realisation of the implications of his aggression and its deadly futility, was, well, beyond entrapment in the grey review pages of the quality Sundays.

Neither the slick Black Panther newsreels nor the ritualistic Hyde Park harangues have ever exposed the intensity of suppressed racial animosity as much as the confrontations between the audience and black members of the cast. The power of this experiment was not verbal. Its eloquence not divisible into cogent packages of 'acting ability', 'choreography' and 'voice projection'. But when the white lady in the front row reacted to the black calloused foot being thrust in front of her eyes with a swift jab at the actors balls; one boggled at the patience and restraint of black power and ached for the sins of one's own race – a tragedy greater than Hamlet's.

Later, a golden haired Dutch cast member went trancelike while his colleagues pummeled him with such convincing symbolic brutality that a girl at his feet tearfully intervened . . . human pyramids writhed and entwined like de Sade's table of flesh, everyone began to dance and chant . . . the evening ended in a communal catharic spasm, the like of which, taken all for all, we may not meet again.

One of my acquaintances could not tune into the Living Theatre because, given their near nudity, he was turned off by the lack of feminine physical attraction, he could not see past the band-aids and appendix scars. That makes him even worse off than Milton Shulman.

A further example of contemporary cultural insularity is evidenced by the decision of every major British publisher to reject Abbie Hoffman's incendiary treatise, Revolution for the Hell of It (Dial Press, New York). Penguin's are said to have justified their refusal with the observation that although they recognised

it as a landmark, Revolution would be slammed by every single established critic, and they did not want that to happen to one of their titles. It has been reprinted three times in the U.S. and stabs have been reproduced in the Black Dwarf and IT. So much for the values of British publishing, which is currently fawning over the name dropping inanities of a failed press tycoon and yet another wanking delineation of the I'm-a-poor-lonely-Jew syndrome which began with Joyce and continues with Bellow, Malamud, Podhoretz etc. threatening the mayoralty of the brashest city in the world and culminating in the gripes of Roth. Revolution for the Hell of It celebrates not the Jewishness of its author, but the lifestyle of tomorrow, and it will infect the culture of today despite the restrictive practices of those literary necrophiliacs who see significance only when they look over their shoulder.

"Teach living at school
And living means understanding"
(from Penguin Education Special:
"The school that I'd like)

SCHOOL STUDENTS: DISCOVER THIS ALTERNATIVE AT THE LIVING SCHOOL. A three day school which is living and not dead . . . a communal experience of discussion – action – ideas – ways of communicating these ideas.

five themes running continuously:

on EDUCATION – the general ideas behind it, teaching methods, class and education, exams, authority, nursery schools; apprentices and industrial training; further education. In all, what it's like now and what it could be.

from the basis of these discussions, a more general programme on POLITICAL ACTION – talks with squatters, tenants, shop stewards, schools, militants – how they started and what their problems have been.

on POLITICAL IDEAS: THE SITUATION HERE AND ABROAD: imperialism and national liberation, Black Power, the industrial scene and the White Paper, the student movement, the position of women.

MAKING PRINTING ACTING DOING: our media: posters leaflets news-sheets street theatre reaching out and being heard and being understood.

AND ALL THE TIME: pop groups, music, play groups, puppet show, films, acting and endless surprises.

July 28, 29, 30 at the London School of Economics. All letters to LIVING SCHOOL c/o LSE Socialist Society, LSE, Houghton Street, Aldwych, WC2.

Despite copious glossy publicity, The Jagger-Fox-Pallenberg film, Performance, never been released. All involved with the film are excited about it, but a Mr Hyman from Warner Brothers is determined *Performance* will never leave the cutting room table. He finds the general tone of the film offensive, as well as intimacy of the co-stars (which apparently shook even hardened camera men). But good news. Warner Brothers has been merged, and in the process, the indomitable will of Hyman broken. See remnants of the original at your local ABC in the Autumn.

& Known as the Genital Disturber, the chair pictured comes yellow and red in stove enamelled metal. The seat and other details are in perspex. An electric motor causes the knob in the seat to rotate once every 2 seconds, producing soft, pleasurable sensations, helping the sitter to "develop mental imagery". Cost 100 gns. Designed by John Kaine, Domestic and Personal Interference, 74 Camden Mews, NW1. 01-267-1000.

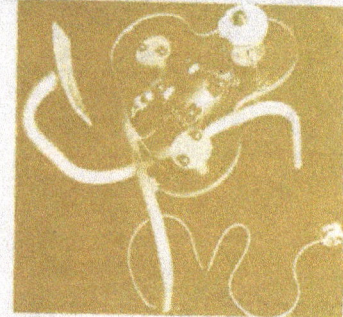

& Bath recreation Ground is a huge grassy corral, and on Saturday, June 28, it was filled with gentle people who paid more than they might spend on food in three days to get in. They queued hundreds deep for the lavatory or warm 'pop' (if they had any money left), or mounds of spun tallow called 'soft-whip'. A conservative estimate, made about noon, said there were 15,000 people. By five o'clock there were many more than that, and a gate in excess of £15,000 for smiling Mr Frederick Bannister.

For their money, the People get nineteen 'Blues' Groups playing non-stop and John Peel labouring to keep them from realising their discomfort and the inadequacy of any facilities offered. No limit on the Gate; they packed them in till they trampled each other down, penned like cattle, thumped into passivity by the music. And–still no protest or complaint. The last train went at 8.30 pm. On the railway station the Penguin orchestra leaving the respectable part of the Festival hooted with derisive laughter at those few of the people who were rich enough to afford the train, as they climbed into their three reserved cars. All the riches of what the Bath and Wiltshire Evening Chronicle called 'the Blues Cult' spilled out to subsidise Mr Frederick Bannister's smile.

& *Real Time* is a new magazine distributed to computer programmers and others, containing murmurs of dissent and messages of hope, from 66 Hargrave Park, London, N19 (1/6).

& Your sons and your daughters are beyond your command *(Dylan):* The son of President Nixon's Chief Aide was recently busted for possession of marijuana. And so too, even more amazingly, was the daughter (wait for it) of Spiro T Agnew.

'As soon as 3 O'clock rolls around You finally lay your burden down . . .' (Schooldays: Chuck Berry)

& Something's happening, Mr Headmaster. More and more schoolchildren are demanding an end to compulsory sport and religion, abolition of examinations and freedom from perverted sex (mis)education. (One schoolboy's typical report: 'We had the vicar to tell us when not to do it. The doctor to tell us how not to do it. The headmaster to tell us where not to do it'). HOD (440 Selby Road, Leeds, LS15) is one of several wild new roneo'd forums of pupil opinion. A recent issue contrasts the verbal permissiveness of Allerton Grange's headmaster ('This is one of the easiest going schools in the country') with the painful realities administered by a

Mr Partridge of the lower school, who beats boys for school uniform irregularities and hairyness. Fifteen pupils of Leeds Grammar School have been threatened with expulsion unless they disassociate themselves from HOD. A temporary teacher, Dave Gibson, was recently fired for selling the magazine outside local schools. Another leaflet, distributed by the Leeds Schools Revolutionary Committee, was recently headlined in the Yorkshire Evening Post; 'Protest Over Sex Leaflets Given to Children'. In fact, the leaflet was mainly concerned with abolition of corporal punishment, prefects and games, pausing in passing to ask: 'Is it the aims of schools to turn out sweetly obedient lesbians and homosexuals?' Last OZ contained a report from a pupil expelled from St Pauls, along with several others, because he was overheard in the corridors talking about pot. Headmasters tend to act on their suspicions, not evidence, as in the recent case of two boys expelled from Rugby, although the police, according to the Daily Telegraph, 'had not been able to satisfy themselves of an offence' (23/6/69). This headmaster, Mr Woodhouse, has expelled fifteen boys in the past two years. Justifying the school's resistence to long hair and changes in fashions, the assistant head, Mr Hunt, said: 'We are paid by a certain class of parent to do a certain job and these parents want their sons brought up in a certain way. It is our job to prevent extremes of modernity'. Rugby seems a suitable case for treatment by the Public Schools Anarchist Committee who last week organised a demonstration at Wellington College, coinciding with a 'minor interior uprising'. This committee can be contacted via the London Arts Laboratory notice board.

& Question seven of the national nursery examination for the certificate of the board asks: 'What contribution can be made by the nursery nurse towards the prevention and treatment of the following conditions: (a)strabisms, (b)otitus, (c)masturbation, (d)eczema.?'

Send 3/6 to 131a Munster Road, Fulham, London S.W.6., for more Pritchard poetry and prose, (see p.13)

& There is something sickening about the easy inevitability with which certain well connected heads are able to buy off a bust. Either go to court and help expose the drug law for what it is, or at least expose police susceptibility to bribery. (One is thinking of the knight's son *caught*, but not arrested, with Mick Jagger). Thom Keyes, author of All Night Stand, has taken the latter alternative. He was arrested for cannabis possession on April 27. The next day he alleges that he handed Detective Sergeant Robin Constable £150 in consecutively marked £10 notes, in return for which it is alleged that Constable offered to

Continued on p.10

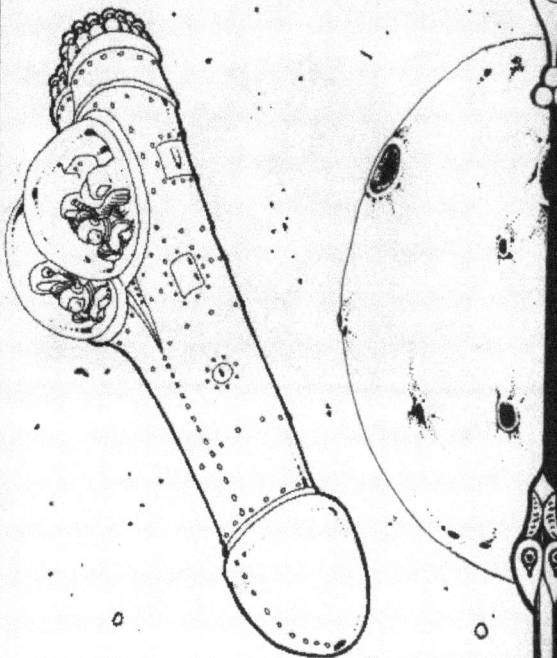

SAVILLE THEATRE
SHAFTESBURY AVENUE W.C.2. TEL: 836-4011
BY ARRANGEMENT WITH BERNARD DELFONT

MICHAEL WHITE PRESENTS
THE NOTTINGHAM PLAYHOUSE PRODUCTION

LEONARD ROSSITER
IN THE RESISTIBLE RISE OF
ARTURo Ui
BY BERTOLT BRECHT DIRECTED BY MICHAEL BLAKEMORE

After its triumphant success in
Glasgow, Edinburgh and Nottingham

Opening July 1st 90/ of seats priced at 5/- to 20/-
Evenings 8.0 p.m. Matinees Thurs & Sat 3.0 pm Previews June 28 & 30 (Prices 5/- to 15/-)

"Heroic acting in gangsterland . . . one of Brecht's finest
comedies" Ronald Bryden, THE OBSERVER

"I am not alone in thinking this the finest English-language
production of Brecht we have yet seen" Irving Wardle, THE TIMES

"Chicago racketeers and Runyon rogues make a fascinating,
vivid and funny study" Eric Shorter, DAILY TELEGRAPH

"From Leonard Rossiter a superlative comic performance in
the title role" Michael Billington, THE TIMES

drop charges against certain people who were arrested at the same time, A few hours after the transfer of money, Scotland Yard visited Thom Keyes at his home and took an 8½ page statement.

One month later the same policeman, Detective Sergeant Robin Constable, led the raid on Mick Jagger and Marianne Faithfull, Meanwhile, some are legally getting high with a little help from *Soma*, the organisation formed to research cannabis and to press for law reform. The active principles of the weed, the tetrahydrocannnabionols (THC), are not yet banned and experiments have already begun with lucky volunteers. Soma is currently appealing for £50,000 to support research and service programmes – 438 Fulham Road, London, S.W.6.

&
The promiscuous relationship of this magazine with the British printing industry has led to an unavoidable neglect of editorial content and a failure to encourage new contributors. What OZ needs most are not garrulous UFO spotters and tripping hippie poets, but probing, eye-shaded nity desk type reporters who can sniff out some of the scene's outrages and follow them through mercilessly. An encouragement to any dormant Lois Lanes or Clarke Kents, we reveal the threads of one story that could be further investigated, elaborated and sent to us: the musicians Union versus Pop, The MU has never forgiven pop or its perpetrators for toppling Perry Como off the hit parades. Its unspoken motto is that the comfort of one redundant session oboe player is more important than the rights of a thousand longhaired pop guitarists. Despite the fact that many of the lesser known pop groups are ruthlessly exploited by the trade and that a vast percentage of the MU's funds derive from pop; the Union is careful to hold its meetings on Friday nights when there is little chance of the pop proletariat being represented. It is also widely known that there is a corrupt relationship between the Union and a leading theatrical agency. Overseas

Last month's issue, OZ No 21 carried an article on Murray Roman. It was written by the very delectable John Leaver from Time Out.

pop groups cannot be imported without the MU's approval, which is rarely forthcoming unless this agency is involved. All this is worth exploring, with examples, quotes and commentary.

&
The Spikeys, or Brushcuts, are summer's new dumb terrorists in jeans, braces and thick leather boots. With sharpened aluminium combs and hair to match they have already wrecked one major free concert. They maraud in large groups, and last month beat up a few longhairs in Hyde Park to the baying accompaniment of vastly outnumbering hippies: "Wow, what a bad scene, man". One compensation: Only the masculine variety have been spotted, so at least they won't breed.

&
If you're tired of computer matching bureaux which seem set out to introduce Cliff Richard to Mary Hopkin; then New York's Head Dating service is for you Sample questions: Which of these drugs have you taken? Grass, hash, keif, opium, THC, speed, smack, acid, mescalin, DMT, DDT, STP, peyote, ups, downs, snappers, glue, yoga, apple pie? Which of these drugs have you balked under? How many times have you been busted? Are you Asexual? Bisexual? Heterosexual? Necrophiliac? Other? For those interested in meeting a hairy, asexual apple pie head, "cats 5 dollars, chicks 2 dollars", write to 67 East 2nd Street, New York, Ny10003.

&
From Political Economy to Women's Liberation, from Social Manipulation to Racism in the Ghetto, SCREW (Support Communications for a Revolutionary Europe and World) has published a lengthy compilation of inflammatory and analytical tracts: write 46 Park Crescent, Brighton, enclosing stamps.

LORDS

The Lord Chancellor took his seat on the Woolsack at 3.30 p.m.

LORD DERWENT (C.) asked whether it was in accordance with the Government's policy to allow entertainments in the Royal Parks which attracted audiences of 70,000 to the detriment of the usual amenities and the peaceful enjoyment of the parks by other citizens, and whether the regulations forbidding sleeping in the parks when they were closed were enforced on the night of June 7-8.

LADY LLEWELYN-DAVIES of HASTOE, Baroness-in-Waiting. - Royal Parks are preserved a places where the public can enjoy relaxation and recreation. It has always been customary to allow a very limited number of events with special appeal and these last two summers concerts of popular music have been arranged as an experiment.

The crowd attracted by these concerts are a measure of their popularity, especially with young people. The behaviour of the audiences has been admirable and comment on the event of June 7 had been overwhelmingly favourable.

However, so many people remained in Hyde Park that it was recognized as impracticable to enforce the regulations and clear the park at night.

LORD DERWENT.—That is an unsatisfactory answer. There are risks to health of a large number of people sleeping in the park all night where children will be playing the next day because of the quite inadequate lavatory accommodation.

LADY LLEWELYN-DAVIES.— On future occasions there will be discussions between the organizers, the police and the park authorities about the provision of lavatories and so on. Considerable help has been offered by the organizers both in the collection of litter and the provision of extra lavatories.

LORD DERWENT. -- Would Lady Llewelyn-Davies consider whether the Royal Parks are suitable for this type of entertainment because although they give pleasure to a large number of young people they prevent a large area of the park being used by other people

LADY WOOTTON of ABINGER.—Is not the implication of Lord Derwent's question that young people are inherently insanitary and objectionable and ought to be done away with? (Laughter.)

LORD BYERS (L.).—The Government should resist this Tory attack on the right of assembly. (Cheers.) It has come to a pretty pass when 70,000 youngsters go to a park and behave responsibly and this House should be seen to be criticizing them. (Renewed cheers.)

LADY LLEWELYN-DAVIES said the dangers of disrupting the ordinary activities of the parks were not great.

She was sure the Opposition had not heard of the groups who took part. They included The Cream, The Move, The Pink Floyd, and one which she was sure would delight Conservative peers, The Election. (Laughter.)

LORD STRABOLGI (Lab.). - Would Lady Llewelyn-Davies assure us that these concerts in the Royal Parks cannot be considered a rival to similar pop concerts organized in the grounds of several stately homes. (Laughter.) The House then debated economic problems in' Scotland and rose at 8.29 p.m.

Hyde Park
sleep-in after pop concert
PARLIAMENT, WEDNESDAY, JUNE 25, 1969

10

WHO CARES ABOUT SEX?

jeremy

The magazine for people who don't care about sex !

SEND FOR DETAILS :

66 BOLSOVER STREET LONDON W.1

OTHER SCENES

by John Wilcock

Tim Leary says that he'll conduct a 'grass roots' campaign for governor of California, beginning with a train tour of the State in September. He already has the support of more than 100 rock bands and 'the four leading newspapers' and explains that though he won't be participating in machine politics 'there may be some smoke-filled rooms'.

At his NYC press conference last week the jubilant acid Guru stoned deadpan into network TV cameras and said the recent Supreme Court axing of the Federal tax proviso on pot meant that heads could smoke legally on Federal property — national parks and FBI offices, for example. The government's recent estimate of 6 million users was about as accurate as their Vietnam casulaty estimates, he suggested, substituting a more likely figure of 40,000,000 smokers.

Chesnut: An old joke reappeared in the LA Free Press. "It is said that the Republicans are considering changing their emblem from an elephant to a condom, because a condom stands for inflation, halts production, encourages co-operation, protects a bunch of pricks, and gives one a false sense of security while being screwed."

Overset: Britain's Noise Abatement Society complained (to the Department of Weights & Measures) that BOAC's ads about its 'silent' jets were dishonest and misleading. And believe it or not the ads were stopped . . . ICI, the British plastics firm, has devised a plastic tombstone . . . Macy's is touting (for 70 bucks) a transistorized belt that massages you while you work (or fuck) . . . The four-year-old Research Committee on Cannabis (write Joe Berke, 31 Randolph Ave, London W9) has almost completed its report after studying the habits of almost one thousand heads . . . Watch 'for the split-second shot of the motor cycle burning about two-thirds of the way thru the marvellous Peter Fonda-Dennis Hopper movie 'Easy Rider'. It's a brilliantly subliminal premonition of how life (and the movie) ends . . . John Harriman writes poems in taxi cabs and titles them with the drivers' names . . .

Eatitup: Cat and dogfood advertising 'are subtly directed towards the appetites of people, not animals' says Connie Sohodski in The Dove, and as evidence she asks why the adds stress that the food is *all meat*? That *dogfood shouldn't taste like dogfood*. That one commercial depicts dogs shopping in a supermarket 'and engaging in all that chitchat that people might engage in'. The fact is, she adds, that petfood manufacturers have discovered that their products sell well in areas inhabited by people who can't afford pets — that they're obviously buying the stuff for themselves.

Extra: Telephone company is refunding thousands of bucks each week to disgruntled customers who lose dimes in broken phones. All you to do is call the operator and ask for your share

Aruba: The nearest island to the South American coast is Aruba (where I dropped out least week to do some work) but like most, islands within our orbit it's predominantly American and totally colourless. No indiginous native food to speak of, no colorful local customs (or costumes), just a dreadful American-type resort conformity as best exem plified by two Sheraton-style hostels — gloomy barns with nothing to offer but plastic

American meals and gambling, Even the entertainment is third-rate Las Vegas acts and this issue, in fact, is the spearhead for an attack on the system by concerned natives who want to see local musicians get a chance, Aruba has one interesting asset: a desalinization plant with oil-powered generators which can supply this almost-barren coral island with almost 3 million gallons of fresh water per day at a monthly cost of about $12 for each family. These plants to extract fresh water from the sea are the wave of the future but very few communities have been far-sighted enough to invest in them.

Smut: Lennox Raphael's 'Che!' (OZ 21) which depicted fucking on stage with honesty, poetry and humor got busted as obscenity whereas Ken Tynan's new hit, 'Oh Calcutta' which depicts fucking somewhat more satirically (and sleazily) will probably make a fortune for all concerned. Which isn't necessarily to put it down: it does present sex more honestly than previous commercial hits and it will free the theatre (and its predominantly middle-class audiences) that much more. But will 'Oh Calcutta' ever see the debt that it owes to 'Che!' And, more importantly, will it ever acknowledge that debt publicly with money or support? ?

A comune: calling itself the Kingdom of Endor tried to plan The Great Aspen Freak Festival in the little Colorado town for this July but carelessly announced that 100,000 hippies could be expected — and that blew the whole thing. Suddenly the available land wasn't available any more and threats of 'vigilante' action scared off what few record company commitments that had been made. What finally brought matters to a head was a claim — untrue — that the Beatles would be coming. Meanwhile, the Colorado legislature passed a special law to allow 90-day jail sentences for kids convicted of squatting on unoccupied property in the mountains west of Boulder. Apparently there was quite a bit of it last year and no law to cope with it.

The Movement: Chicago indictments against the yippies and others charging 'conspiracy' (the first time that the majesty of the US government has been used to make criminal charges against a put-on', says Michael Harrington) is successfully shaping us all into a conspiracy — an open one that freely admits its aim as to be the overthrow of the US 'government'. Heterogenous guest list for the Abbie Hoffman fund-raising party shows how widespread The Conspiracy is becoming . . . Veteran publisher and Peace Eye freak Ed Sanders, meanwhile, is completing his novel about Abbie tracing the growth of the Yippie conspiracy right up to its current position as 'an international cartel of chromose-damaged diplomats, Swedish generals, Yippie agents with the pentagon, war correspondents, bank presidents, nuns, poets, streetfuckers and peace apes' . . . Black Panthers' brilliant (and humane) national campaign to provide breakfasts for undernourished children so they can learn better ('we must survive this evil government so we can build a new one') is outlined in the April 27 issue of their paper, the Black Panther (25c from Box 2967, Custom House, SF, Calif 94126).

Mediamix: If Craig Karpel's profile in the first issue of US is any criterion, David Eisenhower's at least as dumb as his father. And he apparently told the Times that he was marrying Julie Nixon before graduation because he didn't have the 'will power' to wait two years before fucking her . . . As he busted Screw and Kiss for 'obscenity' (his definition), NYC assistant DA Richard Beckler became judge, jury and executioner by threatening

to arrest any newsstand that carried the papers. Apparently he's trying to save money by dispensing with the need for trials although it's doubtful that the US government would agree with him. Al Goldstein and Jim Buckley, the editors of Screw are suing the city for damages, and with help from the New York Civil Liberties Union, plan to take the case to federal court. The first issue of Screw (January 69) is now a collectors item worth 25 dollars, and by the time of the bust, the circulation had jumped from a few thousand to 120,000. Screw was the first into the underground sex field, and is famous for its gutsy down to earth approach, and sense of humour. It exposed male and female genitals and the relative endowments of

PETER METER

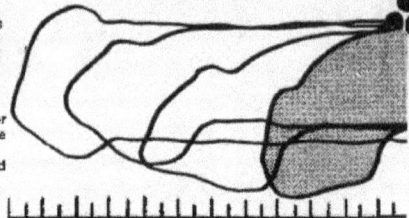

the mayoral candidates, and ran dirty movie reviews which made an assessment, based on a 'peter meter', of the number and quality of erections each one produced.

Are hustlers the only chicks answering those stud-wants-to-fuck ads in the sex classifieds' . . . The Nation doesn't agree with James Forman's campaign to pressure the rich WASP churches for financial reparations. Why? Well, maybe the Nation's financial backers include some of those rich, white churchmen . . . SF's Society for Individual Rights (SIR) is battling with Pacific Telephone for the right to be listed in the Yellow Pages under 'homosexual' . . . Scores of indignant readers complained to Hamburg's Der Spiegel magazine about its ads showing a bloodsuckin chick illustrating the theme that 'Fernet-Branca helps against vampires' — but sales of the aperitif rose 25 per cent . . . The movie, 'If It's Tuesday This Must Be Belgium' ran out of whimsy before it ran out of title, says film critic Burt Prelutsky who suggests renaming it 'Europe On Five Dullards A Day' . . . More financially insolvent u/ground papers can be expected to follow the lead set by Seattle's Helix and SF's Good Times (which has since folded) by reincorporating as a nonprofit religious foundation under the umbrella of the Universal Life Church, staffs thus becoming worker-priests . . . Toby Mamis explains that he asked the copyright people in Washington about the name 'New York Herald Tribune' and was told nobody was using it. And that's why NYC's highschool kids can buy this new, livelier tabloid (110 Riverside Drive NYC 10024). And with the original logo, yet.

LOADED!

Bob Pritchard

There were several members of the County Police Force at each end of the narrow alley. They were hiding behind garden walls, uncomfortable under bushes, and up in the trees, waiting. A Police Psychiatrist had examined the facts in the case of the 'Blackhound Lane Slayings' and had decided that it was inevitable that the killer would attempt to strike again, soon. The Police had therefore decided to prepare a trap. A decoy, Policewoman Elsie Griswold, would walk this way each night until the killer showed. This would be the second night.

The three victims had all been young girls, attractive, and under twenty-three, as was Miss Griswold. The bodies had been found in this lane ten to twelve hours after they had been reported missing. Or, rather, parts of their bodies had, for they had been mutilated beyond recognition. All that had been left of three fine young girls had been a pile of crushed bones, a smear of blood, and a few teeth, from which identification had been proven.

As the policemen waited, a cat stalked the night air across the lane, playing with its tail. It paused at the side, sniffing suspiciously, tail crooked and twitching nervously.

Not one of the policemen noticed when the cat disappeared, nor did one notice later when a small mess of blood and bones lay steaming on the surface of the earth, in the centre of that dark lane.

A car drew up noisily. The decoy alighted, unescorted, and as the men grew tense with anticipation, started to walk along the darkness, heels clicking on the gravel.

There was an earsplitting shriek, then the ground beneath her feet cracked open. Fingers of earth gripped her ankles and started to pull her into the blackness. She screamed, kicking her legs wildly, but the earth entwined around her legs pulling her deeper into its bosom. The men, too stunned to move at first, recovered slightly and raced forward bumping into each other in their haste. Chaos.

As the first man reached her the earth covered her mouth Attempting to scream through the soil she succeeded only in producing a feeble gurgling sound.

Before any man could find a suitable grip on her head it disappeared beneath the soil. The men stood around the bubbling earth, stunned and powerless.

The ground bubbled wildly for a short while, then lay calm and still. Much later the earth convulsed and vomited the remains of the female body. It lay on the ground, a circular mess of bones, framed with a splattering of blood, and one fine pair of N.H.S. dentures.

The earth belched, then fell asleep.

A NIGHT'S DREAM

Her gestures tumble cliches round the room
Filled with examining eyes, while
The pungent stench of cheap perfume
Obscures the blank aftermath of a smile.

In the dark when the light had been fucked off,
I read by my bulbous flame
The story of my life, as if the same
Old fanny had produced a spark,
A fusion of all that glistered in my loins,
Ears, balls, knees and thrusting arse.
It started with a theme —
I call it that — made
Of memories of a randy boy.
Marx only knows the feelings that I had
When all the other lads, my pals,
Kicked footballs in the streets,
Streets filled with paper and with dung,
They wanted to kick balls,
I wanted to rest mine in a cunt
And spinning from the first attempt
To draw the spunk myself
I then remembered Nancy's tits
Big, beautiful, spear —
  Pointed breasts that trembled in my hands
  Like perfect jellies.
    She was not the first I'd felt
    But then she was the best.

    In the privacy of the open night
    One male grasshopper drove
      His point home with a quick shove
      And the lady's shudder. Love?

Alan Bold

THINGS TO SEE IN LONDON

First notice the adverts — London's greatest free show.
One says PROTECT YOUR WIFE
                  INSURE YOUR LIFE
Another says GET A BETTER JOB & MORE PAY
One says that WRIGLEY'S aids concentration
And another says WARNING
          Obstructing the doors of the train causes delay
          and can be dangerous. Any interference with
          the doors is an offence against the BYELAWS
                    If after this show you feel like dining, swallow hard
                        or visit the WIMPY bar in Waterloo station
                            which is run by an Indian in a white hat.
Next day instead of going to the zoo walk down Oxford
          Street and see where the pigeons sit in the road
          like a flock of sheep on a bit of space the stupid
          traffic hasn't noticed.
                    If you feel like a day out try Aldershot.
If you want to see some graphic art, for 9d you can
          visit each of the cubicles of the men's lavatories
          at Waterloo station.
                    One of the best spots if you want to write a postcard
                    or scribble a novel or poem is a bench in the
                    station. This is where I'm writing this.
You can spend the night here.
Don't go to the Brook Green Labour Exchange or the Social
          Security at Holland Park. They won't give you
          anything without you've got enough stamps or waiting
          half a day. I don't have that much time.

It gets rather cold in Waterloo station about 2 am.

But if you stick it out you can see the view from
Waterloo Bridge at dawn. It's OK.

Peter Brown

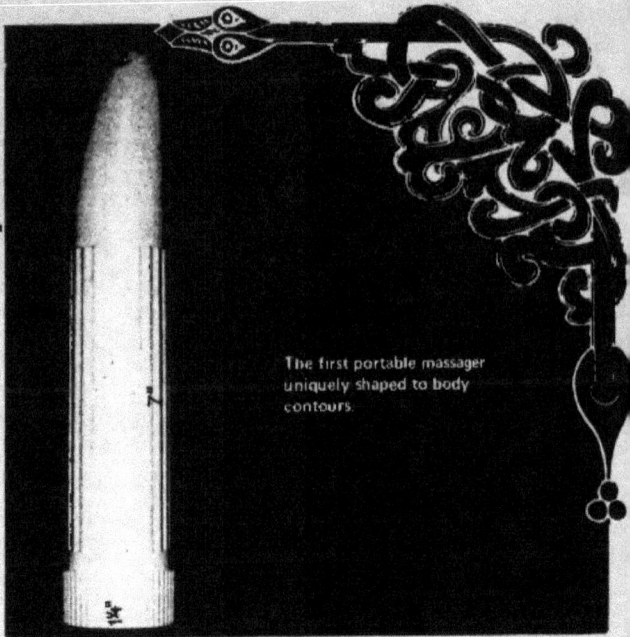

AN EVENING
WITH STEVE DWOSKIN

That's just one page from our new programme!
It takes 35 more to describe the other films on
show in what the Times calls 'a continuous London
Film Festival'. Our presentations are unscheduled
for any public London opening. Some await
distributors, some await cinemas, some have been
banned by the censors. Only New Cinema Club
members can risk tomorrow's films today.

New Cinema Club,
122 Wardour Street, London, W.1. 01-734 5888

* I'm over 16 and I'd like to join The New Cinema Club.
Here's 25s. for my first year's subscription.

* Send me your free illustrated 36-page programme

Name   Date

Address

* Delete as appropriate

hip ocrates

QUESTION: Where can I get myself *CASTRATED*? I'm tired of sex I hate sex, I don't want to be controlled by women any longer! I hate the two-facedness, bouble-think, hypocrisy. I can't stand living in the Sexual Contradiction any longer: sex is condemned, sex is admired; sex is dirty, sex is fun; if I ask her or imply that I want sex, she hates me (What? You think I'm a *WHORE?*) but if I don't ask her and in fact act, like 'I don't want sex' (and I have done this) she says, 'What, I'm *NOT GOOD ENOUGH* for you?

I think all morals should be destroyed, the Church should be destroyed, the educational system, the family, the state, the culture, male supremacy, money, competition, the TV, Power, the police and the courts should be destroyed as the only way in which we can live in a sexually free society. Maybe we should all have to be brought up nude to eliminate the sex hang-ups. And why should we hide it? To protest this social atrocity and hypocrisy, masses of people should fuck in the streets!

But in the meantime, I can't stand it. Will a hospital do it? I don't mean just removing the tubes. I mean cutting off the dick and the sac, so there won't be any more desire for sex. Would I still be able to live? What would happen if I did it myself? Is there any way to put the sex organs to sleep to eliminate the pain?

ANSWER: I think you should call the Department of Mental Health of your county or City Health Department to learn of psychiatric services available to you. Other sources of information are the local medical society or the nearest medical schools. Don't cut off your nose to spite your face.

QUESTION: I am writing to you in regard to my weight problem. I am 22, five feet six inches tall and I weigh 134 pounds. I would like to weigh 125 pounds. I have been as heavy as 145 pounds and really have had no trouble losing the first ten pounds but the second are a problem.

I perform fellatio on my boyfriend an average of four times a day. My girlfriend told me the average caloric value of one ejaculation is 100.

It is true that I am gaining calories by ingesting his semen? Should I keep an account of this and add it to my chart?

ANSWER: Dedicated medical researchers have found that the average ejaculation has a volume of 3 to 5 cubic centimeters — about a teaspoonful. Since the caloric value of a teaspoonful of pure sugar is only 18, it would seem likely that these felonies* committed with your boyfriend lead to a net calorie loss for both of you.
*Fellatio is a crime punishable in California by prison terms of 1 to 14 years for each offence. Most other states have similar penalties.

QUESTION: Could you explain please the results of a conversion operation for either a male or female trans-sexual. Is it possible to develop a penis for a woman or a vagina for a man?

ANSWER: To answer your question briefly, it is possible to construct an artifical vagina for a trans-sexual male but not a penis for a trans-sexual female. In a male the penis and testicles are surgically removed and an artificial vagina constructed, usually from the lining of the scrotum. Female hormones are given to cause enlargement of the breasts and a decrease in facial hair.

In females, male hormones are given to increase the amount of facial hair and to deepen the voice. The breasts are often surgically removed but thus far no technique has been developed to give a penis to a trans-sexual female.

QUESTION: I have six children and would like to find a way to present my soul-mate with a more shrunken area to play in. Dig?

My physician told me that I had an unusually good pelvic floor for having had so many children (whatever that means). I have exercised my vaginal muscles but think I have accomplished all that can be done that way. My husband is sweet and says it doesn't make that much difference, but . . .

Incidentally, I called my doctor to ask if I could have some kind of surgical repair. But the nurse I had to clear it through was grossly offended, wouldn't bother the doctor with it and called me a "perverted slut."

How do them up-tight apples grab ya?

ANSWER: If there's any perversion here it comes from the nurse and not you. I think you should bring this matter directly to the attention of your physician — he may not know the harm being done by his nurse.

Surgical procedures are sometimes performed in a case such as yours and a gynecologist could give you a definitive answer.

HIPPOCRATES is a collection of letters and their answers now published by Grove Press, at $5.00. Dr Schoenfeld welcomes your letters/questions. Write to him c/o PO Box 9002, Berkeley, California, 94709. Mark your letters OZ.

POVERTY COOKING

After the gastronomic excesses of last month, our expert offers a couple of recipes, delightfully simple and morally impeccable, which might have come straight from the pages of George Oshawa's Zen Cookery. Macrobiotics does not necessarily mean brown rice and beatific starvation in a damp North Kensington basement. Eat cheaply, grow happy and fat, and taking into account that you are living in London in the middle of the 20th century, grapple once more with the yin/yang principle.

Backed Rice. Serves four.
Total cost: 2s. Although some healthfood shops charge as much as 2s 9d, you should not have to pay more than 1s 6d a lb. for your rice. *Ingredients:* Two cups of short grain brown rice, three cups of water, ½ teaspoon salt, ½ teaspoon Tamari soy sauce.

Method: After washing the rice, place it in a dry frying pan, and roast it until it is golden and begins to pop. Then place all the ingredients in a casserole and bake for 45 minutes in a 350 degree oven.

If you think that this sounds just too dull for words, melt as much hash as you can afford (but no more than ¼ oz) in a spoon with a little corn or sesame oil, and stir it in instead of the Tamari soy sauce. Call it Rice Delight, and make sure you lick out the bowl.

Eggs in Batter For four.
Total cost: 2s 6d.
Ingredients: 4 eggs. Use only fertile eggs from hens which have been organically fed. Don't despair, cracked eggs from Sainsbury's will do, and despite what you may have heard from your macrobiotic friends, it is not essential that the hens were in the lotus position when the eggs were laid. For the batter: ½ cup of wholewheat flour, ½ cup of water, a pinch of salt, ½ teaspoon corn starch.

Method: Mix the batter, not worrying too much about lumps. Put ¼ of the batter into a small bowl, into which you then break one egg. Gently scoop batter around the egg, and then quickly slip the egg and batter into deep oil, hot enough to cook the batter, but not to overcook the egg. By the time you've done the fourth egg, you've probably worked out how to do it perfectly.

BY JOEL RALEIGH, EDITOR

THE GREAT HIPPIE HOAX

Stripping the petals off the Flower Children reveals them to be floundering in a cesspool of sex, half-crazed with weird drugs, parasitic, selfish, diseased and above all—coldly calculating!

a report to the people

The germination for this book as a public service document began several months ago in San Francisco in the twilight of a raw and blustering day.

In a state of hallucinatory coma, a young woman had been brought by an ambulance to the city hospital. Babbling and screaming, the patient was utterly oblivious of sights and sounds outside of herself.

Stripped of all the verbiage by toxicologists, by officers who had filled in the proper forms, by surgeons, by the hospital's own records as prepared by nurses, the facts of the case were as follows:

For the purpose of this report her name is Ella Willcox, aged 17.

She was listed under the archaic heading of "spinster," but as shall be seen she was anything but that at the time of her arrival at the intensive care sector of the hospital.

She was lying nude when she was found on the grubby floor of a foul tenement basement in the notorious Haight-Ashbury District, feeding grounds of an estimated 60,000 hippies.

Her body was a classic of splendor—except for several factors.

Her belly was distended with pregnancy and it was later determined she was approximately in the fifth month.

Starting at the top and ranging down, her once-golden hair was crawling with body lice. The hair itself was matted and gummy and stank of perspiration.

Her ears were clotted with filth that had accrued on the natural wax and her hearing was somewhat impaired until washing with high-powered syringes brought out blobs of congealed sediments.

Her teeth were rotting and her breath was foul from noxious gases stemming from her stomach and internal organs. Her teeth hadn't been brushed for several months, it was plain to see, and were stained with cigarette and marijuana secretions.

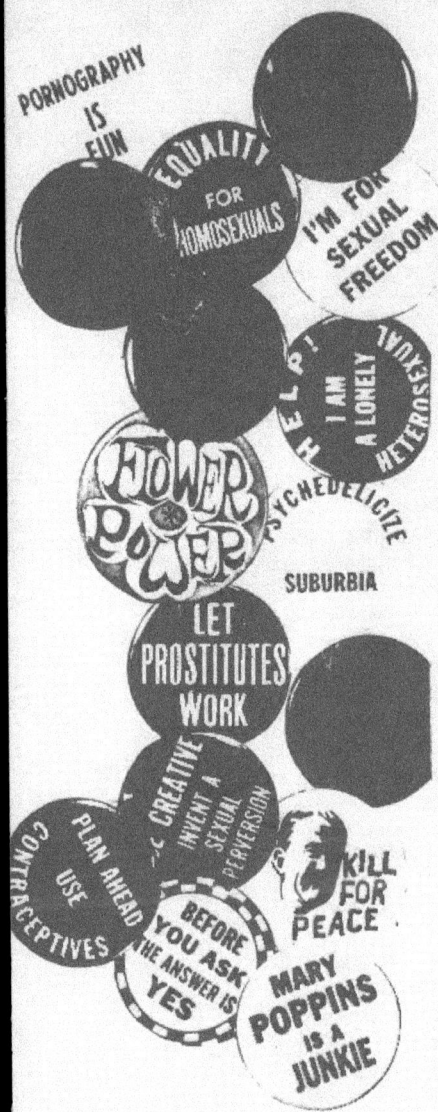

PORNOGRAPHY IS FUN

EQUALITY FOR HOMOSEXUALS

I'M FOR SEXUAL FREEDOM

HELP! I AM A LONELY HETEROSEXUAL

FLOWER POWER

PSYCHEDELICIZE SUBURBIA

LET PROSTITUTES WORK

BE CREATIVE INVENT A SEXUAL PERVERSION

CONTRACEPTIVES

PLAN AHEAD USE

BEFORE YOU ASK THE ANSWER IS YES

KILL FOR PEACE

MARY POPPINS IS A JUNKIE

Her globular breasts were bitten severely and the left one had a festering sore with a tooth mark revealed about the nipple. Lactation had set in and it was apparent that someone had been feeding off her.

Her swollen belly, inflated both by pregnancy and the onset of an early malnutrition, was crisscrossed with scratches presumably made by a sadist. Several of the scratches were oozing with pus.

Her pubic hair was also acrawl with lice of the vulgaris variety familiarly known as "crabs."

The insides of her thighs, which because of her pregnancy showed distended veins, were also bitten severely. From her vagina, a fluid, yellowish in character, flowed.

Her ankles and feet were filthy. The soles of her feet had developed a horny surface of callused skin which indicated the girl had not worn shoes for an extended period.

The room itself, if it can be called that since the boiler of the tenement took up a great deal of space, was a shambles.

Worse, in one corner, someone had defecated and a hole near a steam pipe was obviously used as a urinal. Near this was a tin box that obviously served as the storing place for food.

The air was rank. It sickened the ambulance attendants and officers who had been called to the scene by alarmed neighbors.

No one in the neighborhood would talk. No one would say with whom the girl had been living. An expired driver's license established her identity. She had come from the Middle West and was the daughter of a prosperous hardware merchant. In short, she had come to San Francisco the previous year, had obtained a job, had even written faithfully to her parents until her letters became confusing and discordant.

She had joined the ranks of the hippies, her father, who came posthaste, found. She refused to give up what she called her "new-found freedom," and dropped out of sight except for infrequent appeals for money which was sent her.

It is the goal of this document to show that the hippies —both here and abroad—are nothing but swindlers, liars, conmen, cheats, and that, above all, their primary concern is to keep themselves sensually excited.

They are frauds; they are shams. And the proof is simple, direct and easy.

The proof that the hippie is a hoax may be gathered from those officials who have had close and extended contact with them. With those who know them well and who have remained undeceived by pretensions and by lies.

The hoax that the hippie has perpetrated on the public is enormous.

Hippies are not fun-loving. They are vicious.

They are not saturated with love. They hate.

They are not pure and spiritual. They are degenerate.

They are not kind. They are often insufferably cruel.

They are not simple, natural and spontaneous. They are cold, calculating self-servers who constantly seek to get something for nothing. And they are succeeding. Because society has been gullible and supportive.

That the hippies are this way can be gleaned from the people who assembled, most willingly, to assist in giving from the fund of their knowledge and experiences.

No one has been paid to contribute information to this book. It was given free in the hope that exposure may lead to some concerted public action against a movement now infecting the nation and many countries abroad.

To shield themselves against criticism, to insure that they will not lose their jobs, to make certain that they are not revealing much from confidential files, the names of the authors included here are pseudonyms.

But the facts are true. Some sections which were recorded on tape have been edited only to afford a readable continuity.

We salute, with great gratitude, those who have assisted in this documentation of a great hoax that is running rampant and is, in many serious respects, endangering the nation.

You cannot afford not to be involved.

Your daughter, your son, your wife, your husband may be a victim of the consequences of what the hippie has wrought in this land.

There is a sadness, a disgust and a cold anger in the presentation of this book. ●

BY MR. AND MRS. F. CROWINSHIELD

"please come home! our hearts are breaking!"

The distraught parents of a girl hippie tell of their agony when she vanished into hippie limbo.

We, as parents of a daughter, forever lost and gone to us, stretch forth a hand to other parents who today are bereft of their children.

No, our sweet child is not dead. No, as people who believe in the Almighty, we cannot wish her dead. For it is a sin to wish anyone dead—even though it be for her own good. That must be in the judgment of God, in His hands.

There is little point in recounting what we gave to our dear child, our own Belinda. Suffice it to say she had a good home, a room of her own with her own private bath; her own television set; a wardrobe of fine clothes; charge accounts at the best stores; an allowance of $15 a week; her own little red sports car; a vacation in Europe with three friends; tuition paid for in a famous Eastern college.

Are we wealthy people? No, not as wealth is measured these days. I suppose we are affluent in the sense that we are financially secure and reasonably comfortable.

But we feel we gave Belinda more than material pos-

sessions. We gave her love and tried to inculcate spiritual values.

Where did we go wrong? Where did we fail to keep her on the path of an orderly life so that she turned to the lowest dregs for her companions and threw away a future that may have been a golden one?

Our Belinda ran away from home when she was just 16. Just 16, mind you. It seems like yesterday that she told us triumphantly that she had begun to menstruate. We are not prudes. We discussed sex freely and openly with her. We told her what is known as "the facts of life."

She ran off without a word and we heard from her four days later—after four days of sleeplessness and sorrow. We had an inkling where she had gone. For several months, she seemed to be going about with boys not of her set, not of her class. Untidy looking boys, some of them sporting beards.

This kind of life is not unknown in California today. We did not worry overmuch. The beatnik had his day and we read vaguely and with disinterest about the hippie, the new kind of citizen who despises the world he lives in.

When she left she withdrew her $200 savings and also took money from her father's wallet and her mother's purse. She probably had a total of about $350.

Four days later, she called from Southern California. We live on the Peninsula, about 15 miles south of San Francisco.

Her voice was fuzzy; she giggled hysterically.

"Mom, I'm not a virgin any more." That was her greeting.

Then she began to ramble and used the foulest language we had ever heard in our lives. We listened to her quietly. It was hard to believe she was our daughter.

She said she needed money. We did not ask her what had happened to the $350 in a few days. We did not reprimand her. We just wanted her home.

She said she needed $500 in a hurry. We went to the bank the next day in a state of shock and wired her the money.

Then weeks drew into months and one day a second call was made. This time she wanted just $25. We wired that to her.

In the interim, of course, we had enlisted the police who sent out a Missing Persons alarm over 10 Western states.

The police lieutenant was kindness itself. He warned us exactly what would happen.

"I know the hippies. They'll take her for everything she can get for them. They'll spend in one night what it costs you weeks to earn. They'll threaten to kick her out if she doesn't come up with more money."

Then he cautioned us not to expect to find her.

"Your description is meaningless. She no longer looks like the same girl. She's probably dressed up in one of those weird costumes and it would be hard even for you to pick her out. Moreover, she probably looks different. Drugs do that, you know."

One day we received a letter from her. It was the only one we had ever gotten in almost a year. It reads like this:

"Dear Parents: I think you stink. You make me sick. You make love with the lights out. Are you ashamed of your bodies?

"I'm surprised you ever got pregnant, Mother. You are always so holy and virtuous. Why you never even let Dad take a shower with you, I'll bet. And I'll bet you never let him do the things he would like to do in bed. And I'll bet you would love to do things with him in bed but you're too stupid to tell him that. You're too loused up.

"Mom, did you ever do this with Dad? (And here there was a crudely drawn sketch in the margin of her letter that is too disgusting to describe.)

"Dad, did you ever do this with Mother? (And here was another drawing showing another sexual posture.)

"Send me money. Send me money every week from now on. You'll never hear from me unless you send $25 a week via Western Union. I'm letting you off lightly. I could get more from you. Maybe I'll ask for more later. Belinda."

This from our own daughter. We were torn between sickness and despair. Did she think we had never been young? Did she not stop to think how she was traducing her very own parents who had never harmed her. Why did she do this? Does she hate us that much?

The answer is that she does have a consuming hatred for us.

It took a deal of courage, but we took the letter to a psychiatrist. He twirled his eyeglasses for a while and then spoke.

"Do not for a moment blame yourselves," he said. "You will have a tendency to do so. The girl has completely lost touch with reality."

Then he said something astonishing. "It's not all a matter of drugs either. We have a tendency to blame those peculiar actions, this drive towards self-destruction, on drugs. Don't forget that the very act of taking drugs is a kind of suicide. She hates herself and so she turns the hatred on you.

"There are some women who are desirous in bed and get a deal of joy from their husbands. There are others who are cold and who don't care about sex one way or the other. And there are the tramps, the ones who do do it for sexual passion or for money. Your daughter is the tramp who does it for sheer viciousness. She loves her body and wants to enjoy it to the hilt. Accept the fact that she is a tramp, as is true of all the hippies, and you will understand her all the better."

Of course the question remains this: Would she have become a tramp had there been no hippies?

We are certain she never would have become the tramp the psychiatrist spoke about. She would have gone to college, would have met a man, would have married, had children and gone through life in the familiar pattern. She might have been unhappy in her married life and wanted other men. Perhaps she would have committed adultery many times over. I do not know. But even adultery, even many divorces, even many a mess in her personal life would have been better.

It would have been better than no life at all.

We are not so blind as to say that the hippies ruined her. That would be ridiculous. That would be a lie.

The fact of the matter is she is a hippie herself. Why do we parents always go around blaming the others?

Someone has seen our daughter. We are told she looks like a woman of 35 or more. She has lines beneath her eyes; her skin is grey; her body hangs limply. Drugs will do that, we are told.

We also should like to exhibit another letter she sent us not long ago:

"Dear Has-Beens: Well, you will be glad to hear that I've turned you into grandparents. Yop! You are the happy grandfather and the happy grandmother of a beautiful little baby who was buried this morning. Like that? I thought you would. Love, your ever-loving. Belinda."

Why is she so vicious? Is it the drugs? No. It is Belinda herself. Drugs could not do that. She has a fateful defect somewhere in her makeup, in her composition.

It is therefore with great emotion, with a sense of believing that we are grownups and intelligent, that we indict our own daughter, Belinda, along with all the other hippies.

Our daughter Belinda is to blame for her own destruction and for destroying our lives. We are of course different people. We see no one, go no place. Her presence and her absence hangs over our house.

With heavy hearts, before God, we cannot hold her blameless for this would be an injustice to those whom she probably has harmed in her own, cruel way.

We indict our own daughter Belinda and may God have mercy on her—and on us. •

The indictments have been drawn; the charges have been made; the evidence has been presented. What is to be done now? There is much that can be done—and done right away. A national crisis requires action against the human plague.

what must be done?

During World War II, the United States placed more than 100,000 persons into detention camps. Most people are unaware of this. Today, the U.S. Government should round up draft dodgers and put them into detention camps. Those who interfere with the draft process must be put into other and similar camps. That's what can be done! (UPI)

From **The Great Hippie Hoax**, 'a scalding indictment of the phoney movement that has trapped thousands of teenagers', published by Universal Publishing and Distributing Corporation, 235 East 45 Street, NY 10017; Universal-Tandem Publishing Company Limited, 33 Beauchamp Place, London SW3. This glossy document concludes not only that hippies should be sent to concentration camps, but that their homes be burnt, and the occupants made 'to clean up garbage and thrown into jail'. The book contains eleven 'indictments' of hippiedom, which apart from the one reproduced here include:

Indictment 1, by Sgt Lemuel Parkinson. From sodomy to safe-cracking, from mayhem to murder, from rape to robbery, from prostitution to pilfering, — millions of dollars are spent annually to catch criminals — and a police officer tells why hippies are above the law and get away with their scurrilous acts.

Indictment 2, by Doctor Penn Warran Delaplaine. The hippie activates longings that man has repressed for centuries. These primitive desires make themselves manifest in sexual perversions that appear to dominate the entire movement.

Indictment 3, by Sidonie Grunweld, Phd. They rise at mid-day, perhaps munch on dog food or smear rancid butter all over their tongues, put on some dirty shoes and socks, ignore the stained and filthy bed. Before they set out to pan-handle their way though the day they water the pot on the windowsill.

Indictment 4, by Judge Antonio Bellargia, Magistrate's Court. Then they are hailed into court, the mouth words never before heard in chambers of law. They befoul their cells so horribly that other prisoners refuse to be near them. They wolf down their food like animals, and their probation reports mark the pathological liar. They masturbate openly any place, any time.

Indictment 5, by Doctor Llewelyn Maxfield. A horror of hepatitisis sweeping across the land. Accompanying it is an alarming increase in venereal disease. The dangers of permanent drug damage to an alarming percentage of young people and to the children they will give birth to are terrible to contemplate.

Indictment 6, by Sam D Perriotti. A slum landlord who specializes in hippie tenants tells gleefully how he ravages the girls when they're behind on his gouging rent — and how he watches orgiastic parties at the pads.

Indictment 8, by Arthur Lorge. A self-confessed lecher who preys upon young innocent girls and lives off them until their money runs out, tells what it's like to savour the world's offerings without responsibility. As he puts it: 'I've got life knocked up!'

Indictment 9, by Helen Smithers. She got tired of fumbling on the porch and the hurly-burly of the back of the car. She wanted it what she calls 'straight and hot' without her parents telling her what time to come home and whom to see. This girl hippie freely confesses at 17 that she's had more than 60 lovers in a year!

Indictment 10, by Thomas Eddleworth. The ravaging Hell's Angels, who terrorize whole towns when they go snorting in on their powerful motorcycles, have found new playmates — the hippies. They beat the hippies senseless whenever they want to and use the girl hippies as so many chattels. Here, a member tells of the brutal pleasures they have with the insipid, smiling hippies.

Indictment 11, by Joe L Bushmiller. A famous reporter who has covered everything from dope running to dipsomaniacs, mayhem to marauding tells of his eventful weeks in the sewers of hippiedom where he lived and observed what he calls the 'most depraved people in the history of man.' ●

DRUGS IS A 5 LETTER WORD

By a Sunday Times Reporter

The really serious contemporary scare-mongering over drugs began in 1964, with a speight of articles about the drugs scene at Cambridge and Oxford. It is a rich experience to come across newspaper cuttings showing that 500 Oxford students smoke hash with the familiar remark, in this case Dr Linford Rees, that reefer smoking opens the way to heroin addiction. If all the hash smokers over the years had really turned into heroin addicts we'd probably have an addiction problem numbering tens of thousands.

The activities of undergraduates at our two most respectable university cities continued until 1967 partly due to the Fleet Street trend of employing graduates from these institutions. They brought with them sizzling stories of midnight smoking debauches — good stuff for the gritty editors anxious to please a mass audience which has always felt antagonism towards the privilege associated with Oxford and Cambridge. It's difficult to know whether these newcomers to Fleet Street belonged to the smoking groups — I think not. They were more the establishment student who could hardly wait to rush to London to reveal the distasteful goings-on at their colleges. The Express at the time breathlessly recorded that 'students bought drugs from an attractive Swedish blonde at undergraduate parties'. One couldn't help wondering whether she was the same girl who cropped up in a Daily Telegraph article almost three years earlier. The Telegraph said: 'Reefers ring at Cambridge — inquiries about a Swedish blonde. Six people are suspected of organising the manufacture of reefers for Cambridge undergraduates. They are believed to include a West Indian, a Frenchman and a blonde Swedish girl'.

Needless to say the Baltic beauty was never named; she remains a part of the drug mythology which Fleet Street has constructed over the past ten years. The gutter press did not take an interest in our main university cities until 1967 when the People sent Trevor Aspinall to investigate. 'Drug Sensation at Oxford' was the predictable front-page headline. He quoted the local police chief as saying: 'Only the other day three fathers came to see me about their daughters. All these men were from the upper echelon of society and their anguished state was most distressing. The horrors of this twilight drug world are dreadful.' One of the hallmarks of the gutter press whether discussing drugs, crime or students, is the way the most improbable quotations are attributed to people who are interviewed. Can you imagine any police officer saying 'the horrors of this twilight drug world are dreadful. I have knowledge of previously respectable young ladies selling their bodies to all and sundry to get their next fix.'

In considering sensationalism of the drug scene, no newspaper can be mentioned in the same breath as the News of the World, which employs the remarkable talents of Mr. Simon Regan.

After the Wootton Report on cannabis was released, Mr Regan filed a story which said: 'Foreign dealers flew into London the same morning the Wootton Report was published. In a matter of hours the capital became one of the easiest places in Europe to buy cannabis in the form of hashish concentrate.' In four hours he returned to his office with enough hash to make 500 reefers. No one doubts Mr Regan could buy that amount of hash. But the assertion that London overnight became the drug capital of Europe is arrant nonsense. Mr Regan knows it, and the editor, Mr Somerville, knows it. Yet by a naked political manoeuvre the News of the World was able to mobilise the entire Alf Garnett community against a document which could have gone a long way towards removing myth and misunderstanding from the drug scene.

The authoritative drug specialist on that bastion of Asquithian liberalism, The Times, is a Mr Norman Fowler. He enjoys the confidence of the present Home Secretary, Mr Callaghan, and one cannot help but notice the consistency with which Mr Fowler advocates the Home Office line. Now obviously Mr Fowler cannot be blamed for accurately reflecting Mr Callaghan's views in the Times. It's his job. But as we all know Mr Callaghan has made some notorious errors in his ministerial career since 1964. He, more than any other minister, is more responsible for our present economic chaos. He rejected devaluation thus bringing this country to the brink of economic peril. As Home Secretary he has conceded two fundamental points to the Powellites — the Commonwealth Immigrants Bill and the recent enactment of regulations making entry certificates for dependants mandatory. So while Mr Fowler is slavishly recording Mr Callaghan's personal views of drugs other journalists on the paper are not given the opportunity of perhaps presenting conflicting views. It's a question of office politics. If one reporter has the ear of a cabinet minister he has a tremendous advantage over his colleagues. He is more likely to be trusted by his editor and can exercise conscious or unconscious editorial influence over the paper's policy.

Within the Times organisation it would be difficult for one of the junior reporters to present a view contrary to that of the Home Office or Scotland Yard, so eloquently expressed by Mr Fowler.

A reporter being half-bright about any subject makes difficulties. For instance I have definite views about hard and soft drugs which I have claimed from personal and professional association with the drugs scene. What am I to do then if Dr Elizabeth Tylden the London psychiatrist comes to me with a statement about reefers causing serious psychological disorders? I know already, for instance, that she has claimed that cannabis allegedly leads to genetic malformations. But in the statement she's presenting me she makes no mention of this far graver accusation. And again, if Dr Max Glatt came to me with the story he gave the Daily Mail in January this year I would have serious misgivings about presenting it the way the Mail did.

Dr Glatt said:
'Young people habitually taking hash always claim they have lots of "ideas". But they don't translate these into activity. Their preoccupation with the drug results in the neglect of their interest in furthering their education or training. They don't grow up — they just withdraw into their own hash world.'

I would challenge Dr Glatt's basic assertions. His presumption is that society is being run correctly and that young people are given the fullest opportunities to develop their personalities. From my observations the majority of children in this country are thrown onto the scrap heap at sixteen or seventeen — they're obliged to repress their imaginations and their aspirations to become wage-slaves in a society whose goals are materialist-oriented.

Now, Dr Tylden and Dr Glatt may feel justified in accusing me of misusing the freedom of the press. They could charge me with suppressing their views. My answer is that reporters have a right — more precisely a responsibility — to be sceptical of all views and all information which they receive. It is a common justification of gutter press journalists that they are merely expressing the views of that ubiquitous fellow *the man in the street*. But we all know the man in the street's views.

He wants to send home the blacks, put our youth in the army and rusticate the dissident students.

Exploring the cuttings covering five decades revealed an unbelievably shallow approach to the reporting of drug affairs. For instance in all the thousands of column inches that have been written about drugs I could not find one article which dealt with the reasons why people or individuals took to hard drugs. I want to see explained the social background and the thought processes which makes a teenage boy or girl take a hypodermic needle, fill it and plunge it into his or her arm. It cannot be explained away by slick chat about teenage trends. My own newspaper, the Sunday Times, produced the ultimate in mindless journalism about drugs in a story last year headed 'Crawley has seventy heroin addicts because one boy went to Worthing.' The article recounted how a 16 year old Crawley boy studying in Worthing caught the heroin habit and spread it when he returned home. For all the academics talk about gregarious addicts I am not willing to believe that one boy turned on 70 teenagers. This proposition is intellectually insulting. A more satisfactory reason lies in the sterile environment of Crawley new town, another of the hideous artificial societies created by our town planners.

The mindless coverage of drugs by mass media stems from an inability to understand the problem — the relation between cannabis smoking and alienation of youth from their enforced middle class values. An insight into this estrangement can sometimes be gained from the Underground Press, and Fleet Street journalists should approach this new media — not with a professional abhorrence but in a spirit of compassionate curiosity.

GREEN SHIELD STAMPS FOR RELEASE

Honestly. Release, which needs a fair amount of money to keep in proper working order, can, as a social help organisation, get back 12s instead of 8s per book of stamps. They can also make use of British picture stamps and foreign stamps, and hope soon to get extra money on pink stamps and cigarette coupons. Send stamps, or any other help to: Release, 50a Princedale Road, W11.

Just a cigarette, you'd think, but it was made from a sinister weed and an innocent girl falls victim of this

TERROR!

24 JUL 1939

MARIHUANA

Does that word mean anything to you?

Perhaps you have heard vaguely that marihuana is a plant that is made into a drug.

But do you know that in every city in this country there are addicts of this dangerous drug?

In London there are thousands of them.

Young girls, once beautiful, whose thin faces show the ravages of the weed they started smoking for a thrill.

Young men who, in the throes of a hangover from the drug, find their only relief in dragging at yet another marihuana cigarette.

How do they obtain this drug—since the police are hot on the trail of all suspected traffickers?

They obtain it from so many unexpected sources that as fast as one is closed by the police, so another opens up.

Night clubs, reputable hotels and cafés are frequented by agents. They operate from the least likely places—milliner's shops, hairdressers, antique shops.

But in Soho, in little lodging houses run by coloured men and women, the cigarette can be had for a secret password, and a very small sum of money.

And many terrible tales are told about marihuana addicts.

One girl, just over twenty, known among her friends for her quietness and modesty, suddenly threw all caution to the winds.

She began staying out late at nights. Her parents became anxious when she began to walk about the house without clothes. They stopped her when she attempted to go into the street like that.

At times she became violent and showed abnormal strength. Then she would flop down in a corner, weeping and crouching like an animal. Soon she left home.

No trace could be found of her, but cigarettes and ends in her room were identified as marihuana.

How much does a marihuana cigarette cost? Just a shilling!

Or in a "reefer club," the low haunts where men, usually coloured, sell the cigarette, a puff can be had for sixpence. The fumes of the smoke are caressing, but they leave a somewhat acrid taste and a pungent, sickly smell.

That is, to the beginner. The addict likes it. She likes it, not because of its taste or smell, but because it gives her abnormal strength and makes her indifferent to her surroundings.

One day, passing a narrow street in Soho, I saw a small crowd gazing at the third floor of a dingy house.

A young and lovely woman, her clothes in shreds, stood perilously perched on a window ledge.

Behind her was a man. He, too, was wild-looking and dishevelled. Several times the girl made an effort to jump and the man feebly held her back.

Soon, a third man appeared, coloured and strong, and hauled them both back. They were both marihuana addicts.

As she disappeared, she could be heard screaming: "I can fly. Well, I don't care if I die!"

Unconscious of herself, of any danger, she acted on the impulse to do the impossible.

I heard of one case, a nineteen-year-old dancing girl who was taken to a "reefer club" by a party of friends.

Soon a man was at her side, offering her a cigarette, for which he made no charge. It was a decoy.

Soon she became one of his best customers, spending half her salary on the weed.

She sank lower and lower. Her associates became criminals, drug lunatics, and dope peddlers.

Unlike opium, hashish and other drugs which make their victims seek solitude,

marihuana drives its victims into society forcing them to violence, often murder.

One man, in the delusion that his limbs were going to be cut off, killed his mother, father, brother and two sisters with an axe.

It is easily the most sinister menace to our young people to-day. And to be forewarned about it is certainly to be forearmed. For ignorance is spreading this habit more than anything else.

There's only one way to treat the fellow with the case of "doctored" fags which he offers to young folks. Gaol him! For he's engaged in committing moral murder.

For women, the menace of the cigarette is greater than for men.

Here is a true story that illustrates this fact.

A girl of twenty-one was persuaded by an older man to elope with him.

For months her father searched vainly for his daughter. One night he saw a girl, her eyes staring wildly in front of her, her hands drooping, her head leaning on a man's shoulder.

He was horrified, but even more horrified when a second glance told him that this was his daughter, accompanied by rouged and bloated—

"I am not going home. I'm going to America," she wailed, when she saw her father. The man with her refused to give her up. The girl clung fiercely to him.

There might have been a brawl but the father said:

"I have a friend outside who will call the police if I'm not outside with my daughter in ten minutes."

Reluctantly his daughter went with him. In a few months she was cured of those nightmare weeks.

It may happen to any man or woman. The next victim may be your best friend.

A cigarette seems harmless enough. It is not so easy to check the craving.

For marihuana can turn happy lives into hell.

E. S.

SPECIALLY POSED FOR THE "DAILY MIRROR."

give
acceptable
contexts

lying it to my actions

life

virgo

faster farther

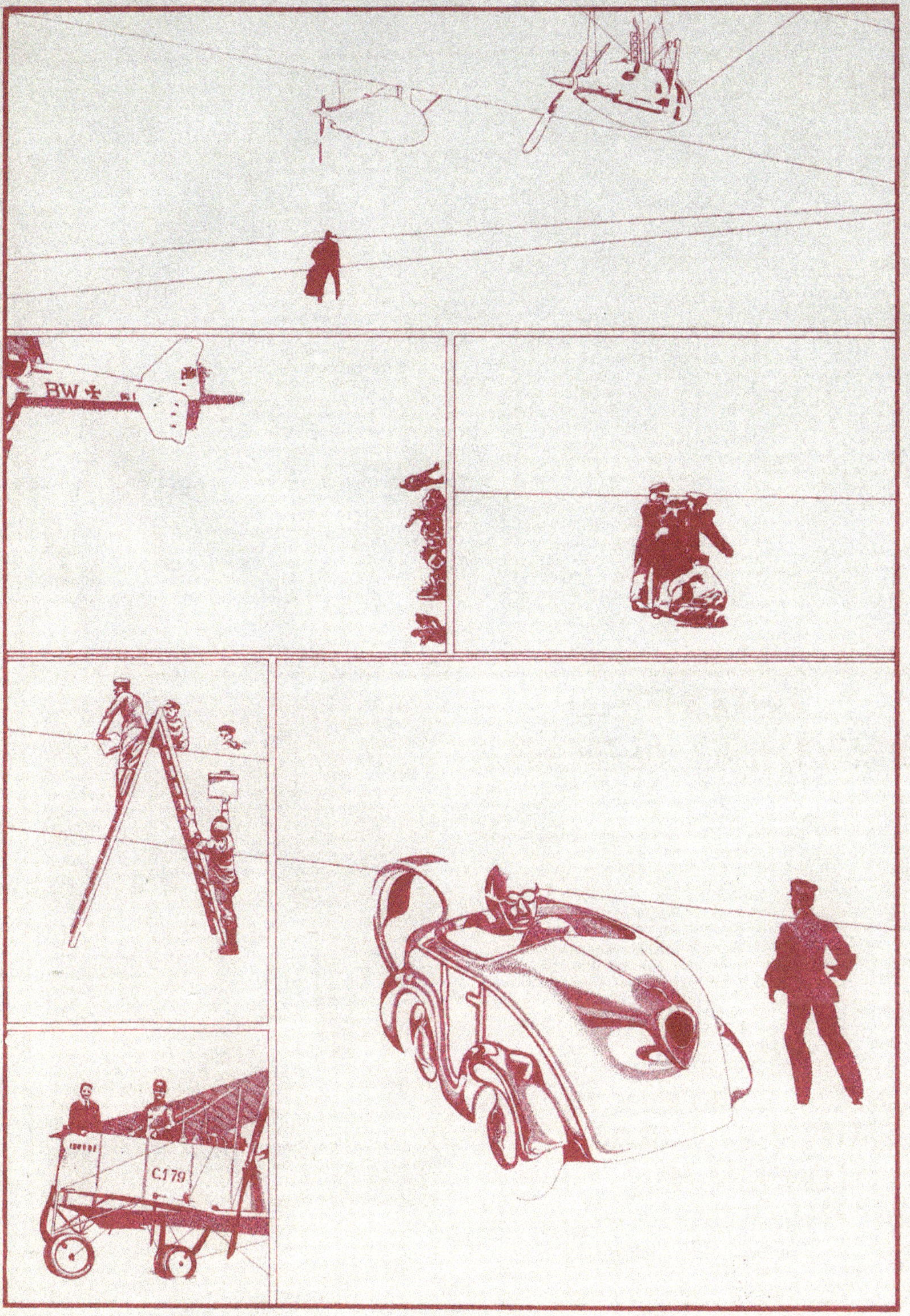
BW
C.179

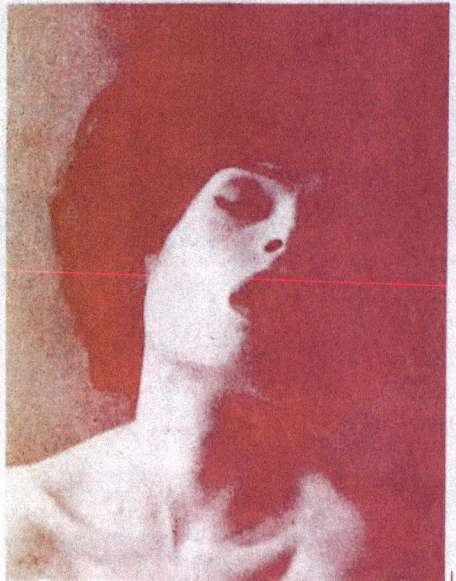

TELEVISION
THE BANKRUPT MEDIUM

OZ TV supplement: introductory notes.

The burgeoning underground press reflects the failure of traditional media to cope with the consciousness of a new generation. Television in particular has repudiated the demands of those supposed to be most affected by it. In the following supplement, Tom Nairn takes the fatalistic view that it is the natural function of a virgin medium to belch forth reactionary propaganda for the first hundred years. Less patiently, others are exploring and developing facilities for an alternative, underground television network (See John Hopkins: Video Now). From the inside, a producer offers hints towards humanisation (A tired producer's notes . . .).

Official reaction to any expression of discontent is (1) "Of Course! But you should have seen how bad it was five years ago", (2) "You speak for a ludicrous minority. Mums & dads who after all buy the soap powder and pay the license fees, *love us*". The same ludicrous minority responsible for escalating the circulations of OZ, IT & Rolling Stone (As those of the New Statesman and the Listener irrevocably subside), who pack Hyde Park for adventurous pop (Could Des O'Connor or Simon Dee fill Sloane Square?), who compel extension of the Living Theatre's Roundhouse season, who nurture arts laboratories all around the country . . . An infinitesimal market? Apparently so. Its existence is not even acknowledged by anything currently on television.

Digression: Who said this: "No single group of viewers, *even if it is the majority*, will be served to the exclusion of all others, no single type of television will predominate . . ." Answer: David Frost and Aidan Crawley when applying to Lord Hill for London Weekend's ITA Contract.

Any week's Radio or TV Times reveals television to be one marathon series of All Our Yesterdays, itself still running. *Peak times*: Show of the Week ("The *good old days*, a special Scandinavian edition of *old time* music hall) yet Once More with Felix, Mirror to a (stone) Age, the Glen Miller Sound, Time to Remember (" . . . as the camera recalls the events of 1919"), The Fifties ("Robert Robinson *looks back* to the death of King Goorve VI"), Film Night ("A Dig into the Past"). Giving a Dinner Party (who *does* anymore?). Princess Grace, *"former film star"* conducts a musical tour of Monte Carlo, Fyfe Robertson asks "Why

Zoos" and the 1969 Methodist conference from the central hall, Coventry, gives us Songs of Praise.

There is nothing new one can say about the pitiful assembly of milk-advertisement celebrities that bounce in and out of each other's shows night after night, except to stress that most are manipulated by a handful of boardroom magnates, who, at the mention of the words quality, originality or culture reach for their export awards. That ex Vaudeville family, the Grade Brothers, know what the public wants. Lew runs ATV and its myriad subsidiaries. His brother, Bernard Delfont, runs everything else and he is a director of EMI, which owns Associated British Pictures (which has TV holdings), which has an interest in the Grade Organisation, which owns Harold Davison Agency (which provides many of the artists appearing on TV) which is connected with countless other showbiz institutions. Even the Daily Express once conceded: "Impressario Bernard Delfont has just done a deal . . . which gives him virtual control over live entertainment in Britain". That was three years ago. The Grades have more control now.

Here's how it works: Bernard Delfont runs the Royal Variety Show, a TV special, which takes place in a theatre (London Palladium) owned by his brother, which raises money for a charity presided over by himself, employing artists managed or promoted by the Grade organisation or Harold Davison and who are often concurrently appearing at theatres run by Delfont or Grade, costumed by Monty Berman, an ATU offshoot, and recorded by EMI.

The same numbing obsession with the gaudy, tinselled, second rate, sentimental, bygone, showbiz glamour era also permeates the BBC. When Billy Cotton died, Mr Tom Sloane, head of Light Entertainment, intoned: "He represented everything good in this country". And certainly the Cotton musical philosophy (viciously anti-rock) still represents the contemporary mood at the BBC, which, politically, is similarly dancing to its own gruesome fox-trot (one step to the right, two steps backwards).

For evidence of the encroaching conservatism of the Corporation see the sour grape memoirs of ex director Kenneth

Adams or compare Lord Hill's BBC charter with that of his predecessor (Encounter, November '68).

One indication of contemporary critical standards is the cultish infatuation with Rowan & Martin, a programme with a dazzling array of human gadgets, of breath-taking pace and intermittent wit, but which is deceptive in its achievements. It is not outspoken. No-one is threatened. No-one is named. A typical 'strong item' consists of a song and dance attack on censorship, with no-one 'exposed', nothing achieved, nothing altered, nothing new sung, nothing publicly uncensored, but all reassured.

Some of those working within media have become so embittered, that they have created the Free Communications Group, which believes that newspaper, television and radio should be under the control of people who produce them. The first issue of their magazine, Open Secret (2/6, 6 Swan Walk, London, S.W.3) publishes almost in full, the hilarious and confidential application by London Weekend Television to ITA. This Group which has also established a committee to enquire into the television industry, seeks to provide a long term alternative for those on the inside. For the rest, it might be more fun to take John Hopkins's advice, and do it in the road with your own portable video.

When the poor-hard-done-by-underground-avant-garde gets on its financial feet its first purchases are, in that order, clothes, hi-fi, colour TV, and a sports car. The last as a joke of course. But why the TV, you ask? Because it nourishes, and extends that boredom with which drop-outs defend their inverted elitism against the facts of life. They never could communicate: now, just like Mr Jones, they've found their excuse not to. And they, they laugh at it, but they keep on watching, whoever calls, while on the phone — the Saint, Jesse James, The Virginian . . . We're all tired businessmen now.

Why do we prefer watching boring TV to our boring friends? Because the picture might change at any moment, while our friends won't.

TV — from a miracle it became a hypnosis, then a habit, and now, wallpaper. Intermittently, a window.

THE TIRED PRODUCER'S NOTES for his testatment

by David Sharp, a tired producer.

I want a television that the people can use, just as they use the town hall, labour exchange, clinic or supermarket. In the mass society people have a need to transfer their experiences, perceptions and frustrations to their fellow citizens, to their functionaries, representatives and leaders. They should no more feel that the apparatus of electronic contact is alien and embarrassing to handle than the dentist's equipment or the garage mechanic's. They have to humanise the media of communication by taking possession of them.

All discussion about television in the past has been about finding means to trammel and control it. Let us talk now about how to free it. Let us stop talking about expanding the area of expression in terms of individual words or actions, watching the area of permitted nudity increase inch by inch over the months, or the total permitted vocabulary of sexuality increase four-letter word by four-letter word. There are no stable yardsticks for the measurement of freedom – there is only the clarity of purpose of communicators determined to say what has to be said. The most powerful form of censorship is the mind of a writer or producer calculating what he can get away with.

Everywhere the content of the television screen is the major guide to what it is possible to think openly with the particular society, the exercise yard in the cultural prison. This is true in Russia, as much as in Portugal, in Britain as much as in America. We are too complacent in the West. Our screens are always just about as open as our societies. Television everywhere is socially controlled, nearly always state-controlled as well. The healthier the society, the better the situation for the professional communicator, the less he is obliged to look over his shoulder. There is therefore, even in Britain with the freest screen and the freest society of all, no room for complacency. The battle-lines merely change from decade to decade. You spend the whole of a professional life pushing them to the farthest extent in one direction and as you pause for breath, turn round – you will see the next generation hemmed in somewhere behind you. In places they are fighting for the right of opposition politicians within the national parliament to use the most powerful medium of all to address their voters; they turn to Britain with admiration and surprise, because here

all the politicians have some right of access to the screen. *Do not be fooled – the next fight is to get the politicians off the screen.*

Be very careful when people speak to you about quality in television, especially if they are critics, shareholders or programme controllers. They are nearly always referring to something that looks good, not on the screen, but in print; they are anxious to adorn their company reports or to achieve the satisfaction of writing patronising passages or simply to appear in the Honours' List. When they talk about quality programmes they are actually talking about programmes which they think 'ought to be out on television'; that is very different from good television, which is almost impossible to legislate for. Good television occurs usually by accident when the producer is merely indulging himself and accidentally succeeds in communicating something to his audience at the same time – when that magical fusion of maker, artifact and public occurs, in which all three are inseparable. Good television isn't even something that can be seen on the screen and later stored in a box; it is a living presence that leaves an indelible impression on the minds of all who saw it and all who were in the first place responsible for it. It is as much the product of the audience acting through the decision-making processes of the producer as a product of the producer reacting to the appreciation-processes of the audience. Good television isn't just a flicker that disappears at midnight; it lives in the way a

Nausea, liberal: Julia or, *"Negresses! Forget the 'ghettoes, for sweet surburban grit will make you Black America's answer to Phyllis Calvert!" (And if you know who Phyllis Calvert is, you shouldn't be reading this article.)*

good person who is dead lives, transmuted through countless half-remembering minds into a piece of history. Good television like history can survive as a gesture, the allusive wave-patterns of the brain. That was nothing at all to do with what the people who try to run television put into their catalogues as quality television.

If you had decided to be a writer of books, papers, plays, films most of your potential public would glance and pass on. That is the way of things. Having made their choice to ignore or reject you, you would trouble them no longer, nor they you. You would be concerned to make a living and gain the serious attention of a few. If you continued not to please the public sufficiently you would soon cease to be

printed. However, you have chosen to produce television instead, and the public will not leave you alone. In vain to suggest that they pass by on the other side. You are not in the print business. That which bores the audience they will turn off. That which pleases them they will eventually turn off. That which impresses them they will try to watch next time. That which enrages them they will watch avidly.

A good proportion of the audience reacts positively to what it feels ought not to have been put on. A smaller proportion reacts passively to what it feels ought to have been put on. You will be exposed without much protection to the ravages of the former. No telephone exchange however

We Needs Must Love the Highest When We See It (Arnold), but

I know what England ought to want because God speaks to me on my Hi Fi (Lord Reith and his Pals), but

inefficient will keep the enraged audience from you. No postal system ever devised will succeed in losing their letters or diverting them from you. No scheduling however late will prevent the chronic sick and their kin from watching your cinematic essay on the benefits of euthenasia; No warning however strong will keep the nervous, or the politically or religiously sensitive from watching the programmes that will most crucially activate their sensitivities. As well to expect the flies to ignore the sores of a beggar. What you must do is work out your own rationale that neither closes your mind to their cries (which would be self-destructive) nor so opens it as to terrify you from calling another shot. The army of the infuriated is the birth cry of your mental offspring; when you hear it you know that you have brought to birth a living thing (and have survived the ordeal yourself). When you have produced something really worth-while and can still feel the stones between your shoulder blades, remember that protest is the outlet of a troubled soul; that section of the audience that cannot cope with the way or the extent to which you have troubled it, is the section that seeks self-reconciliation through abuse. In their abuse lies also the latent demand to control the medium, the frustrated appeal for the right of access, the unconscious demand to give public expression to a social experience. In that demand lies the only real hope there is.

Nausea, Radical: All My Loving, *which sees pop music as the expression – equivalent antithesis of shooting the Vietcong in the head (blows his mind, man). This thesis is sentimental-sensationalist slop, slanted at* News of the World *readers who think they're* New Statesman *readers, at* New Statesman *readers who think they're* Melody Maker *readers, and at* London Magazine *readers who tremble with thrill at the thought of being* Fuck You *readers.*

THE CULTURAL LUDDITES

Tom Nairn

Hand-loom Intellectuals

Among the machine-breakers of 1812, the historian E P Thompson pointed out, 'pride of place went to the hammer-men, who wielded enormous iron sledges called *Enochs* to break open doors and smash the frames'. They had a song which went:

Great Enoch still shall lead the van,
Stop him who dare! Stop him who can!

One feels trepidation, therefore, denouncing the new machine-breakers of 1969. In many circles, both Left and Underground, to hint that new-fangled television machines are good for anything but smashing invites instant Enoch-ing. Raised eyebrows turn one into an accomplice of the system, like the evil West Riding mill-owner who used to wait on the hammer-men coming of a night, with 'barricades of spiked rollers on his stairs, and a tub of oil of vitriol at the top'. But whatever the risk, and without in any way condoning the machine-owners and magistrates, I must condemn the new Luddism. More than that. There is a sinister — and far from revolutionary — significance in the fact that the Underground and part of the Left intelligentsia come together in rare harmony just *here*, of all places. That is, on the lowest possible common denominator of corporate, backward-looking, hopeless, helpless, anti-historical stupidity. Not looking forward to a future together, but weeping over a past. Not in constructive, collective action, but at the point of maximum inertia. Not as revolutionaries, but as pathetic, dispossessed, hand-loom intellectuals menaced by the dread culture-mills of Shepherd's Bush and Kingsway.

Revolt of the Book-worms

The old machine-breakers had a mythical leader called General Ludd. Our new General Ludd, Angelo Quattrocchi, spoke out recently on the front page of the new Paris daily Action (descendant of the revolutionary newsheet of May '68). 'Break your telly into little pieces', he cried. Then, go and see the man who runs the telly, and 'ask him to give you back all the time he has stolen from you, all those hundreds of hours he has taken out of your life'. If he can't do so, break him in little pieces too: you'll find he is full of valves, wires, nuts and bolts — 'Alors tu riras!' The same message scorched the valves and wires in John Goldsmith's recent TV documentary about art students, where suddenly an earnest face loomed out of the set and told the spectator in suitably slow, Dalek-like tones, that there was something even *he* could do to help on the revolution: 'You can smash your television set, now!'

In one sense, the epileptic absurdity of the position is (literally) too obvious.* But the obviousness conceals something else — the real bite of the argument — which has to be concealed, because it conflicts with the apparent revolutionism, the strident libertarianism of the facade. At heart, the neo-Luddites are shamefaced conservatives, timid nostalgics for a lost golden age of safe cultural elitism.

Looking first at the facade, it must be obvious indeed that the modern cultural machine-breakers are as doomed to defeat as the weavers of 1812. Like the latter, they have identified the new machine-system as being evil *in itself*: an affront to humanity, and to all the decent values of human intimacy and spontaneity. The confusion is the same in both cases. The gigantic new cotton and wool mills did create a sort of hell, laying waste large tracts of England, and destroying an older (and in some ways preferable) culture. Yet they also forged the modern world, and were the only possibility of liberating mankind from want and raising him in time to a vastly superior social culture. Once the process had got under way, there was only ever one thing for the workers to try and do: control it, in their own interests, and develop it further. To break the machines and kill the men who owned them merely distracted people from the real, difficult revolution which had to be accomplished: trade unions, political organization, the formation of a new culture. Instead, General Ludd's men tried to resurrect a dying world, a culture forever lost of independent men living beside their work in small village communities.

As they did with the early mass-production of material goods, so the new Luddites would do with the growing mass-production of mental goods. But there is a difference. Confusion could be forgiven the starving weavers of 1812, illiterate villagers caught in the vice of contradictory forces they did not understand. It is much harder to forgive their new descendants, intellectuals whose wilful ignorance extends to their own work and values, their own backgrounds, their own natures, in an unbroken tide of bad faith.

The hammer-men of 1812 did not represent (as they tended to think) an ageless and natural way of life, now criminally threatened by the satanic mills. They represented a transitional form of industry, small-scale domestic production which had

*The obviousness is frequently underlined by the astonishing number of such wreckers who turn out to be addicts of Radio 1 and hardened movie-goers. I know one incapable of thought unless the radio is on. Another is, without exception, the worst telly-addict discovered in a long experience of viewing and viewers: reduced to total subjection by a test-card, he will watch anything. But because these earlier mass media have been around for some time, and are partly absorbed by 'culture', they rarely seem to disturb the Luddites.

the seeds of the new monsters inside it all along. In exactly the same way, the telly-despising intellectual of our day does not in the least represent ageless, 'true' culture. By and large, he represents the culture of *books*. That is, the first, transitional form of mental industry: the old-fashioned, artisan production of ideas now menaced with extinction (or at least, radical transformation) by the mass media. But once there was print, it was really inevitable that there should be such new media sooner or later. And it is impossible to turn back upstream again: one's hammer will simply part the waters.

You Can Burn All Your Books, Now!

General Ludd II and his men have forgotten what the fate of print-culture was, in its own early existence. They have forgotten that, as McLuhan pointed out, it was the most reactionary of cultural phenomena for long after its birth. For a century it propagated little but mediaeval bigotry and prejudice, treatises on the detection and torture of witches, unreadable Reformation and Counter-Reformation polemics, and assorted theological rubbish. It put the manuscript-scribes out of business and (I don't doubt) made them feel like smashing the presses.

Would they have been justified in doing so? How alien the coldly impersonal, lead-stamped book must have seemed, after the unique, lovingly transcribed, *human* manuscript! To a progressive manuscript-clerk the situation must have been intolerable: the devices had not only put him out of work, they were filling the world with cultural junk! Imagine his withering scorn on seeing printed books in a friend's home. How — to employ General Ludd II's favourite term — how *plastic* book culture must have looked: neatly-packaged brain-poison from faceless leaden men, a new barbarism spreading into every home . . .

But we know — and certainly the telly-haters ought to know — that this 'barbarism' contained the industrial revolution and political democracy within itself. Neither could have existed without it. It also signified the end of an ancient elite culture founded on mediaeval ignorance and squalor. Opponents of the presses looked back to Dante; but the presses themselves looked forward to Shakespeare, Marx, and Joyce. And of course, to Quattrocchi & Co. too, the new elite threatened by a newer barbarism, solemnly identifying its own senile decrepitude with the ever-shining light of human culture.

Bubbles in the Primeval Ooze

It would be too much to expect originality

from the TV wreckers. They are in the unfortunate historical position of being able to enunciate only cliches, the receding echoes of a (fortunately) moribund culture. When television was younger, even good-bad writers like Raymond Chandler denounced it more effectively:

Television is really what we've been looking for all our lives . . . television's perfect. You

Bad Money Drives Out Good (Hoggart), but

All I Want Is One Station Broadcasting Light Intelligent Music All Day And Night And I Might Just Be Able To Bear A Commercial Station With Snide Anti-Left Propaganda To Get It, And Then I'd Happily Send My Colour TV To The Starving Biafrans.

turn a few knobs, a few of those mechanical adjustments at which the higher apes are so proficient, and lean back and drain your mind of all thought. And there you are watching the bubbles in the primeval ooze. You don't have to concentrate. You don't have to react. You don't have to remember. You don't miss your brain because you don't need it. Your heart and liver and lungs continue to function normally. Apart from that, all is peace and quiet. You are in the

Satire stagnated because the next step was a radical critique, a constructive rethinking, which the satirists couldn't manage and the BBC headed off. But beware: sub-Fascist realpolitik peeps silently, but grinningly, over the Marxist shoulder. Alf Garnett is its old-fashioned, nostalgic, and all too human, face.

poor man's nirvana. And if some nasty minded person comes along and says you look like a fly on a can of garbage, pay him no mind. He probably hasn't got the price of a television set . . . (Letter to C W Morton, 1950)

The apparent novelty of the new Luddites is their pretence that machine-breaking is revolutionary. An attack on totalitarian garbage-can culture, no less: hitting back at the great brain-washer and his sinister agent

crouching in the corner of the living-room. In a society like this, to expect most TV programmes to be other than garbage would be naive. But the responsibility for this plainly lies with society, which manufactures the TV that suits it. And society includes us. Chandler understood that, at least:

To me, television is just one more facet of that considerable segment of our civilization that never had any standard but the soft buck. Hasn't today and probably never will have . . . Perhaps in some ways the worse television is, the better . . . Perhaps enough of those people will realize after a while that what they're really looking at is themselves. (ibid)

To think that cracking a few telly-valves will stop or cure this state of affairs is even more naive. To think the valves are somehow responsible for it carries one perilously close to that traditional Right which has always thought that 'more' means 'worse'.

Yet this is what the neo-Luddites really think: a culture forced on the defensive is in fact capable of such regressions. If they were really interested in a revolutionary attack on the corporate capitalist state, the correct strategy would be – naturally – to fight for power within the media, and ultimately for control over them. It has not been sufficiently recognised that one of the central weaknesses of the May '68 revolt in France was its indifference to such issues. France, where conventional bourgeois print-culture was at its most powerful, where the old apparatus of literary academicism has left a deep mark on the whole intelligentsia and infected the Left with its archaic narcissism, where the most rabid revolutionaries retained until 1968 the fossilized cultural mentality of a 19th century village schoolmaster – France was, in this one vital respect, the last country where a 20th century revolution should have occurred. Marx said that the Communard revolutionaries of 1871 failed when they hesitated at the gates of the Banque de France, and did not appropriate it. The revolutionaries of 1968 failed because they hesitated too long before the gates of the ORTF, the Paris telecommunications centre. They wrote bravely on walls, like mediaeval scribes. But they despised the electronic walls in every living room too much to write on them. No other revolution can afford to make the same mistake.

Concern for minority audiences is a minor matter. All mass media exploit the overlap between middle and working class culture. The best ideas admit these tensions, within and between them with the banalities conceal. Wrestling is the last outpost, in this middleclass medium, of pure lower working class roughness.

Contrary to intellectual misreporting, whereby the good guys always win, the real anti-heroes are the hateable, unbeatable villains, like McManus, Pallo and Rann. For those blissfully ignorant of how it's fixed, wrestling can hurt, in the sense that the old fashioned boxing booths could hurt, when plucky innocent lads were ready to have a go against the booth pluggily.

True, French television may have been the most odious and cretinous of any western country. Yet even in the ORTF, the television workers showed they had more in them than valves, wires, nuts and bolts. Does Ludd II believe that the journalists and technicians who waged one of the most stubborn of the May-June strikes, and later lost their jobs, are machine-men who would →

ITALICISED QUOTES BY
RAYMOND DURGNAT

be better employed wielding quill-pens? In other countries like Britain, where even the existing structure of the medium is more flexible, and the contradictions in its functioning are consequently greater, where TV could obviously be something quite other than what it is — here similar attitudes on the Left are inexcusable. They are only a hair's breadth from being frankly counter-revolutionary.

Narcissists with Hatchets

As print-culture contained the possibility of the bourgeois-democratic world, so the electronic media contain the possibility of a communist world within themselves. That is, of an effective common culture which can overcome the last vestiges of restrictive elitism *without* thereby reducing humanity to a lowest common level of mechanical conformity. Television is still in its earliest, crudest phase, corresponding to that of the printed word a century or so after Gutenberg. The great developments certain to come, in technique, transmission, reception, educational and local-community use, personal recording and projection, will transform the medium and its social meaning. They will realize its (literally) revolutionary possibilities. Through them, technology will itself help to shatter the primitive bourgeois social framework, by generating within it the foundations of the first great and truly communal culture — the first free culture — tomorrow.

But this is just what the Luddites fear, though they cannot portray the fear openly without betraying themselves! What contempt for technology lies in the disparaging picture of the 'valves, wires, nuts and bolts' in the telly-man's brain! What dismal fear of the mass culture which would remove for ever their own pretentions to the inheritance of 'art', their own aristocratic, last-ditch elitism masquerading as the avant-garde! In brutal fact, their own bookish world is founded upon the mechanical debasement of popular sensibility, upon that wretched, mindless conformity inseparable from the mass exploitation of the printed world as a means of domination. How many hours has the printed page stolen from humanity's lifetime? Who will restore to us our ten years insufferable tedium of miseducation by literature?

They are therefore incapable of seeing that the new medium might be different: that it might be more than an infinite, calamitous extension of the reign of books over the earth. They too, in other words, are 'really looking at themselves', as they pick up their hammers or hatchets and make angrily for the flickering screen to darken it for ever. But like Narcissus, all they will ever destroy is their own dark reflection.

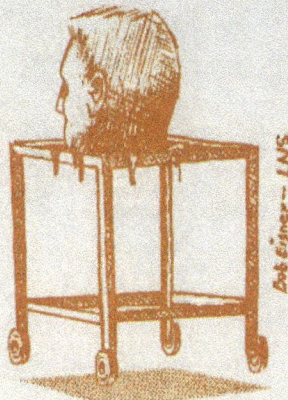

VISUAL WANK

Bob Eijner — LNS

Sorry OZ, I really tried. When you rang up on Wednesday about doing a piece on TV entertainment, I got onto it right away. I called Keith Smith at BBC publicity and said OZ was doing a survey of TV programmes, and could he tell me about Light Entertainment? Yes he could — What week did I want; I said Monday to Sunday. He started chuckling and said 'You know We've never had a call from OZ before, can you hear all right with all that hair?' (Chuckle). I could hear papers rustling, and then he said '22nd of June — Ah yes, the first of a new Lulu series recorded in Sweden.' I remembered what you said about showing how the same artists appear on every show and asked him who the guests were. He chuckled again and said — 'well, My Generation, — the Rolf Harris dancers — they're very good'. Anyone else, I said, yawning. 'No', he said 'they're all foreigners and you wouldn't know them'.

More paper rustling. 'You must send us a copy of OZ — I haven't seen it since the first issue. Very hippie, isn't it?' I said it wasn't but couldn't raise the energy to say why. (Send him a copy will you.) But by this time he was telling me about the N F Simpson show with Ned Sherrin producing. 'Of course we're not trying to send anyone up — if you want an intellectual name for the type of show, its parody — oh no, not satire — parody in the best sense. But, really, if we make people laugh we're happy.'

By this time he was humming catchy little tunes and the papers were rustling like crazy. It was time for a joke again — 'If you like tennis you have Wimbledon every night for a week.' I started awake. What — a satire on Wimbledon? But he said 'no no just a joke.' 'On Wednesday night we have the second of the Bobbie Gentry shows, (she wrote Billy Joe) which is very good if you like that sort of thing,' he said, archly. I thought briefly that perhaps she stripped, but already he was giving a list of guests — 'I've got Joe South, Billy Preston, Alan Price and James Taylor, and also John Hartford.' He said something about John Hartford but I couldn't catch that.

'On Thursday and Friday we've got nothing'. He didn't seem particularly upset by this catastrophe, and went on to tell me that BBC1 were repeating Not in front of the Children.

'Wednesday, there's a fifty minute show of Les Reed's greatest hits — he did all Tom Jones' big songs — he must be a very wealthy man by now. Humperdinck, Donald Peers, Cleo Laine, and Jackie Trent are going to sing the songs. On the same night there's the third programme in the Beryl Reid series'. I said I liked Beryl Reid, and he said the show had had mixed reviews and really wasn't very funny, 'Some people seemed to like it.'

The papers were still rustling at the same breakneck pace, when we came to Saturday.

'The Ken Dodd show' he said with a slight catch in his voice 'with Vince Hill'. Who else I said, and he countered with 'Being Ken Dodd there won't be much of anyone else'. 'Also a profile of Peter Ustinov and fifty minutes of Nana Mouscorie — she wrote the White Rose of Athens — which is a special programme recorded at the Top of the Town in cabaret.'

He was still singing softly when he came up with his last morsel — 'fifty minutes of Herb Alpert and his Tijuana Brass recorded in the US'. I rallied and asked — 'Does he sing as well' and was rewarded with another stanza of the Yellow Rose of Texas and 'Yes'. I thanked him and promised to send the copy of OZ (don't forget to send it) and hung up. Well, that night I decided I'd try to watch some of the programmes. So I turned on 'the Good Old Days' on BBC1 where a magician was talking to an audience dressed in Edwardian clothes and very false moustaches and they were all laughing so I turned it off. I guess I'm not ready for that kind of camp. I forgot to turn it on again, so I went up to the Roundhouse. I didn't watch any more TV on Wednesday, because I went to hear Dick Gregory at the Arts Lab. Gregory was really rapping — talking about how he was going to picket the peace conference in East Berlin, how the CIA put black agents onto him and they have to invent stuff because the jobs for black CIA agents are rare, about food needs, and food poisons, and how a soldier who is ready to die will always beat one who is only able to kill. Gregory is great — he's a prophet of an age and really so musical that it's impossible to tell you what he says because the *way* he says it is so beautiful. And *he's* so beautiful — like a sacred scarabin in this dunghill of a city. Thursday was a hassle, so I didn't think about the piece until I got in at around seven. I turned on 'Top of the Pops' and there was Tony Blackburn smiling his capped teeth smile and looking as if he had filled his pants on screen — very nervous — but the show started with the lousy new Beatles number and pimply kids jerked on the screen (only when they *were sure* the camera was on them) and a few bubblegum groups mimed their songs badly, and that was the pop ration for the week now that Colour Me Pop has ended. Following that was the First Lady, which I bore for about five minutes. Later I watched some of the BBC's films of the fifties but a guy came round and we talked till late.

I'm really sorry I didn't get the piece done but tonight I'm leaving for Stonehenge and the Druid's Summer Solstice. There is going to be a big ceremony at midnight and dawn and someone told me that a virgin will be deflowered).

It means missing the Alfred Hitchcock movie, and not finishing your article, but it should be fun. Sorry.

Ian Stocks.

SHOOT IT, SHOW IT ! VIDEO NOW!

John Hopkins, Co-ordinator of TVX.

Funny thing about our society is that most of the machines we need are all around us, and it's just a case of figuring out how to get hold of them. This article helps fill the information gap about what machines there are, what they can do: the figuring is your business.

In a word, portable TV is here. By portable I mean that there is an outfit consisting of a shoulder-pack videotape recorder (weighs 13 lbs) and a hand held TV camera (weighs about 5 lbs) which works off its own internal batteries. A microphone mounted on the camera picks up sound, and synchronised sound and vision are recorded on a half inch wide videotape, running time 20 minutes.

The batteries last an hour and are rechargeable. Cost, about £575. To see what you've recorded, the tape is put onto a larger record/playback machine, rewound, and played back through a TV set adapted to the larger machine's output. The total cost is just under £1000, including accessories like battery charger etc. Made by the Japanese company Sony, whose head office (01.695 0021) will tell you where your local Sony dealer is.

For the technically minded, it works to 405-line standard, with 220 line definition, bandwidth of about 3MHz, negative modulation, automatic gain control for audio, automatic exposure compensation for video. Standard C-mount lens is a 4:1 TV zoom, viewfinder is a miniature 1" screen mounted at the back of the camera. The portable camera and recorder code no. DVK 2400, playback machine code no. CV 2000. A similar machine made by Japanese company Shibaden will be on the market soon, which uses 625 line system. UK distribution by GVS (01.202 8056). The real differences between Sony and Shibaden emerge when you look at the overall systems developed by these two companies, and how the portable recorders fit into these systems. The tapes from a Sony portable can only be played back on one machine, as it was produced originally for the domestic market. The tapes from the Shibaden portable can be played back on a variety of machines, all of which are compatible with the entire range of Shibaden equipment. In certain applications these differences in back-up systems are important, and the Sony system has greater limitations.

There's another difference too. Each time you edit in the camera (stop shooting and then start again) you make a discontinuity in the sequence of control pulses put onto the tape when you record. When playing back, this discontinuity causes the picture hold to be lost for a short time. With Sony, this can 'tear' the picture for up to 2 seconds, but with Shibaden all you get is a 'flash' lasting perhaps a tenth of a second. It means that on Shibaden you can do a series of very short jump outs and get away with it, which on Sony will produce just jagged torn pictures. And with Shibaden you can also dub on sound at the playback stage. To be fair, the Sony felt better balanced and easier to operate, a question of design hipness: and the actual picture quality is at least as good as Shibaden if not better.

Well that's as concise as I can make it. Now read on. Two other questions. Can I play back from one of these machines thru my ordinary TV set? Not without modification, cost £35 or if you know a friendly electronics freak, maybe £10. The manufacturers ought to produce a cheap connector box for this purpose, but they don't. Can I go to a shop and buy this equipment as an individual? No. You've got to buy it thru a company and prove educational or industrial use. What happened was that the UK electronics lobby, realising that they couldn't produce equivalent machines, pushed a restrictive law thru Parliament to protect their sales of what I'm reliably told is relatively inferior equipment. Well, what do you expect from a country whose economy is on its last legs?

Where do we go from here?

The cat's out of the bag. Although certain technical problems remain, the chief of which is electronic editing, *we can now make our own television*. What's more, the mystique of TV studios, technicians and administrators, and hard-to-acquire expertise, and the hurdle of the ACTT (cameraman's union), have been exposed for the bullshit they are, in one fell swoop. Want to join the ACTT so you can work in TV or films? It'll cost you plenty in free drinks and expensive meals. Want to do a Granada TV directors course? You need a degree.

Well, it's all downhill from now on. The speed with which we can develop alternative circuits in Universities, Arts Laboratories and Neighborhood-Local situations depends now only on our resourcefulness, the figuring-it-out I spoke of earlier.

It's interesting to compare the obvious stirrings of grass-roots TV with the statements made by our beloved Minister of Technology, Mr Wedgewood Benn.

He seems to understand better than most of his colleagues the inevitable nature of electric technology which is to decentralise the media. He also expresses concern (on TV !!) that TV in particular needs to be made more available to more people, and that this is a social necessity. Fine words. Well, unlike the administrators who hold the reins of commercial TV — and that includes the BBC — we haven't got vested interests in prolonging our own jobs where they are obviously due for a shake-up.

What's more, we are now beginning to produce the answers to the questions that Mr Wedgewood Benn has been asking.

OK Mr smart guy, how *would* you run local TV? Actually it's quite simple. To start, a couple of portable recorders. Two rooms to operate from: one a small studio for interviews, the other with editing facilities. Your *video journalist* goes out shooting: children, entertainment, revolution, town hall meetings, conversations, opinions . . . he comes back to the editing room, rewinds, edits if necessary, makes duplicates, and the tapes are sent out to various parts of the district where playback sets are located. Pubs, cinemas, meeting places, dances: places where people are used to get together. Pay for it from advertising (no sweat to put ads together), maybe paid admission if it's at a cinema, and public funds. Yes, you heard me, PUBLIC FUNDS.

This is the point where the town councils have got to fork out some cash, and it's not much, to provide a public service. Within a short time any basic system of local TV like the one I just described could undergo considerable sophistication. Instead of sending tapes to the playback points, you tap the existing GPO video lines already laid down for this sort of use. Then, you can transmit without the tedious business of trapesing across town three times a day.

Then, you might set up a low power transmitter to use one of the broadcast bands not used in that place.

The point about all this is that *it is possible now*. So let's go ahead and do it.

So what are the prospects?

On the level of local TV, all that has to be done is to find one town or borough council that will give support to a scheme that will turn a lot of people on. The difficulty that they may actually want to *control* what is put out on local TV can be avoided by giving the council as much time as it thinks it wants to tell the people whatever it wants to tell them. In fact, it's not down to a them-or-us control battle: it's down to letting as many people, factions, opinions as possible be aired, and this in itself is the opposite of a potentially dangerous influence. It would be just as socially harmful to allow the 'revolutionaries' to control such a facility as it would be for the 'reactionaries' to control it. Before my colleagues on Black Dwarf — long may they thrive -- get uptight, here's an example. Imagine a situation where Mr Barry Quartermain is allowed to give his opinion of how to treat squatters and earn his living, and Squatters who have been set upon by his men are allowed to say what they think. Give a man enough rope and he'll hang himself. The trouble with broadcasting is the moment things get interesting, the interviewer closes the conversation with some neutral remark. What would happen if you let Enoch Powell and Tariq Ali talk it out, all day if need be? Or the local grocer or pusher starts to say where he's really at?

In some respects we have a better idea of what not to do than what to do. Why is the news always read in a serious tone of voice, and religious programmes held in the atmosphere of a morgue? Could it be that they really think 'the news' has much relevance to the man in the street? Or that god vanishes when you crack jokes about him?

On the level of Universities, Sussex, Brunel, Leeds, Strathclyde, Birmingham, York and Imperial College London, and Brighton and Plymouth technical colleges have their own closed circuit systems, and there are probably more I don't know about. I'm under the impression that TV in these places is still treated as something available to only a few people, which has to be done in a studio, and by means of which only 'neutral' topics may be discussed. However, what is more important is the very existence of the systems themselves.

Jim Haynes announced at the recent FACOP meeting at St Katherine's dock that the Arts Labs throughout the country want to set up a circuit and exchange material, and the first steps have already been taken. The open-ended no-holds-barred attitude in the London Arts Lab is going to be very

productive when it comes to exploring the possible uses of video.

Recently a meeting was held at the ICA between film makers and the setting up of a parallel video circuit was mentioned.

So we can see that already there is a number of small circuits and viewing situations, which with a little co-ordination form the basis of an alternative network. The task at present seems to be to promote mutual awareness and realisation that, once again, what we are looking for is all around us, and all we have to do is *to get it together*.

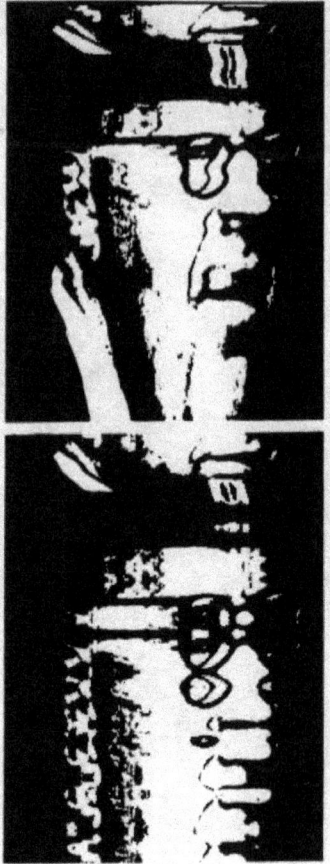

Mid July London:

A group of people will be asking the Government for a local London TV station. The detailed plans will be set out at a press conference to be held shortly. Information from TVX, 1 Robert Street, London NW1.

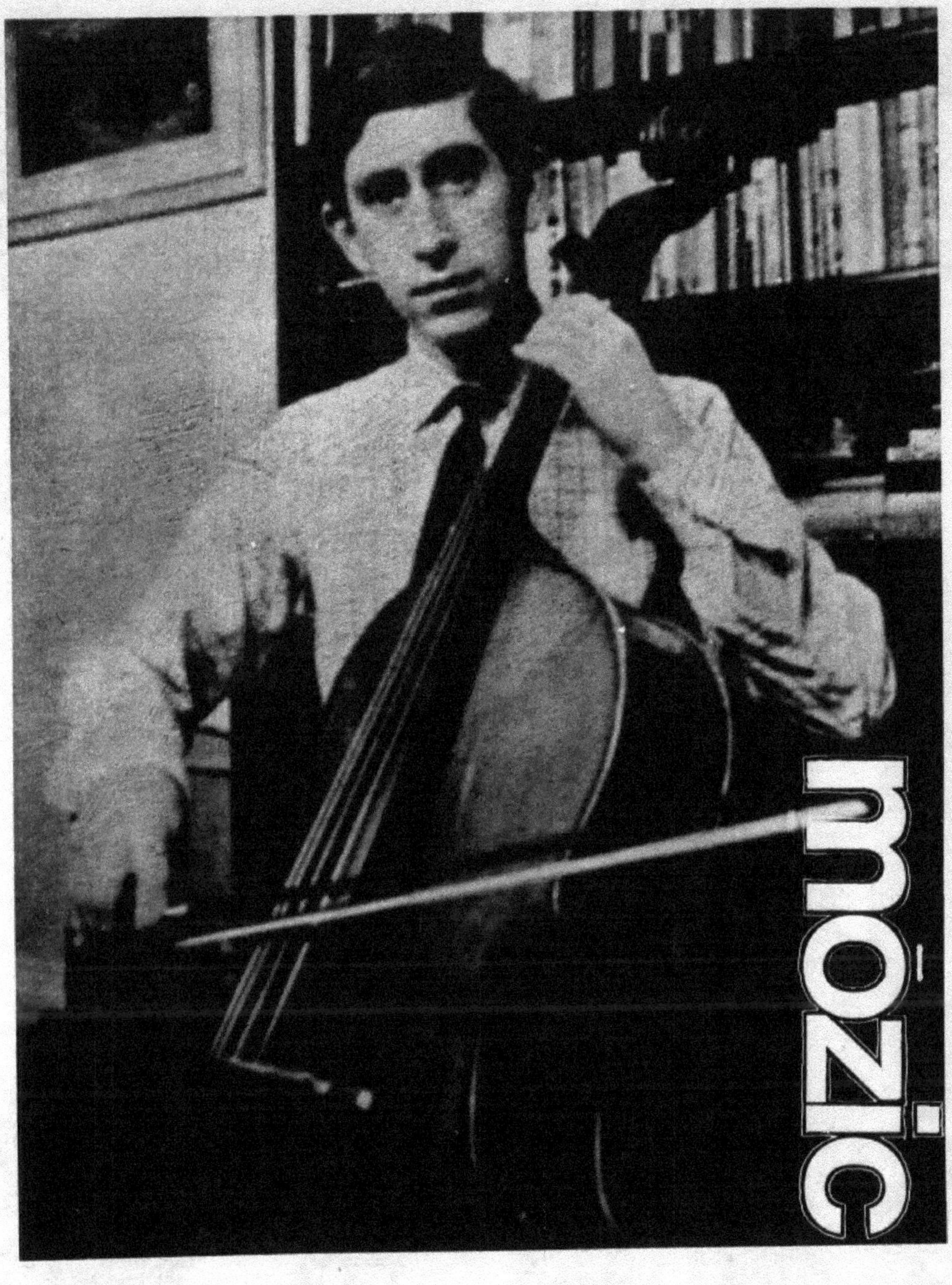
mōnic

To Begin with could you tell us something about the film you've made?

We made a movie called 'Uncle Meat'. It's got a lot of pictures of the Mothers in it, it also has a very strange plot which will require some straight-life-type actors to execute and we need some more money to finish it.

Isn't the plot explained on the sleeve of the Uncle Meat LP?

The beginning and the end is in there – the middle isn't.

Was the album written with the film in mind?

It's quite possible to make a film to match music, so I made some music and I made up the story line around it.

Basically what sort of a film is it?

It's a fantasy film with political and sociological overtones!

Sounds very deep. Is it?

Yeh, quite.

And we are all going to be able to see it?

We've got a couple of negotiations with people trying to raise the money to do it but it isn't that easy – you can't just come out and say 'Fred, will you give me the money?' He says 'OK' and then you go and make it. It's really involved with a lot of paper work and bullshit.

Are you pleased with the way that the concerts have been going?

Yes, it's been amazingly good considering the type of stuff we are playing which isn't, you know, major minor chords with a steady beat which is what most pop music is made up of – a couple of suspensions here and there. We've some things that don't operate in a key signature, and more things that use chords that don't appear in your everyday harmony book, and some rhythms which are difficult to tap your foot to. So it puts it a little bit out of the ordinary frame of reference of the average teenage audience or the average adult audience, if they ever came to see this kind of stuff. But strangely the kids here, even out in the provinces, were very open to the music and listened to it, I don't know

whether they understood it, but they liked it.

Did you put a lot of work into the music?

No, as a matter of fact I wrote most of it on the plane on the way over here, and I-er-usually just get some paper out and start drawing dots on it, and wait for someone to play it so that I know what it sounds like. That's the chamber music stuff. You know there's a difference between songs and compositions, songs are put together a different way, but these little bitty pieces that we are doing, they are based on another technique.

In the first concert you performed in this country why did you bring on members of a straight orchestra?

Well I like to play with straight musicians, you know, it gives us a little contrast material, and it also displays the fact that there are some members of the group who really are very skilled players and could exist just as easily in a symphony orchestra as on rock and roll stage; so we brought them out to er sort of bridge the gap between electric music and the other kind. Unfortunately there was one old fart in the string section that kept playing out of tune on purpose, trying to make the stuff sound ugly – so it turned into a carnival at the end. And it turned out that way because I wasn't going to let this guy spoil the show, so we made some use of the fact that the music was turning out a little bit sour, and I thought I'd stretch it to its illogical conclusion, and we went up dancing around on stage with them and having them, you know, do various things that you wouldn't expect a person in a tuxedo to do, like blowing farts through a microphone towards the audience, that's one way you can save the show when you have an unco-operative violinist!

I was reading in one of the 'pop' papers that you are now considered to be not a load of hairy freaks making rude noises, but talented musicians. Does it amaze you to read about yourselves in this way?

It's sort of funny, you know, they never would have discovered that we were musicians if I didn't do those interviews with those people and talking like hours on end trying to explain to them in detail what it is we are doing, because most people who write about music don't know what music is. They have certain tastes about the pop stuff that they listen to, and they don't have a broad based musical background that they could use as criteria by which to judge new music. It's pretty easy to judge a rock and roll song you know – like – does it make you tap your foot? Does it have the kind of words you want to hear? – in the boy/girl situation which is usually the plot basis of most of the lyrics, does it turn out all right

in the end for you? You know, those are the things you look for when you are reviewing a song. But if we come along and we are playing some electric chamber music or if we are experimenting with electronic sounds where we are into percussion constructions, or we are into unaccompanied arias on stage which are spontaneous, or we are doing some sort of visual thing with a gas mask. You know, if you are a rock and roll critic in one of those pop papers what do you write about? What kind of musical background do you have to assess this, how much Stockhausen have you heard, how much er John Cage do you know about?

You have obviously listened to these serious musicians, but are they interested in what you're doing?

Of course not, because that's one of the things that's really sick about the so-called serious musicians' world. It completely ignores rock music. You know, they think that 'we have it all, we are the avant garde and we are the forefront of musical experimentation,' say serious composers you know, and they're foolish to think that way because we in the rock world have equipment at our disposal that they don't even know about, that we use on the bandstand all the time. I am sure that a lot of the composers who are sweating now in their little isolated garrets don't know about electric woodwind instruments or what you can do with them. Even the electric guitar hasn't been touched by serious composers, and this whole thing has happened right under their noses. They ignore it. They think that electric music is something that you make with a synthesiser and amplified music is a completely different world. The composer has been writing for bassoons for a long time, but the way it sounds in our ensemble is completely different. It's executed the same way, the only thing we added was electricity. The same with the flugel-horn, clarinet, flute and other things we use. The trouble with the serious music world is that they're too narrow

$\frac{1}{4}$ oz	hash
2 $\frac{1}{2}$	cups of flour.
1	cup of honey.
1	cup of treacle.
1 $\frac{1}{2}$	cup sugar.
1	egg.
1 tsp	cinnamon.
1 tsp	baking soda.
1	cup water.
$\frac{1}{4}$ lb.	butter.

Finely powder hash add cup of water bring to boil and simmer
for five mins. stirring all the time.
Beat the egg in sugar add and mix flour. baking soda. ginger, cinnamon.
melted butter. honey. treacle and hash water. pour into a greased
baking dish. cook for one hour at 350° or regulo 5.

eat. wait.
and listen to

A BLIND MAN'S MOVIE
MURRAY ROMAN
Track 613 015

DISTRIBUTED BY POLYDOR RECORDS LTD

minded. They should go to the rock concerts. That's one of the reasons why their music is out of touch with the youth. And it shouldn't be, because I think that they are doing important things artistically, but it's very difficult to bring that to the attention of large numbers of people; And the largest single body of people are the teenies -- and how we get our music across without lowering our standard is that we just play it in places where the serious composers never go. We go to the Fillmore, and we play in all those little psychedelic dungeons all over the United States. We play schools and we play hockey rinks and we play bowling alleys and we also happen to play concert halls when we come to Europe.

How much of your music is notated?

50 per cent of it. The other 50 per cent is improvised and it's very carefully structured, and the live shows we do are all different, not just because of the improvisation but because of the way the building blocks of the show can be assembled.

Could you explain some of the lyrics on the album?

I am very interested in things which are absurd, and so the lyrics of that album are absurd, but some people think they are too sophisticated to appreciate an absurdity now and then.

Some people may think that there's some deep sociological significance in the lyrics.

Well, as a matter of fact they do have sociological significance but it isn't as literal as most of the intellectuals would like to make it. You know, it's a pretty subtle thing. First of all it's an art statement that we are working in this medium, and it's also an art statement that the package looks like it does for that record. It's an art statement that the words are what they are against the music being what it is. It's all very carefully balanced out.

So the lyrics are used also for a pure 'sound' purpose?

Right. Rundy rundy rundy doody mop mop sounds very well in that context, it looks stupid on paper but that's the thing with lyrics you know, lyrics on paper generally speaking don't look well at all, like, why did any body bother to put them down on paper. In fact usually cringe when I write 'em, but it's a different thing when you realise it as a sound and especially

depending on what register the voice is singing it in and all those other variables like the reference in the Uncle Meat variations to 'fuzzy dice and bongos, fuzzy dice, I got 'em at the pep boys at the boys, brodie knobs and spinners, chromium plated'. OK now those words on paper don't look like very much and if you say them they don't sound like very much, but if you take 'chromium plated' and sing it on an operatic melisma like the soprano is doing in that thing it becomes something really absurd you know. What she's singing there is a very difficult piece of music and she's being forced to sing those words on it. Of course I don't think you even know what brodie knobs are over here which makes it even less accessible.

What are they?

A brodie knob is a plastic knob which is screwed on to the steering wheel of a teenage automobile, generally it's clear blue plastic — some old men have them too, and they have these little pictures you know that you turn one way then you turn the other way and the picture moves, and the picture is generally a nude girl, her hands behind her head, so that it looks like she bounces her tits up and down for you when you turn your wheel.

Frank Zappa/Pete Drummond

THE ROLLING STONES

You can't always get what you want
Honky Tonk Women

45 rpm   F12952   DECCA

Lenny Bruce THE BERKELEY CONCERT *Bizarre Tra 195*

Somewhere along the line Lenny Bruce became known as a "dirty comedian". Well, he's no comedian – he was the first to admit that. One night he apologised to an audience 'I'm sorry I haven't been very funny – but you see I'm not a comedian, I'm Lenny Bruce'. But THEY all thought he was dirty, after his first season in the Establishment Club he drew these comments 'the man with a sewer for a mind', 'America's vilest export', and 'a fountain of filth at £600 a week'. When he tried to come back to London he was met with a deportation order at the airport as the Home Secretary had decided that his presence in England was "not conducive to the public interest". In Sydney there was much of the same. Lenny Bruce had several attempts at giving performances and was stopped by police, once in a theatre, and once in a club when he got into a hassle with some female who didn't appreciate him, and then finally when a University concert was organised, the Vice Chancellor stepped in and cancelled it. So Lenny went back to the States, where he didn't exactly get it easy. What with drugs and obscenity, he was always getting busted. Everywhere he spoke, the audience was half fuzz, waiting for him to drop one of the magic words they had written down in their little books as 'obscene'. And sure enough, drop one he did – he wouldn't let a challenge like that go by. Once in court, he always insisted on acting as his own lawyer, which only complicated things for everyone.

Well, he's dead now, and he died a lonely and unnecessary death, but this album is, if anything could be, a good memorial. This is Lenny Bruce talking to you, and somehow it's like listening to someone you know and like and respect, someone who's got something important to say, and manages to make it funny as well. As I said, he's no comedian, there's nothing facile about him, no well-rehearsed patter produced by a battery of scriptwriters – it's all him, it wouldn't do any good trying to get down anything he says, you've got to hear it for yourself. He just talks about things that concern him, like justice, and the law, religion, girls, and being Jewish, etc. Some people are saying that Lenny Bruce on record is dated (well, he does talk about Vietnam), but this album is now, as if was when it was recorded, just a man getting up and talking openly and thoughtfully – and fast, funny and frenetic as well – about some pretty timeless subjects. Recording quality is okay, no frills – in fact it's just edge to edge Lenny Bruce. The abrupt cut-off at the end, as if the original tape just ran out, is pretty exasperating, though. Ralph Gleason, his old friend and patron and one who stuck by him, writes some very good sleeve notes. But he was lucky enough to know Lenny Bruce first-hand. This album is the closest we'll get.
Gina Paul

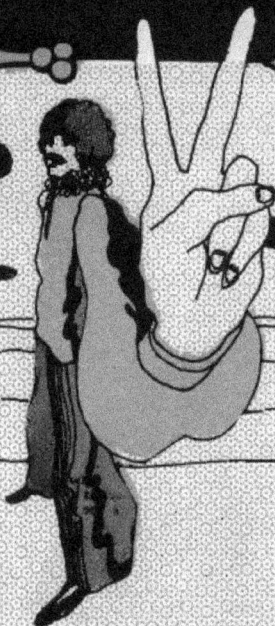

VELVET UNDERGROUND. Velvet Underground *MGM CS 8108.*

The Velvet Underground have always been a group who turned as many stomachs as they blew minds: not everyone can groove on them. Their attraction (or repulsion) lies in the extreme areas in which they operate: insistent, relentless rhythms . . . hysterical organ and guitar . . . wrecked vocals. A cut like Sister Ray on their last album makes a direct bid on the metabolism; you either escape or surrender. Their music is always unsettling and disturbing, their heads adrift somewhere in William Burroughs-land, a sickly sweet, rotten smell in the air . . . songs of Strange Pleasures, subversive and corrupt.

Yet here we are with Jesus, a long way to travel from Heroin in the space of one LP. Have they really hung up their spurs and the whip of shiny, shiny leather with the sailor's suit and cap? Have the Flowers of Evil started to bloom? Perhaps they haven't gone through 'changes' so much as 'modifications'; the wolf and the lamb walk hand in hand. For the first time 'velvet' shares top billing with 'underground'. They've stopped 'rushing on their run' and slowed the pace to a processional dawdle. But though everything has been toned in low key it's still unmistakably them. It's got 'feel' alright, but it's a kind of ghoulish, corpselike feel. Gone are the walls of sound and vast textural contrasts; in comes a sad, liturgical droning, the wailing of the converted sinner (but with his tongue slyly in his cheek). One doesn't really have faith in their faith, and it's probably wisest to give up very early trying. Cop out of value judgements, write it off as some variation on camp (which VU have always been strong on anyway), and you can relax and enjoy it. Songs on this album are divided between heaven and hell, and the casual listener will be forgiven if he doesn't quite notice the difference. Jesus is pure, simple, moving and undeniably sincere. But then there's Some Kinda Love, which is another thing altogether . . . shall we say 'hard core necrophilia'? The lyrics are filthiest – 'Put jelly on your shoulders and lie down on the carpet . . .', or, 'In some kinds of love the possibilities are endless, and for me to miss one of them would be groundless . . .' Murder Mystery, in which chick / drummer Maureen Tucker takes to song, is a cross between the Mothers and the Billy Cotton Band Show, and reminiscent of the saga of Walter Jeffries on White Light/White Heat. Maureen also takes the honours on Afterhours, and gets into a nice Vera Lynn bag . . . in fact she warbles delightfully.

Velvet Underground don't really sound together on this album, either as a group or as individuals, which I have a sneaking suspicion was what they might have been aiming at. Luckily too, for if they made it they would lose their quality as a group . . . fragmentation is more their scene. The style of this album is the antithesis of their style before. By replacing blatant freak-value with subtler means they end up sounding more bizarre than ever. Tired cliche, but this album really does grow on you . . . like a malignant tumor.
Adrian Ribolla

KING OF THE BLUES GUITAR Albert King *Atlantic 588173*

While both BB and Freddy King have visited this country and have more than lived up to their reputations, Albert, the most recent of the Kings to emerge, has yet to make a trip to Europe. However, when he does, he should be a sensation, at least if his records are anything to go by. After the excellent live set, Live Wire/Blues Power, comes his latest release in this country, 'King of the Blues Guitar', which though on Atlantic is in fact, a reissue of some of his Stax work of a couple of years ago, five tracks of which were released on the Stax album, Born Under a Bad Sign. If you haven't the Stax LP, this is the better buy, excluding as it does, the two mawkish ballads, The Very Thought of You' and 'I Almost Lost My Mind', which so marred the first album: and including several of his excellent single releases such as 'Lucy' and 'Cold Feet'. Recording for the Memphis based Stax label, King has been influenced by the soul sound for which the label is famous; and on his studio work he uses Booker T and the usual house musicians. As some blues purists in this country object even to the use of horns, they might find this hard to take. Nevertheless, they must one day come to terms

ROCK QUIZ

Here are sixteen authentic quotes about rock music, ranging from 1956 through to 1969. Each quote has three possible alternative origins. Tick your choice and turn to the astounding answers on page 44.

1) 'Rock 'n' Roll is a means of pulling down the white man to the level of the negro. It is part of a plot to undermine the morals of the youth of our nation.'

The Secretary of the North Alabama White Citizen's Council
Richard Daley, Mayor of Chicago
Judy Garland

2) 'I don't know anything about music. In my line I don't have to'

Yoko Ono
Elvis Presley
Timothy Leary

3) 'Viewed as a social phenomenon, the current craze for rock and roll material is one of the most terrifying things ever to have happened to popular music. Musically speaking, of course, the whole thing is laughable.'

Billy Cotton
Frankie Vaughan
Steve Race

4) 'Nothing really affected me musically until Elvis.'

Eric Burdon
John Lennon
Donald Peers

5) 'The kids accept almost any form of rock and roll, even the lowest and most distasteful . . . It seems to encourage sloppy clothes that become the accepted uniform. It's one step from Fascism.'

Malcolm Muggeridge
Mitch Miller
The Editor of the New Musical Express

6) 'I am one-hundred per cent Christian and everything I do is done with my religion in mind'

Billy Graham
Little Richard
Cliff Richard

7) 'It's so fabulous being young and a girl and you can have nice clothes and can dress up, and that's the nicest part about it, being famous and people admiring you.'

Sandie Shaw
Mrs Jeff Banks
Sandra Goodrich

8) 'In the old days you'd drag your old man out on the lawn and kick the shit out of each other, and he'd say, 'Be home by midnight!' and you'd be home by midnight. Today, parents don't dare tell you what time to get in — they're frightened you won't come back.'

Dick Gregory
Frank Zappa
Simon Dee

9) 'The same goes for my stripper routine. Nobody has ever objected . . . why should they? All that happens is that the stripping music plays and then I take off my jacket and . . .'

Engelbert Humperdinck
Janis Joplin
Danny La Rue

10) 'The effect of rock and roll in young people is to turn them into devil worshippers to stimulate self-expression through sex; to provoke lawlessness, impair nervous stability and destroy the sanctity of marriage. It is an evil influence on the youth of our country.'

R D Gaiman, Public Relations Officer to the Church of Scientology.
Rev Albert Carter, Minister of the Pentacostal Church.
Marjorie Proops

(Compiled by Felix Dennis & Jim Anderson).

11) "Uh-oh, I think I exposed myself out there . . .'

P.J. Proby
Jim Morrison
Judith Durham, ("Big Boobs" to her friends)

12) 'Too many people are becoming obsessed with pop music. The position of rock and roll in our sub-culture has become far too important, especially in the delving for philosophical content.'

Mick Jagger
Tiny Tim
Jan Wenner

13) 'Pop's not a culture, it isn't an art. If rock and roll is a culture it's a great big boil and when it bursts it will leave a nasty scar.'

Mick Farren
Simon Dupree
Che Guevara

14) 'When I perform am I producing art? Am I *fuck!*'

Mary Hopkin
Terry Reid
Jimi Hendrix

15) 'Pop is the perfect religious vehicle. It's as if God had come down to earth and seen all the ugliness that was being created and chosen pop to be the great force for love and beauty.'

Mike Heron
Donovan
Liberace

16) 'I had a banana band in highschool.'

Bob Dylan
Duane Eddy
Sir Malcolm Sargent

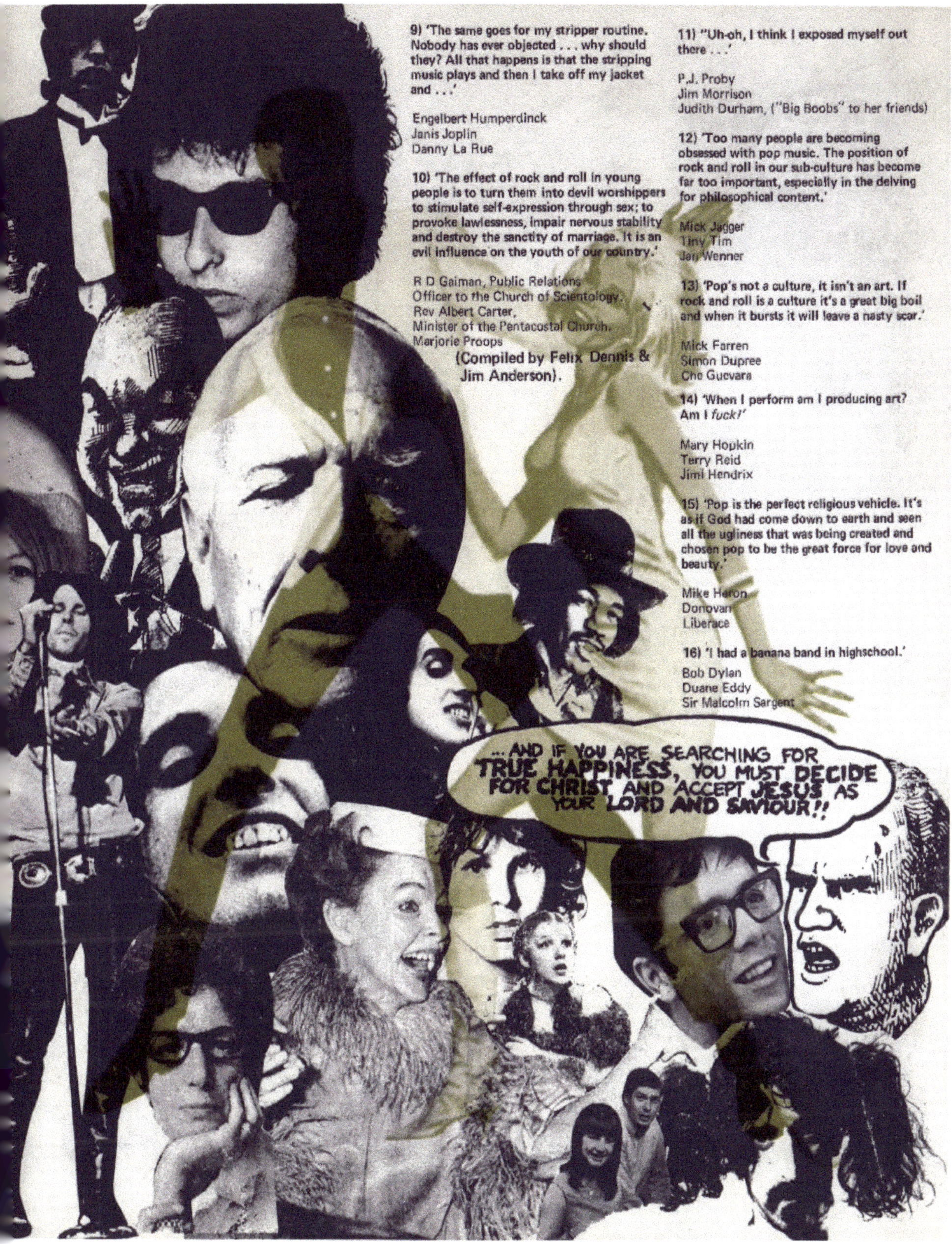

... AND IF YOU ARE SEARCHING FOR TRUE HAPPINESS, YOU MUST DECIDE FOR CHRIST AND ACCEPT JESUS AS YOUR LORD AND SAVIOUR!!

with the fact that most of the post BB King bluesmen and even BB himself have made use of horns, and are influenced by gospel and soul styles. This can, as in the case of Buddy Guy's treatment of Knock On Wood, be simply a commercial ploy to retain the interest of soul conscious black youth, or it can, as in Albert King's case, be an extension and development of the blues form, in the same way as BB King extended it by introducing gospel influenced vocal mannerisms and a strongly jazz influenced guitar style, derived from Django Reinhardt as well as T-Bone Walker. Albert's guitar style has its root in BB's, but it has a thicker, meatier tone to it: a more limited guitarist, certainly (at least on record), but none the less effective. He owes a lot to BB, but without being too derivitive. Of all the newer bluesmen, Magic Sam, Jnr Wells, Albert Collins, Buddy Guy etc, Albert King has probably the freshest approach, his is almost certainly the most interesting development of the BB King style while still remaining within the strict blues form. 'Born Under A Bad Sign' is best known to most people through Cream's version, but the version contained here is the original and one of the album's standouts. Other highlights include two brilliant slow blues, Personal Manager and Laundromat Blues. In complete contrast to the slow moodiness of those two tracks are Lucy, a tribute to his guitar in which he speaks of her as a woman, and Cold Feet, where he bemoans his lack of hits while his soul brothers at Stax are all high in the charts.

One of the most welcome by-products of the current success of white blues bands has been the revival of interest in both the older and younger negro bluesmen. While Albert will never receive the adulation or financial reward of the Claptons of this world, he is now at least playing to a wider audience and his album sales are picking up. Of the Albert King albums available (five, including imports) this is the most representative of his work at it's best.

Peter Dalton

A MEAL YOU CAN SHAKE HANDS WITH IN THE DARK. Pete Brown and his Battered Ornaments. *Harvest SHVL 752 Stereo.*

The whole process of reviewing is really a product of the popular mass media with its demands for 'instant copy' and so on. It's incapable of dealing with anything less ephemeral than yesterday's headlines since it's based on first impressions, and first impressions are so often not worth the paper they're printed on. Anybody who's noticed that a child can get more comfort and enjoyment out of a cheap, dog-eared and ancient teddy bear than from a whole roomful of bright and shiny, but unfamiliar, new toys will realize why. Some things can become more important to us than their external appearance and our first experience of them might ever suggest. It's this long term effect – the quality of art (or the teddy bear, or that lucky penny in your pocket, or whatever . . .) that makes it live and continue to influence us – that the short review just can't account for. It's what makes the short review ultimately worthless, something to be taken with the largest pinch of salt

you can find.

Understand me, I'm not saying Pete Brown's LP is art (or not art), or even that it is good music of its kind (or bad music of its kind). I'm only trying to be objectively honest, and the trick, as I see it, is not to be put off by one's first impressions of this album. They're likely to be unfavourable. Like Captain Beefheart, Pete Brown often taxes the ear-drums and frequently strains the sense of credulity. On the third time round I've just begun to detect saving graces: some of the lyrics really do have an appealing directness, and on some of the tracks the band really *does* appear to be rapping, interacting, constructing something valid. On the other hand some initial pessimisms seem to be borne out: on the whole I'd say the musicianship is weak and on the two tracks where the lyrics are in part and most obviously improvised, Politician and Travelling Blues, Pete strives too consciously to be evil and ends up as merely ridiculous, 'That's on three hearings. You may get this, or something different, quicker than I did. You may get it after a good while longer. You may never get it at all. And even if you do consider the whole thing merely abrrtive it shouldn't automatically be precluded from your collection. If it's true that by our mistakes we become lovable, then it may merely mean that this album has a better chance than most.

Graham Charnock

IF ONLY FOR A MOMENT Blossom Toes *Marmalade 608010 Stereo.*

There is a side to me that doesn't like record reviews, particularly underground reviews. Nine times out of ten they just end up as a kind of public wank by the reviewer who is living out his fantasy as best he can. However now and again an album comes along which although not a point of departure for other people's dreams, achieves something beautiful and unique in such a personal way that those of us who have heard feel a need to ask those who haven't to listen.

It's about two years since Blossom Toes' first album was released and on the evidence of this. their second album, it was two years spent growing musically and growing together, for after a very long listen I find this one of the best albums I have heard for months, and if a few levels and production points had been smoothed out and the track Just above my hobby horse's head taken out, it could possibly have been the best.

The feel of the album is very positively West Coast in terms of the colour and structure of the music; occasionally there are momentary glimpses of America and Americans, a suggestion of the Airplane, a hint of Beefheart, something which made me think of Steve Miller, but these are just the memories from which musical language is made and communication established, the imagery is essentially English, an experience drawn from an environment that includes us all, acid freaks, politicians, warriors and children moving in a world that sways between dream and reality without ever belonging to either.

With an album where people working as a group achieve a high level of performance as a group its rather contradictory to single out parts of the whole. However, my personal highs were Jim Cregan's playing on Indian Summer, harmony guitars, Billy Boo, Brian Godding's guitar solo on Wait a Minute, the rhythm section throughout and perhaps Giorgio Gomelsky's greatest contribution to pop music so far, bass vocal harmony on Love Bomb.

Blossom Toes have listened, lived, evaluated and evolved into their own thing, I hope you like it as much as I do. *K*

Answers to Quiz

1) The Secretary of the North Alabama White Citizen's Council, May 1956
2) Elvis Presley, April 1957
3) Steve Race, May 1956
4) John Lennon, February 1967
5) Mitch Miller, November 1957
6) Cliff Richard, April 1969
7) The three alternatives are Sandie Shaw's maiden, married and stage names, December 1967
8) Frank Zappa, June 1968
9) Engelbert Humperdinck, May 1969
10) Rev. Albert Carter, Minister of the Pentacostal Church, Oct. 1956
11) Jim Morrison, March 1969
12) Mick Jagger, February 1969
13) Simon Dupree, April 1969
14) Terry Reid, Jan. 1969
15) Donovan, 1968
16) Bob Dylan, June 1966

OUR FIRST SPIRITUAL EFFLUENCES,

OUR FIRST MUMMY-MADE MEDICINE,

SHALL BE PHYSIC MADE FROM THOSE

WHO SHOWED THEIR ECCENTRICITY

BY THEIR UNNATURAL PERSISTANCE

IN RETAINING THE APPEARANCE OF

LIFE, AND FROM THOSE, WHO WHILE

IN THIS LIFE, MIMIC'D MORTALITY.

A MEAL YOU CAN SHAKE
HANDS WITH IN THE DARK
PETE BROWN AND HIS
BATTERED ORNAMENTS
SHVL 752

WASA-WASA
EDGAR BROUGHTON BAND
SHVL 757

ALCHEMY
THIRD EAR BAND
SHVL 756

HARVEST
EMI

BLACKHILL ENTERPRISES LIMITED

E.M.I. RECORDS (THE GRAMAPHONE CO. LTD.)

MARSHA

Do you think of your hair as an aggressive sign?
No. Listen, how did my hair happen? My hair happened because I was wearing it in Shirley Temple curls and it rained one day and got very frizzy. I looked in the mirror and saw how easy it was going to be to keep it that way. The manager, or somebody at

Hair said: 'It would be very nice for you to wear that in the show.' I said maybe sometimes I'll wear it that way and sometimes I won't. I found it was easy to maintain it that way and then I really got into it, like totally into it. It got a lot of work for me and I've been able to exploit it.

But as far as the political thing goes that's not your object in wearing it.
Definitely not. Somebody came to me saying that one of the large newspapers was doing a story about 'naturals' and black girls going into this very heavy identity with African heritage and whatever. I told the man I couldn't possibly discuss that with him because that wasn't why I was wearing my hair like that. Of course it's kind of nice for people to associate that with me, but that's not really where it's at in my head at all, because my hair could just as easily be straight as kinked. There are a lot of things happening down on the plantations and there are a lot of things that the hair can do.

How are your relationships with the black activist groups in London. Have they approached you or have you wanted to do something with them?
It's very strange. They approached me on a very naive and beautiful level, really. Somebody from the black power group came up to me and said: 'We're doing a show, can you come?' and 'We're having a meeting, can you come?' and I went down to see what was happening. I went down in face because I wanted to set up a nursery for black children in London since I had this nursery in Berkeley. I thought that I could tie it in with the Movement and that in some way it might help, but when I got to the meeting I just felt that it was going to take so much time and energy to make them aware of the fact that I wasn't a foreigner and that I wasn't standing apart from the Movement – our Movement – that I just didn't get into it. I found the vibrations very funny at that meeting. I was treated like an outsider and I didn't expect that, you know. I expected that being black, I would be treated like everybody else in that room.

Was the reason that you were treated like an outsider that you had made it in . . .
I don't know. Perhaps it was the fact that being American sets me apart from the blacks in England. I didn't really understand why I was treated like I was, but I did definitely feel some strange attitude towards me.

Many black musicians coming to England, mainly rock, but jazz as well, often say, in press releases anyway, that they really dig England more than the States and that they feel much less of a prejudice here. What do you think of that sort of statement?
I think they feel that way because they don't really live here. Unfortunately nearly everywhere in the world there's this really blind prejudice. I thought when I first arrived here that none existed, but as soon as you start looking for a flat, as soon as you start talking about anything, as soon as people start asking you about music, about your hair, about the entirety of your being, you realise that there are great prejudices existing in almost everybody's mind.

You find this less now or not, I mean for you at the moment?
My position is really very strange because I find that before Englishmen identify me with being black they first identify me with being American, you know. Perhaps if I were West Indian the treatment I would get would be totally, but totally different. But when you get into the working class and the middle class society, you find that all the prejudices are the same. In fact, because I lived in Berkeley, I find more here than there. I think the prejudice in England is diabolical because nobody really discusses it. Ladbroke Grove really exists but nobody does anything about it. Discrimination in housing is an accepted thing and is something that everybody is very courteous about and refuses to discuss. They try to throw it off as being irrelevant or whatever. I can't understand the English position on the racial situation at all, but there is definitely a very strong problem here, which I think makes the blacks position here worse than in America. At least we're getting out there and discussing it, at least we're hassling over it.

What's discussed here is always in Enoch Powell's terms, too, that's the level of discussion.
Oh, exactly. Unfortunately there's somebody in that position to lay something like that down and have, seemingly, most of public opinion with him, and yet there's no black back-lash, there's no liberal back-lash, nobody seems to get upset about it. I mean Powell can make these statements and nobody blows him off the face of the earth. I don't understand it.

Vogue Magazine had some beautiful pictures of you awhile back but their little precis talked about you as a golliwog, as if you were some kind of man from the moon. How do you feel about that sort of thing? And also about the way IT ran your ad, with emphasis on WOGS for Walk on Gilded Splinters, which probably was a mistake.
Yeah, there was a mistake, in that before that happened I wasn't wise enough to approve all my ads before they went out. I mean, that Vogue article happened because Ray Connolly did an article about me in the Evening Standard and the

46

headlines were that I was the prettiest golliwog in London. Unfortunately I can't get upset about the word 'wog' because it doesn't seem real to me. If they were talking about 'niggers' there would be some very heavy anti-vibrations coming, but 'wog' doesn't mean anything. The word has no bad connotations for me. It's just some English thing. The only reason I was opposed to them calling me a wog was because I realise that in this country the word is used adversely against dark-skinned people. That's what made me up-tight. Whoever made that ad had a lot of bitching to cope with from me because of it.

Your first single, Walk on Gilded Splinters – you took Dr John's sly, jazz orientation and made it into a real voodoo chant.
I left the Hair evening show at 12 and I got to the studios to record and found that there was a group in the studios so I had to wait for another hour and so by the time it happened I was really uptight and I must have sung that fucking song about twenty times. I realised I was getting very uptight about something I really believed in, so I sat in this funny little room, and it was so hot it was ridiculous. I always smoke when I'm recording, cigarettes, and I couldn't smoke because there was no ventilation. I couldn't sing because it was too hot, it didn't work with my clothes off, so I put my clothes back on, it still didn't work so I decided to sit down and calm down, and get into the motion of the music, which to me was a very spiritual thing.

It sounds like a heat trance.
No. Three years ago I met these two Americans who said that they had had a seance and that there were spirits in their house. I went over there laughingly to prove how wrong they were about seances and spirits and this whole thing happened and since then I have had great communication with something that's with me all the time, and that's how I eventually got into the song.
When the song was recorded by me it had nothing to do with voodoo, it had to do with something that I have that's greater than that. Because when I think of voodoo I think of poisonous snakes, you know, and what I did with that record had venom in the lyrics, but not in the over-all feeling.

You were talking before about the whole pop scene in terms of the super-star scene.
I mean what is that, what is a super-star? If someone uses that word again I'm going to like freak-out, because I should think the people who are called super-stars are considered super-stars simply because they play their instruments very well, but to even allow themselves to be associated with that label takes a hell of a lot out of it.

The real super-stars have very little to do with that label.
Yeah, I guess you're right. I mean, nobody calls Jagger a super-star.

But he is one.
You're joking, he is one. In my heart and in everybody else's I don't know. There's so little happening in the business at the moment. Things are stagnant – I don't mean that in somebody's back yard somebody isn't creating something beautiful, something new, something really fresh – so what they're doing now is to get cults going around super-stars, and super-stars don't exist. As soon as you call yourself a star, you're really taking yourself seriously aren't you.

It means you make a lot more money.

I don't know. I seem to keep the taxi-cab company going but other than that I don't seem to have a whole lot of money. A lot of us are here because we were running away from middle class society. I left the University of California because I was really tired of estate cars and I get here to find that that's exactly what you ride in to go up to Leicester to do a gig, and that a push bike isn't good enough for you. And you can't go out of the house without any make up because of your image. I don't have any image because one day my hair is going to fall out.

That's not exactly fair, Marsha. Marsha Hunt playing with White Trash is the merging of two incredible images.
I'd rather call myself Mabel. If Marsha Hunt means something to someone other than what it means to me which is like this name my mother gave me because she couldn't think of a better one, I can't get involved with that. It's very hard to explain, but none of that is real, none of that is why I came here. I'm just happy to know that I'm not at Berkeley any more. I left it because it was becoming to me everything that the armchair philosophers said they didn't want to become a part of. Like the Free Speech Movement, we were fighting the system, and before we knew it, like within three weeks, we had committees, and sub-committees and anti-sub-committees and the sub-committee to the sub-committee. And I thought, 'Well, this definitely isn't happening' and I came over her to breathe again. It's frightening when I think I might slip back into that thing again.

How do you find you're fighting it? How do you try not to slip into it?
If I can just keep laughing, you know. If people can get good vibrations from my energy, from what I do because I'm happy. I'm sad, then that's a nice thing, but as soon as I get involved with projecting what I think they want me to feel then I'm going to be in a very bad way and I hope that I never get the. If I see it coming, I'm going to split again.

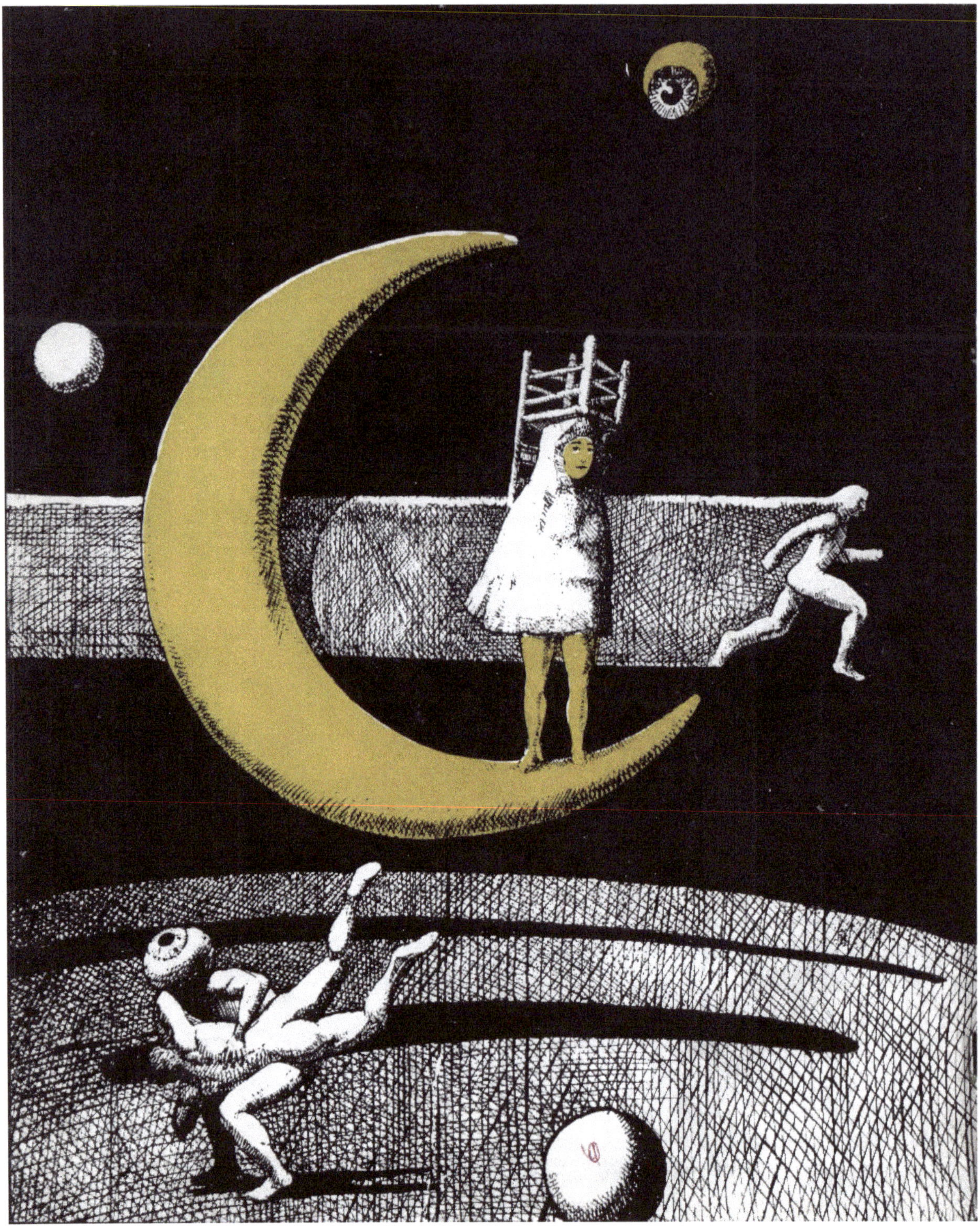

23

3/6

OZ

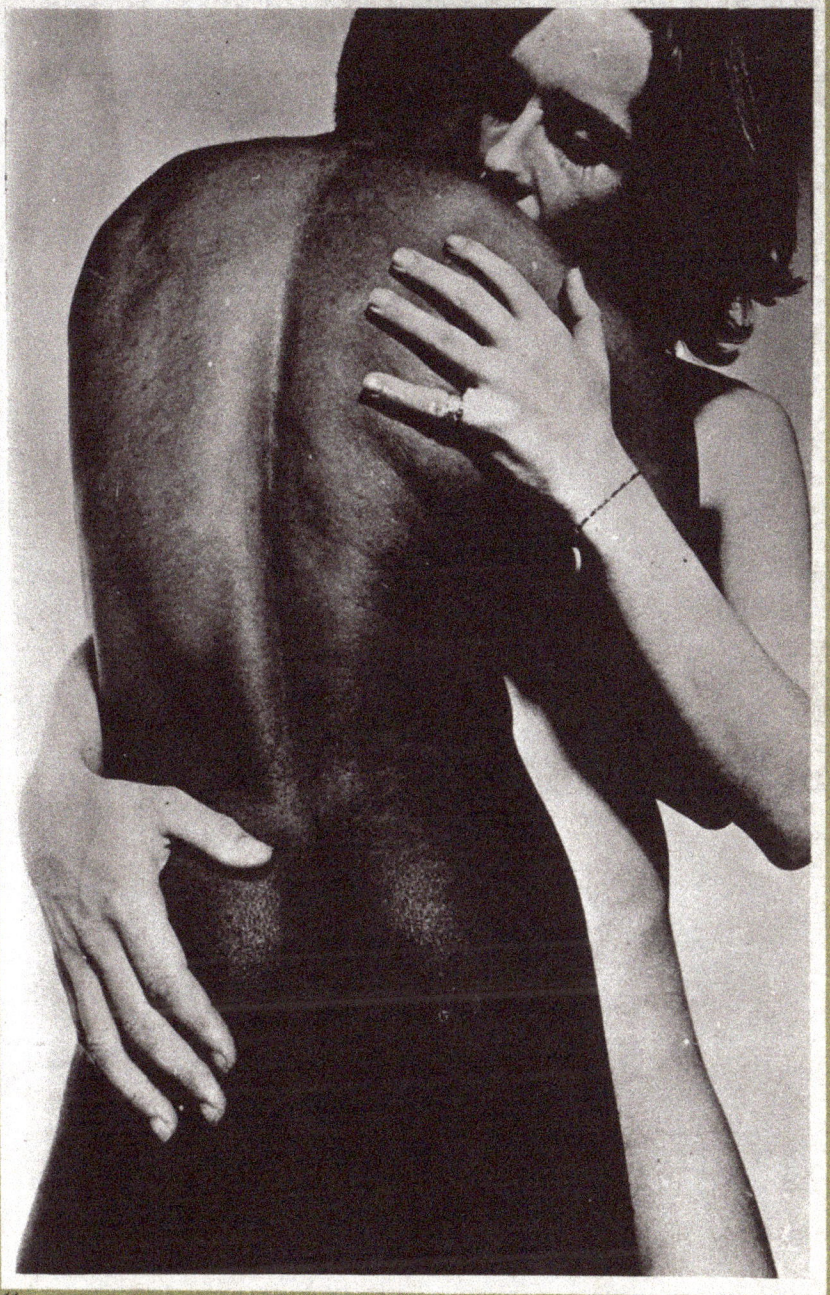

"yet each man kills the thing He loves..."

OZ 23
August/Sept 1969
OZ is published by
OZ Publications Ink
52 Princedale Road, London W11.
Telephone 229 7541

Printed by OZ Publications Ink.

Advertising: Contact Felix Dennis @ 727-8456

This issue appears with the help of Sebastian
Jorgensen, Richard Neville, Felix Dennis, Jon
Goodchild, Louise Ferrier, Jim Anderson,
Ken Petty, Miss Murphy, Keith Morris, Tina
Locke, Martin Sharp, Thom Keyes, Robert
Owen, Jim Callaghan, "Buzz" Aldrin & the
Policeman at Heathrow.

Distribution:
UK: Moore Harness Ltd. 11 Lever Street,
London EC1, CLE 4882. ECAL, 22 Betterton
Street, London WC2, TEM 8606. Trans-
mutation, Guildford 65894. California:
Rattner Distributors, 2428 McGee Street,
Berkeley, California 94703. Holland: Thomas
Rap, Reguliewarstraat 91, Amsterdam, Tel:
020-227065. Denmark: George Streston, The
Underground, Larsbjorn Straede 13,
Copenhagen K. France: Impossible.

Allen Ginsberg, Ted Heath, Robert Frazer, David Litvinov,
Christopher Gibbs, John Frazer, Alan Bates, William Burroughs, Jean
Genet, Long John Baldry, Desmond Dekker, W. H. Auden,
Andrew Loog Oldham, Cliff Richard, Billy Graham, Chris Denning, Tony
Windsor, Jim Anderson, David Hockney, Mark Lancaster,
Robert Helpmann, Michael Bentine, Kenneth Williams, Wild Child, Beverley
Nichols, Godfrey Winn, Donovan, Jeremy Thorpe, Pierre Trudeau,
Robert Stigwood, Maurice Gibb, Steve McQueen, Alain Delon,
Detective Sergeant "groupie" Pilcher, Paul McCartney, Karim Khan,
Rufus Collins, Lionel Bart, Truman Capote, Robert Carrier,
the Duke of Edinburgh, Dusty Springfield, Elvis Presley, Plato,
Andy Warhol, Rock Hudson, Lord Snowdon, J. Edgar Hoover,
Marc Bolan, His Highness the Prince of Baroda, Jimmy Young,
Norman St John Stevas, Walter Bagehot, Tariq Ali?

FIERY CREATIONS LIMITED
present

Bob Dylan & The band
Ritchie Havens

The who Moody blues Fat mattress Joe cocker Family Pretty things
Free Marsha hunt & white trash Battered ornaments Blodwyn pig
Aynsley dunbar retaliation Gypsy Blonde on blonde King crimson
Edgar broughton band Bonzo dog band _____ august 30   25/-

Bob dylan The band Ritchie havens Tom paxton Pentangle julie felix ____
Gary farr Liverpool scene Indo jazz fusions Third ear band ___ august 31 £2
two day ticket ____ 35/-

tickets in advance from
FIERY CREATIONS LIMITED   TAVISTOCK HOUSE   WARD ROAD   TOTLAND BAY   ISLE OF WIGHT

3

Correspondence

4

PORNO SWEDEN

Yes, you still have to send to Sweden for your Porno. For £1. we will send you our Glossy samples, Richly coloured catalogues on Films, Colour-Slides, Photos, Magazines and Books. We accept I.R.C.s International Reply coupons which you can buy at any Post Office. Cash Postal Orders and cheques are also acceptable, but leave all payee columns blank.
MAYFAIR DESIGN, BOX 9077, 12109 JOHANNESHOV 9, SWEDEN.

Dear OZ,

Reading your mag makes me feel very small, it's alright for the Living Theatre to take off their clothes, but I've got a few nasty spots which I am very embarrassed about, and have to drink lots of milk and eat out in the sum (what fucking sun?)

The fucking scene out here in the country is non-existent, we have to do it with our hands, which leads to a red raw tool and aching balls, legs and back — bad temper and nerves, and it does drive you crazy because you know what you're missing every time you masturbate.

The smoking scene? One of the most efficient drugs squads in the country is working in this area. So who needs paranoia as well?

Then there was the time I turned up at the Arts Lab (first and last time) to see the Dylan film and couldn't afford it. 15 bob for a fucking film! I was thrown out by some irate trendy who kept muttering something about Royalties.

I thought the idea of kids doing their own thing was that it would be cheap and for everybody, not a clique.

I can't play the guitar, I can't write poetry, act, paint, or sing and my understanding of politics and economics is very limited. So what happens to me in the great cultural revolution.

In my 19 years I've had 3 women, a nervous breakdown and some poor education. Can't you people in London realize that 20 miles north of IT, OZ, Arts Labs, etc, NOTHING HAS CHANGED! So what's all the fuss about?

Do I hear smug laughter.

JF

Dear OZ,

Rugby is breaking bravely away from tradition, is being democratically reformed with the boys in mind, and is in no need of an anarchist revolt, thank you. So please tell the Public Schools Anarchist Committee where to get off.

Love,
Peter James,
Springfield House,
West Clandon,
Surrey.

Dear OZ

On June 22nd the Sunday Telegraph revealed that over 30 boys at Rugby School were expelled because they were 'hippy rebels' — they were wearing their hair long and preferred mod clothing and they had tried to introduce 'hippy ideas and literature' into the school. Two boys had also been expelled for smoking pot, and for circulating OZ and IT. They also published their own magazine, Lucifer, which was halted after three issues. A 'Rugby Freedom Movement' had been formed and the boys involved went around smashing windows and light bulbs and generally wrecking the place. The following day the Rugby authorities issued a statement admitting that there had been some trouble recently, but that the number of boys involved had been exaggerated.

Next Sunday, the Telegraph — now giving more attention to the whole business than either of the supposedly troublemaking OZ and IT — announced that on the following Saturday (July 5th) an anti-public schools demonstration would be held by the London-based Public Schools Anarchist Committee at Wellington College. The demo, would take the form of a minor uprising. An advert in the Drury Lane Arts Lab, called for support. It stated: 'In each of the country's public schools there is a tiny group of heads trying to destroy inequality and petty tyranny. They need your help.' The headmaster of Wellington said that he

bitterly resented 'the intrusion of professional agitators into the affairs of a private institution.' Meanwhile the headmaster of Aldenham Public School at Elstree announced that he was banning both OZ and IT from the school.

And for the next gripping instalment read the Sunday Telegraph?

Seriously, an attack on the public school is not just an attack on the school authorities, but also an attack on some of the pupils, their parents, and the rich and powerful upper crust of our society. No attack should be taken lightly by those who plan it — any small group from outside the school stands little chance anyway faced with such opposition. In society's present state, it is best that the public school pupils themselves attempt to change their environment into something more free and sensible.

Yours,
Tristan Wood & Julian Ledbury,
c/o Rugby School.

Dear OZ

It's a lie to say television is a 'bankrupt medium' (OZ 22). It's like saying TV does not exist. It's an example of idiotic non-think. What you seem to have totally forgotten is that the medium is only 15 years old — virtually nothing compared to the cinema, and nothing at all compared with theatre, literature, painting, sculpture or theatre. You are dealing with something whose potential is unknown, whose capabilities are unknown, whose resources are unknown.

I resent very much one quote in this unfortunate supplement — I think by David Sharp in his 'tired producer's notes.' He claims that the point I have made above is not a useful one. On the contrary I regard it as an extremely useful and important argument because when you compare the

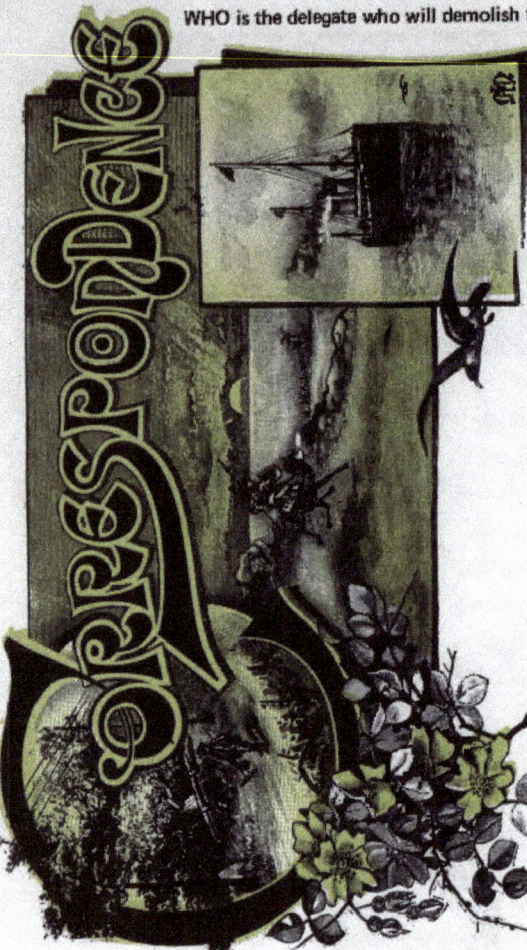

improvements made in cinema from the time it first started, around 1890, with a film made 15 years later, say 1965, you find they are minimal compared with what TV has achieved in the same period of time.

I've worked in TV for three years and can remember thinking how extraordinary it was to see live TV pictures from New York. And now of course I can watch pictures from the moon. The technological possibilities of this are beyond one's imagination.

That's not to say that the ideas being made of TV at the moment are necessarily the best. But as a contribution to the debate your supplement is worse than non-existent. It's positively damaging. OZ has merely screwed up a real issue — at stake. Most of your criticisms of the BBC are absolute and total fictions. The BBC has in fact worked out the most amazing British compromise.

There is a Board of Directors which involves a director of television, a director of radio, a director of administration and so on. They run the BBC and they are the group of people to whom all those who work for the corporation are responsible. But the Board of Governors is responsible to nobody at all except the Government. So you have the State, and the Board of Governors who are there to interpret what the State wants, you like, except that they consist of a lot of people who are not political appointees.

Some are totally opposed to the Labour government and when the Conservatives come in they will be totally opposed to them.

These people have their representative on the Board in the person of the Director General, and he exists, as it were, as a filter and he goes back to the Board who tell him they want this and that and go chortle, chortle, chortle, and ask how can such and such be watered down. Then the Director General goes chortle, chortle, chortle, how can I water that down and this is passed down to the

head of a department who says chortle, chortle how can I water that down. The net result is that the people who are actually making the programmes are not controlled in any way at all by anyone.

Often what the BBC tends to do, by and large, is to go half a step forwards while seeming to go half a step backwards. It was the BBC who first said 'fuck', not ITV. It's the BBC who shows nude women, not ITV. It was the BBC who saw 'Man shot in the head in Vietnam', not ITV. And the BBC produced 'Till Death Do Us Part', etc. etc. So it's absolute nonsense to write off the BBC as a reactionary organisation.

Of course I'm not denying the validity of some of your criticisms. Certainly the subculture of pop music, organisations like Release, Shelter, Bit and magazines like yours and what they are supposed to stand for, are largely ignored. And the BBC is completely at fault in this.

But if your David Sharp (known to me, by another name, to be a very senior producer who should know better), your Raymond Durgnat and all the particularly whoever was responsible for that introduction are assuming that behind all this there is some kind of corporation conspiracy then they the hell didn't you conduct a debate along those lines. Such an approach could have yielded infinite possibilities. If there is a next time I may suggest you change your misleading heading to 'TV is the medium' and run a supplement which has been thoroughly and intelligently thought-out; not just another compilation of uninformed sneers.

Yours,
Tony Palmer
Ladbroke Grove.

FROGFEED

verbrechen oder wunder: ein vollständiger mensch
A crime or a miracle : a complete human being

Dear Oz,
I was down at the Midnight Court last Friday taking pictures of the groups, then a small army of fuzz moved in and started making people feel a bit uncomfortable. I got a couple of shots of them engaged in their usual activities, and promptly had my film confiscated by the management of the Lyceum.
So much for yet another 'underground' organization. They should stick to bingo-halls and the Hammersmith Palais.
To be fair, I did get compensation for the film, but that isn't the point.
It is interesting that they let me take pictures for three weeks without any interference, but as soon as the fuzz appear?
Love,
(Name and address withheld by request)

Dear OZ,
Just one small point about something Marsha Hunt said in OZ 22. Namely: she didn't know why the British blacks gave her the cool reception. Now, the answer to this is not because she is American, or any kind of nationalist or race thing, but because of CLASS. And it is because of class conflict that the whites hate/fear the blacks (and, of course, vice versa). Marsha's like the duchess who couldn't understand why the peasants didn't smile when she brought them windfalls every summer. By making a bit of money she's put herself even more firmly in the middle class than she was when she was a swinging student at Berkeley — a small wonder the labouring blokes from Ladbroke Grove didn't exactly feel that she was one of them.
And, of course, they would be right in viewing her as being largely uncommitted to THEIR problem she, after all, has risen above it. Now, she will attract only a few sophisticated shreds of white racialism (no greasy landlords to fight with, no getting refused drinks, no being thrown off buses by yobs, etc; etc.) — her public is black and white, and her money and success will attract the usual arse-licking crowd of admirers from both colours — because, in her case, the primary base for racialism (i.e. economic) will have been destroyed. Marsha had better start learning that you can't succeed by the values of a rotten society and then try joining those who are being crushed by that society. Easier by far to have carnal relations with oneself.
luv,
Bob Ritchie
Osborne Cottage
Cassington
Oxford

Dear OZ,
Well, waddaya know, the Great English Romantic Revival has just hit the vinyl. Called Jethro Tull they will play sweet songs and merry ditties to soothe your cells. Bring not your nasty Clearwater near, nor your vulgar Waters, give me a cup of tea, a Jethro, and a good lie down.
With heart-shaped Fenders and a posy of violet Marshalls they assault our ears with a cupid's kiss. Out with bodies, hit the pits with Mum.
Get Stand Up, it's the best English album for some time and reading between the grooves is a pleasure.
T. R. Zelinka,
10 Argyll Mansions,
Hammersmith Road,
London W14

Dear OZ
The Secondary Schools' Unions were unable to achieve any serious mobilization of youth. Since its collapse the vestiges of SSU's in the North-West, e.g., Manchester, Stockport, Oldham, etc., with the help of a radical newspaper 'Seed Eye' now hope to re-start the movement. The new campaign will be based on a £3 minimum wage demand for school students who choose to stay on beyond the school-leaving age.
The campaign will be called WAGE — We Ain't Getting Educated. A research group is currently being established in Manchester. Its purpose is to churn out facts which will prove to people that our present educational system ignores the needs of the individual student.
A festival is being arranged for the North-West. The idea of the festival is to have an exciting setting. Blues festival at the beginning of the new term (September 12-14) to draw attention to campaign aims. Earlier, Sept 6-7, there will be a meeting of militant leaders in Manchester — ideas needed.
Yours fraternally,
Naomi Winthorne
(Manchester SSU)

Dear OZ
With reference to your article on Spikeys, OZ 22, I fear you are sadly misled as to their numbers and sexual division. The Skinheads have appeared in large numbers since last September.
It is not surprising that this violent movement has arisen: man is fundamentally a violent creature, and a re-action to the peace-love culture thing was inevitable.
Let us not dismiss these people as morons however. We both have a uniform. We are all reacting to the confusion and pressures brought about by the Neo-industrial Revolution, which is still in its infancy. We all use the soft drug: the Cropper's favourite tripe is acid, he has contempt for the

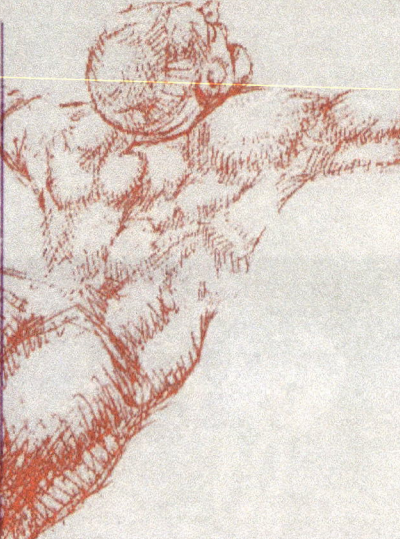

sacred weed. But where is the fundamental difference?
Isn't our reaction to Skinheads remarkably like the Normal's reaction to us? Are we utter hypocrites, or do we echo the words of Frank Zappa:
'Who cares if hair is long or short, or partly grey.
We know that hair ain't where its at!'
Yours wrongly
A Friend.

Dear Oz
While the over-adorned carriage of the Prince of Wales meandered through the servile sycophants some discordant notes issued from three "heads" nearby. The procession meanwhile continued on its way. But as soon as the "pram" turned into another street the trio were immediately pounced upon by the fuzz. The scenes which followed were grotesque. Swarms of navy, silver-buttoned, truncheoned sadists — whose faces were contorted with fury — broke loose with abuse and blows. This went on for five minutes. The 'heads' emerged with bedraggled clothes and bloody faces. The Press, who were onlookers, didn't even bother to mention this in any of the 'national deceptives'.
Yours
Thomas Jenkins,
130 St Helens Avenue,
Swansea, Glamorgan.

Dear OZ,
Concerning your recent issue (OZ 22) I have just been reading The Hippie Hoax thing (Pages 17–23). Marijuana turns happy lives into hell! Is this all true?
Surely this is CRAP! Love and peace and freedom to all.
Andrew

Dear OZ
I am editing, for Panther Books, an anthology of revolutionary and radical poetry by young British poets. The book will, I believe, demonstrate, justify and reflect the political aspirations of young people today. I would like to hear from your readers who should send contributions, with sae, directly to me.
Alan Bold
19 Gayfield Square
Edinburgh 1

Dear Germaine
Revolution is a happening thing. Lets not be so serious about it.
I hope you won't be stuck in you bag of defending 'the underground'. Like the man says, lets make it for the hell of it.
Love
Gene Mahon
Rolling Stone
19 Hanover Square
London W1

6

Dear OZ
Right. Fuck the Lyceum. Thank the stars that Explosion burst on us. So, now we must all STAY AWAY from that Moon shithole.
Dave Carey
nr Piccadilly Circus
London W1

Dear Germaine
Perhaps you could know how it feels if you find the Steely Dan III from Yokohama.
But it's a commercial proposition.
Jane Nicholson
Rolling Stone

Dear Oz
I was pleased to feel the fire of germaine's observations. Obvious they may be, but it's heartening to see them reiterated simply and strongly. We all need to be reminded from time to time how so fucking easy it is to conveniently forget the principles which we profess to believe. Compromise is a hell of an insidious thing. Thus we all agree on the occasional necessary for it, but once you don't, it rots you like gangrene, slowly really inch by inch. And you adjust. You didn't even notice...
International Times is a far better example. At least Rolling Stone doesn't pretend — it's on the bandwagon, that's all, and doesn't even get that together!
But keep off your one OZ, lest you forget too — and the enemy is there. With you the senility syndrome is setting in.
Having said what you said . . .
Sincerely
Glenn
London

Ozzie —
Your efforts to bring such luxuries as food into the reach of the impoverished multitudes are ingenious and admirable. But you've done it again, human flesh (at least in the US) is UNFIT FOR HUMAN CONSUMPTION due to the large amounts of DDT in the body. Better luck next month
Catherine Pontabo
7600 Merrill
Chicago, Ill. USA 60649

Dear OZ,
Sure, pepper in a vagina is a certainty for kicks, and freedom without responsibility degenerates into license.
OK, so you don't know the SDS is prepared to the use of explosives and sabotage also they're linked up with Black Panthers for the spread of urban violence. Further OZ proclaims it is revolutionary, but then so was Jesus.
Of course these words are used by the 'boys', but if you possess a bit of intelligence with a healthy imagination combine with the half a million words you select the correct one, i.e. 'bullshit'.
However, we all need go your way towards a humanized society; whereas I'll defend 'Civilized Society' because despite its warts it's worth defending.
May the best side win.
Alan Donn
35 Marlborough Road
Woodthorpe, Notts. NG5 4GE.

P.S. I am a man of principle, with positive values and standards, i.e. integrity, fidelity, the dignity of labour etc. etc.

Dear OZ
I am fifty-four. I was brought up strictly Church of England and a Royalist. At the age of four "correctly" refusing chocolates from a stranger I to and I accepted them immediately on being told that they were from 'The King' (King George VI). No problem there, as the 'stranger' was in uniform (actually a friend of my father's) — 'The King's Army'.
I am still a Royalist. I no longer consider myself a practising Christian.
I am more Christian than I ever was, old age? I don't think so, the example of the young.
I have tried once, I meet their friends. I went to the Rolling Stones gathering in Hyde Park because

it was an 'event', because my eldest son is a disc-jockey.
I would never have believed that I could be broad-minded, standing, happy and safe.
I've read through 'Lucia de Lammermoor' at Covent Garden, through 'Lize' at Stratford-upon-Avon, through Wimbledon — but a crowd of 'Hippies'?
The wonderful impersonal goodness of the young. An old-fashioned world? No longer so.
Let us be grateful that at last Christ's teaching (not St Paul's) is alive in the land.
Yours truly,
Harriet Ravenscroft
Jameson Street
London W8

Dear OZ,
I find it frustrating that whilst up to 500,000 can turn out for free concerts — many of whom seem to be under the impression that they are taking part in a revolutionary act that will topple the society sitting in the sunshine for five hours and listening (most whose position lies firmly within the System. Less than a hundred found the energy to go and protest against the mass-murderer Nixon when he came to London last February, and less than fifty turned up at a recent march on the Spanish Embassy to show solidarity with those people under Franco's regime who are condemned to spend the rest of their lives in rat-holes for the crime of opposing Fascism. Or are we supposed to let Nixon, Franco, Wilson, Vorster, Mao, and all the rest of the politicians who consider it their duty to run our own brains for us, do their own thing?
Yours fraternally,
Geoff Trodd

Dear OZ
Rumour has it that Barry Quaterman is going to re-open UFO. Would you care to comment?
Love,
Peter

Dear OZ,
Many thanks to you, and your readers. Since your publication of my request, I've received from OZ readers six pairs of spectacles, which is a very good effort indeed.
Yours sincerely,
Albert Bailey
Almstead Optical Mission
Marrow Brook Lane,
W. Farnborough, Hants

Dear OZ,
Maybe we're all a little too tied up on this sex-revolution thing. Maybe on this whole revolution thing. Maybe we should all just go off and sit on a lonely cliff-top or something and think. Maybe we should all read Huxley's 'Brave New World' and see if that's what we want.
'Squib'
1 Valley Road,
Harrogate, Yorkshire

Dear editor,
70,000 copies of a questionnaire have been sent out by Martin Zeki to people whom he considers the 'Underground'. The questions he asks are either extremely stupid or potentially dangerous. Any innocent studies of dissidents in the past have later been used to control blacks, workers, homosexuals, and students. This type of questionnaire is subject to the same kind of repression. For example, this seems to be one of the first studies of how the members of the underground get enough money to eat, to sleep, etc. Depending on the results, it could well be, that people with long hair will have additional difficulties next time they go to the National Assistance. And the big question could not have been better disguised by the fuzz itself. If the results show that 75% are addicted to heroin, then any member of the 'underground' can rest assured that the fuzz will estimate that out of

every four houses, they will come three.
What one is to do with questions like the following, we don't know. The space race is a waste of time and money. (For the Underground, regrettably and, if politics is ignored by the minority, it will slowly die.) But if the money is wasted on the questionnaire, Martin adds a list of books that he tries to sell by soap powder commercial advertising.
We then feel, that there are a number of things that Zeki should publicly explain. Since these results will be published whom are they meant to benefit? What is his relationship to the Underground Press Syndicate Europe? Where does his money come from? A careful estimation from people who should know indicate that some £540 have been spent on the printing, posting, and paper for this project. Certainly this amount of money could be more usefully used to satisfy the needs and aspirations of the alternative society.
It might be better right now if people simply ignored the questionnaire or had a little fun at Martin's expense and sent back the five oard envelope empty.
Love,
Alexander Hofer
48 Park Crescent
Brighton

Dear OZ
I have enjoyed reading OZ, and have done so since issue number ten, the first issue I bought. I had no idea what it was going to be like — it just looked interesting. I have read it since because I proved to be, for want of a better word, good. I regard myself as one of the comparatively few people who stayed with the peace movement after the over-publicized summer of 1967. Of course, the movement had to change its original idea slightly. We must be realists.
Recently, we have had to put up with more publicity than is good for us, I say this as one who is really an outsider, who is still conforming (for educational reasons). I have watched the fuzz raid IT etc. with a worried mind. The music of the underground is gaining numerous new followers like myself. Not all these, are exactly peace-loving, or anything like it. Some are sadists. We were a group of drop-outs but are being infiltrated by those who aren't.
Now, and I'll say, we may talk about increased readership but I am shocked at the way some of my autophiliac friends and others I have seen, are using OZ etc. They use them and treat them as dirt, rubbish and cheap thrills. As a person, I like to, and do, observe people and things. I am convinced that things are becoming rotten. I speak mainly of the Midlands. You seek to spread the message but as you do so it becomes subject to change. Some people can't be convinced, some won't and some are just stupid. I dearly hope that destruction doesn't come as a result of adventurous creation, as it often does.
Love and Good Luck,
Malcolm

101 Flood Street,
London, S.W.3.
August 19'69.

~~Dear Richard,~~
Dear Richard,

~~Thanks a million for staying away,~~

Thanks a million for staying away, lost in that enormous book you're writing, letting me edit this issue with a sense of total freedom. But of course the established (established? Watch it!) guide-lines were there and, brother, ~~did I smurth~~
~~did I sometimes need to cool off by clinging to them! Also, and particul~~
~~why, the~~
~~did I sometimes~~
did I sometimes need to cool off by ~~clinging to them! Also, and particul~~
~~did I somethi~~

did I sometimes need to cool off by clinging to them! Also, and particularly, to your aides and abetters – Jon, Felix, Ken and the beautiful Brigitte. They've given me incredible support. ~~Register that. These last three-lay-out~~ ~~Register that. These last three-lay-out~~ Register that. These last three layout nights we've logged-up a sum total of say three winks sleep between us. The straight press was never like this! From the "complimentary" copy I'll make sure the office sends you (c.o.d. ho) you'll find OZ has tripped out over homosexuality, considered the American-on-the-Moon thing in terms of a Faustit wank-off into space, then of a Faustit wank-off into space, then re-considered it as but the first hesit-ant step towards an inter-planetary consciousness. Throughout in fact consciousness. Throughout in fact

you'll find traces of rampant schizo-phrenia, yin and yang nt consciousness. Throughout in fact you'll find traces of rampant schizo-phrenia, yin and yang not quite to-gether. Isn't that what most of us are into, after all.

~~White~~
into, after all. Why pretend otherwise?
White

While collecting graphic metaphors for all this I took the liberty of moving in on both Martin and Philippe at the Pheasantry where of course they were deep into their own independent work. (Molopolis gets advance exposure here, too, though it looks as though we'll have to leave out the pic. of you as movie-starin movie-star-in-the-making. Sorry.)

He took a leap, a head leap, into someone else's shoes and turning up-side down glimpsed the moon-shot through "alien" eyes: not all a his through "alien" eyes: not all his wave-length these days, though it might once have been.

Same thing, in a way, happened in compiling the homo section. If Keith's photographs are journalistically effect-ive but perhaps not as convincing as usual it's most likely because we posed them and there was quite a bit of self-consciousness about or at that stage.
Felix, for example, is terrified on
Felix, for examp
Felix, for example, is terrified out of his wits that little old news-stalls ladies will not display any magazine woti tje cpver O t with the cover I take the with the cover I take responsibility with the cover I take responsibility for choosing. "We'll sell a tenth our with the o with the cover I take responsibility

for choosing. "We'll sell a tenth our usual number," he moans. Then gets straight back to working his arse off. Hope he's wrong…

Same girl-lover, mother, sister – once challenged most of us into our first fuck; someone else into our first mind-wrecker. V.I.P.s without pens. Now, short of a one-way ticket right through to the other side, way, way out there, what's next for us beautiful earth-bound cripples? Under the heading. (Dylan) "You can have your cake and eat it too" you'll find a suggestion or two.

That drug clinic doctor I inter-viewed proved extraordinarily persuas-ive. It took place well after midnight in his straight, cramped, wide-awake little flat, both of us flattened to the backs of our skulls by too much of this and/or too little of that. I felt, on leaving for Tina and baby blue, like I must be one of the most hung-up-over-sex individuals in town. I didn't feel alone either.

Conclusion of the moment: the hero scene is not only absurdly limit-ing but unnatural as well. Why, for Christ sake, way is history littered with the bodies of men who chose to communicate with sticks and stones, with knives and napalm, rather than with love.

Blake wrote somewhere something about not trusting generalised forms of love; trust only that love which manifests itself in 'minute part manifests itself in manifests itself in "minute particulars", he preached. De-conceptualised love. Hello John. Hi Yoko.

Thus I've dedicated this guest editor issue to the proposition that (every-thing else having been tried, space apart, new break-through alchemicals

apart) making love means not making war ONLY if that love can transcend, physically, erotically, orgasmically, sexual distinctions. So get your Button writers down to it: Make Men, Not War (for guys) and Make Women, Not War (for dollies).

As for the rest of the contents there are a few put-downs of IT that I hope aren't misinterpreted because that's one underground publication, that, early on anyway, meant more to me than any of the others. IT.

This is ridu
This is ridiculous. Everything else is type-set but Spike. Ad
This is ridiculous. Everything else is type-set but Spk

This is ridiculous. Everything else is type-set but Spike. And here I am writing exclusively to you while all the awakening world awaits non-exclu-sive OZ. If I don't get the usual to-gether in time I guess this will have to take its place. I wonder if the "Daily Mail" will every employ me again Mail" will ever employ me again?

All love to Louise and yourself,
Sebastian
(Perhaps I meant to get out of it this way all along. Games!)

8

MAN
MAKETH
MAN

SUCK FOR PEACE

Prostitutes are the most myth-ridden people imaginable, and not particularly bright. It may be because their sexual lives are reality, while the opposite is true of most Americans. I mean, they are forced to pawn their dreams daily and get enough to eat. They always remind me of "disposables," a type of merchandise that was quite new when I was young, but which now has swept the country: disposable plates, dresses, shirts. The Kleenex people seem to have begun it, and their rational for the product they sold bearing the famous name works for "disposable" men too.

When thumbing through the yellow pages under "P", ask yourself these questions:

Is he soft? Strong? Does he pop up?

See? For softness, think of maileability and submissiveness: his ability to conform to your wishes. Strength? Let's call that sexual endurance or virility. This guy, as a pro, should possess a physical strength that best expresses itself in the sexual act. Now, "pops up." He's got to have a prick that stiffens at the sight, sound, or mention of money. After all, from his point of view and yours, it isn't necessary that he respond to you on a level of personal attraction. That might even be unpleasant. Right? But he has got to become aroused, for your convenience, at the prospect of earning some of your money. Therefore, have no truck with limber dicks and excuses. He's got to be there in the full masculine condition as often as you need him so. And let's not forget size while we're at it. A good sportsman will always throw back the minnow, believing it unworthy of his equipment and expecting it to grow by next season.

Simple test. When auditioning your glandular technician, see how many silver dollars he can support on his stiff cock.

Ah, disposable people! Doesn't that

play music in your ear? It gives one a feeling of infinite power and of cleanliness. One appreciates, uses, and discards toilet tissue. The cost is immaterial No matter how much of the stuff we use or how dependent upon it we become, we are never obliged to cherish it after use. The thought is or should be repellent. But sexual pleasure is the legitimate end of any intercourse, and any means to that end is acceptable. Prostitutes, therefore, conveniently provide that service which may neutralize the temptation or necessity of complicating legitimate friendships, or even loves, with the pyrotechnics of unbridled license.

Male prostitutes are currently called 'hustlers'. In Oscar Wilde's time, they were

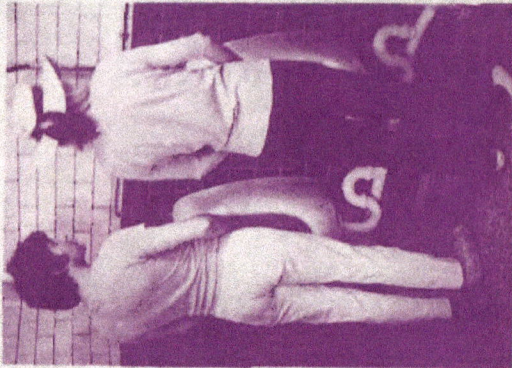

called 'renters,' because one paid them periodically. Paid them either for sex, or afterward, because of blackmail.

If you live in a small city or town, you may find them with difficulty. They thrive in the larger cities. Nevertheless, If you hang around the bus stations, swimming pools, train stations and airports, you're sure to find them, along with various social diseases and embarrassment. Use with caution. Avoid the taste for trash, if possible. Of course, they'll probably be parttime or advantage hustlers. They won't often ask you for x number of dollars, but will be inclined to grant their favors in exchange for dinners, drinks, trips and nights out.

Your best candidate, in my opinion, is the American College Boy as opposed to the professional prostitute: we'll get him a little later. And American college life being what it is, he will be anywhere from eighteen to twenty-eight. Strong, healthy, often good-looking, he is the flower of the philosophy of extended adolescence. He will bud but not bloom for a decade or two, then bloat and go to seed.

Get yourself a house or apartment. Call in a faggot decorator. Check him out and have him do something marvelous. Stock your bar. Serve perfect cocktails and get a superb car. Learn to cook or hire one. When you entertain, get the most incredible, the most amusing and the most intelligent people to your house. They may be vicious. These Medusas thrive where the currents are strongest, on a rapidly changing atmosphere, and are consequently perfect at parties where prolonged conversation is to be avoided in favor of the quip, pun, lash and flourish of repartee.

Now, the stage being set, go down to that restaurant, bar, or parking lot, to that corner of eternally patrolling cars, and hook yourself an attractive college boy. Strike up

everywhere, though curiously enough they may be neither illiterate, unschooled or idle. Indeed, to make a living in this business these men must work unceasingly and at very low rates for long hours. In fact, because the scale of pay is low, say five bucks, or about as much as you'd pay for a slum female, the market being at all times glutted, they must work every waking hour, and are always, should you ask, waiting for someone . . . a call . . . a contact . . . a John.

The difference between a trick and a John, for instance, is largely a matter of time. Generally a trick, as in cards, is turned quickly; one may have several in one night. A John, however, may be the main who keeps one or with whom one has a standing arrangement.

Prostitutes of both sexes and all economic categories are what I call "Telephone People." I've never known one of them that didn't hang around the house calling, waiting to be called, and answering calls, not necessarily from customers, but blend as business. If I didn't know better, and I'm not sure I do, I might believe that it's all a conspiracy engineered by the Bell Telephone Company. For surely if whores were all rounded up and put in nice clean comfortable houses designed for the purpose, there wouldn't be such a need for negotiation by wire, neither would the sidewalks be so littered with idle flesh.

. . . Resourcefulness plays a cheery part in masturbation too. Heaven knows, if you simply have but one position for it, one approach to it, you'll bore yourself just as you'd bore a lover with only one position to have sex in. Since masturbation is something you do by yourself that stimulates voluptuous reveries, you naturally use devices and implements to help things along. Hasn't everybody at one time or another turned on the vacuum cleaner for a good clean blowjob? I certainly have.

While I was in school, I met a very resourceful jack-off. Resourceful in that at this point Bimbo was perhaps too shy to have as many actual contacts as he wanted, and consequently made up for it by himself. One evening as we were exciting ourselves with talk, Bimbo told me he fucked Baggies. This was years ago and I hadn't even seen Baggies. They'd only just appeared in the supermarkets.

"Well, tell me," I said, "how you do it and where I can get them and what the hell are they?"

"It's very, very simple," he cooed, puffing on one of his colored, scented cigarettes. "Baggies are sort of filmy plastic bag-things you buy to put sandwiches in. Amazing. Keeps 'em fresh too!" Another sip of the cocktail. "The idea came to me while I was making my lunch one morning. They're very cheap. Anyway, you take a Baggie and a very large sponge, either an artificial one or a natural sponge, and you cut a narrow slot or slit in the sponge about, oh . . . as long as your dick is. Then, you take the Baggie and insert it in the sponge. Then moisten and soften the sponge with water, not hot water – warm water – and put the sponge into a larger plastic bag." His eyes had begun to sparkle, and a smile played about what he liked to think of his "cruel" lips. "Now, take a tube of KY and squirt a lot of it into the Baggie inside the sponge and knead it a little. Now what I do is put the sponge between the inner-spring and the mattress of the bed. That's just the right height when you're on your knees, but slip in your pi-pi, and fuck away! The softness of the bed and the warmth and sponginess of the Baggie dear make it feel just like one of those weak little people I like fucking in the ass so much. In fact, you can even tighten it by leaning forward and putting all your weight on the mattress."

I must admit it piqued my imagination. I had an erection by this time the sure test for any idea. We were just finishing our drinks. We rose.

"Oh, and one more thing."

"What?" I asked a little blearily.

"They're disposable. Neat, eh? So cheap you just throw them away."

"Oh," I mumbled. "Yes, yes."

"And none of that stupid clap business."

The extracts reprinted above are taken from a brilliant book of rare humour and raw vitality entitled *The Homosexual Handbook*, by Angelo d'Arcangelo, published by Ophelia Press Inc. If you wish to obtain copies of the book, or any others in the Ophelia or Olympia Press catalogues, write to 67-69 Irving Place, New York, NY 10003, USA. Price $2.95

Angelo d'Arcangelo.

SILENCE

John Cage

POVERTY OF FUCKING, argues a young West London drug addiction clinic doctor, is a greater hang-up for most of the world than poverty of eating. In short, bodies are starving. And good men for sheer lack of complete loving. Aroused by unknowing dreads they make contact with sticks and stones when it could be, should be, must be with cocks and balls. The author of this piece has, in more ways than one, been turned-on by his "patients": his convential medical training — homosexuality, like drug-taking is a sickness, horror, horror, etc. etc. has been thoroughly arse-upped. From his words with OZ you get the impression that he's headed for that space opened by Reich & Laing and maybe further. Here he exposes the Vice Anglais not as inadequacy, deviation or whatever, but as a hope for the future, the most obvious, most natural, most ready-to-hand, most necessary, most inevitable breakthrough for butch and brutal mankind. Read on, girls, read on:

TAKE IT LIKE A MAN

Sex since general

Freud has become confused with the life-force. Talking about any other animal, sex is just concerned with reproduction something

which cannot be achieved by two men. The sex organs are generally referred to as sort of genital urinals. I think in fact they've got three purposes rather than two: there is the ordinary urinal function, then your genital function which is reproductive, sexual for having babies. But then you've got your orgasms and you can have orgasms with anyone. So orgasms can't be related to sex if you look at it in natural terms, if you look at it in the terms of what nature intended. Orgasms can serve another function.

The thing is that man is primarily an animal. And he's an animal that loves the elaboration of his environment that he's made by using his cervical hemispheres which makes him think that he's not an animal any longer. But I figure that there must be some level at which all men are the same.

Everyone now is coming to look at things in terms of duality. You know, you can talk about what's natural for Man but you've got to specify whether you mean natural for Mankind as a whole on a biological level or natural for our society.

That is Man as he is in a society which has been made by thinking, as a result of his cervical hemisphere. And the two are not the same. And because the two are not the same, each individual is confused and I think this is very fundamental not only to homosexuality, but to all illness. The thing about societies is that they're defensive and you can illustrate the gap between what's natural for Mankind and what's natural for society when you consider killing. A man has to be *trained* to kill and it requires rigid by rigid discipline and all the rest of it, therefore it is not natural for Man to kill another man. In order to make a man defensive, you've got to tinker around with his motivating forces and instinct. Its as if

Man has reached a compromise between being defensive and being loving, so that he's never allowed to love to the extent that he's capable of and yet he's able to love sufficiently in order to keep society together.

I use the word homo-erotic rather than homosexual because it has more love connotations. This is so important — words have so many emotional connotations. I mean the word homosexual arouses so much anger and resentment. I believe the love force between men is equivalent to the love force between a mother and her child, and I think it would be in Nature's interest to have such a love force. And if this love force was enabled to express itself the whole balance of society would swing right round. You would in fact accomplish a revolution, because the Revolution that people keep talking about doesn't, to me anyway, mean tearing things down. I mean I don't have visions of 1917, the French Revolution and so on — blood and all that nonsense. You have a switch inside and people's outlook changes from being defensive to being loving. This is usually what the hippy what's-it is all about. Then you have accomplished the revolution. And this change of heart is fundamental to the success of whatever change in cultural patterns takes place in the next few years. If you were in a society where loving awareness instead of defensive awareness, was the 'law', then homosexuality would never be noticed. Unfortunately, however, there's no model to look to. When you consider why did Man become defensive, why became Man's enemy in the first place, I think you've got to say, well, there's certain organic causes for insanity. I think it's insanity for Man to do an anti-instinctive act, i.e. to kill another man. It's not Nature's filing their legs in the air in order to get a man, the way they have to now. This is the big complaint of women. They are so despondent, because women are missing out badly.

When you start encouraging people to be themselves, that is natural for mankind as a whole, you find that homosexuality becomes something natural. You have, in fact, got a cure for "homosexuality". Whereas most young people have very open minds, when it comes to homo-eroticism their homo-erotic 'drive' or 'instinct' has already been suppressed by the time they start verbalizing and talking about freedom and so on, so that the whole range of erotic freedom tends to be neglected. I've noticed there is in fact a considerable amount of self-consciousness about this even among "underground" people. Almost to a man the possibility that they might be queer has crossed their minds but they've just brushed it aside. Men just can't admit that they love other men. And quite obviously if Man is not allowed to love his fellow men it's easier for him to kill them.

man*") And this involves all sorts of things like being able to fight and not loving other men, not going to bed with other men.

I think you could probably say ... men were (innocent but they were about as ... but being ignorant they didn't know about dietary deficiencies etc. For example the Vitamin B complex. One of the symptoms of this ... homocidal mania, so quite obviously, right from the earliest times, one man ... one another for no particular ... and from then on Man has had to defend himself from ... you get culture which are very loving, like the ancient Greeks, but they always seem to be ... from outside. When a ... sees preying in the jungle ... another lion, whereas when a man goes out to work the chances are that he is preying on another man. So that somewhere along the line man in our society is not being loved ... for Mankind as a whole. He's encouraged to ... give up defensive ... Children are taught to fight ... bullied at school for example. So that men are taught not to be cowards. Its 'unmanly' to be a coward. So again the brainwashing goes on, 'you must be a

a woman. But every time a handshake and ends in an orgasm. ... any orgasm. There are degrees of friendship, as with a woman with a woman. In a natural state if you have an orgasm with a woman there are three people present who are to be considered ... because of the fertility thing, so here again it is safer to have orgasms with men to take some of the pressures off the women.

True homo-eroticism is going to become extremely fashionable, which will be the best thing that can happen for women, because for the first time, probably ever, men will learn properly how to make love. Most men of any age seem to use women as sort of complicated masturbating machines and the first thought that enters their head when they see a woman is fucking her, with very little consideration for the woman, for 'turning her on' or really making friends with her and developing a deep emotional thing. But I think that men will learn how to seduce women properly, so that women don't just have to

1.
ELEVEN YEARS OLDER
THAN BIRTH
AND WITH THAT SEXLESS INNOCENCE
I BEGUILE YOU FRANCIS —

MOVE YOUR ATHLETIC HANDS
AND WITH MY SPARKLING EYES
INFLATE YOUR MAN-SIZE EGO
MAYBE NOW THERE IS A WOMAN
WHO PUTS YOUR HEAD ON OLYMPUS
AND YOU FUCK
LIKE THE GOD YOU BELIEVE YOU ARE
OR MAYBE YOU STILL RAPE SMALL BOYS
AFTER TRAINING
IN THE PAVILION SHOWERS

2.
THEN YOU PAUL
WITH YOUR THIN WHITE FACE
YOUR LEARNING AND YOUR
INTELLECTUAL
CALLING TO THE CHURCH
LONG HOURS BY CANDLELIGHT
TALKING THEOLOGY OSCAR WILDE
WOMEN OSCAR WILDE
MOVING ME IN MY NAIVE ADOLESCENT DREAM
TO NESTLE AT YOUR FEET RESPONDING
TO MY ADORATION

WHY DID YOU EARTH YOURSELF
BY TOUCHING ME WITH YOUR CLAMMY
HANDS IN THE EMBARRASSED DARK OF SLEEP

3.
THESE ARE TWO
TWO IN MILLIONS
ALL NEEDING ORGASMS
ALL NEEDING ORGASMS
ALL FRUSTRATED
ALL CONDEMNED
ANOTHER SEX THAT WEEPS
FOR SIMPLE ACCEPTANCE

4.
GREEN URINALS ROWS OF MALE
URINATORS HOLDING THEMSELVES
TIGHT
LEANING OVER TO CATCH A GLIMPSE
HANDS IN POCKETS MASTURBATING OVER
RUDOLPH HOPING FOR THE PRETTY BOY
BY THE MIRROR
WHO HOPES FOR THE PEACE OF A ROOM
SOMEWHERE AND A GIRL
TO STROKE HIS BROW

YET NOW

AS I LIVE AND LEARN
I SEE THAT IT IS NOT A DISEASE
OF THE MIND THAT THE NEWS OF THE WORLD
OR PENGUIN FREUD SUGGEST

5.
NOT BRUTAL SISTER
OR CRUEL MOTHER OR DOMINANT
FATHER OR PERSUASIVE COUSIN
BUT SOCIETY
THAT CRUSHES GOOD NATURAL LOVE
BETWEEN MEN THAT CREATES PERVERSITY
AND SORDITY THAT PREVENTS NARCISSUS
AND GOLDMUND AND GIOVANNI AND
WILDE FROM BEING AS BEAUTIFUL AS
ROMEO AND JULIET DON JUAN AND VALENTINO

michael j w storey, the last supper

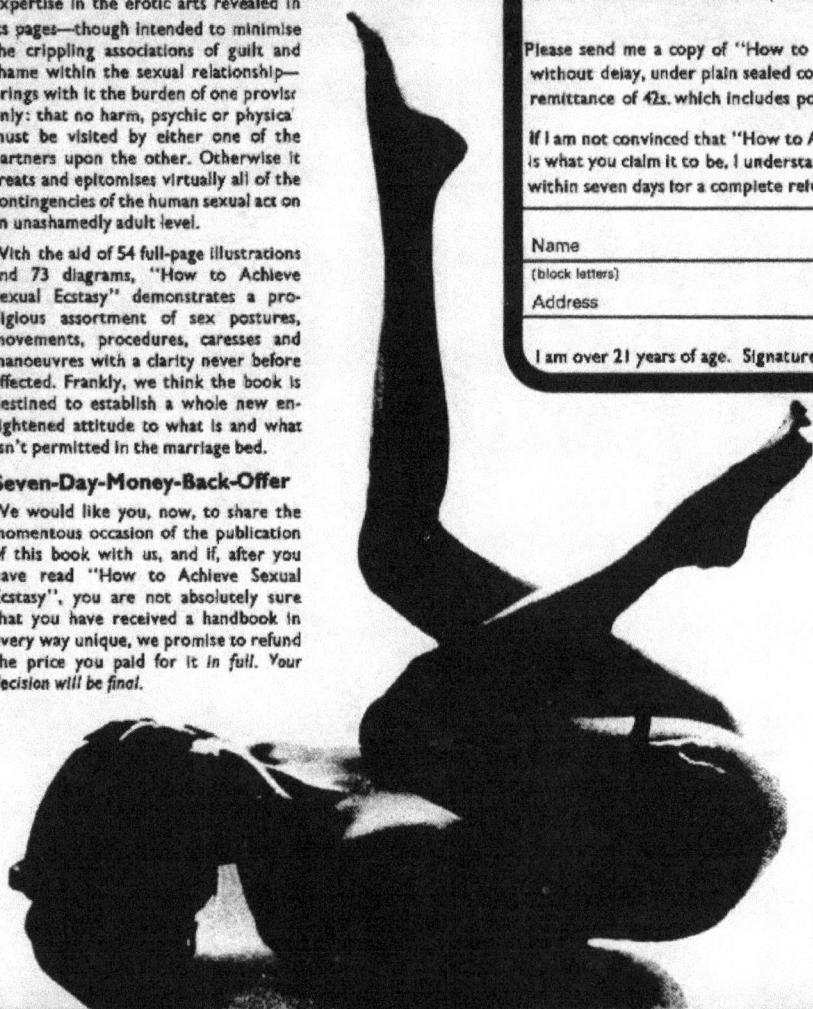

Did you feel the Moon move Little Rabbit?

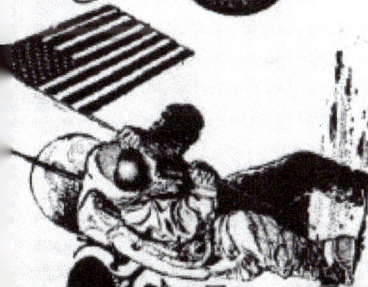

By Bob Hughes

The god Apollo, mythology teaches us, pursued the goddess Luna constantly but never caught up with her. It was not weakness on his part; one may assume that Apollo never wanted to copulate with that barren, meteor-pocked virgin; but the pursuit had a ritual function, and it ensured, among other things, that the sun rose each morning. What Apollo did not want to do, Apollo 11 has achieved.

"I think," said the Emperor Caligula, on his deathbed, "that I am becoming a god"; and in becoming a minegod, what gifts did homo sapiens, as represented by those two cybernetic beasts swaddled in tinfoil and high-absorbency diapers, leave for Luna? It is a depressing list. Billions upon billions of dollars were expended so that our Faustian technocrats might leave behind them the culminating traces of several million years of evolution:

several plastic bags of urine,
two pairs of discarded boots,
a plaque inscribed with a cliché,
a few pounds of waste metal,
and an American flag.

There is little enough reason to suppose that it actually happened. As filtered through the TV screen, science fact was frustrating after the science fiction to which, from childhood, we were all used.

Once more, life set out to imitate art: this time it almost succeeded.

Armstrong and Aldrin, loping and galumphing like Michelin men from one rock to the next, while David Frost intoned his banalities and Courrèges's models waddled to and fro in moonsuits and Revlon churned out its ads for frosty moonstruct lipstick ... one became aware that nothing had happened on the screen which could not have been done in a television studio for £30,000. The special effects were so far below the Kubrick level that they seemed unreal. Such are the perversions that media impose on actuality; but the moonshot was conceived in terms of media, as the greatest and most expensive public relations exercise in the history of man. The intention was to demonstrate, to a fifth of the human race, via TV, that America cannot lie and cannot fail. It was partly because of this that a curious failure arose in the project itself: earlier PR defeated its own ends. The moonshot was not a dramatic event because it only involved human protagonists at the most superficial level. It was advertised as drama; but a football match is not drama. One was aware from the beginning that either the astronauts would get there or they would not; and that it hardly mattered. For the purposes of public relations, whether they did or not, since in the former event it would be a Triumph of Science and Will and in the latter day, we had all been so indoctrinated in the technological omnipotence of NASA that success was expected automatically, and our only catharsis could have arisen from failure.

Naturally, nobody hoped for failure, since that would have meant the deaths of Armstrong, Aldrin and Collins and we are all - are we not? - against death, especially the death of men whom we vicariously "know", though prolonged exposure in TV and the press, the number of lives that might have been saved if the money spent in establishing (I speak only of overt scientific purposes, which, in the case of Moonshot, were secondary) that some lunar rocks contain 6% titanium, is of course, beside the point: it does not accord with the mythological structure established by the First Church of Brain Scientist.

Very few people who followed the moonshot could have escaped the feeling that it all was pre-ordained; that the astronauts were running down a groove in space like slot-cars; that they would land and return, and that they were in no way responsible for their fate. No doubt it was to cut this heresy that Armstrong took over manual control of the module just before landing - otherwise his audience would have assumed that the only role of man in space was a symbolic one; just

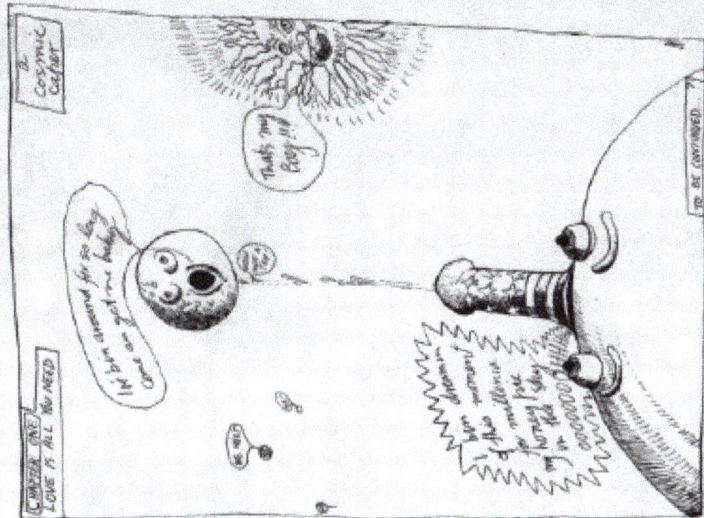

Lunar Eclipse, August 27, 1909
Washington, D. C.

a machine for planning, American flags. "Even despite our computers, Armstrong thus proclaimed. 'We are existential beings, even in Space.' And yet, now that it is over, I can only think of one picture which Armstrong could have made which would have qualified as unquestionably heroic. Suppose he had planted the Flag, and then poured petrol over it and burnt it? Impossible, alas; there being no oxygen on the moon. But if Luna does not justify a lunatic gesture, what will?

(which, in this context, meant the collective Will of the US Government) appropriate enough. Nothing was adequate to the grandeur of those banks of colour—several thousand parameters of billions had been left to chance. So science only reminds us that the dullness in Armstrong and Aldrin behind them was trained to fear to see symbolic value.

The Rubik became relics.

Whatcan they mean? 'One, unhappily has already disappeared — the First Footprint, which a [?] footnote after the small step for man, can be viewed... That's one small step for man,' the New Statesman observed, 'the word "was" and "mankind" had until then been thought synonymous, and henceforth "mankind" could only mean the new general class of astronauts. Perhaps NASA was warmed by such implications; in any case, NASA & Armstrong have agreed to rewrite the sentence, which will go down in the history books — with luck and PR pressure — as "That's one small step for a man". This change, Time Magazine was swift to point out, reflected the humility of the first mortal to reach the moon. Curiously enough, this was virtually the first time the word 'mortal' had been applied to Armstrong in an English-language magazine; the previous assumption having been that Armstrong was nothing of the kind. What we have been witnessing is a reinvigoration of the Christ myth: the redeemer from space who, as soon as he utters a word, sees it dissected for

religious significance by squads of acolytes. There is some evidence that even the President of the United States believed that otherwise, why would his team proclaimed that the descent of the Holy Boot was the most important event in universal history since the creation of the world?

Indeed, the whole atmosphere of Moonshot was saturated with religious panoply: consider the ritual significance of the flight. Encamped at the end of the flight, considering fear disinfection. On the third day, he rose again ... But the parallel here is not so much with Christianity as with the cult of the pharaohs of ancient Egypt. As seen in the complete teaching the sacred body of the astro [?] the observation-room, with its [?] for mythological attention is with its [?] mummified likeness a few hundred miles above.

The two moon men ... and they likewise, however, fear Plague and ... said the Holy Poo ... for ... by some Virgin ... to show in the ... prime form of ... under ... sacred territory by Plague and ...

CAIN IN PEACE FOR ALL MANKIND. This was agreed by Armstrong, Collins and Aldrin, at one Blessed Millennium, Nixon, who confined it the rub ... difficult though it is to appreciate, so circumstance either when they agreed that there is nobody and nothing to come to (which seemed to be so with Luna), or else when they have buried the last Indian. However, nobody in NASA could be certain that the moon might not have some inhabitant, in case the astronauts brought some back: elaborate Auschwitzers of sterilizers and UV radiation were prepared for them on earth. We come in peace for all mankind, but emphatically not for any life-form which we find below 'bed' level, in this way, the Plague summed up the most exquisite of all contradictions in colonial self-justification; and the fact that none of us can much about microbes, not even moon microbes, should not blind us to the profound truth of the Plague's cliche.

But the flag — there was the rub of the whole performance, the failure of imagination represented by sending 19th-century sensibilities to the Moon. It was

beyond its first proportions: the confident phantasy that man, by his technological achievement, will and must dominate the future. Act III, opening with Moonshot, will also show another, even the great silver panic which the great silent astronauts (number 11 to be projected in mid-flight) will be directed into the sun, and there be vapourised, thus initiating on the rewind and compressed can; so of Werner von Braun and all his fellow-Americans the symbolic illustration which American and Russian hubris has so long sought.

In the meantime, we need monuments of an absurdity overt enough to suit the reports. How much better it would have been if Apollo 11 instead of leaving its collage of symbols behind on Luna, had settled for one great image! Clare Oldenberg should have been commissioned to design a gigantic Feathersmade plastic tube, it could had for instance, a Reclining Fig ... or Luna 7 ... a sundries has of Dick ... pneumatic frame. To see ... 70,000 faces milked youth so it at last some that, it would be worth going to the Moon.

Mother Earth

MILES

becoming possible. The corresponding experience in thought can only come after the continental experience has been felt by enough people, either in person or through the media.

And we all know the next step after that. Planetary thought can only come when Man can see the planets and when he is aware of the next step, which is interplanetary thought. The only place to see the planet is from outer space.

Man's supreme and latest concern is ... just started

der himmel nimmt zweimal den hut ab (I)
The sky takes the hat off twice

20

MAX
ERNST

A WARNING?

THE JULIAN PRESS
issue a warning:

the photographic illustrations from "Variations on a Sexual Theme" of the variations of position possible in sexual intercourse contained in this book are posed by unclothed human models, together. This book called simply "Variations on a Sexual Theme" is the most intimate and enlightened mannual ever to be published in this country. It contains 40 beautifully posed photographs by a top photographer, showing the basic coital positions, the knowledge of which are essential to ensure maximum sexual satisfaction. It is a book that could not have been published even a year ago; it is no hype.

Each photograph is accompanied by a frank commentary suggesting the movements and carresses likely to heighten each others enjoyment. Because of the beauty of the photographs and the couple portrayed; the exquisite binding, and quality of print, it is undoubtedley going to be a run away best seller. At the moment only a limited edition has been published and is only available by mail order, direct from Julian Press. On receipt of the coupon below and 60s. you will be sent, under a plain seal cover, one copy, which carries with it a seven day money back guarantee if you do not find it as good as we say it is.

THE MEDIA PIRATES

RETURN OF THE

caroline news SWN

In the usual field Ronan O'Rhaily who runs Radio Caroline together is going into television. He plans to operate from a Super Constellation aircraft which will be standing by in case of break-down) above the ground. He is to transmit programmes which will commence over the North Sea to the U.K. area. It will run from 6 p.m. to 2 a.m. the first few hours will be all music, in a variety of things. 'The sort of things,' said O'Rhaily told OZ just now, 'That you don't to get the whole thing off the ground... anyone, could like anyone, could like the place where he wanted, uncensored...

will be taken up by features and films. It will be a 625 line picture in colour, and you can adjust any 625 line set to receive it.

The advertising will be done in the same way as Radio Caroline and O'Rhaily seems pretty confident that this is virtually a licence to print money and also he creative. He speaks in terms of a gradual shifting balance between making the radio for the promotion of 'gentle anarchy'... company a profitable concern and using the make people, especially the young, aware of the need to gradually help those in need, like the aged. He has his Super Cons. lined up and hopes to be on the air by the coming Spring.

ALAN REID

die säf
the lu

eigen
ds rise

ROYAL AIR FORCE

INNS/438
RAF FORM 4216

OFFICIAL SECRETS ACTS

DECLARATION

TO BE SIGNED:
(i)   In duplicate, by officers, on first appointment.
(ii)   By officers, airmen and airwomen, during service, as and when required, including such occasions when personnel are posted to and from Ministry of Defence (Air)
(iii) In duplicate, by officers, airmen and airwomen on leaving Her Majesty's Air Force.

1. My attention has been drawn to the provisions of the Official Secrets Acts, 1911 and 1920, which are set out on the back of this document, and I am fully aware of the serious consequences which may follow any breach of those provisions.

2. I understand that:
   a. The sections of the Official Secrets Acts set out on the back of this document cover also articles published in the Press and in book form.
   b. I must not divulge any information gained by me as a result of my service in Her Majesty's Air Forces to any unauthorised person, either civilian or member of HM Forces, orally or in writing, without the previous authority of the Ministry of Defence (Air), as laid down in QR 991.
   c. I must surrender any documents etc referred to in Section 2(b) of the Acts on transfer from one post to another, save such as have been issued to me for my personal retention.
   d. These provisions apply not only during the period of my service with Her Majesty's Air Forces, but also after that service has ceased.
   e. All the information which I acquire or to which I have access owing to my official position is information which is covered by Section 2 of the Official Secrets Act, 1911, as amended by the Official Secrets Act, 1920, and that it would be a contravention of those Acts for me after I have left Her Majesty's Air Forces:

       (1) To publish without lawful authority any such information in any form, whether orally or in any document, book, newspaper or magazine article, play, film, broadcast or otherwise in the United Kingdom or abroad.

       (2) To communicate without Lawful authority any such information to any other person whether or not such person is or has been employed in the service of the State.

   In the event of my wishing to publish such information in any form after I have left Her Majesty's Air Forces, whether orally or in any document, book, newspaper or magazine article, play, film, broadcast or otherwise, I should, in my own interest, as well as that of the Crown, write to the Under-Secretary of State, Ministry of Defence (Air), for permission, forwarding a copy of the material it is desired to publish.

3. I hereby declare, on leaving Her Majesty's Air Forces that I have surrendered any sketch, plan, model, article, note or document (whether or not classified) made or acquired by me in the course of my official duties, save such as I have due written authority from the Ministry of Defence (Air) to retain.

4. This declaration is made this......5th.......day of....NOVEMBER.............1968.* and I have received a copy for my retention.

Unit Stamp

TRANSIT SQUADRON
RELEASE/DISCHARGE
5 NOV 1968
R.A.F. INNSWORTH

Signed: ....

Rank: ....

RAF No: ...B42780022..............

ROBERT PETER KELLEY
(Full name in block letters)

Witnessed: ....

Rank: ....

*Delete as necessary

26

Nine months after being given (buying) my freedom from the RAF I find it increasingly difficult to recapture and put into words the hatred and contempt that I then felt against the air force. These days I can feel only sadness and pity for them: "For they know not what they do". Shit. They know very well for once you've signed that innocent-looking piece of paper (for five, nine or, wait for it — even twelve years) you're theirs. You really are. At first one belongs to them in body only (in that they may order you where they will, to do what they will, while providing 'fresh meat' for the sadists in charge of the 'basic-training' camp). But that is nothing. It's when you realize that it's your mind they're after, when their foul oh-so-subtle process of British indoctrination runs again and again. How did I get into this? You ask yourself again and again.

Let's go back four and a half years. I'm seventeen and a half and I've just left grammar school, my boredom relieved only by the occasional knee-tremble in some back-alley in the town of my birth. Depressed area: managing to keep a couple of steps ahead of the accountancy-type career plans my parents have so carefully laid out for me. Anyway, Christmas '64 passed in a drunken haze and I'm still around. Then my mother, kind soul, unearths some air force propaganda/literature that I'd had orgasms over at the age of 14 or was it 12? The sight of the 'men in blue' turns me off a little but to keep the peace at home I decide to give the local CIC (Careers Information Centre) a visit.

'Interested in languages son?' (I'll murder my old French master). Various aptitude tests (even Mike Same got in the same trade), the promise of a £250 bounty at the end of a year's crash-course in Russian, visions of James Bond-like activities, (all in civilian clothes they said) and three and a half weeks later there I am, a student in blue, receiving my six-week basic-training. Very h-a-s-e sick.

I survive. Bull-shit had abroad do and went on to a new camp where 13 aircraft flew.

To give those who may never have visited the course, who may never materialized of course, nor this misinterpretation of the facts. Those facts being of course that all such beauties had ceased (two years beforehand and the civilian suit but was reserved only for those with brown noses, or maybe an Air Vice Marshall type uncle?

Accelerated promotion to sergeant at the end of the course? That too had ended two years before, or so they said. In actual fact the promotion that I did achieve was that of Airman to Junior Technician, missing two intermediates, those of LAC & SAC. Part of the 'social elite'.

Berlin hit me like a new world where Vodka cost 10/- a bottle & 1/5d got you 20 cigarettes but after a few months the alcohol wasn't enough to dispel the increasing disenchantment. Not just the degradation of waking up still pissed next morning but also the incredible amount of bullshit that was seemingly of more importance to the RAF than the job for which I had been trained. A friend turned me on to Dylan and I decided to take leave and hitch-hike to Morocco, where on February 8th, 1967 I turned-on in Tangiers for the first time. Four days later in Marrakech I was invited to live with a Moroccan family and from that moment on it was a one-way trip. I left three weeks later still stoned and with the firm intention of conducting an intensive campaign to turn-on as many of my RAF colleagues as possible and somehow obtain my discharge from what had by then become the 'air force'.

Unfortunately because of short-hair etc... it took a while to make contact with the dope-scene back in Germany, so it was back to drunken oblivion and ever-increasing frustration in my efforts to obtain a premature discharge. It was about this period that I began to explore every possible means of being discharged, thrown out, anything would have sufficed. The official reply to my repeated requests for a discharge were that I must first serve three years from my 18th birthday and then apply to purchase my release, the cost being £150. This served only to plunge me into weeks of depression, alleviated only by the occasional smoke and the various pills prescribed for me by the station Medical Officer. His answers to my frequent visits and pleas for help in obtaining a release on the grounds of depression were that I should accept the fact that I was 'in' and 'had better watch my step or face the consequences'.

'67 dragged on and passed into '68, by which time I had passed through a Married phase and defection was more or less a permanent thought in my head. A glimmer of hope entered my life when I was given my first official warning to change my attitude, improve my standard of dress and also to produce a standard of work of which I was known to be capable. How did they expect me to get it together when I was spaced on Lebanese Red? Failure would result in a review of my future employment in the service. Beautiful, my first natural high! The Cream said it in 'What a Bringdown' — Soon after this I had leave and was stoned in Turkey a week after I'd left. The scene in Greece was too reminiscent of the RAF so back to the land of Hashish Economic Miracle where the best buzz of all was waiting to be fed into my head. I was no longer wanted, my application for 'purchase of discharge' had been accepted and I was on my way. Seven weeks later and £150 poorer (I'll work out at around 4/6d a day over two years) I was back in England being handed a little blue book, a discharge book. I soon lost it, I've even forgotten my ID card number. A feeling of pride.

Parting word. The day I cleared from the camp I had a final interview with the Wing Co. He asked me if I had enjoyed my stay on the camp.

I grinned at him. He offered me a cigarette. I grinned and lit my own. He then asked me what my ideal society would be. At the time my head was in Cuba, so I told him. We digressed and started rapping about socialism. 'A h maisuil come from a working class famlich', he said, and look at the position I've got to. I grinned again and didn't ask him why his nose was brown, or how many floors he'd scraped with razor blades or who had bullied his toes and forced his uniform for him. I stood up to leave. His final words were: "Lenin was a THUG". I grinned and I left.

IN YOUR CASE, IT IS OBVIOUSLY *TOO LATE* TO EMPLOY 'STANDARD' TECHNIQUES!

tune in
Radio Red

turn on
lebanese red

fall out
cost: £150

MEN IT CAN BE DONE!

hip pocrates

Copyright 1968 Eugene Schoenfeld MD

QUESTION: I think my girlfriend and I have been screwing too much. The reason I believe this is lately I've been almost continuously tired.

Could it be that too much sex is wearing me out? We only screw once a day, six or so times a week. As far as I know, I'm getting a balanced diet and plenty of sleep.

What do you think?

PS1. I'm 20 years old.

PS2. We've been living together 4 months.

PS3. I'm six feet tall and weight 130 lbs.

ANSWER: "Too much sex" for one person may be too little for another. But newly coupled couples sometimes feel they must have sex every day, even if they're not in the mood, just to prove to each other they're in love. Anyway, sex is not as lethal as we've been led to believe.

Perhaps you're not really eating a proper diet. Six feet tall and 130 lbs? Eat! Eat!

Chronic fatigue may stem from any one of several causes. Have a physician give you a thorough physical examination.

QUESTION: I am a serviceman in Vietnam and my wife thinks I am having sexual relations here. Not so, but after arriving I noticed some pimple-like protrusions in my public area. I went to sick bay where the corpsman laughed them off as venereal warts.

This worried me so I wrote to my wife who is a Registered Nurse. She gave me a rather long medical term and said they were caused by gonorrhea. Now she is going to sue for divorce, I have checked with a few other medical sources and they all say the warts are not caused by sexual contact.

I am rather puzzled by the whole thing and would like to find out who is right. It doesn't seem possible that the service and civilian doctors could be 780 degrees out of line in diagnosing this problem. Pray for peace.

ANSWER: Condyloma acuminata are warty growths thought to be caused by a virus. Their common name, "venereal warts," tends to perpetuate the false belief that they are caused by venereal disease such as gonorrhea.

Venereal warts are seen more frequently in women than men and may appear anywhere on the vulva or within the vagina. At first the warts are small elevated growths the size, perhaps, of a mole. Later they become quite large giving a mulberry-like appearance. Conditions which seem to favour growth of venereal warts in females are a profuse vaginal discharge, obesity, infrequent bathing and pregnancy.

Treatment for venereal warts is similar in males and females. A solution is applied directly to the warts which causes them to shrink and disappear. Often one or more reapplications are necessary. Some mild discomfort may be noted in the surrounding area but the procedure is much less painful than one might imagine.

QUESTION: William Baird, birth control expert, is quoted in the May, 1969 Ramparts as saying: "You'd be surprised how naive about sex some of those bright college kids are. Some of them believe

they can prevent pregnancy by withdrawal. Now, just what is wrong with "pulling out" as a means of contraception?

ANSWER: Coitus interruptus is a risky means of contraception — and a drag as well.

Small amounts of semen may be deposited in the vagina before the sensation of ejaculation occurs. Studies have shown this fluid contains thousands of spermatozoa.

QUESTION: I've been married for five years now. A little over seven years ago, my husband, he was 18 then, had a vasectomy (clip job, he calls it) in order to make him sterile.

He has been sorry that he did it but what was done was done. We decided we would adopt a couple of children next year or the year after.

But believe it or not, I am pregnant. Missed last March but I didn't worry. Finally my doctor insisted on a test at the end of May and that proved it.

My husband won't believe that he is the father. I have no reason to lie to you — I don't know why nor you me. Another man hasn't touched me in 6 years. My doctor told him it was possible for the vasectomy to help and asked to examine him but he thinks my MD would lie (I think maybe he suspects my doctor).

Now he has said that he does not blame me for wanting a child but insists on knowing who this "mythical" man is.

It would make him the happiest man on earth if he just knew it was his baby.

ANSWER: A vasectomy is a simple surgical procedure often performed in a physician's office. Two small cuttings are made in the scrotum in order to cut and tie off both vas deferens, the spaghetti-like tubes which transport sperm from the testicles.

Vasectomies ALMOST always cause permanent sterility. Since attempts to reunite the severed ends of the vas deferens are usually unsuccessful, few physicians would perform a vasectomy on an 18 year old.

Rarely, the severed ends reunite spontaneously and this apparently has happened in your husband's case. Any family physician or urologist could examine your husband's semen microscopically and assure him he could father a child.

QUESTION: I have a question that is very important for me to learn the answer. When a boy is eating me what should I do?

ANSWER: Do unto others as you would have others do unto you . . .

DEAR DR HIP POCRATES is a collection of letters and answers published by Grove Press. $5. Send your questions to OZ.

POVERTY COOKING

955. **Asceticism** — N. asceticism, puritanism, sabbatarianism; cynicism, austerity; total abstinence.

mortification, maceration, sackcloth and ashes, flagellation; penance &c. 952; fasting &c. 956; martyrdom.

ascetic; anchorite; martyr; hermit &c. 893; puritan, sabbatarian, cynic. Adj. ascetic, austere, puritanical; cynical; over-religious.

*

956. **Fasting** — N. fasting; famishment, starvation; banting.

fast; fast day; Lent; spare —, meagre- diet; lenten -diet; — entertainment; short -rations, — commons; Barmecide feast; hunger strike.

V. fast, starve, famish, perish with hunger; make two bites of a cherry. Adj. lenten; unfed; starved &c. v.; half-starved; fasting &c. v.; hungry &c. 865.

957. **Gluttony** — N. gluttony; greed; greediness &c. adj.; voracity. epicurism; good –, high- living; crapulence; guzzling; over-indulgence. good cheer, blow-out; feast &c. 298; gastronomy.

epicure, gourmand; glutton, hog, gastronome, gormandizer.

V. gormandize, gorge; overeat oneself; engorge, eat one's fill, cram, stuff, stodge, glut, satiate; guzzle; bolt, devour, gobble up; gulp &c. 298; raven, eat out of house and home.

have the stomach of an ostrich; play a good knife and fork &c. 865. pamper, indulge.

Germaine

Some of IT — ed. David Mairowitz, Kistler, 25/-
New Numbers, Christopher Logue, Jonathan Cape, 12/-
Watchwords, Roger McGough, Jonathan Cape, 10/-
Turning On, Rosa Guffasch, Weidenfeld & Nicholson, 45/-
Pop from the Beginning, Nik Cohn, Weidenfeld & Nicholson, 25/-

The most salient fact about Some of IT is what it costs. The cost of a book is normally not a salient feature except that David Z Mairowitz admits in his shifty backward (backward-looking foreword) that the book begins as a 'necessity for cash'. OK so it is a moneyspinner. As one isn't anxious to write totally irrelevantly I suppose I ought to assimilate about its propositions as a moneymaker. Well, for one, there's no way of making it. It is a mausoleum, built of chunks of prose from the first ten issues (there have been six story) which were assistant-edited by blue-sky soul, David Z. himself, who made a less than spectacular comeback recently to pirate No. 51. Those nearly new issues were stiff

with waydirt and big names and even more than usually dazzling examples of the international low-down that have been the sort best thing in IT to the day in day summarology of the community here and now. The chief value of IT is that it is ephemeral Mairowitz has obviously chosen the least up-to-date material for his mausoleum, and sent a hasty now to the direction of underground notions of co-operativeness and freedom from critical pre-suppositions and personality cult, by refraining from calling it the Best of IT although the only other principle reason he can have used would need to be mere copies. Why on earth anyone

Felix's letter from No. 49 Other Scenes inside the reason for Michael de Freitas's Abdul Malik's withdrawal of World, a organisation only slightly too high-minded than Mairowitz's, indeed for wanting to include it in the first place. Any movement of literature rising out of the blood first lies flowed beneath IT's indigo must necessarily be very little like the newspaper that flopped out to the street regularly as enormous cool to unwound and sometimes unintelligible character. Incoherence obliterated Mairowitz even if to the import and unusing works to reproduce the graphic a lost of will anyhow appeared in the original to see the layout partly because just forgetting becoming the trade paper of the underground pop promoters it might be better served by everybody bought a dozen copies of the next issue and sent them to clergymen, male nurses, politicians, schoolteachers, dustmen and skinheads everywhere.

New Numbers is from Logue and London. *Watch...* from McGough and Liverpool. Logue ... a mythmaker, a camera eye seizing on the characteristic images of his Kulturkampf ... cut of focus always slick and contained on paper a Nova/Queen poet. One wills however he's something else One graffiti on roughcast is worth this whole slimy vacant pink and black and white thing The value of McGough is that he deep into words a loosed ment memories tangled in familiarities of sound and touch and feeling less poent ... sure wit ... is wit ... words ... not real withawd. Logue ... of his and her, McGough, for me and you, something plaintive colloquial joy, cock in hand, a noticed confused head-board but only wonderfully Logue's cut struck poet is never curiously enough or struck enough. It's never really there. The textures are the mannerism ... idea ... before however showed up. McCough's poetry is a snarl of dream. f.b. confession the difference is the difftiest coaxing number and word. Take your pick. You know what mine is.

Raaa Ou ... it is really did her book. Up and down the ment ... turning on to everybody she was ... going is the book Three hundred and twenty-one mags of well-returned subjects and predictios clauses, colon, phrases, spitfies reported conversation paragraphs, parentheses not a flood of freedom, brilliance not a single verbal gesture more ... tive than a its cold heart ... th th accusation by the all over getting ... cries t'slop ... not a fust-... or blow ... s drag with this chi ... s ... et ....

and mostly because it is simply incompetent. is less effective (that is to say lovely) than it was when it was originally hurled together. Even Alex Gross's unremittingly brilliant journalism appears here as not so much still-born as new dead. The shape of the book suggests a quality of liveliness that it does not have, for it is wrapped in slippery silver plastic foil which slides out of the holder's nerveless paw like wet soap: if only it did contain a paragraph or two from Hamburger Mary or Middling Sue, a reminder of the most hallucinating weeks of events, the weirdest of the small ads, a collage of the confident plans and predictions that never materialised some follow through on the voices that disappeared. (Where are you Tom McGrath now that we really need you?) The real strength of IT is not small-time journalism by big-time people, but the simulation of good word-power from people who might otherwise not have written at all. All that remains of the attempts to give IT into the hands of its workers is the mendacious masthead, and a volume like this repudiates even those attempts. It might have been a more successful money-spinner to make up a cut-out theatre of IT's daily battle for survival with all its dishonourable truces and its casualties. If IT is to be rescued from

Blackhill and Harvest are getting it together
Blackhill and Harvest are getting it together
Blackhill and Harvest are getting it together
Blackhill and Harvest are getting it together
Blackhill and Harvest are getting it together
Blackhill and Harvest are getting it together
Blackhill and Harvest are getting it together
Blackhill and Harvest are getting it together
Blackhill and Harvest are getting it together
Blackhill and Harvest are getting it together
Blackhill and Harvest are getting it together
Blackhill and Harvest are getting it together
Blackhill and Harvest are getting it together
Blackhill and Harvest are getting it together
Blackhill and Harvest are getting it together
Blackhill and Harvest are getting it together
Blackhill and Harvest are getting it together
Blackhill and Harvest are getting it together
Blackhill and Harvest are getting it together
Blackhill and Harvest are getting it together
Blackhill and Harvest are getting it together
Blackhill and Harvest are getting it together
Blackhill and Harvest are getting it together

"A MEAL YOU CAN SHAKE HANDS WITH IN THE DARK" - SHVL 752
PETE BROWN & HIS BATTERED ORNAMENTS

"A WASA-WASA" - SHVL 757 - EDGAR BROUGHTON BAND

"ALCHEMY" - SHVL 756 - THIRD EAR BAND

BLACKHILL ENTERPRISES LTD.
E.M.I. RECORDS (THE GRAMAPHONE CO. LTD.)

EMI

AMERICAN record dealers say they
will refuse to stock the new Blind
Faith album which portrays a picture
of a nude eleven-year-old girl on its
sleeve.
I hope British record dealers will show
the same sense when the album is
issued here. It's in outrageous bad
taste and should be withdrawn.
Don Short, Daily Mirror

Mōzic

33

Campaign Against Psychiatric Atrocities, c/- 194 Clarence Gate Gardens, Glentworth Street, London NW1

Meanwhile Farren, once gutsy enough to launch the Social Deviants on their very own label and, what's more, get away with it commercially, wants to take the orgasm out of his cunt and put it into his head. England's first organs transplant he's not calling the operation MCA No, it's the Pink Fairies (see our black and white supplement) and one or two of the old Deviants. Tyrannosaurus Rex and, yes, the Pretty Things are going to be there with him. He wants to feel Lud again

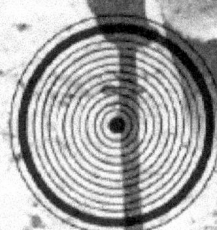

Ochs once ordered out of Dylan's chauffeur-driven Cadillac for suggesting the master would never be as big as Elvis no matter how hard Colonel Tom Grossman tried, had been tramping the streets of Edinburgh looking for a hotel To buy To own To be Master of an ever-changing community of one-night stand salesmen and their whores, Glasgow Rangers supporters, whisky freaks, Yankee tourists, American friends, other friends. Human hearts and assorted Gifted fantasies. He wants to feel loved again

PHIL OCHS (b. El Paso, Texas, 1940, d. Chicago, 1968) chose an East London bomb site to tell the girl he was trying to screw that he couldn't been destroyed MICK FARREN (b. Brighton, England, 1944, d. —) chose a Chelsea double-bed to tell the girl she was screwing that he'd like to shoot a policeman stone dead.

One American. One Englishman. One. They've never met. They do so for the first time! — in this issue of OZ. Head to Head Hearts Bleeding. Wounded by fact and fantasy. Interviewers Alan Reid and Chris Robbins (see Spike) caught the gush. Suicide is homicide is suicide is homicide is suicide. Liberation has always meant dying.

for rebirth are rehearsals for representation are rehearsals for resurrection are rehearsals for redress are rehearsals for containment are rehearsals for reside are rehearsals for revolution are rehearsals for remission are rehearsals for confirmation are rehearsals for redemption are rehearsals

The Rock & Roll business is ideologically in a very sorry state in Britain. You just walk into the Speakeasy and half the freaky, hip people in there are straights masquerading. They're just guitar technicians. And they are just controlling themselves in terms of rock and roll as one of the last non-controlled medium. So when I thought all this out I realised that the Speak divided itself into the ones who are getting uptight and the ones who are getting the others uptight. We seemed to be the latter group so we thought that a corporate identity might be a good thing.

'One of the first principles in everybody's mind is to put the orgasm back into Rock. I can remember the days when chicks used to rub themselves up and down the seat arms in cinemas and that was great. Rock & Roll is really like a conditioned energy release, it's like Voodoo or something, it's got a lot of things over the kids. There's just so little balls in it these days.'

Then Dylan freaked out and decided that all politics was a joke around '65. The change in Dylan had no effect on me at all, being the other political song writer I was asked that question at that time, I didn't think it was terrible because I'd always admired Dylan as a writer and the only question was Dylan a writer getting better or worse and it definitely was getting better — as if Tambourine Man, I was one of the first people to hear Tambourine Man, he came over to my house and sang it, I just couldn't believe it, you know, then he sang it at Newport.) I was glued to the stage.

A band can be used to block a street. It's very difficult to move it, especially if it's got a generator, because it's a peaceful audience which blocks the street. It's very easy for the cops to break up an angry crowd and hit them over the head with clubs, but if they are all happy and groovy it's very difficult to break them up. So it's a thing that can be swung into use when the situation arises. This is just simple time-wasting strategy.

'We want to just bomb out and do something. We have at least six drummers, seven guitarists, seven bass players, four or five singers and maybe two organists. So, say at three o'clock closing time you come out of the bar and you think, "Heh, it would be good to go and play." So you shoot down to the nearest open space and you play.'

The heating off into the bands, the musicians of that period, eventually, all grew up into groups, and then in came psychedelic — which I don't like — all the things that have happened. I consider it to be the least important and the most damaging. Another sudden euphoria and a huge let-down, we are now in the process of is the let-down of pop disintegration.

I think drugs made my music more essential. I might have done that without drugs. I mean I took some drugs and my music became more essential, I never overdid drugs and I never got onto speed at all, so I never really gave myself over to it. I am glad I didn't. I think drugs have ruined very many people in music and I am saying that as somebody who would advocate the legalization of Marijuana, but still I think that the effect of drugs got out of hand and killed people and music got out of hand and obviously sexual.

'The idea of violence has been happening off and on for God knows how many years since the war, but it's only lately that community violence has gotten to the level of us,' Jamie says. 'So it stands to reason that within the next two fucking years some schmuck in fucking Wall Street is going to start marketing violence. They've been doing it for years of course but so far they are in control of sweet fuck all on our level. We have just got to make goddam fucking sure that they don't get control which is where another faction of the Pink Fairies comes in. The Fairies have to open all the kids' heads. It won't be us that's in the forefront though – it will be the unification of all that the Pink Fairies have managed to do that will be in the forefront. You know — the million kids that have risen to hear Mick sing "Fuck it!" and stand up and piss in the street.'

'The Pink Fairies are organising a musical attack on authority, like the MC5 in Chicago, a strategic, organised and effective attack on the straights. The real purpose is basically to try and be outrageous. In terms of the fact that most of us have money, or access to money, we're a lot less vulnerable than the average kid on the street. We press the cops and in many ways throw out an outrageous smoke screen which covers up a lot of useful things that can be going on at the same time. It means the heat can be taken off the underground press for instance. If it looks like we're causing most of the trouble the underground press will look really peachy then.'

Mick Jagger is the best pop singer in many ways and the best rock singer, but Mick Jagger is still a form of copy of Elvis. Mick Jagger is the perfect sixties answer but, good as he gets, its not as simple as quality unless you were so good to wipe out everything. Elvis was conditioned by the Army — King Creole was a good movie and good music, and Jailhouse Rock, was a good movie with good music. He was really good then, but the Army conditioned and straightened him out and when he got out of the Army he was totally packaged and plasticised by Tom Parker and so for 10 years Elvis made sugar movies and was totally plastic but the point is that Elvis survived this and this is what's obvious now with US Mail and and In The Ghetto and Guitar Man and his TV special. Of course the pop scene is deteriorating which is not necessarily sad because all scene's deteriorate, you know, folk music came and was huge and degenerated; jazz music came and was huge and degenerated; and now pop music is doing the same. It's all processed, I am glad things were created out of it. But the last stage, the stage of the frantic sexuality, you know of Jimi Hendrix of the Cream, of all these people; personally I don't get excited or moved by the music — it doesn't strike me as human. You know all the great music often is very human. The great Elvis. You know, Heartbreak Hotel. Those songs as garish as they are — the thing is I think great music comes from great personalities.

'Take the Hell's Angels. They are in the situation where they have been taken out of the boozer, away from their brown ale, and given acid. And they're still trying to sort it out. They are in the same space that 80 per cent of the English kids buying records are in at the moment. Once that record buying public has been given the push they will reach that violent level, the violent stage the Angels are in now. And at that time they're going to need some sort of organised format like the Pink Fairies which will be able to voice some sort of direction.'

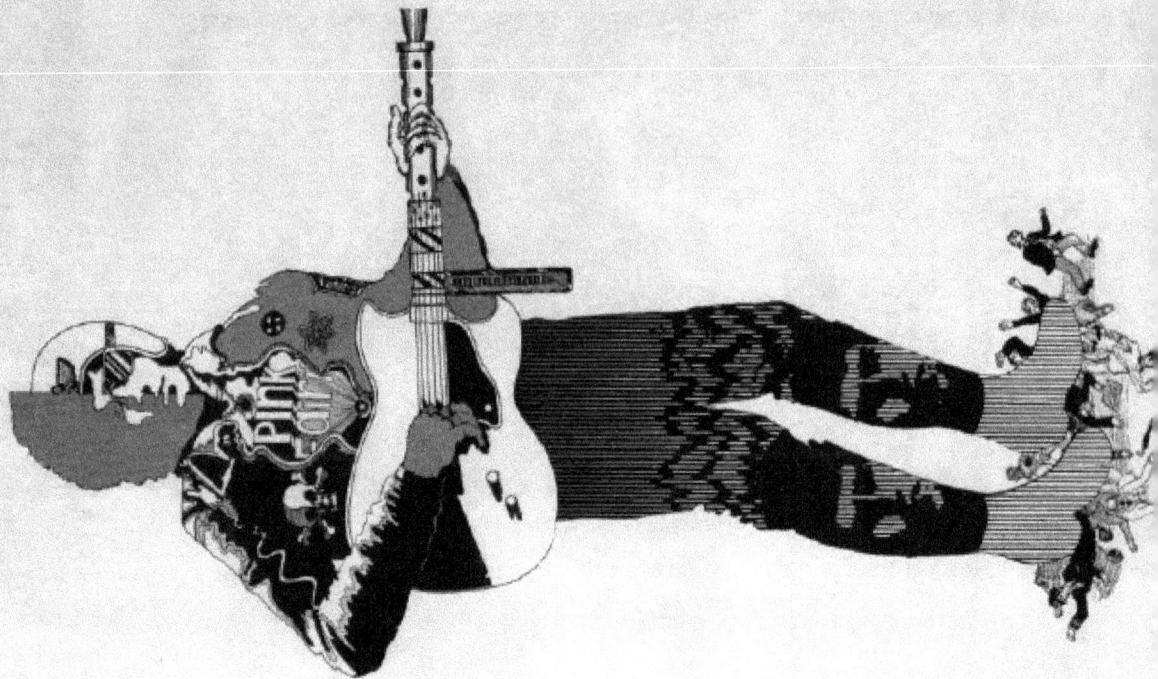

'At demonstrations there is no example. If you have somebody who is easily identifiable – this is where the One Percent Colours come in – and acts in a certain pattern in the face of a certain situation, then the people immediately around them will follow. Which is groovy – it gives us another guide. So when the horses come down we can say, "Link hands, stand still." People listen to you. They say, "That cat is a member of an organisation, he is standing still, that means standing still is where it's at.'

Then the assassination happened, which is still the primary factor of the whole thing in America, it's the most psychologically damaging thing that's happened to the Western mind that I can think of. In a sense its almost like a personalised world war 2, because the image to the Western man of a movie star president, intelligent, you know, all things that a lot of people want to be, is totally wiped out for no apparent reason, and this is the main thing everybody is intimately aware of through the media. Everybody's seen Kennedy, even people that didn't like him said, well, he's pretty, and then he was killed ... brutally, bloodily, in public, so then, in a sense, it drove everybody crazy in retrospect. I think people are still suffering from that, and this generation will always carry this shock with us. Especially as American culture spreads out to everyone else accordingly, you know people crying and breaking down when they heard. I cried too. The whole thing in a sense is a bloodbath of attractive public figures. This is what the game is, Robert Kennedy, Martin Luther King and Malcolm X, you know, being wiped out. My feeling is that America has got to a certain point of wealth, and you know, wealth can be very destructive, and at a certain point the cancerous aspect of America just got out of the secret Government in America and the Public Government which is the PR firm. What was slowly dawning on Kennedy was that he didn't have as much power as he thought he had, he came to be President and as soon as he came in he was involved with the final stages of the plan to attack Cuba and this and that and don't worry about it. Unimpeachable military advice which as soon as the attack was launched was immediately untrue – they told him that as soon as they landed the people would desert Castro and the opposite happened, people rushed with rakes down to the beach.

'Yeah sure you can have a dirty magazine as long as it doesn't go over 30,000 circulation. If it goes over that you're in trouble. And sure, you can carry as much politics as you like – but no faggot ads. But faggots mags are okay just as long as they don't carry any politics. The idea is to keep everything in cages like the zoo. That's going down all the time. And one of the reasons it goes on is because there are some real chicken shit musicians about, particularly some of the top musicians but they're frightened to open their mouths. It may mean that their teeny bopper sales will go.'

A room mate of mine called Jim Glover played a guitar so I started playing the guitar and this is when folk music was just coming in. The Kingston Trio was coming in and Baez was coming in – the early folk is different from the village scene and the village came after the folk boon hit. Then more and more people moved to Greenwich Village. This is where Dylan comes in. This is where Tim Hardin comes in. This is where all the big rock groups came in as straggling folk groups, Mamas and Pappas, Byrds.

'Politicians ... I don't mean Wilson, I mean Rudi Dutschke are so fucking depressing in their life-style. The new left are a bunch of shits, really boring shits. It's the same with actors ... actors are going right down the pan. James Dean was the last real life-style, with maybe Steve McQueen and James Coburn now. But they are very secondary to Jagger, or Hendrix or Townshend.'

The death of the American which is what all this has been about through the 60's, you know, the starting out as heavenly and ending up as hell which is the death of the American, the death of the Kennedy's, finally the death in Chicago of the all out middle class attempt to still be liberal and human and go through the electoral system and the utter and public and brutal failure of that experiment. That's what's happened and that's what brought this album (Ochs' 6th – Rehearsals for Retirement) which is the swan songs of the country. It's like the soul of the country has been killed and I feel myself partially murdered – songs about the death of a country. So the album ends not with the revolutionary call but it ends though I've been killed. It's like you retire and pull back and it's like it says 'now comes the rabble – if the future's out hordes take over and craziest takes over'. The social obligation is that this must be stopped, you know, it's like you don't have the heart left to try and stop it, it's like it doesn't matter the mental state, the final point of everything.

There ought to be roach party that takes the audience from HAIR down after the show to see a few speed freak kids. You know the whole thing – songs like, "We Ain't Got a Barrel of Money", and all those songs about money doesn't get you happiness, "Mother Kelly's Doorstep", and "Buddy Can You Spare a Dime". The poor are really grooving on it. They really dig being poor. So don't worry about them folks – they've got something you haven't got, they've got poverty. They've got integrity. They may not have anything to eat, but they have not integrity. And it's the same old shit over again ... you know.'

I mean I'm half political and half musical and I go back and forth between the two and I go along and sing my concerts every year. I do some concerts and every year I make a record or so and it comes out and it does well, I never get a hit single and I never go on television – but I'm not that kind of artist.

The average straight thinks twice before he kicks the shit out of a hippie because they don't know which type of hippie it is. You've got two breeds of hippie walking the streets – one will chain whip the guy who beats him up and the other will fall down and turn the other cheek. The 50 per cent risk is too much for the average straight. It's just the threat of it. I don't really see us beating anybody up ever – but the fact that we're on motorcycles, we have belts with heavy studs, so that we are not into a peace and love situation, you're in at least an "I will resist situation." GEO ROMAK

PHIL OCHS
REHEARSALS FOR RETIREMENT

BLIND FAITH Blind Faith ATCO SD 333004A

A super first album by a super new supergroup. Stevie Winwood sounds superbly spontaneous, Ginger Baker is superbly rythmic, Eric Clapton superbly unhalant and Ric Grech tries superbly hard. The whole thing sounds pleasantly enough like a cross between the Cream and the Band. They'll be nice about it at the Speakeasy, totally uncritical in the suburbs and finally non-comprehending on Radio One. Seriously, it's very good – better than we had been led to expect by all the ill-informed detractors who saw them in the park, and worse than all those column inches in the music papers would have you believe.

Super. Cathy McGowan should review it, not us.

John Leaner

FIENDS AND ANGELS, Martha Velez LONDON SHK 8395

First opinions of this album were none-too-enthusiastic after playing through various tracks during a day interspersed with a heady dose of Messiaen at the Albert Hall and a further bite into Uncle Meat – compared to which Martha Velez and Fiends and Angels appeared, well smooth, predictable, competent and cosh a bit sick, maybe a little too predictable. Perhaps about right for the Revolution discotheque.

However, first impressions being what they are, I played the album several more times, over two or three days of varying moods, but those first impressions still linger. To consider the credit side first: Martha Velez has a good bluesy voice, a bit velvety expressive – a good way with words. She has had a wide experience in the States, and turned down a part in *Hair* which can't be bad. But without wishing to put Martha down, what is really interesting about the album is the backing she gets. Her Angels (and Fiends?) are some of the best known artists on the British scene – on "I'm gonna leave you" and "Feel so bad" there's the unmistakable sound of Eric Clapton and Jack Bruce, and with the addition of Mitch Miller and Duster Bennett, it's almost inevitable that these should be two of the best tracks instrumentally. In "Swamp Man", Martha is backed by Cupid's and Chris Wood, and on "In my garish days" it's Chicken Shack with Martha instead of Christine Perfect up front. On the Dylan track "It takes a lot to laugh, it takes a train to cry", there's the distinctive organ of Brian Auger.

Backing of this quality might even redeem fom some, and it's hardly surprising that the sort of really excellent instrumental work of those who should, like Billy Preston's, That's the way God planned it from being merely a bible-punching bore.

One major criticism of the album as a whole, in fact, is really this — that the variety is provided by the accompaniment rather than the singer — the distinctive feel of each track is either that of Clapton and Bruce, or of the sound associated with Traffic, with Brian Auger or whoever.

Still all in all, this is a competent and well-produced first album even if Martha might have been a little lost without her illustrious friends. It would be fair to say that there are some interesting things going on, musically at the moment, particularly in the States, and it would be good to see more than the present more flavour of British Artists (some of them on the present album) being really adventurous. The Mothers have shown how you can carry the kids with you when you stray from the home key, and (to adapt Frank Zappa) pop is only the best vehicle for expression we have at the moment, not a tradition or a faith, so it must move on. This album doesn't. Everyone seems happy to stick (albeit smoothly and professionally) in that same old groove.

Two postscripts: from the cover, Martha looks a beautiful chick, and a bitch about the sleeve note. The cover layout's good, but why can't we be given a little more straight information about Martha Velez and the musicians other than that this is her voice over which predominately means something to Martha even if it means nothing to Decussy or to the likes — but let us all into the secret, or leave it to the publicity men.

Mike Hirst

TIM BUCKLEY Happy Sad EKS 74045

The liner notes to Tim Buckley's last album, "Goodbye & Hello", were short and anonymous. "I love and think fondly... Tim will sing you his ten takes and then wander off again. I'm these few wearing Buckley has obviously been through a few interesting experiences.

Firstly, he's baked a chick in Room 109 at the Blasker, (a motel/hotel?), on the Pacific Coast Highway and dug her enough to take ten minutes and forty-seven seconds to thank her for, and change an old man, full of self-pity back to nearly eleven minutes of Elektra Records' time speaks for itself.

Secondly, he's been balling grass.

Thirdly and possibly (?) most important of all, he seems to have made some sort of shift in his philosophy. Comment on the complexities and frustrations of an artist working in our present time has been faded, to explore the infinity more interesting and surreal territories briefly touched before in songs like "Morning Glory" and "Carnival Song".

He's no longer singing about wars anymore, at least not the kind of Two-star generals and Dow Chemicals – no, he's just not concerned any longer in the widening cracks of a current society, of its inhabitants, those of modern and geekish direction lies beneath daily on their minds and speaks.

Buckley has forsaken pessimism, evil or otherwise. "I wave goodbye to America and while hello to the world". McLuhan's "Fantasy Global Village" is his front sitting room.

Like any number of rock artists, Dylan and Lennon among them, he's back to personal relationship. 'Room 109', for example, compares with 'I Threw It All Away' on Nashville Skyline or is less Obvious, but no less tangible way with the blend of John & Yoko which is basically the story of real-life love affair. All of a sudden we think about it!You just can't do without it, well, you know the song as well as I do. And T.B. has learned it off by heart.

Musically speaking, this album is just slightly less adventuring than before. The arrangements are still as absorbing and fastidiously constructed as ever, with the usual emphasis on Buckley's triple-time twelve string backing, through the berserk congas of Carter Collins, and Lee Underwood's fine electric guitar work, but often and especially the acoustic work of the eerie voice is suffocated strange animal inflections of sound insensitive and badly lost by over-running and/or insensitive instrumental work. Buckley too, seems to have been concentrating far too hard on the profundity and delivery of his lyrics, and in the process tends himself to his own worst enemy, overstatement.

Mike Hirst

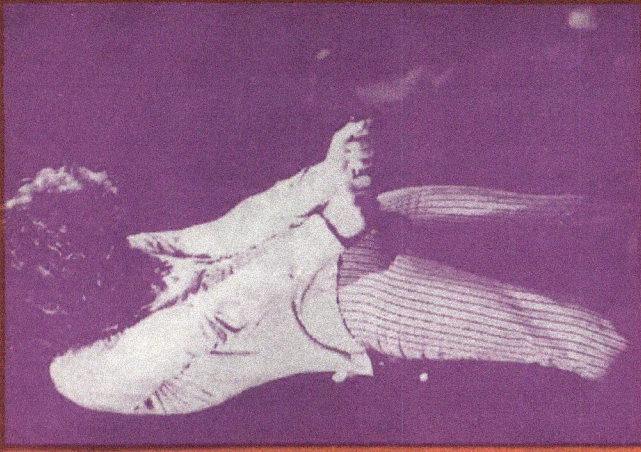

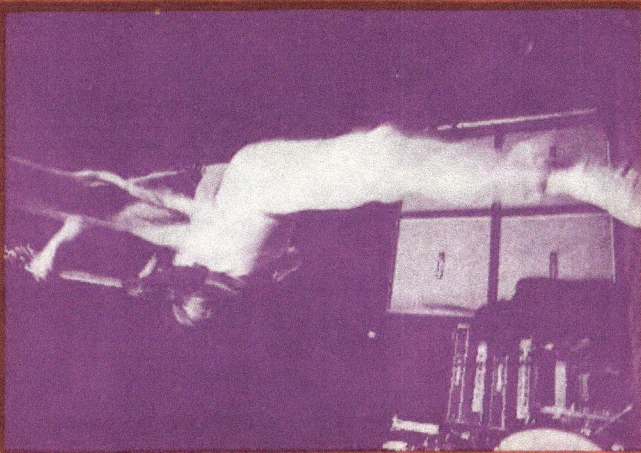

A PHILIPPE VON MORA FILM

starring

JOHN IVOR GOLDING   BILLIE DIXON   MICHAEL RAMSDEN

and introducing

MAYOR UMBERTO HUMP, SHIRLEY HUMP,
JACK "STEALTHY" HUMP (ALIAS CHIEF OF
POLICE HUMP), PIANO, GERBER MOTIFART,
THE SINGER IN THE MILK EASY, TWITCH,
MAD MICK, ANDREW THE ANARCHIST, DAVY
CROCKETT, FUDZY, MOLOPOLIS CREATIVE
DIRECTOR, THE STEALTHIES, STREET
FIGHTERS AND ASSORTED DISTINGUISHED
EXTRAS

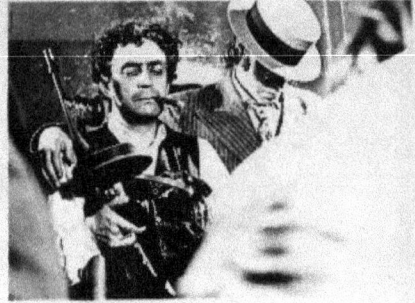

"Do Underground Sam Spiegels read
Mandrake?" Sunday Telegraph.

"There is something deeply satisfying about it!!!" sighed Lady Click.

STILLS   HARRY YOULDEN

director
VON MORA

prod. manager
JOHN WEDLEY

script
PETER SMALLEY-MORA

musical director   cameraman
TONY CAHILL   TOM COWAN

sound
ROBERT ALLEN

editor
STEPHEN CARTHEW

assistant directors
FRANK KENNINGTON-WEILEY

money
ERIC CLAPTON

40   SHOWING SOON AT YOUR FAVOURITE LOCAL CINEMA

COHEN
The Beautiful Loser

Raymond Durgnat

Cohen's beautiful LP's are the flowers of towers of which his poems are the outworks. He can't sing. Lady Day can't sing. A but revalidates the (in her case) pmet what may seem (in his) a t miserabilism. Yet his songs needs the his work just as the best of P rest of Keats.
His Selected Poems 1956-19 pulled between free verse, prose, so

nibbling onwards and upwards into one's gut.
Beautiful Losers centres on a bookish anthropologist, whose stream of consciousness recalls uneasy ecstasies with his suicided wife. Edith: her lover, F. who is also his fellow orphan, friend and guru (hence Master Song); and a martyred Iroquois Saint, Catherine Tekakwitha (1656-1680), who seems at once a lost moral ideal (having the stiff clear will of brave and cult) and alter ego (masochistic insolently dient squaw).

Beautiful Losers is prose poems in narrative (just as much free verse is prose justified so that you'll read is comic-strip faux-camp, post-lonesp, Burrovian science-metap and that Fuck You poem where Orlo ubes Ginsberg jerk off on a Tangiers bed

Its first 50

paradox-packed pages be the mood and even when. See wind, if turns to the seductie only to trace his sance masochisme

monologues as to prie and parody will jerk off volley, a fist a pissed phrenesi. (The wit and teasers of am that jerkoff his rhapsody(like that part there wa a rul pret di with dictionary (erotasam mewn) (and the minimm inst lehdkiosss (and so ann) (and so ann)

Fig poetry j mady swims in the Solomon deep log (by the the Song Bea LP's mantra to be of to get for it (serious) and then, you it to be not by not (serious) at dennation (ways (The mecess then was Fr

Historia de (Calif ernin in the Penguin Olympia Pr Satisfied Desire), Ribb C ard B (as (he du Clef Georges Batts dry rose flesh(the thin Cohen is has practice man sized in carries the temptatin of each and every gentility will com mdy sig pores Flesh as mud into immanery-pore tragic

The earliest ms are are and so/to man had to ent it s pep fre represented by meth with classical Gr tery Himself and over For you,/I will be a   now he was quite eradica or co is

sands ms old of pro any (fesliq In the P For Hitler se is my of of fact and s st s open anguish and s deeper watches the academic watt kite pulls gentle enough to call you master/strong enough to call you fool (x the gulls slowly writhing, slowly sinq/On the spears of wind. I can   Cohen in a movie called Song of V folksinger is seeking the who will believe in a sufficiently to thrust the spike his sleeping this alienated aprt   the Wandering th Flying Dutchman the ears of Mrs Moteson.

P Some reason sound fan of th Master Song on the first LP. Is the Cohen(vyed nough Vancou) keep able to find his Firm The Farnal Gam rerbing by Leo the in progress of it's sunny Hai the author. Its mist this is a demonstratio the essence of the Norway poems preverty and dawn its thing he songs properly here day date The gentlest e   pal he reses (1alm brazely on the great repua kinown a single me exiles in the arriving friendly sisters, he's affably impotent, and interested only in symbolic and actual modes of suicide. There's a moral in that somewhere and maybe it's this. Curious yins and yangs link Calvinist (ultra-WASP) and Jewish (un-WASP) modes. Calvinism: 'I must match my father', Judaism: 'I must placate my father'. Calvinism's internal repressions match Judaism's intra-family tensions.

It's because we're all Calvinists and Jews (father-religions) without fathers (poor old pop) that we're driven to feminise everything – including the male body (called the polymorphous Paradise). Yet it's arguable that if God had meant men to feel themselves, they wouldn't have organs pointing like arrowheads out to the avid wounds, but winding round their own bodies like a spider's web of fleshly remorse. Other space leads to self-sacrifice, inner space leads to suicide.

Cohen's sense of guilt and failure, as authentic as Greene's, is maintained in the teeth of adverse circumstances. (his family are rich. he was offered the Governor-General's prize for poetry, and the National Film Board of Canada's intelligent, yet intriguingly unrevealing, documentary shows him prettily melancholy, hummily sensitive and well at ease with all. Yet his work's weakness is an over-reaction against all consolation, however nearly less when he writes as Judas feeling the nails go in.

It's where narrative rears its old hat head (as when a couple are dominated by a rodent-like robot sex manager: orgasm cannot wither, nor exhaustion stale, its implacable, variety) that the novel leaps into its real lunacy. If Cohen's LPs offer the essence of his written word, it's not because the latter is redundant. Indeed the songs' undertones unfold their dirty dozens here. It's because the song forms controls the sprawl (Cohen's generous muse needs a very strict corset) and encourages the idiomatic against the literary.

In mid-'66 Cohen turned to C & W and cut his first disc at Nashville. His sad, drifting soliloquies heal the breach between psalm and song. Monotonal, liturgical, cyclical, like a post-Reichian wailing wall in words, they're sardonic, watchful, self-critical. Harshly tender, seemingly sad, they have their element of moral prophecy, and assert the opposite pole to Dylan's John Wesley Harding, whose surrender to TV-Western banality is either impenetrably ironic or spiritually senile.

Among the 7 deadly sins of the hippie era one may list: indifference disguised as tolerance ("Do your own thing – Jack!"), suicide disguised as self-abandonment; and a snidely pitiful repudiation of fatherly qualities (geniality, responsibility, consistency) disguised as humility, femininity and spontaneity. Cohen's bad conscience has got their number. Lady Midnight ... pointed at me where I kneeled on her floor/She said, 'Don't try to use me/Or slyly refuse me/Just write me or lose me/It is this that the darkness is for.'

An ex-Calvinist friend confessed that the best years of his life were the naively puritan ones. Then sexuality, guilt, ascetism and misogyny balanced one other so nicely that he was incessantly erect, indifferent to his own pleasure, and rarely capable of ejaculation. This delighted, and awed, the girls, and asked his old-fashioned pride, with remorse doing the job of masochism. The less puritanical he became, the more he allowed himself a full-body-and-mind orgasm, the more the thrills of guilt shifted to anti-life attitudes. Now all women are his

LPs: Leonard Cohen, CBS 63421,
        1967. Songs From A Room,
        CBS 63587, 1969. Poems
        Folkways 9805, 1969.
        Selected Poems 1956-68
        (Jonathan Cape, 35/s). The
        Favorite Game (Viking 1966).
        Beautiful Losers (Viking, 1966.
        Bantam, 1967).

Books: Ladies And Gentlemen, Mr.
        Leonard Cohen; Poem; Angel.
        All from National Film Board of
        Canada, London, 16mm.
        Songs Sacred And Profane, in
        Look Magazine 6/10/68. Ian
        Munn, Leonard Cohen's Novel
        Beautiful Losers, Zig Zag No 1.

Films:

Articles:

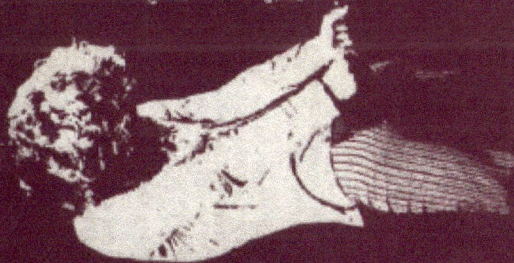

heads & Reds

SAVE £1

BRITAIN'S BEST VALUE!

Due to fire, flood, holocaust and a police raid, OZ is sacrificing its ENTIRE REMAINING STOCKS of back numbers... RIDICULOUS SAVINGS. Although these back issues have actually INCREASED in value, we are throwing them out at the original price (plus postage) — maybe this is your chance to make up a COMPLETE SET (Present Sotheby's value — £16,750.) THIS OFFER MAY NEVER BE REPEATED! Our accountants say we're crazy — what do YOU think?

BIG GROOVE

OZ 1. Sorry, absolutely unavailable.

OZ 2. Slashed to 3s! Mammoth colour poster: Wilson of Toad Hall. Mark (Rush to Judgment) Lane tears the BBC to shreds. Peter Porter's pungent Metamorphoses. Ludicrous interview Malcolm Muggeridge. Disgusting British Breasts Competition. SEE HOW THEY SAG.

OZ 3. Unobtainable. A priceless relic of a bygone extravagance.

OZ 4. PURE GOLD! Rush this one! Very few left. Pure gold pornographic fold-out cover by the earthquaking Hapshash and the Coloured Coat. Scientology exposed. Fuck de Gaulle. A Bastard's Guide. A marriage Snakes and Ladders. OZ's own set of TAROT CARDS! 10s. only.

OZ 5. SAVE 2s 6d! KING SIZE JUMBO POSTER — Plant a Flower Child in psychedelic pink or tropical yellow. Hurry, hurr, hurry, stocks dwindling fast. Price tumbles from £1 — a sacrifice at 17s. 6d! EXTRA BONUS — Great Alf Conspiracy on reverse.

OZ 6. 3s. — OZ + John Wilcock's OTHER SCENES — two for the price of one — Dope Sheet — how to drop acid. Leary in Disneyland. John Peel spills the beans — a prophetic interview before he hit the BIG TIME. Ruthless expose of the King of Nepal ('It nearly caused a bloody war.' Foreign Office.) Letter from a Greek Gaol. McLuhan's One Eyed Electric Kingdom — Raymond Durgnat. PLUS! Unique rainbow colour process throughout — every issue different (BUY THEM ALL!)

OZ 7. 50 ONLY TO CLEAR! Famous Bob Dylan cover. Black Power — Michael X meets the Flower Children. Wog Beach Shock! How the Sun Maims. In Bed with the Americans. A real blow-job at 3s.

OZ 8. Originally 5s, sensational value at 3s. Bumper double issue + free copy of infamous wrongly spelled Guevara poster (sick 'humour at its worst). Quattrocchi on the failure of the Russian Revolution. Richard Meltzer's raunchy Epistemology of Rock. 'The most unreadable OZ ever.' (Stevie Wonder)

OZ 9. 3s. Unidentified Flying Objects — the weird horrifying world of the Flying Saucer Society — a collector's item. Laing poetry page PLUS (ravishing inside expose of St Paul's School horror camp. A TRIP!

OZ 10. The Pornography of Violence — the issue with the blood spattered cover. Roger McGough's Summer with the Monarch. Amnesty report on torture in Greece. BBC transcript of sadism in Arkansas. LBJ's Chessboard of Death. WARNING: Adult material only — keep away from children. Orgasmic at 5s.

OZ 11. 3s. Fluorescent gummed sticker cover (now stuck to inside page) Vietloon Conspiracy. Famous, much discussed New Statesman parody ('Most amusing', Paul Johnson). Jerry Rubin's historic call to arms: 'Yippies are stoned idealists, searching for a vision of Utopia.' The first OZ with 9 grain of intelligence.

OZ 12. Three GIANT-SIZE colour posters. Unstitch them, play games, have fun. Reach Nirvana. TECHNICAL TRIUMPH... took three years to print. A fool and his 3s. are soon parted. The Lord loveth a cheerful buyer.

OZ 13. The whole French revolution for 3s. Gold, (fucked-up) fold-out cover by Michael English. Mammoth AGIT-OZ supplement prepared by GENUINE British militants. (Nine months after this OZ appeared, students tore down the gates of the LSE) Extensive, incisive and deeply moving review of 2001. Lengthy libelous extract from Dylan film. Don't Look Back.

OZ 14. 48 pages. At 3s. this is less than a penny per page. Down on the Farm with Emmanuel Petrakis. Herman Kahn sees the future ('I don't like it.') What happened when Fabian Douglas went to school with long hair — world scoop! Shock story of Diggers delivering own babies — Electric Circus is stillborn. An unforgettable, unforgivable OZ.

OZ 15. Martin Sharp's award winning portrait of Mick Jagger in full cry — in glorious technicolour. Flip Top Legal Pot. BFI Bulletin. All about Meher Baba. Original Jimi Hendrix doing things with his guitar. NEON POP OZ and connoisseur's choice of the early OZ style. All for 3s.

OZ 16. MAGIC THEATRE OZ ... 'What does matter, and makes the Magic Theatre the only first class issue of OZ in the last sixteen, is that at last a magazine has broken the mould in a lyrical and decisive way. As a frequent non-reader I can promise you that readers OZ losses through such an experiment are no loss.' Robert Hughes. 3s. for a new high in magazines.

OZ 17. Manfred Mann. Smash Cash. ICA Blast. Indian Ashrams. South African Queens. Greek Gaols. Don't let your Chick Blow Your Balls. Does Shelter Really Shelter? Is Tiny Tim What he Eats? Black Eagles. A virtual Encyclopaedia Britannica of contemporary life — an amazing, unbelievable, suicidal 3s.

OZ 18. Experimental format warped straight from Rolling Stone. Michael X talks. Any verbal torch ! ... Revolutionary Militant Student. Appalachian Finn — SQ ! ! ! in and build a barricade. Terry Reid. The Soft Machine. The real horrorment of Marrakech and much much more for a mad 3s.

OZ 19. NEWS OF THE WORLD exposed this OZ but we still have a few left — The universal Tongue-Bath. A groupie's Vision. Why Metropolitan Sergeant Pilcher knows so many pop stars. World's only living Dylanologist writes about the world's only Bob Dylan. The Food Explosion. FRELIMO. Why the Press Council is a Dangerous Hoax. This OZ is still being sold contrary to legal advice. For 3s. it's a cheap and dangerous buy.

OZ 20. HELL'S ANGELS — Hippies jape as they menace Arts Lab in drug orgy rape gang bang loot shock! PLUS Situationist 'Supplement' direct from Paris. Out of the Psychodrama by David Widgery. Inside Jann Wenner's Head there is a Stone Rolling. Roast Trafalgar Pigeon. Dirty pictures and a bad of cheap thrills for 3s.

"—but I was the one who smiled when I got it !"

BIOGRAPHY OF THE SIMEON SYNTHESIZER

by SIMEON of Silver Apples

Both Danny and I were bored with conventional musical instruments – not so much how they are played, like we can really get into a good guitar's player's technique and all that – but the *sounds* that the guitar itself makes. I don't care how many fuzzes, wah-wahs, or vari-tones you run it through, it still sounds like a guitar. And that can still be very groovy. Don't get me wrong. I'm not putting the guitar down, or anything like that, I'm just saying that we wanted to find something new, and we knew it had to be electronic just because that seemed to be the area most open to experimentation.

A friend of ours gave us World War II surplus audio signal generator and we went to work from there. Not having any electronics training, we had to go step by step, shock by shock, learning how to hook it up – vary its sound, key it in, make it go. This old generator is the nucleus of what is now the Simeon synthesizer. At the time we had never heard of a synthesizer.

This was, I guess, somewhere in late 1967. The main problem was that of pitch control. It has to be played like a fretless instrument, 'cello or like a slide trombone. So it was a matter of finding various positions on the sweep dial so a melody could be played. After I got to be pretty good at that it occurred to me that I had a few more generators, beyond the one board that I might be able to get some bass lines figured out with my feet. So we got the cheap ... found ... and stacked them on ... started practicing. Next ... my feet were busy, and my right hand ... doop-ah-doo ... my left hand play ... some more generators ... combinations of ... through telegraph keys. The more generators I had keyboard. I found ... I could play, so we hooked something else and got some more – plus some more telegraph keys.

The Simeon now was a heap of wires, keys, with walls, and generators piled up on a table. It was obvious that if we were ever going to do anything with it, it would have to have a console. So we hooked something else, this time I think it was my guitar, and got some plywood and glue and screws and made a big flat box with everything mounted down on it – and in it. God was it heavy, but the Simeon was not a "thing." We had a few tunes we could play, so Barry Bryant, our manager, got us a job playing at Max's Kansas City's upstairs discothek. We drove a few people out and some stayed and danced and had fun. But at least it was a beginning, and also someone from the Gibson guitar and amp company heard us and suggested that with one of these tone units we could get ... effects. We found ... that anybody could play it ...

... most like ... to play it ... I practiced ... elbow. At first ... to get the ... opponents ... imitate on ... the melody going ... time I keep ... going ... with my right hand, and sing ... Now I can do ... Danny, in the meantime, had gotten hold of a whole bunch of drums and turned them chromatically so that instead of just playing percussion drums he could now only keep a beat but also play in key with me. If you ... on our version of Mustang Sally ... as good during a little 3/4 break. A big break as far as the Simeon is concerned occurred while we were playing a gig at the Cafe Au Go Go and one of the

guys on the bill gave us the name of a friend of his who had built a little voltage control keyboard. We quickly made contact and bought it from him. That soon was mounted down into the box. Shortly, thereafter, another friend showed us that a walkie-talkie unit made a good white noise sound (we had so far been using an FM tuner for white noise) so we mounted down a walkie-talkie – being sure to yank out the aerial as not to get any transmissions through it. This put through the squelch knob sounds like ocean waves or wind, depending on how you play it.

... the Simeon is a conglomeration of ... that anybody could sit down at ... – or if anyone were to ... you would practice a piano ... music on it. The instrument ... lots of freedom in that each ... can be easily tuned ... be heard by the human ... once struck a high ... low and blasted ... been flying ... that we're supposed to ... right? ... "Bubbio," but it ... to see two ... too-a-loo on the ... an unconfirmed acid sighting.

We are the first to admit that the Simeon is a crude little monster. It was never meant to be a Moog-like creature, in fact it was recently in the same recording studio with a Moog and it didn't blush a bit. Someone called it the result of hippie technology and it flexed its muscle. It is made to be a live performance instrument, and leaves all the multi-overdubbing tricks to the sophisticated fancy black boxes with blinking lights and myriads of patch cords.

The Simeon loves to crouch out in the middle of a stage and have someone pull out all of its stops.

It's an energy machine – getting it together – it once tried to mount the Moog, with love in its tubes.

UPS.

From Other Scenes

obstruction to the full enjoyment of the record, which basically consists of D. S. S. being musically very tight a together, using strong tunes and interesting harmonies. Here and there the odd line comes through, the most successful track being the frighteningly ominous 'Ship Of Fools'. After a few plays, of course, one tends to remember more and the tunes come through quite clearly, the words, important and unimportant in their nonsense, receding into the background. Now even the dog has decided to remain in the room and sleep surrounded by beautiful tunes.

Cousin Caterpillar

None of the tracks here have quite the absolute sincerity and above all conviction that made 'Morning Glory' one of the musical highs for me last year. At least, not up to now. Buckley's material always takes time, and it's easy. It's difficult to judge. He does have an incredible voice, capable at times of almost unbelievable variations in tone and pitch. It's a shame that he still appears to lack the confidence to resist completely proving the point. Only on one cut, the last and shortest, 'Sing A Song For You', does he in fact relax enough to let the words flow straight out of his head without running them through the gauntlet of his indisputable but stuttering vocal abilities.

But if that is a fault, and certainly Tim Buckley and his producers do not appear to consider it to be one, then it can be the only major fault in Happy Sad. For Happy Sad is a whole LP, as have been all Buckley's albums. Hours of thought and concentrated work must have gone into the making of it. There is not an ounce of hype here. As a poet and a musician T.B. is getting better all the time. Just a few more '1069's' and another gypsy woman could do it.

Felix Dennis.

KIP OF THE SERENES Dr Strangely Strange (Island ILPS 9016)

The first time I placed this record on the turntable the dog sat up and howled. It's the first album by an Irish group called Dr. Strangely Strange, a record produced by Joe Boyd and, (according to the advertisements), a group raised and informed by the Incredible String Band (whom they sound a lot like). But it didn't make any difference.

Although a keen listener to the Incredibles, the dog showed then left the room. He was uneasy.

The trouble was the words. The importance of the words to their music would be quite indeterminate... So definitely is a mute accompanist would lose Dylan, but this isn't the answer. The words, though excellent musicians would lose many people regard words as being as important as Pop people seem to be quite so indirect in their efforts to avoid it Some of the great fear of words around. So although a keen listener to their music were taken away.

And every time I've listened to this L.P, I've found my mind unable to concentrate on the words and running onto the tunes, the harmonies and the instrumentation. Or even the tone of the voice, but hardly ever what that voice is saying. Dr. Strangely Strange's lyrics are a crowd of instant images, few of them seem to need any close examination, (the easy couplet form is frequently used) so that the words are so superficial, so unimportant, in fact, giving way to a hint or a ba-ba, which only goes to make one regret that the words are there — the voice is needed, but the words only form an

WE WERE HAPPY THERE

MCA MUPS 375 STEREO

MCA RECORDS LTD., 139 Piccadilly London W1 England

47

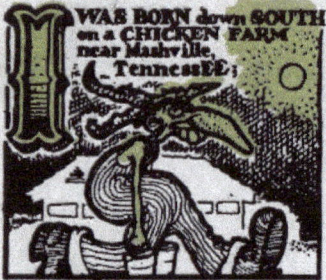

The Beautiful Freaks

OZ
24

3'6

Welcome to

the OZ Freak Show. A gallery of beautiful people, whose wildly original world-view flows into their life style. Freaks are anti-hypocrites; who abolish the barriers between theory and action, fantasy and reality, politics and play, sanity and madness . . .

With media turning the world into that global village, plugging us into the same experiences — we all risk growing into the same person. In such a world, freaks restore the Individual

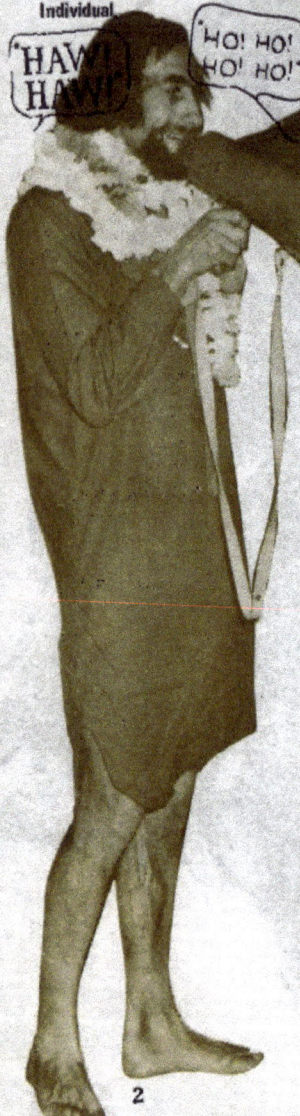

'HAW! HAW!'

'HO! HO! HO! HO!'

The wonderful wizard of Auss

THE only conventional thing about Ian Channell was the manner of his arrival at Heathrow Airport yesterday. He flew in from Australia by jet.

As resident wizard at the University of New South Wales, he might have been expected to arrive on a broomstick. But he explained: "I do not scatter powder and make spells. I am an illusion broker."

He lives in a special house at the university and is supported, he said, by the students and the Vice-chancellor's fund.

The exact purpose of his unusual post is not entirely clear. The wizard of Aussie said simply: "They need me for almost everything."

A strange figure in most curious clothes, he is on his way to a students' conference in Hamburg. He carries flowers and rolled umbrella, and wears whistles round

his neck and a plastic hammer in his belt.

"My house," he said, "is called the ALF house. It stands for Action for Love and Freedom. Members of ALF are for freedom without the use of drugs."

The whistles, he said, were to make everything go quiet while he explained to policemen that he is not dangerous.

Ian was tarred and feathered by students recently, but the experi-

THE FOOL

THE ACTING

ACTING

THE FOOL

If it is illegal to sleep in the open air, sit on the pavement, read certain books, to miss a day at school, to run away from home under the age of 16, to laugh and sing in the street, and punishable (by refusal of employment) to grow one's hair to a pre-1914 length, then it is obvious that the insanity of our civilisation requires very special handling.

Without face to lose, there is a great freedom of opportunity for a fundamental critique of all social relations and ethics. There is a great deal of license permitted a Fool provided he is seen as having nothing to gain by his activity. Just to do absurd things that harm no one, perhaps make a sly comment on a puritanical practice in a friendly way, let people have a laugh at your expense if nothing else. If you are generous and wealthy in this area of personality, then you have achieved something towards alleviating the tension and anxiety of life in this decaying culture. Who loses?

This leads me into an outline of the theory and practice of the fun revolution or politics of the absurd. The kingdom of heaven on earth in this eschatology is of course the Fool's Paradise — Cockayne or the Bum's Heaven that Burl Ives used to sing of.

THE THEORY AND PRACTICE OF POLITICS OF THE ABSURD
Some fragments to be filled in by others

Need for an Alf [Australian Liberation Front — ed] cadre of tough hobbit type detached expressive actors on the stage of life. Optimistic existentialists assuming as a base line the sort of model of the universal man that can be derived from many religious thinkers, artists, philosophers and humane livers.

The new tactics of guerrilla warfare of the mind can be seen as having a tradition — see Czech history especially, the British fun war against Hitler 1939-1942, the Danish response to the Nazi invasion and attempt to eliminate Danish Jews, the defence of Mafeking by the founder of the immortal Boy Scouts, the retreat from Gallipoli, the Emden, early days in the Vietcong guerrilla warfare against the Americans and South Vietnamese Government troops, in the subculture the heroes are Good Soldier Schweik, Brer Rabbit, Bugs Bunny, Tweetie Pie, The Road Runner, the simple elf peasant in Grimm's Household Tales, the universal figure of Jack pitted against the powerful aggressive greedy but simple-minded giants.

Chaplin, Laurel and Hardy and most of the silent clowns starting in the Mack Sennet stables. Ulysses is the hero rather than Agamemnon or Achilles; Jesus rather than the priestly and political bureaucrats he had to outwit. Was the crucifixion a Houdini-type hoax and did Jesus make his getaway to India with Thomas? Socrates played his game with the whole of Athens as his opponents and finally got them to kill him to save

himself from the sinful act of committing suicide so that he could go on with his search for the universal human essence in the world of the soul — why couldn't he wait until the usual time, the impatient old devil?

IN THE FUN REVOLUTION EVERYONE WINS
In the fun revolution everyone wins or it is immoral and inhumane. Social relationships are transformed, individual organisms are not hurt, maimed or killed. Man is a role-player, not a one-dimensional White Anglo-Saxon Protestant Adult Male Bourgeois Business Executive with the rest of mankind as an inferior residual category. Man can be liberated from seriousness and self-hypnosis encouraged by over-dependence on print, education, nationalism, symbols of success, cleanliness, whiteness and achievement and Pythagorean overreliance on quantitative criteria of meaning. Man as free from oral dependdency hangups, anal control and order hangups, castration anxiety and sexual inadequacy hangups. Man neither as free to hurt others nor as forced to love them. It's all in the mind and understanding can liberate us and all mankind.

Heads I win Tails you lose tactics to give the aggressive puritans enough rope to hang themselves and then to love them instead of hurting them is the basic tactic and ethic of the Alf fun revolution, e.g., placard in one of last year's fun Demos, "Let Professors use student toilets". The use of stickers as detonators of authoritarian, teacher figures disguised as individuals loving man and wishing to liberate him.

Love the Americans in Vietnam, help them to get home to their friends, etc., or

to desert safely if this is the only way out. Martyrs are manipulating pity to get their cause accepted not by reason but through Black Magic (emotional control). Going to gaol is no sign of being right, going into a mental institution is no sign of being wrong (see Laing and Goffman on this). Work it out free of social control by the "Lonely Crowd" around you.

THE FUNCTION OF DEMONSTRATION
Postulate: Demonstrations have at least two functions:-
(i) Instrumental — to attempt to persuade other people that your point of view is right.
(ii) Affective — the emotional satisfaction of demonstrating itself.

How can this twin objective be best satisfied? THIS is the issue — not bourgois considerations of respectability or puritan self-fulfilling prophecies that all men are basically aggressive and not to be trusted (including themselves, of course), nor traditional hanging-on to outmoded ideal models of the good old time demos and revolutions that worked (did they? — if so why did things get worse) for our grandfathers?

Banners are only one sort of props that can be used in a demo and have as many disadvantages, if not more, as other props. They produce an aching in the arms, inhibition of freedom of movement during the march, procession, dance, ritual, etc., or in any rapid tactical withdrawal which may have to be made. Other gear for demos include:- Hats: Helmets (affective or decorative Roman, medieval, Goth, Vikings, etc., and/or instrumental-protective, e.g., modern Japanese, police or firemen's), bowlers and top hats (capitalist absurd), flying helmets (curse you, Red Baron), boy scout hats (be

2

DAILY MIRROR, Thursday, September 11, 1969

ie

prepared), pith helmets (colonialist absurd), medieval headgear (women's hats in opportunity shops are often suitable).

Clothing: Academic gowns (educational absurd), military dress uniforms (militarist absurd), white lab coats (technocrat absurd), sporting attire (competitive sporting absurd), nightshirts (anti-puritan trousers demo), old-style male swimming costumes (ensuring male nipples are covered, puritan shame of the body absurd), cloaks, kimonos, inscribed T-shirts, long gowns, baggy trousers, ankle-length riding skirts with boots, mini-skirts still a powerful revolutionary weapon; suits of armour (plastic, metal or cardboard), (Quixote absurd).

Hair: Let it all hang out. The existentialist self expression of hair resisting the demon barber's symbolic castration. The male ("the birthright of his sex") can again reveal his essential nature as the display expert and show-off. The return of the pre-1914 colourful male as revolutionary in the grey flabby masculine world. Wigs may be used by the successful segmented role-players.

Attention-getters and harmonisers: Clickers, bells and various other portable instruments that are easy to play whilst on the move. Not pianos, those bourgeois symbols of success with their constipated size and thundering sound which displaced the beautiful harps. Other suggestions include drums, harmonicas, whistles, trumpets, trombones, sousaphones, tubas, swanee whistles, bird callers, auto harps, rattles, jew's harps, dustbins, violins, cymbals, triangles, etc. Also bubble-blowing apparatus, smoke machines, etc.

Transport: Walking, running, skipping, dancing, roller skates, skate boards, pogo sticks, go-karts, scooters (pedal-type), old prams, tricycles, cardboard tanks, horses, camels and other absurd animals, etc.

Improvisation centrepieces: This is virtually an unlimited field, depending on the luck of finding and recognising certain objects (ready-mades) and deploying them in environments where their impact is maximal in detonating the false consciousness of the petty bourgeoisie.

A few items I have personally tried out in a variety of social contexts, both inside and outside the university, have provided excellent foci for living theatre experiments. These are a tailor's headless dummy, a wooden aspidistra stand, a long amplifier horn, a dustbin, a Roman standard (SPQR) and a beach umbrella. I am looking for a large clock face at present.

FUN DEMONSTRATIONS ARE AVANT-GARDE

In all the latest in the happening art scenes, John Lennon, John Cage, Pop Art, Ready-mades, Living Theatre, Retribalisation, Implosion, re-emergence of living in the mythical dimensions. The WASP's are in retreat. Art as puritan manipulation of materials in the mimetic, scientific experiment to capture a disenchanted, predictable, controlled environment has freaked out into icons, myths, action painting, ambiguity, and sheer play with materials. Paintings are being recognise; again as traces of the artist's life activity in doing his thing - and the painting of the first pin-up, the Mona Lisa, and its hoarding as an alienated object by Da Vinci as inhuman as the Roman collections of objets d'art.

Paintings are the excreta of the artist. It is the existential act of creation that is the valuable thing, not the anal retentive behaviour of collecting others' paintings.

I could go on but where would it all end? Think for a moment of self-destructive sculpture. What is the artist doing? Why pop art? At least the idiot alfs on their pogo sticks and with their childish clickers are somewhere in the mid-twentieth century. There is something charming and quaint about the old-time radicals still haggling over Trotsky and trying to cope with Marx's Economic and Philosophical Manuscripts which I'm sure they wish had remained undiscovered or suppressed as in Russia. They are remarkably like traditional leaders in the Church and Education faced with the new theology and the student-power phenomenon.

THE "LUMPEN" DIALECTIC

The contradictions inherent in the one-dimensional communist-capitalist bourgeois, puritan, nation-states are revealed only when negated by the recognition of a true dialectical alternative.

This is now present — and to Marcuse's consternation turns out to be the hippies, yippies, dropouts, temporary workers, children and some women. These are the "Lumpen" or "uncontrollable ratbag" proletariat today. They are increasingly being revealed as having valid world views and ethics of interpersonal behaviour, they exemplify their philosophy rather than preach it and their message is the possibility of liberation through cutting down alienated work commitments and simple but transcending forms of leisure. Thus the phoney class struggle by competing bourgeois groups for the meaningless symbolic spoils of the overdeveloped welfare warfare states may end.

IAN CHANNELL

Rufus Collins Living Theatre Black Freak Beautiful

On the surface his skin shines ebony and his charm is as mannered as Noel Coward but he doesn't go to Savile Row drink champagne stay at the Savoy, does take drugs, and dig them, fuck whoever he pleases, spout the revolutionary dream in a stream of express poetry that's impossible to stem, shout skinheads from the car window at any passing short hair, and support your local filth most particularly when there is a large car full of large dyed people. He does hold you in thrall with spittle and blazing eyes, and muscles that bulge estatically through shimmering robes . . . he does believe in change . . . and has been charged often with psychic violence although his flag is non-violent anarchy and his heart pacifist.

"Say I am aggressive. Say I have my own particular kind of violence. I think it's not violence but energy. An attempt to change the smug attitude. When you react against something you have to take a step beyond the thing you are reacting against . . . the step further is the one that labels you freak – but that's the one that brings about the change. The only way is to become physically involved with what you're saying so that you let the grief and sweat and perspiration you feel when say, some-one has been killed, come out – let it come out so that you can re-channel the energy instead of sucking it back, sitting back and sucking it in and keeping it under a calm cover until the pot boils over and you have another confrontation where you kill off fifteen million people".

When you pass him on the street he's so charged with energy it's like passing a pent up explosion and when you see him in Paradise Now he bursts like lava over the upturned faces of the psychodrama . . . using the theatre as an arena, to challenge the human state with the force of his convictions, dancing the red cape before your eyes so that you charge him with your answers and so find them out under the merciless glare of the fanatic revolutionary.

"We attempt to arouse people out of their lethargy because once they can stand up on their own feet and shout 'NO' loud and strong, then they can no longer talk about death in a calm and civilised way. You hear about Vietnamese children starving, you hear about African children starving, you hear about Mexican or South American children being fed poison, being gassed planes hunting them down in the jungle just because they are Indians, and you know if you kill off so many you'll be given a piece of property as a prize. It's the human animal hunt, and the hunters come back to talk perfectly calmly about – how many Indians did you kill today? I've killed 1,500 and that means 1,500 acres more land, we're reacting against this kind of calmness that's smothering the Universe. The calmest places you can go are the places where there's most killing. You get a conference between two heads of state, Nixon and the Queen of England, or Nixon meeting the Russians . . . and what they come to meet about is how many people are going to die. The calm way is the way of the killer".

He says "Yes I'm a freak" because people have labelled him that since he bled out of his mother's womb in freakdom 30 years ago in Harlem. "My father drank, my mother slaved and my brother and sister and I nearly starved, but my mother always taught us table manners, and which fork to lay where, even though there was no food to eat. I began to take dancing lessons and became a child star. That's very far out in Harlem. Even then the way I looked put people uptight. I'd walk into a store and the manager would say to the shop assistants – don't "speak to that nigger just get him outta here.

"Anyone is a freak who has not adjusted to society as created by the media – anyone who tries to look for his own freedom, anyone who tries to follow the principles and precepts in fact set out by society is consistently put down, but it's society itself that's directly opposed to the freedom of the individual. If you protest against wars against polluted air against food which destroys your body – then you are a freak – theft is something the Government itself created, they being the thieves. Individual freedom is bullshit. I'm called a freak because with my life I demonstrate what I believe. Nowadays people get into the same jibbering rages over hippies as they did blacks. These people think everytime they see a black man he's screaming black power – well maybe every black man is saying black power in his own way, but it certainly has NOTHING to do with the horrible violence they associate with it, these people who believe in a strong class system of inequality, believe in money, war, and competition.

At thirteen he went to a monastery after meeting the only man he had ever seen who looked happy, a monk. He stayed there for seven years but exasperated with the isolation, and rigidity decided his evolution must take place outside the sheltering walls. The religious influence remains.

"I'm trying to bring up life so it's more beautiful, even the washing of dishes takes on a new significance so that nothing is trivia – drugs teach us that – there is no trivia in life. I'm saying: find a new ritual because the ritual you bathe yourself in now is the ritual of blood. Each action of man should take on the beauty of the elevated state so that instead of rituals like the Chicago massacre written in the blood of America, we can heighten perception and the very life we are living. You can wash dishes, and it's as holy and sanctified as meditation. Something everyday like shitting – your have to get away from these strained shits you've been brought up to when you HAVE to go to the bathroom every morning after breakfast, and be out in five minutes. You should totally relax and allow this thing to happen to you – allow the relief that the whole body feels with the bowel movement. Why do we always shut the door? Because it stinks? My dear we all shit, and it's not an alien smell. If people ate better food they wouldn't have such bad odours."

Yes – the quintessence of black sexuality that makes male and female quiver with expectancy, cast downward shivers at his extraordinary perfectly formed body. He sees them.

"It's a constant battle to free myself from my own sexual mores but each time I overcome in that particular

4

battle I am opened up further. When one finally realises that everything is sexual and most of the frustrations of the world are sexual frustrations then it becomes absolutely necessary to hammer on the door of the sexual revolution. People see us walking around the streets being friendly, holding each others' hands, whether male or female, kissing, loving – and then they feel the freedom we have in the use of each others' bodies and touching each other – but it frightens them.

"Psychedelics are very important because they open you up – ram you into contact with the reality that you most of the time try to escape. Drugs are a quick way to the visions and if you don't come from a history of 2,000 years meditating to get to the visions – drugs help – o yes".

Acid laughter bubbling up through the top of his wire head.

"The great revolution in America is because of marijuana ... because more and more people are turning on and finding the vision of another life. They see that they were living their lives to die. What angers me most about society is that the moment a voice is raised against anything felt to be wrong it's violence – it's insanity ...

"The real violence of the world is the violence of death, the violence of killing, the violence of the underprivileged, the violence of starvation. We must use our energies to transform the world and make it more beautiful".

He's living the revolution. Dig it.

DANAE

MARCIA HERSCOVITZ INTERVIEWS HERSELF IN THE PRESENCE OF IAN STOCKS

"A tragic-comic novel, poignant and unforgettable, a rich and bawdy masterpiece."

I'm alone now in her room, a tiny silver space in the Angel, a dream-factory with gold and silver mirrors. Cosmic draperies and fringes hang down over a satin bed strewn with foxes. The window looks down on the garden and on the opposite wall is painted a trompe L'oeil window: blue sky and white lace. There's artificial grass on the floor and real blue hydrangeas. Pictures and toys are strewn with precision to reflect in mirrors and dangle precariously. Sarah Bernhardt in her bedroom, Anna Pavlova with a deck of cards. A Forties mannikin casts her eyes downwards on a box of Black Magic chocolates whose partially open lid reveals its contents of black lace. Everywhere there are collages made from old photographs, pictures about daily rituals with a twinge of surrealist irony. And erased photographs of people with the light in their eyes, women sporting lemniscates, children manifesting out of thin air.

I.S.: How do you get these effects?

M.H.: By erasing with a pencil eraser.

I.S.: Who is Stan Stunning?

M.H.: Jay Landesman. Books are strewn all over the place. An original edition of "Magick in Theory and Practice" by Aleister Crowley, "The Equinox," Vol. 1., No. 1., by Aleister Crowley, "The Book of Lies" by Aleister Crowley, "777, a quabalistic guide to ceremonial magick" by the same. "The Selected Poems of Andre Breton" and "The Projection of the Astral Body."

I.S.: Did you really come to London to find the Great Beast?

M.H.: No, I came because Julian Beck bought me a ticket, but I decided to

stay and look up some old friends. The Atlantis Bookshop window and my house are the only two places where Aleister Crowley and Marilyn Monroe sit side by side.

I.S.: Are you a witch?

M.H.: No, but I believe in magic and the power of the will and I'm very interested in cults and secret societies. Especially the Golden Dawn which existed in London around 1910 and had as its members W. B. Yeats, Samuel Mathers, Florence Farr, Bram Stoker, Arthur Machen, Crowley: I wanted to know how this form of ritual secret society manifested itself today and I discovered it in the Rolling Stones. Kenneth Anger came to Paradise Now with Lucifer tattooed on his chest and his new film "Lucifer Rising" is about Brian Jones.

I.S.: What about magic spells, bewitchments, enchantments?

M.H.: I used to play with red candles and home made dolls as a child and recite invocations from the Key of Solomon. Now I'm into better and more subtle realities, or dreams. They put Artaud away for casting dispersions on the butchers' wives. Note to girl troubled by vampires: Remember, dearie, you made them and make something beautiful instead. There's a lot of amphetamine sorcery on the Lower East Side, whirling dervishes and take-off artists. Also secret readings on Sunday mornings of the Zohar and Kichl's

Pharmacy where I used to buy manna. Splendor in the artificial grass.

I.S.: Let's not get carried away. Tell me about the Tarot cards.

M.H.: (fondling a bulky deck of 78 handpainted cards, closing her 'gold-lidded eyes and pulling out the Ace of Cups): I made these cards in 1965 in New York. I had been reading with the Marseille Deck but felt the need to make my own deck with new designs. Everyone has to make his own wheel. I used to be Michael McClure's reader-advisor. I always make the subject cross my palm with silver to prove I'm just a cheap gypsy hustler and don't bear responsibility for what the cards say. The Tarot never lies. It's a perfect system with the four elements and cycles represented in the four suits and the Hebrew alphabet on the Greater Arcana. A set of pictures, representing everything in life, that can be read by the literate and illiterate alike. Everyone wants to find the system of the universe. Taro means rota wheel, which sounds pretty-right to me. Wheel, calendar, cycle, circle, earth, moon, stars, movie stars, beds, bodies, astral bodies . . .

I.S.: What are you doing?

M.H.: (sucking her thumb): I'm making a dream book called "Magic in Bed."

It's a series of images which tell a story with eyes closed. It started with an assignment from the Times

Sunday Magazine to do sixteen dream pictures and now it's growing into a book I'm dedicating to one of my benefactors, Max Ernst.

While I'm still on the camera I'd like to say hello to Kasoundra in New York and Mom and Dad in L.A. There used to be an afternoon television show in Los Angeles called "Queen for a Day". Six different women would get up and tell Jack Bailey why they were the neediest and the studio audience would vote by applause meter. The winner was Queen for a Day. They used to drape her in a red velvet cape, put 24 long-stemmed roses in her arms and show close-ups of the tears streaming down her cheeks. They gave her a washing machine, a bedroom ensemble, new clothes, a facial, luggage and a night on the Sunset Strip.

The Sibyl at Delphi was another chick on a big trip. Once a year the Church would dress her in a bride's dress and take her to a cavern underground where she sat on a tripod and inhaled the fumes of laurel leaves. As God's bride she would go into a trance and utter the prophesies for the year which all the priests would write down. Unfortunately she committed the sin of falling in love with a mortal man and was expelled from the town. She lived the rest of her life with the goats on the mountain.

"I imagine she's a pretty nice girl but she doesn't have much to say."

This girl's back is bent until it is uncomfortable, her lungs are crowded so that she can't breathe well. Her head is tilted so that blood does not flow easily to her brain and she can't think well.

5

JOHN IVOR GOLDING

UROLOGICAL NURTUREMENT

JOHN IVOR GOLDING: *Welsh genius drop-out, lateral talking drifter. When in town resides at a men's hostel near Drury Lane. Lives off disability pension of less than £4 a week.*
One time: Photographer for Picture Post. Gunner in Singapore. Dancer in BBC chorus line.
Recently discovered by prodigy Chelsea film maker, Mr. Golding ("call me J.G.") is renowned for his unscheduled guest appearances at such social hot-spots as the Ritz – for the christening of Lord Harlech's grand-daughter – and George Harrison's home – where the new-cool pop-celebrities were not amused.

With all due respect to Christian Barnard and what he was trying to do with that dental surgeon, I have to say nature is a very sensitive thing. It's like its own species. I had quite a few years studying tropical medicine while I was overseas. I was, shall we say, a cheap labour BMO. You see, a lot of people have this monstrous idea about nature – oh, you've gone three years of age now, no more napkins to put on, no more Johnson's Baby Powder, now that's the weakness today.

I agree one must have a sense of porportion because of, shall we say, the Alsace Lorraine hetero principles, constitutional principles which a lot of people are conditioned by . . . another name for an Alsatian dog with a one track mind. Alsatian dogs are trained by the police and only the person that disciplines that dog in feeding him, hygiene, in every way, he only obeys the instructions of his handler. The very same thing, you see is this. It's not a matter of the neighbours that you get. A lot of people, the Inner Outer Mongolian people and some parts of Tibet but let me tell you I only noticed in one or two parts of Australia but I did notice it in South America mainly especially in Uruguay – a lot of this: the urological nurturement of those that were married similar to the French. The point is this you see. It's not a matter of mollycoddling. I know the majority of people turn round. You see, as Richard Marsh says, he's glad that he left the Wilson cabinet. This earth is three thousand million years old. Now the nearest thing you can go to, apart from the ice age elephant, is your cyclovan which was caught in a place I know very well, Port Louise, Mauritius, and three hundred and fifty thousand years old they are, you see, but nature is a very fragile thing and just because people say ooh, there's a lovely motor car, Bluebird on the salt lake flats, Malcolm Campbell's son, or shall we say, going to the moon. We've actually got the computers now, but look at these pressurised suits that people have to wear. There is a limit you see, for which, in the crevices and the catacombs of the cortex that you can accept even an aberration or its hallucinations of its own inspirations even if you have to have a . . . to some . . . to the violent one by all means but don't give it to the meek and mild. It's dangerous, my dear, don't give it to the meek and mild. Oh don't upset nature. I think that dentist that we had from Pretoria, you know the one I mean, Christian Barnard's friend – I think myself you see, it's a very delicate thing. He may have had bulbous disease of the heart, but at the same time, the thing is this; milk causes cancer in mice and . . .

I was fourteen at the time. Cut it up hijacked, if you like, but believe me, you had to be in bed at half past four in those days, and I suppose it takes quite a long time, I mean to say, for example: I was challenged a couple of months ago when we were doing a film. A friend of Robin Day's happened to be in the Chiswick Town Hall when I was in those House of Lords robes. You know, the Coronation Gown. And he said "I think you'd be first class on the Panorama, with Harold James Wilson." And I said: "I remember him well, he was just like a boy scout." Yes, I remember him and Griffiths from Llanelly. A yes man, His grandfather was a workhouse superintendent in Huddersfield. Allright I said, I think I can go a bit better with my current affairs than he can.

Lord Harlech asked me what I had in mind – I said automatically, it's there automatically. In other words, we're trying to get a pari passu with what we had on the old Sunday shows. In other words, for sixty minutes it was vibrating. Oh yes, it was vibrating. It really gives that adrenaline, that bromide effect, that metatone, that europhosphate. You have to give a catatonic, shall I say a narcissistic religious scene, you see, because it's a Sunday show so you've got to throw all that in to please the geriatrics. In other words, the calvinists, the Methodists, them of all denominations you see, you've got something, believe me, that is why we had it as I mentioned to you in the Inner Region Formation and when we had the BBC Come Dancing, the doors used to clash open and the cameras, just like South Pacific, were going and then the chandeliers coming down la di la, and then of course you're all dressed up and you have this sort of scintillation with the music which gets everybody going. Of all ages, everybody in tails, all the girls are in crinoline dresses and the point is this, that it used to take me like the National Anthem. It can make one very agile. You understand, it really gives a better agility than the Spanish dancers that you see in the Spanish restaurants, or should I say what you see in Barcelona on the Costa Brava for tourists. I mean to say when you've actually been to these places, when you're actually with a compere like Allan Williams, and the main three taking on the South Constituency from Callaghan, very well known, and they've all been out to Australia by the way, J.G. Wynn Jones, Wilfred Wolner, the insurance broker, that's Lady Plymouth's last husband, and of course Cliff Morgan.

We used to have a mascot, she was sweet 16 Angelina, and was always dancing on the village green, when the boys come out you can hear them shout, poor little Angelina, but the point is this, that you then open out with the Romancy marches or something like that, and the main point is this, the leaders you can take to satisfy the Radio doctor, now chairman of BBC, Dr. Charles.

THOSE FABULOUS FREAK BROTHERS IN PASSIONS & PARANOID

LEE....

Once upon a time, Lee was drafted to Korea and like most soldiers, was killed in action. He was shipped back home to California where a kindly old buddy gave him a hallucinogenic kiss of life. He was re-born as one of Sgt. Pepper's Band, joining Lucy and a million others who, in that sparkling summer of 1967, overflowed into public parks, glossy magazines and each other's arms.

Towards the end of 1967, he left California for India, where the Brothers of Eternal Love had told him he would find his guru.

"In Hong Kong I bought some ginseng root, the purest thing in the world. It is very rare. Eaten over a period of 21 days it is like taking acid, only a body purifier as well. It glows in the night. The guy in the shop didn't think I had enough money for it. I went next door, which looked like it hadn't had no customers for about 20 years. They had it for 250 dollars. I went to the bank, and when I got back to the store, the whole family was waiting to see me buy the stuff. It was in a tin box. Inside the tin box was another old, wooden one, and inside that were about thirty long sticks. When I opened the box in Calcutta, everyone in the hotel wanted some. You know: "I got a sick mother," and all that. Next thing I knew I was down to one piece. When I got to Katmandu I had to camp outside the town. There was a Danish photographer there taking pictures, so I showed him my ginseng root and Indian statue I had. I left the box open when I went to show him around the camp and when I got back, the kids had broken the root up into little pieces and passed it round. It blew my mind. All gone, and I didn't get to eat a single piece."

In Katmandu, Lee spent his days in the Blue Tibetan restaurant, playing his records, stoned out of his mind on Government hashish, and paying his friends' bills. His attempt to start a commune ended when he was put on a bus and dumped at the Indian border.

"The Times" 12 December 1967

"Katmandu — a hippy camp at Dhulikhel, a mountain village 19 miles from here on the Katmandu-Tibet Highway, has been disbanded by the Nepal police. They are said to have deported the camp leader and warned others to leave the country soon. The camp was to have become an international temple for the hippie cult. It had been decorated with photographs of King Mahendra and Queen Sita, but these proved of no avail against police action."

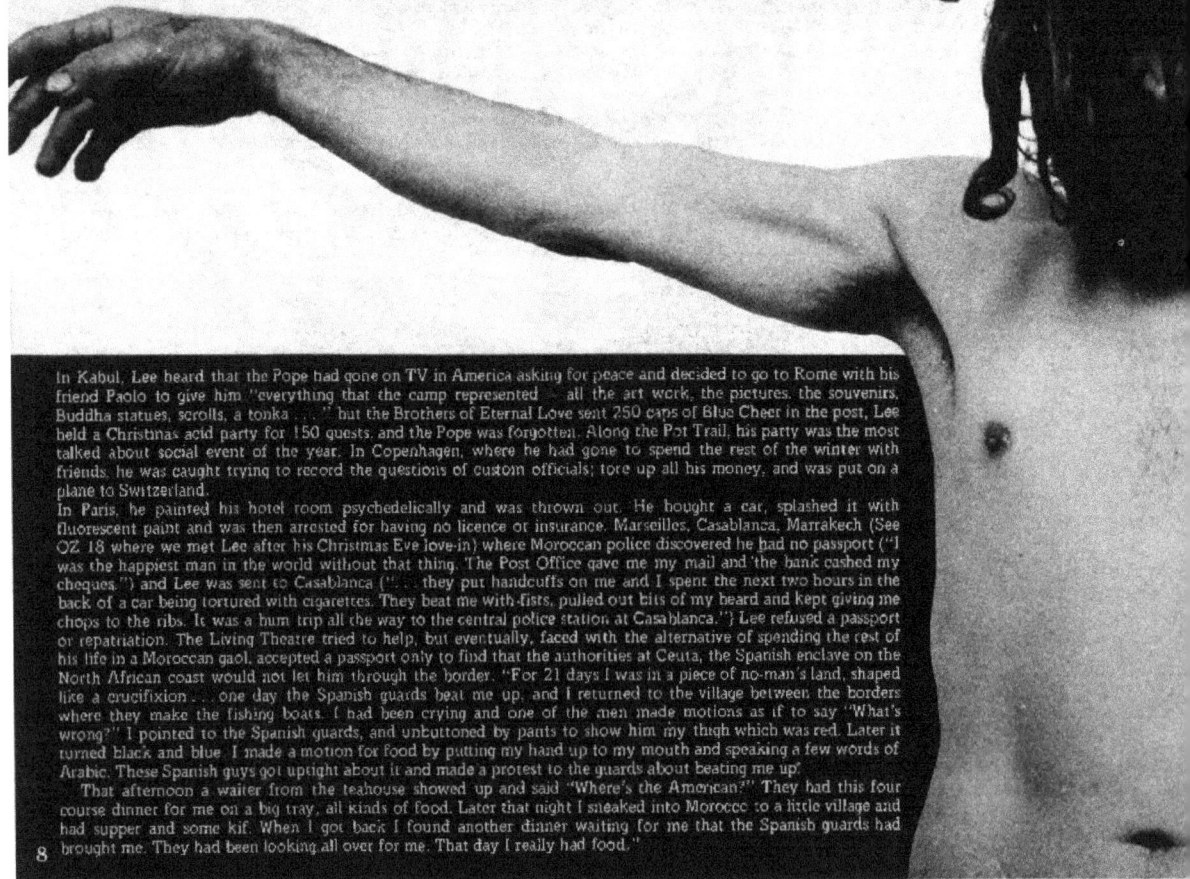

In Kabul, Lee heard that the Pope had gone on TV in America asking for peace and decided to go to Rome with his friend Paolo to give him "everything that the camp represented — all the art work, the pictures, the souvenirs, Buddha statues, scrolls, a tonka . . ." but the Brothers of Eternal Love sent 250 caps of Blue Cheer in the post, Lee held a Christmas acid party for 150 guests, and the Pope was forgotten. Along the Pot Trail, his party was the most talked about social event of the year. In Copenhagen, where he had gone to spend the rest of the winter with friends, he was caught trying to record the questions of custom officials; tore up all his money, and was put on a plane to Switzerland.

In Paris, he painted his hotel room psychedelically and was thrown out. He bought a car, splashed it with fluorescent paint and was then arrested for having no licence or insurance. Marseilles, Casablanca, Marrakech (See OZ 18 where we met Lee after his Christmas Eve love-in) where Moroccan police discovered he had no passport ("I was the happiest man in the world without that thing. The Post Office gave me my mail and the bank cashed my cheques.") and Lee was sent to Casablanca (". . . they put handcuffs on me and I spent the next two hours in the back of a car being tortured with cigarettes. They beat me with fists, pulled out bits of my beard and kept giving me chops to the ribs. It was a bum trip all the way to the central police station at Casablanca.") Lee refused a passport or repatriation. The Living Theatre tried to help, but eventually, faced with the alternative of spending the rest of his life in a Moroccan gaol, accepted a passport only to find that the authorities at Ceuta, the Spanish enclave on the North African coast would not let him through the border. "For 21 days I was in a piece of no-man's land, shaped like a crucifixion . . . one day the Spanish guards beat me up, and I returned to the village between the borders where they make the fishing boats. I had been crying and one of the men made motions as if to say "What's wrong?" I pointed to the Spanish guards, and unbuttoned by pants to show him my thigh which was red. Later it turned black and blue. I made a motion for food by putting my hand up to my mouth and speaking a few words of Arabic. These Spanish guys got uptight about it and made a protest to the guards about beating me up.'

That afternoon a waiter from the teahouse showed up and said "Where's the American?" They had this four course dinner for me on a big tray, all kinds of food. Later that night I sneaked into Morocco to a little village and had supper and some kif. When I got back I found another dinner waiting for me that the Spanish guards had brought me. They had been looking all over for me. That day I really had food."

8

IN THE SKY WITH DIAMONDS

Back in Paris, he managed to get a room for one night by wrapping his head up in a towel and pretending to be ill, but otherwise found himself relegated to gutters and suburban churchyards. London, since his arrival three months ago, he has found more sympathetic. He was told not to play his record player in Hyde Park, was photographed at a window of the 144 Picadilly's squat-in as a 'defiant hippie, symbolising total rejection of society', and he found the vibrations at the Isle of Wight 'outasight'. "There's no way I can express my feeling for what I seen out there. It really is a message, a spiritual message."

But not everyone received it: October '69:

"A very good friend from the other side of the Grove came over with his sitar, and that was when we were just coming on acid. And that guy was really outasight on his Indian sitar. Anyway all day long it was just beautiful, just fantastic vibes and about three o'clock that morning, they came in. They had come over that afternoon, looking for a man for questioning about some deal or other. I let him in. He didn't look like no policeman. I thought he was an insurance salesman. He came in and after he got inside he said he was a policeman. I sat there talking for a minute to him. I asked him if he went to church on Sunday, I said looks like you eat good. He was getting fat, you know, that downhill drag they get from over-using their whatever. We were playing a game to get the house organised. We were thinking of games we could play in the room to keep the kids that come there open-minded. Like if they got something to trip on in the room with their music, like fish. A tank of fish. Kitty cats, Doggies. Real trips. Keeps them going in the right direction, towards nature. I found a fish tank upstairs and I'm going to move it down. I was talking to the girls about moving it down today. I've got it all ready. Soon as I get this motor going to keep the water warm and filtered. And we decided to put coloured glass in the windows. We already had the guy over. He looked at it. Gonna cut the glass and put it all in. Red glass, blue, green. But I think everyone is down on anything being done on this house. I ordered this money specially from the states just to do all these things. To make it a nice trip room.

Well, that morning, I went to the bathroom, the kids remained in my cubby hole next door to the bathroom. And while I was in the bathroom, I heard this voice saying as I was sitting there, all you people out! In that real old British accent, and I knew something was up. I looked out the door and I seen these three or four cops right inside the big room but still right at the doorway. I jumped inside my little closet, shut the door and locked it. Blew the

candles out and said the fuzz is here busting us. Then we heard all this rumble outside the door, somebody smashing something. Then voices and some moaning and groaning. In the panic and excitement, we opened the window, and there was the drainpipe. I slid down it, hit bottom and said, "Come on, Man, follow me, it's groovy." I cut out the front way. As I made it out through the bushes, and was just making my turn to split down the road, I heard this cop say, "There goes one down the road. Get him," and I put on extra speed, it was like putting myself in overdrive. Completely man. Like I was on the racetrack of the world. About three thousand yards later, I ducked inside of an alley way going in between two buildings. I lay down under some stairs there and lay panting like mad until I could catch my breath. As I got up from resting, I seen them put somebody in the paddy wagon. They had several police cars and I think two of those big vans, those ice cream wagons. Black ice cream wagons. What's that cat's name who makes all those busts. It was in a cartoon in that paper Black Dwarf. Well, he struck again last night. That motherfucker right there in that cartoon strikes again. What's his name. Attention all heads in this area. Whoever reads this magazine, be on the look-out for P.C. Frank and that motherfucking ice cream wagon with the red light on the top and the blue uniforms. Don't let them close your mind. Please don't let 'em close your mind. Keep an open mind. All things pass. Outasight, outasight, outasight. I can't win. I can't lose. I got nothing to lose. One to me is fame and shame. One to me is pleasure and pain. One to me is lose or gain. They're all the same says my brain. The Tao says that, or words to that effect."

The following night, Lee received 100 dollars from an American friend and Lee spent it all on an acid party. He mixed it with punch and turned on fellow squatters and forty guests. Bongos, flutes, drums, a sitar, plenty of food, and with everyone tripping beautifully, the arrival of twenty fuzz seemed a matter of little importance. Heads were lined up against walls, shaken down, hash was confiscated, roaches collected, but surprisingly no arrests were made. "We was all laughing. The music still going and no one was getting paranoic. Only them cops. Anyhow, I don't know how, but they just left those roaches and walked out. It was just outasight. The magic of acid and they just didn't know what to do. Fantastic." Lee was jubilant, but the following afternoon they got him. At the moment, he is in Brixton gaol, awaiting trial on two charges of resisting arrest, and possession. Bail was refused.

"I don't know. Why? A guy just wants to practice his religion, just wants to do his things, man. All I want to do is smoke, stay stoned, and just groove. Why is it so hard for a man to breathe . . . this damp air in England."

9

A Very SPECIAL Freak

This is a very special Freak. It is the edited result of a series of taped interviews with a young man who works in a London travel office.

Surprisingly as it may seem, I am not completely opposed to the capers of today's young. I'm 26 years old in December and that means I collect on an insurance policy which my father took out for me when I was five. With the £1,000 I intend making some sort of business investment. Perhaps I'll buy some growth stock or put some money into a small business. You can't do much with a £1,000, as you know, so I need to treble it at least. I'm lucky in that my wife is completely behind me in this, she thinks the risk is worth it. While we're young, why not take a gamble — that's our attitude.

People are entitled to conduct their lives in whatever fashion they like. If they want to grow their hair long, or wear ridiculous clothes, let them. If they want to be unwashed and filthy and unhealthy, I'm not going to stand in their way. If they want to sleep together in deserted premises in sleeping bags, that's their problem. These are questions of personal taste and hygiene which each of us has to decide, for personal taste and hygiene which each of us has to decide for ourselves.

And if we are brought up correctly we should act normally as most of us do.

But what irritates me is the fact that the small minority of young people who freak out don't work. Instead, they prefer to live off the State; to sponge off people like me who work and pay taxes. This is extremely unjust and I wish the Government would do everything to stop hippies from bleeding the rest of us. I hope I'm not sounding like a Fascist or anything. I don't want everyone rounded up and put into work gangs. But if young drop-outs were encouraged into industry they would soon realise that there is another, worthwhile existence. It's nothing to be ashamed of to be a wage earner. In fact, it is ennobling to work during the day and return home at night to be a sort of father and protector in the home. This is

the principle on which our civilisation is founded.

What would happen to my life if I suddenly decided to stop work. First of all my wife would almost certainly leave me. She wouldn't have any time for a man who wasn't prepared to pull his weight. (And I wouldn't blame her!) Secondly, my family would ostracise me, and I can hardly think of anything more devastating than losing the respect of my close relatives by becoming a sponger. Thirdly, I would feel decadent. I would ask myself why aren't I giving all my energy to helping Britain to grow strong? I would be swamped with guilt because I feel it is everyone's duty to help preserve Western civilisation. The alternative is handing over our civilisation to the communists.

And lastly, without working I would lose my dignity and the need to maintain a private and public standard of behaviour which enables me to be respected by my relatives and friends and provides the firm foundation of my marriage. I would find it intolerable to throw off my dignity and allow my own petty individualism to run wild. If we all did that, our country would be in the hands of the anarchists.

I can't for the life of me see why these youngsters don't want to settle down and get a decent job like the rest of us. There would be far less tension in our society if they conformed and this is surely in the best interests of law and order. And I am concerned about those who have practically made a religion out of their drop-out existence. You hear them worshipping Love and Peace as if we could all have it for nothing. It's not as easy as that — you have to work for it.

I'm working for Love and Peace at my office every day of the week. I don't get in anybody's way and I don't break any rules or regulations. And my wife and I are in love like any other young married couples. We may not be as madly in love as we were when we first got married, of course, but we respect each other and that's what counts.

We live in Blackheath on a council estate and we

try to live in peace particularly with the neighbours. To this end, we try never to mix with them; I always think it's best to keep out the hair of your neighbours otherwise you'ry just asking for trouble. So we keep our own counsel and don't bother anybody around us. What more can you ask a man to do? I'm loving — I'm giving peace a chance!

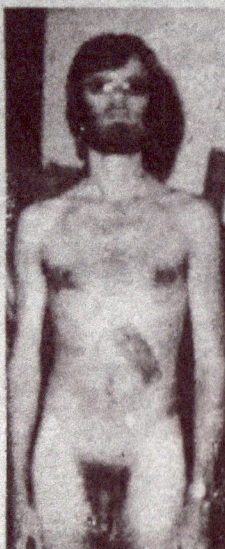

Absence makes the Peter Fonda.

DON'T WORRY — BE HAPPY.

A VERY ABBREVIATED DIRECTORY OF INTER-NATIONAL FREAKS — not all of them beautiful.

USA: Tuli Kupferberg, Emmett Grogan, Frank Zappa, Abbie Hoffman, Paul Krassner, John Wilcock, Valerie Solanas, Louis Abolafia, The Living Theatre, Little Richard, Ken Kesey, Reverend Jefferson Fuck Poland, Jerry Rubin, Playmate of the Month.

EUROPE: Simon Vinkenoog, Robert Jasper Grootveld, Jean-Jacques Lebel, Danny Cohn-Bendit, Fritz Teufel.

AUSTRALIA: Mad Mel, Bea Miles, Rosaleen Norton, Richard O'Sullivan, Francis James, Barry Humphries, Zara Holt.

UK: Michael Chapman, Jimmy Saville, Arthur Brown, Jack Henry Moore, Robin Farquarson, Mick Lesser, Simon Tugwell, Wendy Sharkey, Spike Milligan, Hoppy & Suzy, Wild Child, Muzz Murray, Edward Heath.

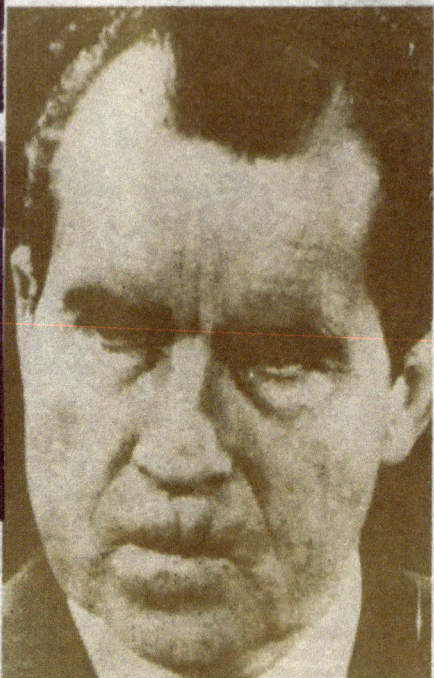

10

Anthony Haden-Guest

Bruce's Paradise

Bruce is a familiar figure around Chelsea, and has been for several years. He is thin, with a shortish beard, and a pre-occupied manner, and he holds his right arm rigidly above his head at almost all times. This is an 'Indian Thaumaturgical Exercise' which he learnt from a devotee of Gurdjieff (mystical author of ALL AND EVERYTHING) and has practiced since the age of 22. He is now 36.

Bruce gets £7 a week unemployment benefit, which he supplements by begging small loans. His clothing is nondescript, though right now he is wearing a well-cut jacket, a present from his father, who is an established painter. Bruce also used to be a professional painter, and was doing well . . . a delicate realist, with a spidery line. Nothing surreal or bizarre in either imagery or treatment.

His writing too is delicate rather than surreal. He handed me this book rather diffidently. "It's all I've got to play with" he said. The book is a Lion Brand exercise book, with a Royal Blue cover, and ruled white pages, much thumbed. Bruce's handwriting is small, educated — he went to a public school — but nonetheless the book is difficult to read because it is written both in pencil, now smudged to near illegibility, and various colours of biro. Also a great deal is altered and crossed out, so that sentences and even words do not invariably finish.

Some extracts of the book follow. I have done very little to the text. Obviously I have selected what seems (to me) the best, and where there has been a great deal of rewriting, crossing-out, and re-crossing-out, a certain amount of editing has been necessary. Apart from that, all I can say is that I wouldn't mind having written it myself.

The title-page is very heavily scored with crossings-out. It did read 'Heaven' adding a Battersea address. This has been crossed out, and now large blue capitals say PARADISE.

I went into a tavern in Battersea, began
To practice the piano when the
Earth-Being had agreed. After approx three five six five minutes
The E-B. asked me to leave
He told me that he preferred television. I went out, of course, I never pick quarrels with E-Bs.

Signed on. No job. Collected my
postal draft. My unemployment benefit? doesn't amount to enough for lunch every day
Oh, dear. Charity
I stopped to give a lady
Suffering from cancer of the bones my
remaining sixpence and my

film
and music address

There are several little Scars on my r.h. (right hand) How on
earth did they appear?

Heard about an Irish play on the wireless. I'll enquire.

Wrong Connections
I told the Earth-Beings around me as I walked on Earth
Streets "I don't own you. Nor do I own
Your possessions. Also I don't wish
to bother you.
I never drink anything containing alcohol and I never smoke
My health has been appalling.

I am wearing my dark brown or
plain chocolate-coloured trousers, my
brown socks, my brown shoes, my pale-
olive-green and white shirt and my Eagle
jacket . . . I eat and drink regularly and I sleep well. I handle
and play with my possessions,

all of which
I keep just beyond my bed, mercifully and carefully

I avoid Romance completely
My health has been appalling
I must buy a laurel garland
For my head.

I went to the V & A & A Museum where I bought a strawberry milkshake, consumed it? at my leisure, decided that it would be an excellent idea if Princess Margaret
were to play one or two songs on an harpsichord
(or a piano)
and the Earl of Snowdon and to sing with
Michelmore . . . and also if possible
(Prince) Charles (with his guitar) would become members
of my immense group, The Spiders

To be sung . . . Undesirable to the tune of Unforgettable

A jam sandwich and a plate of soup

"I do music every day. I do play the piano every day" explains Bruce *"In the*

Western mode, I play anything, like Liberace" (laughs) "No, I never improvise. I think to improvise one must have quite a knowledge . . . Although I can play a Classical tune, I have to play a popular tune simply because I haven't got as much as one platonic girlfriend. The thing is that popular music appeals to girls" (Appealingly) "Doesn't it?" And Bruce breaks, with unexpected control and harmony, into popular song.*

My I.T.E.
More Word-Jewels
"Any money, no?" Denis asked me,
"No" I replied "I'm completely
'broke'" (to use the slang word Linda
Christian once used in a television film)
I've been more or less broke for the last
fifteen years because I've never
aquired work which paid enough
My last girl friend killed herself because
I wasn't Cliff Richard
I've had a difficult time

getting into pop show business at my age

Bought Denis's shopping, as usual.
He nearly always gives me breakfast and supper. I am grateful, He works
with Mr Parle. In the evenings he studies his pile of possible film scripts (Aldous Huxley, Graham Greene, Christopher Isherwood, Scott Fitz
gerald and other writers). Unfortunately
the film camera which Nell Dunn, Sir Philip Dunn's daughter, lent me was damaged. Because I haven't been
able to sell my drawings of Harmless
Machinery (including me using Harmless Machinery and Self Portraits)
I haven't been able to buy another. Now
Denis is looking out of his window.

(Denis, says Bruce, is Irish, and they share a room in a boarding house in Battersea. This boarding house is to be the subject of a documentary which, Bruce thinks, he will shortly be making with the Earl of Snowdon and Cliff Michelmore. "Yes . . . Yes" he says — there is an element of repetition in conversation, which is also very self-effacing, almost apologetic. "Yes . . . I suppose one Idea I've got is . . . is to ask Princess Margaret who I saw playing the piano . . . playing the piano . . . I'd like her to play the piano in my documentary".

Anyway, the reason that Bruce is on the streets so much is to leave some room for Denis . . . "Talking about painting, well, I can't paint there . . . Because it gets in Denis's way. He needs the chance to (A) study Aldous Huxley and (B) practice his singing. He'll probably sing the tunes I select for him. He doesn't have a platonic girl friend either. I want to suggest that this documentary should get him and me into Show Business. The fact is that I want to get into Show Business to film Aldous Huxley novels, with a view to doing a film this Summer. Yes, something like EYELESS IN GAZA . . . "Does Bruce think

11

there is something extra special about Huxley? "No. The fact is I do not. He seems as good a person as any. He does write novels..."

And what incidentally of Bruce's parents..."I think they are a little disappointed... I think that they are wondering how it is that I can't afford a FRAML... a, a frame for my drawings of Tame Machinery... I enjoy doing drawings of Tame Machinery... The sort of machinery that appears in SCIENTIFIC AMERICAN. I used to buy one or two SCIENTIFIC AMERICANS but then I ran out of food and drink... I mean by tame, machinery that isn't war machinery. I wouldn't draw war machinery, not me... Personally I am a preacher of peace" (apologetically) "Personally I don't rate myself with his paintings" Who? "Leonardo da Vinci... I don't like his paintings of war machinery. I don't suppose he did." (Laughs) "It must be a joke... I saw Yoko Ono walk into Paul McCartney's office. At any rate" (appealingly) "It's better than Hiroshima..."

"Will you ever make it, do you think?" Denis asked me. If the Earl of Snowdon accepts this script that could be the "start of something big" for me in the film line. I may get film and recording offers.

(The Snowdons again. Curiously enough, Bruce is only one acquaintance who fantasises about the Snowdons. The Snowdons are in this not unlike the Kennedys. The brighter an image, the more intense (and sometimes macabre) the feedback).

My I.T.E. (My Earth life-aim) I'm holding my right arm up in The Air until in this or another ?re-incarnation

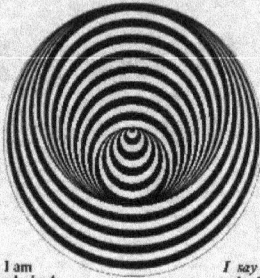

I am admired by nine hundred million young girls that is, of course an Earth - aim, but I keep it in mind, although apart from my main quest (Good Health)

Several of Bruce's pre-occupations occur in this passage. The I.T.E. are Indian Thaumaturgical Exercises. Bruce holds his arm in the air. If he stands still, he may, instead, outstretch his foot... "It's supposed to keep up the vibrations" he explains. He has been doing these exercises since he was 23! "I was given it as an exercise by one of M. Gurdjieff's followers and friends... Madam Loubchansky... She suggested it as a remedy for Philosophic Confusion. In the police they call it a Skyhook. It does heal people. It has cured me of my stomach-ache" Is Bruce sicker than other people? Yes, he says, than asks, with alarm "I haven't said anything obscene, have I?".

I say No. "An Earth-Aim of mine" he says "Is to hold my arm up until I am admired by nine hundred million girls". Does he want to go to bed with them? "No. My health has been appalling. Nice of you to ask me". Bruce divides activity with the other sex rigorously enough, with Love, Romance, and Sex. Sex is Sex, Love is Platonic, and Romance is betwixt and between. Bruce does not have a Platonic girlfriend. We would be very happy if some girls, as many as possible (The magic number seems to be nine hundred million) could write platonic love-notes to Bruce c/o OZ.

I gave the match-man in Brompton Road what remained of the shilling Tim had given me. I passed a street violinist and a second match-man but I had no money left..., I went to Luba's Bistrot in Yeoman's Row, just the road where Luba gave me a beautiful soup (soup of the day – beautiful soup) when I had finished my soup I went next door to Richard Temple's galleries where I spoke to one of his assistants "Would it be all right for the Earl of Snowdon to visit these galleries?" "Yes, if he is interested in it" "I suppose that one might install an harpsichord (temporarily)"

is alive and well...

I AGREE WITH YOUR TACTICS BUT I DON'T KNOW ABOUT YOUR GOALS

A preview chapter from a soon-to-be-published but as-yet-untitled book by Jerry Rubin — veretan Berkeley activist, yippie founder and the running mate of one-time Presidential candidate Eldridge Cleaver.

People who say, "I agree with your goals. I don't like your tactics" are full of horseshit. The goals are always excuses — it's the tactics that are critical. The means of the revolution are the revolution. If we had to decide beforehand what our goals were, we'd be arguing about the future society for the next 1000 years, but we can all agree what to do. Do. Do. Do. The movement gets its greatest unity around tactics. We come to action with different experiences, and through collective action we grow together and become a movement.

I never knew what the issues were at demonstrations. They were all decided by leaders who went to boring meetings to debate each other for hours. What we wanted from those meetings were demands that the establishment could never satisfy. If they satisfied our demands, we lost. The purpose of demonstrations is confrontation, the demands are secondary. What makes the demands radical is the fact that the Establishment would not satisfy them. Just in case, we should always have a supplementary set of demands tacked on to the original. "Amnesty" is always good, because amnesty takes away the power of the power structure to punish. That's a hard one for them to swallow.

Remember those early civil rights demonstrations? The demands actually were jobs for black people in hotels and auto showrooms. The people picketing and sitting-in were not the people who wanted the jobs; in fact, we spent our lives avoiding such jobs. We were fighting for demands which we didn't even believe in. It was the means that were important: the picket line, the sit-in, the rally, the demonstration. If the power structure were smart, it would have satisfied all our demands without a fight. But that's what makes power structures power structures, they can't do that.

We liberate ourselves by fighting for what we believe in. The job of good leadership is to put forth demands which won't be satisfied, but which are reasonable enough to get a lot of people, especially the liberals, on our side. We scream furiously when our demands are not met, as if we had expected them to be in the first place. We know we're actors and we must believe in our act.

Why do people go to long meetings debating for hours what the demands of a demonstration will be and what will be the specific words on a leaflet? None of those things are important. Nobody reads leaflets. What's important is the theatre. Scripts are for shit. Ours is a do-it-yourself revolution.

Revolution is not the satisfaction of a "program." Revolution is the arrival of new classes and generations on to the stage of history through struggle, the changing of people from spectators to actors. As Castro puts it, "The goal of the Cuban revolution is to turn every individual into a legislator." *Representative* democracy is the enemy. The goal is each-man-his-own-revolution. We do not want concessions from our leaders: we want to run our own lives. We achieve the revolution by *making* it.

We free ourselves by first realizing how unfree we are. You only find out how unfree you are when you start fighting for your freedom by breaking rules. We have as much freedom as we don't fight for. The dilemma is most people in America *think* they are *free* because they can't even imagine freedom. They think reading lines verbatim from a pre-written script is freedom. Stop reading the lines as they're written; you'll get fired and find out how free you are.

Vietnam has been the best thing that has happened to America in a long time. Vietnam has demonstrated emotionally to the American people how little control they have over their own government. In fighting to end the war the American people have begun to achieve their own liberation. The longer the war continues, the greater freedom we will achieve fighting to end it.

Truth emerges in crisis, and Vietnam is America's truth. We can understand America by looking at Vietnam where it all comes clear as a crisis. The goal of the revolution is to create crisis.

The only way to know if your tactics are successful is to see how many people you alienate. In America, it is normal daily life which is the enemy, and we've got to alienate people by shaking up their daily lives. If you don't alienate people, you're not reaching them. Ineffective protest is protest which gains no one's attention, makes no one unhappy, alienates nobody. Effective protest gets people upset — therefore it's usually illegal.

America puts people in prison through carefully defined roles. We are students and teachers, workers and managers, bureaucrats, lawyers, judges. Everybody is defined by his role and told how to act. The freest people in the country are the "not-students." We are known by what we are *not*! That should be everybody's goal, to be known by what he is *not*.

How do you know what a man's role is? By his clothes. Want to be a lawyer? Get yourself a blue suit, a couple of yellow legal pads, a brief case, a client and go to court next week and identify yourself as a lawyer. Nobody will ask for your diploma; print your own. All you need to do any job in America is the clothes. If you get the clothes, you're the job.

As a transitional stage towards communism, the yippies demand that everybody changes his job every year. Everybody should do what everybody else does in society so we can all understand and feel the experiences of other people.

Everybody should drive a cab, run an elevator, work on a newspaper, grow food. The world has gone full circle from non-specialization to industrialization and specialization, to computerization and back to non-specialization. Communism ushers in the universal, renaissance man. The expert and specialist will be a museum piece.

The yippies try to liberate people by getting them to change their clothes. We relate to other people through their clothes. A judge puts on black robes and all of a sudden everyone starts treating him like a god. He takes off his robes and he's just like any other schmuck on the street.

The suit and tie is the essence of the class society. Ties will be illegal in our communist society. The Marx Brothers are our leaders as they go into restaurants cutting people's ties. The be-in represents the goal of our revolution — the be-in is a costume ball. Everybody comes as ballplayers, queens, generals, pirates. We're trying out different lives and fantasies.

The purpose of the revolution is to create theatre-in-the-streets. You are the stage. You are the actor. Everything is for real. There is no audience. The goal is to turn on everybody who can be turned on and turn off everybody who cannot be turned on. Theatre has no rules, forms, structures, standards, traditions — it is pure, natural energy, impulse, anarchy. The revolutionary's best impulse is his first impulse. Do it! Worry about it, analyse it later.

The yippies declare war on Hollywood and Broadway. We are out to put them out of business. Theatre belongs on the streets. America tries to get people to feel artificial experiences, and purge their emotions through catharsis with television, movies and plays, so there is little emotion left for one in his daily life. We live our lives through John Wayne. The role of revolution is to break the stage, start a fire in the movie theatre and then start screaming, "Fire! Fire!" How can theatre compete with life in this era? How do you outdo Vietnam? The only way to match Vietnam is to bring Vietnam home. The theatrical producers of today are creating theatres of Vietnam on the college campuses of America.

When we first got the idea of Chicago, we went to hip theatre people to get them out of their auditoriums and into the streets. There was interest, but not enough. It was not the professional theatre people who created the Theatre of Chicago; it was the amateurs. The yippies feel knowledge can be dangerous, because knowledge forecloses possibilities. Experts are masters, and prisoners of previous forms. No real advances are made by experts. Our leaders are children and blind people. The revolution makes "expertise" a crime.

The Living Theatre came to Berkeley the same week the people had spent fighting the National Guard in the streets in a Theatre of Blood. Being pacifists, the Living Theatre thought this was the wrong way.

The Living Theatre liberates the audience and the auditorium as much as is physically possible within the medium of paying money to go to an auditorium with a regular starting and closing time. Actors merge themselves with the audience, eliminating the stage. "We're not allowed to smoke pot," one Living Theatre member screamed out, whereupon he was offered a joint from five different directions in the Berkeley audience. Another Living Theatre member shouted, "I can't take off my clothes!" All around him people started taking off their clothes. "I can't travel without a passport." That struck a lot of people in the room odd, because for some of us it's a crime to even cross a state line.

People were angry at the contradiction of revolution-in-the-auditorium — taking all our energy and putting it into a play in one place at one time for a price. The theatre medium is archaic. Shouting "freedom!" in a theatre is a contradiction in terms. The only role of theatre is to take people out of the theatre and into the streets. The role of the revolutionary theatre group is to make the revolution. The role of the revolutionary rock group is to make the revolution. The role of this book is to get you to make the revolution.

The newspaper editors of America in their annual conferences call on the "experts" to explain to them what their children are doing. They would never think of asking the criminals themselves to come to discuss their crimes. Although the panels are called "Conferences on Student Unrest", the editors call as participants people who spend their days in the library and their nights sleeping very soundly. Why don't they call those of us who are restless and can't sleep?

The College Editors can't get away with that because it would be too embarrassing for them to call on older people to explain what people their own age are doing. They usually have to invite a token yippie who brings all his friends. When you ask for one, you get 20.

We freaked out as soon as we arrived. The editors were carbon copies of each other. Is there a factory somewhere producing college editors? Their faces had the same tired, bureaucratic expressions. They talked as if they were talking to each other on the telephone. There they were, person to person in a fancy Washington D.C. Hotel, and they had talking-on-the-telephone personalities. They related to each other not as human beings, but as fellow professionals. They came from campuses that had been burning down all year, and the main question on their minds was: Should college newspapers editorialize on the Vietnam war or would it compromise journalistic integrity?

Just keeping our voices in a moderate tone in talking to these editors was a sell-out, I felt. It implied the discussion was "reasonable". Is the Vietnam war a difference between reasonable men? Do these editors think a dispute between a Southern redneck cop and a black slave is a disagreement between reasonable men?

Paul Krassner got so hysterical over their matter-of-factness that in the middle of one of their discussions he began to cry. "People are dying in Vietnam and you're talking like this", Paul kept sobbing. He was on acid at the time and the unconscious truth of the situation burst forth.

We woke up Saturday morning and dropped tabs of acid, ready for battle. What the editors did not know was how conspiratorial we yippies are. We had seized their conference completely and we were setting up a rigged debate for the afternoon: "Should the College Newspaper Editors Association Take a Stand on the War?" The editors had no idea that some people in suits, short hair and ties pretending to be college newspaper editors were members of the Washington Street Theatre group.

I went to the show myself not knowing who were the editors and who were the actors. I'd be able to figure it out, I thought.

But everybody sounded like an actor. I couldn't believe anybody was a real editor. It was the most insane discussion I'd ever heard: Should we take a stand standing up? Sitting down? On the toilet? For negotiations? For the war? Against the war? They were all playing at being editors. Who was real and who was unreal? I knew only 15 of the 150 people in the room were actors, but I couldn't tell who.

Finally the vote was ready to be taken. The lights suddenly went off. Flashed across the wall were scenes of burning Vietnamese babies, torture scenes, napalm. The room was full of hysterical screams. It was a torture chamber. Everybody started screaming. "Stop it! Stop it! Stop it!"

The film stopped and a voice came over a bullhorn: "This is Sgt. Haggerty of the District Washington Police. We arrested the man who put on this film and we have charged him with obscenity. Everyone in this hall is under arrest for conspiracy to watch obscene movies. Stay where you are. Please do not resist arrest."

The editors started fleeing the room. They thought so little of their country that they believed immediately that they were going to be arrested en masse for seeing a film. They believe they live in a Nazi country.

A crewcut husky guy in a suit-and-tie jumped on top of a chair, identified himself as editor from Notre Dame, and yelled at the top of his lungs: "I've just come back from Vietnam. I've seen my brothers dying. We've got to stop this killing. The men in the White House are sending us all to die for nothing. I'm a college editor and you're a college editor. We have power. Are we brave? Can we be brave?"

Is this guy real? Or part of the Washington theatre group? I didn't know. But finally it struck me — it made no difference. Everything was real and unreal.

The editors finally realized they had been the subjects of a huge dose of Reality Theatre. They were furious that their "democratic dialogue" had been disrupted. They were ready to expel the chairman of the afternoon session who had conspired with the yippies to put on the show. They went through a torturous meeting, screaming and yelling at each other. Through the meeting they realized they had learned something about themselves that day. People started talking to one another off the telephone. It was an emotional breakthrough.

Senator Eugene McCarthy was coming in two hours to a press conference for the editors. They were going to run a real "Meet the Press" show, the way their Big Daddies do it. They started going around to us, begging us not to disrupt it.

I thought to myself: Bullshit. The press conference is free theatre to be used by anybody who can make the best use of it. The purpose of a press conference is to make news. News is free. Why assume that the only person who can make news is the presidential candidates who answers questions? McCarthy is just an actor, and we're all actors. There is no stage.

Theatre uses whatever props it needs to most dramatically make its point. The most effective theatre breaks rules, throwing people into a new situation without guides to behaviour. It wouldn't be effective just asking McCarthy a question. McCarthy could co-opt any question. Anyway, what offends us most is not McCarthy's content, but his style. The most oppressive thing about it is the format of the press conference treating the candidate as an authority.

It was a few minutes before McCarthy was due to arrive and I had no props and no ideas. I was on acid and I stood to the side jogging like a boxer, working up enough confidence to act out of the roles that everybody else would be respecting. When you break a set theatre like a press conference or a classroom, you got to have a lot of confidence in yourself because everybody's going to be looking at you as if you're crazy. You got to be crazy.

Somebody was holding a newspaper and I saw the heading: JAIL-BREAK IN HUE, 2000 VIET CONG FREE. I was delirious! 2000 people who were in jail a few hours ago were now free! McCarthy says he's against the war, doesn't he? For what other reason could he be against the war except to see the Viet Cong free?

McCarthy came in just as I heard he was: distant, distinguished, reserved, unemotional. He had no Secret Service protection. Didn't the word reach him that the crazies had infiltrated the college editors' conference?

He finished his 15 minute speech and was getting ready to answer questions, when I started running towards him.

I jumped on the stage, put my arm around him, and started screaming, "People are free, Gene. Gene, people are free. Aren't you happy? Isn't that great!" The television cameras were buzzing away. My arm was around his shoulder. I'd intended to kiss him — really I did —

but it just didn't work out because he was so cold. I felt like an unrequited lover, my emotion unreturned. McCarthy actually tried to ignore me, continuing the press conference as if I weren't there.

Within ten seconds there were five more yippies and diggers on all fours around his feet, barking like little animals. The editors went out of their minds. The organizers of the conference tried to plead with us reasonably to move away, but it didn't work. We were delirious that human beings were free in Vietnam, and we wanted to celebrate, not have some boring press conference.

Gene was surrounded by the Marx Brothers. We tried to unnerve him psychologically, making faces at his every answer, booing and cheering things he said. But he went on — trying to be the master defuser of crisis.

We heard an Indian drum in the background. Dum-dum-dum. People were carrying a coffin towards us. As they got closer and closer, I saw McCarthy get edgier and edgier. "Don't worry, Gene," I said. But he was trying to act as if I didn't exist. The coffin-carriers reached McCarthy and emptied the coffin upside down. Hundreds of McCarthy buttons came flying out wrapped in an American flag. The coffin read: "Electoral Politics". At this point McCarthy just turned away, left the stage and cut the press conference short.

The college editors started moving towards me, hungry for blood. They were seething with an emotion that I'd never seen them express over the war in Vietnam. Their professional reputations had been spoiled. They went beserk. "What are you so angry about?" I screamed. "McCarthy paid us to do this. His campaign is dull, dull, dull. It's the best thing that's happened to his campaign. Finally he's going to make national television. Don't worry. McCarthy's not pissed at you. He's happy!"

"If this is your revolution, Rubin, you can have it," one editor said. I didn't know he was that interested in the revolution in the first place. "If this is your newspaper business, you can have it," I replied.

Being an ex-reporter I felt self-righteous: "We gave you a news story and you're angry. What kind of reporters are you? Fuck you. What is this shit, objective journalism? What are you trying to do, be reporters like your daddies? These press conference formats are dead!"

I was furious at these editors because I finally realized their game: they want to be popular. "Go home and watch television!" I screamed, "you're corpses. TV is putting you all out of business. Hah, hah. TV is making you useless!"

The editors just couldn't keep the niggers out of their conferences — or their newspapers — no matter how hard they tried.

Good theatre is the unexpected. Everybody always expects radicals to march in a circle, carrying picket signs and shouting slogans. Radicals have got to put away their picket signs and use their imagination.

Bobby Kennedy was coming to San Francisco to speak at a $500 a plate dinner for the Big Democrats. I can never understand those $500 and $1000 dinners. Are some people that hungry? What do these Democrats do? — starve themselves for weeks and then come in like hungry lions, devouring everything on their plate, and then putting it aside, and saying, "Now that was worth $500"? I guess I look at them through my son-of-a-working man eyes. To them $1000 is pocket money. They see it the way I see a quarter.

We got to Kennedy's dinner an hour early and set up a table with bread, bologna and mustard, and we made free sandwiches to give to all the necklaced, fancy-dressed, tail-coated men and women coming to eat Senator Kennedy's big dinner. It sounded like a rotten deal to us, paying $500 for dinner inside, when you could get a free bologna sandwich outside. When people arrived, we shouted, "Have a free bologna sandwich. Why pay $500 for bologna inside when you can get free bologna right here?"

I never saw so many "influential" people get so angry in my life. "You scum, you dirt, you filth!" they screamed at us. I yelled back, "I thought only Republicans talked like that!" The women were scandalized. They moved away from us as if we were a snake about to coil.

Kennedy attracts a lot of Jack Newfield-types, liberal-dupes who come on to revolutionaries real chummy-chum-chum. "We're really fo-

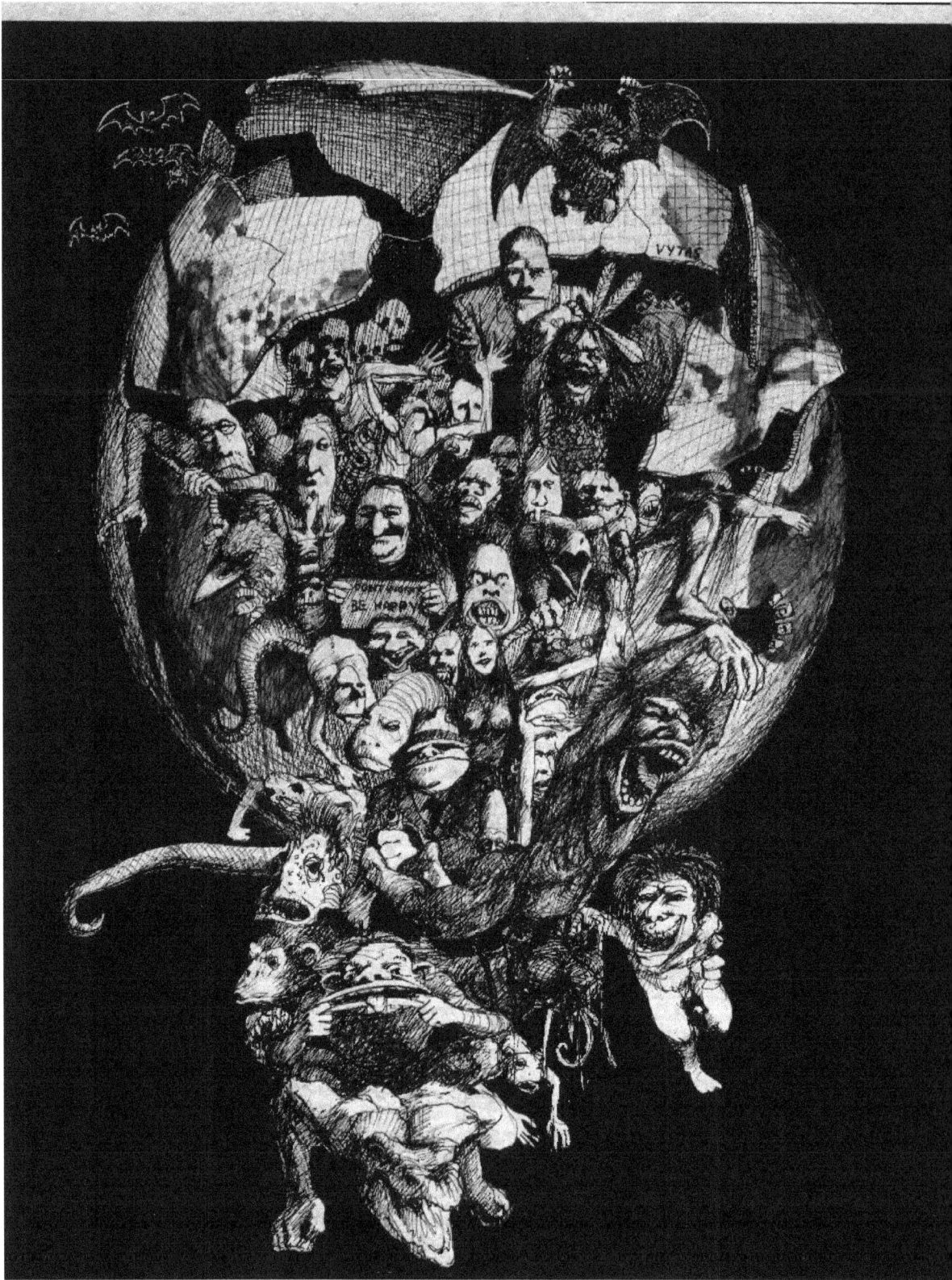

astro, but we're working for Kennedy so that we can make things
asier for revolutionaries, don't you know?" And then they added,
and we got free tickets." But this time the revolutionaries had a great
actic. The liberals had to prove their friendship to us by eating our
ologna sandwiches. If they ate the bologna it would ruin their
ppetites for sure, and we could be certain they would be repulsed by
obby Kennedy's dinner. You are what you eat.

What if one day 5000 sound trucks travelled throughout a city
announcing, "The war in Vietnam is over. Turn on your radio for
urther information." The telephone wires would be buzzing. Within
wo minutes everybody would be calling his mother telling her "The
var is over!" Nixon would hae to come on television to reassure the
American people that the war is still on, despite the vicious rumour-
nongers.

The peace movement is not bureaucratically organized well
nough to carry out such a project, and is also too locked into ideology
o let its imagination go crazy. Phil Ochs went around from peace group
o peace group in spring of 1967 trying to convince them that it was
ime for the peace movement to celebrate the end of the war. The
umour started going around that Phil Ochs had become an apolitical
cid-head, which was not true. Phil just sees too many movies. "How
an we deal with the absurdity of Vietnam except with our own
bsurdity?" asked Ochs. Finally Ochs gave up on the politicos and
eace people, and started working with the freaks.

Posters of a sailor kissing his girl on V-D day, WW II vintage, were
lastered all over New York City, announcing the celebration of the
nd of the Vietnam war. 2000 teenagers and assorted nuts showed up at
Vashington Square Park — for most of whom the war had never even
egun. We didn't know what to do with ourselves, so we went around
laying our noisemakers and telling each other that "The war is over!"
Ve got in a huddle and started counting backwards: 100-99-98-97, and
s we got into the 20s more joined us and when we hit 1, we screamed
The war is over!" and we started running up Fifth Avenue to share the
ood news with our fellow New Yorkers.

The cops were unprepared. They thought we were going to be
ice boys and girls and celebrate the end of the war by playing in the
Vashington Square sandbox all afternoon. We ran through the streets
creaming, "The war is over!" Cab drivers honked their horns. People
topped their cars and got out to ask, "What did you say?" Even
ro-war types waved and said, "Is it really? How did you know?" Alan
insberg ran into automats, threw his hands to the sky in that special
insberg handspring, and screamed at the top of his lungs, "The war is
ver! The war is over!"

Everything became part of the celebration. New York cops on
orses and with sirens blazing came after us to clear the streets. We
hought the police were celebrating the end of the war, too, bringing
heir own noisemakers and props. Red lights, green lights, traffic jams
nd noises all became part of the celebration.

Nobody was unhappy the war was over. And what was even more
mazing: Nobody asked: Who won? Nobody gave a damn.

We should have broken into Broadway plays and screamed, "The
var is over!" People there would have turned to us and said, "Ssssh,
ou're interrupting the play. Ssssh." We'd respond, "We're part of the
lay."

"Demonstrations should turn you on, not off," says Phil Ochs.

The demonstration broke people out of their expected roles.
ro-war people couldn't figure out how to react to this psychological
ssault on their minds. How much more effective than parading around
vith signs saying, "End the war."

The key to theatre is timing. Theatre grows out of the situation
nd the key to theatre is timing. In the summer of '67 it was appro-
riate to scream the war is over. But then LBJ pulled a theatrical trick
n us. He said the war is over. The role of the peace movement during
he time of negotiations is to show people that the war is still on. The
ippie demonstration in Chicago was the reverse of the War is Over
emonstration. We ran through the streets shouting, "The War is On!"

The power to define is the power to control. Over 99% of the
iolence that takes place in America is by the State through its cops and
rmies. But when a cop shoots a nigger, that's "law and order." When a

continued page 19

black man defends himself against a cop, that's "violence." Is the same moral act performed when a Jew kills a Nazi as when a Nazi kills a Jew? Why aren't there different words to describe the violence of the oppressor and the violence of the oppressed? The power structure creates the frame of reference which forces the people to see things from their point of view. The role of the revolutionary is to create actions which force a revolutionary frame of reference.

Huey P. Newton determined what millions of people would think and talk about for years when one October morning in 1967 in Oakland, California, he shot and killed an Oakland cop who had stopped his car and was bullying him, ready to kill.

Not a million books, articles or speeches could have defined the situation so clearly as Huey's action. Huey forced people throughout the world to ask themselves: What would I do if I were Huey Newton? What would I do if I were an Oakland black terrorized by Oakland police? Thousands of people identified not with the dead Oakland policeman but with Huey Newton. A massive response from black people, white liberals, white radicals, students, professors, doctors, housewives throughout California formed the Huey Newton Defense Committee and argued that black people should arm themselves and defend themselves from the violence of the white police.

The white power structure tried to react business-as-usual. One white life is worth 1000 black lives. They made plans to execute Huey P. Newton.

The Oakland courts were unable to execute Huey. Huey was convicted of voluntary manslaughter and sentenced to 2-to 15 years in jail — a compromise.

Huey Newton has become a symbol of the liberated, black revolutionary acting for his people. The battle to free Huey is the battle to free ourselves, because Huey did something that was right, but that we are as yet afraid to do, and he redefined the situation for all of us.

The Black Panthers have been able to take actions that have created legends throughout America. The Panther uniform — beret, black leather jacket, gun — gave the Panther myth incredible force. Three Panthers on the street became an army of thousands. When the jackasses of the California state legislature were meeting in Sacramento to deliberate a bill to leave guns in the hands of the cops but take them out of the hands of the victims of the cops, the blacks, the Panthers armed themselves, drove to Sacramento and invaded the Chamber to personally pay a visit on their Congressmen to discuss their grievances.

The idea of armed mad niggers invading their Sacramento sanctuary must be a nightmare of every congressman. But the Panthers were acting out of common sense. How else can a citizen talk to congressmen? By writing a letter which is answered mechanically by machine? Our legislators have cut themselves off from the experience of the people. They represent special interest groups and see the people only on guided tours. They don't experience the life of the people, so we have to bring our way of life to them.

Fear and paranoia is the luxury of the suburban leftists, the armchair intellectual, the graduate student, the uninvolved. The further away you are from the movement, the more scared you are. The Black Panthers aren't afraid. The yippies aren't afraid. The Viet Cong aren't afraid. In your living room, you're scared to death. In the middle of a riot, I've never found anybody who's scared. The way to eliminate fear is to do what you're afraid of. The goal of theater is to get as many people to overcome their fear, through action, as possible.

We create reality wherever we go by living our fantasies.

(See Oz 18 for Jerry Rubin's Emergency Letter)

NUTTER STUDIOS

hip pocrates

QUESTION: Some time ago a doctor injected silicone into my nose just above the left nostril. The silicone started to come out.

I went back to the doctor and he removed an inch of hard white substance hanging out of a pore in my right nostril. But he couldn't remove the rest of it.

My nose is now both uncomfortable and unbecoming. What should I do?

ANSWER: Silicone injections are still experimental procedures in this country. Even the experimental work was stopped for a time while the Food and Drug Administration investigated possible dangers.

Permission was recently granted to resume the experiments in all parts of the body except the breasts. Breasts were excluded because the presence of silicone makes cancer diagnoses more difficult.

Silicone injections are thought to be useful in correcting certain cosmetic imperfections, but any experimental procedure may back-fire. Your physician has undoubtedly consulted with other researchers in this field regarding your case. Or he may wish to refer you to another plastic surgeon for a second opinion.

QUESTION: My girlfriend had a very unfortunate pregnancy before I met her. She had a Caesarian section and because of complications her uterus had to be removed. She does have her ovaries, however.

I would like to impregnate my girlfriend but obviously can't. Can you advise me on the pros and cons of her getting a uterine transplant or similar therapy?

ANSWER: I'm sorry to tell you that no operation for a uterine transplant yet exists. But adopting a child can be as fulfilling to a couple (and the child) as one born to them.

Adopted children even come to resemble their adoptive parents because of similar facial mannerisms and body movements.

QUESTION: Whenever I eat in a Chinese restaurant the upper part of my body feels numb, I feel weak all over and my heart seems to pound.

What could be wrong?

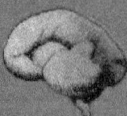

3 months

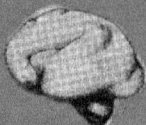

4 months

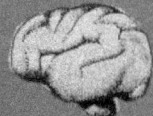

5 months

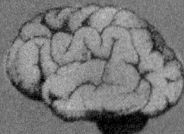

6 months

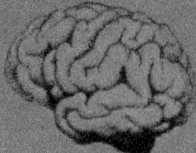

7 months

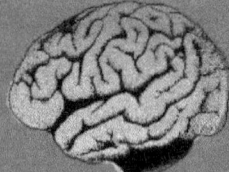

8 months

9 months

ANSWER: Chinese Restaurant Syndrome came to public attention last year with the publication of a letter in the "New England Journal of Medicine" from a Chinese physician. Dr. Robert Ho Man Kwok noted these symptoms when dining in Chinese restaurants but not when eating home-cooked Chinese food.

Even before Dr. Kwok's letter appeared, a Yale gastroenterologist had found a connection between Chinese food and headaches in some individuals. Dr. Martin Gordon and seven brave volunteers (all of whom had previously been victims of Chinese Restaurant Syndrome) ate in a Chinese restaurant in New Haven, Connecticut. You know they're brave.

Halfway through the meal they noticed headaches, numbness of the face, palpitation of the heart, sweating, clenched jaws and flushed faces.

The culprit seems to be monosodium glutamate which is generously used in such delicacies as won ton soup. Most people are not sensitive to this seasoning, but those who are sufferers from the dreaded Chinese Restaurant Syndrome.

Don't worry too much about it. One or two hours after the symptoms begin they disappear and you'll be hungry again.

DEAR DR. HIP POCRATES is a collection of letters and answers published by Grove Press, $5.

Dr. Schoenfeld welcomes your letters. Write to him c/o OZ.

QUESTION: I have a friend who smokes marijuana almost every day and has fallen behind in his school work.

What can I tell him to make him smoke less?

ANSWER: You can tell him any drug can be abused, including marijuana.

"Thinking About Using Pot" is a booklet containing scientific facts about marijuana prepared by Tod Mikuriya, M.D. and Kathleen Goss. Copies cost $1 each and are available from the San Francisco Psychiatric Medical Clinic, 1840 Grove St, San Calif. 94117.

Does marijuana impair driving ability? Not in experienced users, according to a study published in the May 16th SCIENCE Members of the Division of Research of the Washington State Department of Motor Vehicles and Departments of Pharmacology and Psychiatry of the University of Washington School of Medicine gave tests simulating actual driving conditions to 36 marijuana fiends.

The group scored no more total errors on the simulated driving test when stoned than when they were straight. Alcohol, however, caused them to score significantly more driving errors.

The driver-training simulator consisted of a mockup of a car facing a 6 by 18 foot screen in a totally darkened room.

"The test film gave the subject a driver's eye view of the road as it led him through normal and emergency driving situations on freeways and urban and surburban streets."

Alfred Crancer, Jr., of the Washington Department of Motor Vehicles, had previously found in a five year study that a driving simulator test could predict future driving skills (an actual behind-the-wheel test could not). Factors tested during the 23 minute driving film were accelerator, brake, turn signals, steering and speedometer.

The average age of the 36 heads was 22.9 years: 7 were female and 29 male. Each subject had three "treatments." One treatment consisted of waiting in a comfortable lounge with no drug administered before taking the simulator test. The second consisted of drinking 2 Bloody Marys or 2 Screwdrivers of a concentration sufficient to cause a 0.10 per cent blood alcohol level (nearly half of drivers fatally injured in auto accidents have been found to have a blood alcohol level of 0.05 per cent or more). The third seemed to be a treat as well as a treatment and consisted of smoking 2 joints of a batch of marijuana kindly provided by the National Institute of Health.

More "speedometer errors" were made when stoned than when straight but in this test speedometer errors mean not speeding but amount of time looking at the speedometer. The authors of the study believe that drivers high on marijuana spend less time looking at the speedometer because their sense of time perception is altered by the drug.

"They often report alteration of time and space perceptions, leading to a different sense of speed which generally results in driving more slowly."

The conclusions of this paper coincide with observations often reported by chronic marijuana users. Some individuals greatly fear driving under the influence of marijuana; others enjoy driving while stoned and believe they perform at least as well as when straight. Driving under the influence of any drug is best avoided but it seems as if another marijuana myth has been shattered.

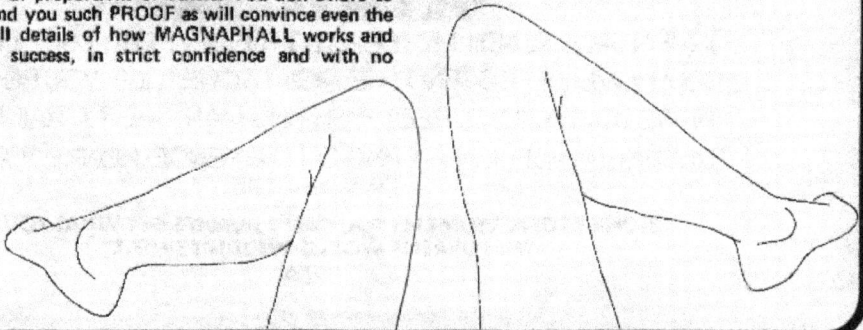

INTERVIEW WITH: *ILSE OLLENDORFF REICH BY HARVEY MATUSOW* September 1969

Your book (Wilhelm Reich: A Personal Biography – Elek Books) is coming out this month

Today Reich is a sort of folk-hero for many thousands of young people both here and in America, and many of them don't even know why.

REICH: My guess would be his attitude towards sexual liberation, which, today of course, is a matter of fact. In Reich's early twenties, the Victorian influence was still very strong, and he was really the first one who tried to liberate youth from Victorian attitudes. He made it quite clear that he felt that sexual liberation was very closely allied to political liberation. Also his work, Democracy Concepts, directed against the professional politician. I don't know whether it's as much in Europe as in America . . . but youths are so fed up with the professional politicians whom they see as ruining everything; that there is, whether they know it or not, an appeal in Reich's book.

Then the attacks on Reich which were perpetrated by the press and by government agencies, not only in the United States, but n Norway, Denmark, Sweden, Austria and Germany were because he was breaking the bonds of Victorian morality?

REICH: Yes, I would think so. They were afraid – evidently rightly so – they were afraid once the liberation came about in the sexual field, that the political liberation would follow. They were afraid for their status quo. Reich was a great rebel, against everything they stood for, and that's where the attacks came from. Of course, their 'attacks' are one of Reich's concepts of the emotional plague, which was completely distorted, again by his disciples. The fact is that you attack someone where you feel yourself attacked – and they felt themselves attacked in their moral concepts, their sexual views, and rightly so. So they attacked Reich in that same field, and made him a sex maniac and what have you.

What was it that Reich was doing with, what the popular press called the Orgone Box, or Orgone Accumulator?

REICH: As I try to explain in my book, the Orgone Energy Accumulator, (its real name,) was an experimental device the function of which was to get the biological energy of the body, a sick body, strengthened. That was its only purpose, to strengthen the biological functioning of a body. Now, it worked out that if, for instance, someone was very anaemic, it would do something to strengthen the haemoglobin content of the blood. It would enhance the biological energy and help the body to fight any disease. It was never claimed by Reich to be a cure-all. He never claimed it could cure anything, and it most certainly wasn't ever mentioned by Reich in connexion with sexual energy or potency which is claimed again and again by the popular sex magazines. Even the United States Food and Drug Administration tried to make it look as if it were a sexual racket. All these allegations against Reich and his work started in an article which appeared in the New Republic in 1947.

Did Reich feel that his work with the Orgone Energy Accumulator was stopped too soon for the kind of results that such experiments could get? That they were never fulfilled because of the Government's injunction which allowed the destruction of the boxes, and the burning of his books? That he really needed more time?

REICH: Again and again, Reich asked the Government to do large scale experimentation with the accumulators in a hospital. Nobody really took it seriously enough to help him and we really didn't have the means to do it on a large scale. Reich had done a lot of large scale experimentation with mice, and it seemed to warrant experimentation on human beings, but it never came to it. He asked again and again for help from large-scale organisations and foundations, but it never came to anything.

So to a great extent it would be true to say that the work on the O.E.A. was never fulfilled? Stilted as a result of ignorance and misconceptions partly derived from over emphasis on sex in a press that attracted certain types of people who had only sex on their mind?

REICH: I think you're very right. The number of people who were on the fringes. It was very distressing to Reich. He didn't want to have anything to do with them, and actually he said that it became such a burden, that in a way he was almost glad when the Government injunction came. To that extent he was freed of that burden, he was beyond that point, it had just been one experiment. He was already in outer space with his experiments at that time. The Accummulator, and human beings, to some extent irritated him. Do I make myself clear?

Yes! You mentioned just now, Reich's moving on to his experiments in outer space, and we know that the Russian Sputnik was launched just one month before he died – he at least lived to witness it. What of his experiments in space?

REICH: I don't actually know very much about it because all the experiments came after I left, or at the time I left, I just couldn't follow his work in outer space. With Reich, life, work, was all one – and if you were not fully with him, it was just impossible to continue living with him. It was beyond me. I just couldn't accept for instance, UFO's as reality. And these he definitely accepted as reality, I couldn't. They may be right, they may not. I don't know enough about it. But Reich claimed to have, not talked, but made contact via his cloud-buster space gun. He claimed to have been able to, not destroy them, but push them away, to chase them away. And he insisted that they came over Organon (Maine, USA) that he saw them hovering overhead, and I couldn't accept that. I am maybe too much of a realist.

Well in prison he used to stand in the yard and look up at the sun, partially shielding his eyes, and if you spoke to him he'd say, "Don't you see them? They're coming, Something has to be done. They're there, can't you see them?"

REICH: Yes. He was convinced that the earth was under attack from outer space. He was absolutely convinced about that and as I said, he thought the whole flight in space could only be done with orgone theory. He was convinced of that. He made big calculations. I didn't understand anything about it, and I couldn't follow it. I know that he wrote that the Sputnik was a game, a toy, compared with what was going on. He was convinced also that the American Air Force and the Space Agencies were aware of this work. I don't know where he took that belief from, but to me these were illusions.

Today you hear talk that the Space Agencies are experimenting secretly with some of Reich's experiments.

REICH: Well, I haven't heard any of that. This is complete news to me. I haven't even heard the rumours!

What do you think his reaction would be to the fact that man has finally reached the moon?

REICH: I can't even speculate. Absolutely no way of telling.

Do you think, if Reich were alive today – or if Reich's spirit were here, looking at the world today, what do you think his reaction would be, seeing the youth in this new anti-political revolution – do you think he might be smiling somewhere as he looks on?

REICH: I think he would. That would be a very positive thing for him. This anti-political ideal.

About spiritualism, that is, when the body dies, does the spirit continue to live? What were his attitudes?

REICH: Well, he wouldn't talk about the spirit going on living. He would say that orgone energy that fills the body, I mean, what makes us alive, in his opinion, was the orgone energy. He said that you can move, that you are standing erect, that whatever makes life is the energy in you – that's orgone energy. When you are dead, you fall down – the energy leaves your body, and his idea was that this amount of orgone energy which is in the individual body merges with the general orgone ocean outside of us. That was as far as he went. I don't think he believed in the spiritual world. I would accept this idea, that what they call soul or spirit, or whatever leaves the body when it is dead, I have accepted the concept of orgone energy completely, in that sense. As for living matter, I can see that this merges with the general orgone energy ocean.

For instance, talking about total orgasm, which is a fusion really of the totality of the energy, moving outside of oneself, almost to create a new life form, which is to infuse the energy into another life form, and if you feel this, the totality is sort of what he was about – transfering the energy.

REICH: That is what he explained, I think in "Either God or Devil", and what is it there, the cosmic superimposition. This is what he had in mind – the identity of all living matter whether it's in space or in the human body. This is the same energy that moves.

I know that many people have told me who've taken LSD that they're able to go back in their minds to where they're only a dot – they sometimes can't explain what it is – but that its a dot of energy, like a star – and in a sense they become totally immersed in the universe and they feel that this experience is very similar to what they've read in Reich.

REICH: I would think that this is so. I can't judge because I don't know anything about this experience with drugs, but I think that the experience would be the same. When people talk about it, and Reich wrote about the oceanic streamings and things like that, this is all part of the same idea, of the same energy concept.

23

THE NAVY LARK

When I arrived in London on leave I made straight for the pubs in the West End with the intention of getting pissed and maybe finding a bird. I got pissed alright but someone in the bar suggested that the best place to pick up a chick in London wasn't the pubs but in Hyde Park on Saturday afternoon. So I slept off my hangover and tooled down Oxford Street just after lunch on Saturday and found the place crowded with people. Not my sort of people, mind you. You see after six years in the Navy (I joined when I was 15) you tend to think and react in very conservative, orthodox ways. What I mean is you get a sort of short-back-and-sides approach to life.

The people I found in the park were something new to me. I was wearing my wellpressed uniform and feeling very choked up in this unreal atmosphere. We had been at sea for 18 weeks — a long time without birds, music or someone sensible to talk to. I'm on submarines. There's none of this join the Navy and see the world crap. You're trapped in this cold, black prison and suspended under the sea doing jobs you're told nothing about. If you believe the lectures they give you at Portsmouth we're helping NATO — defending western civilisation and the British way of life I suppose. But it's all so ridiculous.

One night I got drinking with some old hands and they absolutely believe that if there's a war it will be over so quickly we won't have a chance to survive. So what's it all about?

Well, I'm in Hyde Park on this Saturday afternoon and there's a guy up front singing and he's asking the same thing — What's It All About? Whether it was drunken remorse or not I can't say but I was feeling pretty lonely and depressed. That's fairly typical with sailors. Have you ever thought why sailors have such a reputation for being drunks? They can't like the stuff — nobody *really* does. Have you ever thought why sailors have such bad relationships with women? Why do their girlfriends and wives always run off with other blokes?

Their love affairs don't only break up because they are away so much. It's more than that. I've been on ships and watched the anxiety turn to jealousy and then hate. The Navy doesn't want anybody who can't hate. So when the average sailor comes ashore he's never looking for love or affection he just wants to get all the hate out of his system. Hence the fights, the boozing and the sickening nights in the brothels of Gosport. I was really trying to work all this out in my head when three people sat down near me to listen to the concert. I had the usual reaction — I thought they would stare at my uniform and end up making some smart comment. That's how the fights usually start. But this was altogether different. We somehow started to talk and then when the concert was over they asked me to join them for coffee.

I won't bore you with the Big Romantic Story but by Sunday morning I was in another world from the one that had held me captive for six years. We spent the day visiting people and smoking. At 11 o'clock on Sunday night I knew it was time to get ready to go back to my base. We all drove down to Charing Cross. It was midnight and the streets outside were all pretty deserted. On the platform there were mainly sailors standing around or sitting on their suitcases waiting for the "Special" to take us back. It was the most depressing, empty moment of my life. No one was laughing or joking, all the sailors were trying desperately not to catch the eyes of the person next to him. They were all like executioners going off — in terrible shame — to work the gas ovens. My friends were looking at all the faces and I could tell they were horrified.

I knew immediately what I had to do. "I'm not going back," I said, "let's get out of here." That was a month ago. My life has now changed altogether and it's not just because of the girl I met in the Park and the scene we've now got going. And it's not just smoking — although this has certainly helped to broaden the levels of my consciousness.

For instance, I now go to operas just as much as I go to pop sessions. I want to study for "A" levels to get some sort of education. The only thing I'm sure about is that I don't want to have to return to the Navy. They've got a warrant out for my arrest now and I have to keep changing my address. And every time I go for a job I am asked for my insurance cards. I can usually work for a fortnight before the boss gets edgy and starts to ask too many questions. Then I have to move on. One day they will catch up on me; I'll be arrested on a demonstration or turned over after a party and then I'll have to go back and face a spell in jail. But that's not the worst of it. My contract with the Navy — the *minimum* contract by the way — is nine years from my eighteenth birthday. This means I will have to serve another six years *plus* the time I was absent without leave. So I could be in until I was 30. The best years of my life wasted in the Navy is an appalling thought. I dread the thought of being captured.

I read the other day in one of the papers that there are about 200 sailors, soldiers and air men who want to get out of the services. (The exact figures on deserters isn't known because the Government is too frightened to give it). I know how all of those 200 feel — frightened and frustrated. I guess I'm really one of the lucky ones — I'm outside trying to lose myself in the Underground while they're still inside roosting. The only organisation, apart from the anarchy of the Underground, helping servicemen like me is the National Council for Civil Liberties. Officially they've got to give you a lecture and tell you to give yourself up but then they try to offer any help.

The Underground can help a little more by being a little more sympathetic. If you see some sailors or soldiers around the scene, don't immediately assume they are nasty, vicious bastards. Some of them may be having severe personality crises; they may be genuinely searching for a life-style that is more fulfilling than helping to organise the destruction of mankind. Behind those uniforms of death there may be souls of life.

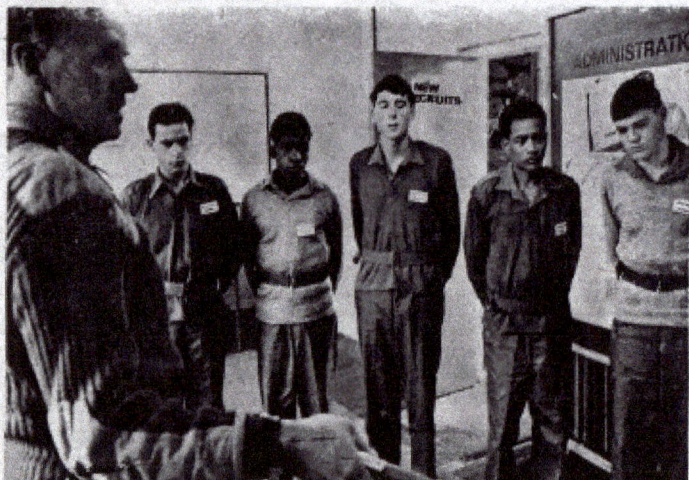

If the Alternative Society is really to be an alternative, then we must redefine our relationships with one another. Oh, but something is happening, Mr. Jones, look at the Isle of Wight/Woodstock, where half a million young, stoned, broke, anti-careerists sat non-violently and smiled at each other, yakkety yak. It is easy to demonstrate that thousands of people are not football hooligans, wear bright clothes and relate to each other with more warmth than stockbrokers; but when it comes to resolving disagreements deeper Underground, then this new morality is swiftly swamped by the old hypocrisy.

In the US major Underground disputes (LNS, Berkeley Barb, Fillmore East) have not been settled with daffodils and lysergic acid, but with punch-ups, lawyers and lies. In the UK, behind-the-scenes power struggles have often degenerated to a level which would make the occupants of Westminster shudder with envy. Because the participants are often neurotically aware that their private behaviour contradicts their public philosophy, the mud is slung with excoriating intensity.

Last week a crisis has raged at IT, and there has at least been an attempt by some to settle it in a spirit not entirely contradictory to that expounded in the paper's editorial pages. As OZ lumbers off to press, the situation changes every minute, so we cannot offer a full report. It is difficult to present the facts objectively, as personal friendships with some of the IT people tend to colour our interpretation. Herewith a cursory and semi-accurate resumé of events, an attempt to present the conflicting points of view and some of the issues raised:

– On Sunday October 13, the IT offices were occupied by some members of the IT staff and friends, who announced that the paper would be taken over from the editors. The London Street Commune was invited to join the occupiers, which it did, and both groups issued the following statement.

The International Times was liberated by the staff of the paper from the offices at 27 Endell Street and is now being run from address below. Since Love Books relinquished control of IT the paper deteriorated to the point where Peter Stansill, David Hall, and Graham Keene claimed to be the legal owners and bosses of the paper. We, the staff of the paper declare that IT is now a workers' group and we will continue to represent the alternative society against any attempts to gain control. Our solicitors have been instructed to take the necessary steps to halt any action the self-styled directors may take. The International Times, workers group have invited the London Street Commune to occupy and use the building in our absence. The Commune will use the building for its own purposes which include the setting up of a Street Newspaper for skinheads, Angels, Beats, and other beasties.

NOW *The International Times is again* YOUR PAPER. *This is a vital move in the history of the time – the so called* UNDERGROUND IS SURFACING. *We hope to work closely with the Commune, and the other groups that are helping redefine our society. The new IT will not have editors, typesetters, etc., the roles will go* BUT THE WORK WILL BEGIN

–Those involved in the takeover included David Warren, a former art director and Ian Dallas, a former guest editor, Charlotte & Malcolm Jackson (switchboard & distribution), Joe Bareboim (part-time distribution), Gareth Bartlett (general helper), Philip Cohen ("Dr John") of the Commune and others.

–When Graham Keen, Mark Williams and others of the editorial staff discovered that they were were unable to enter the building, that the advertising girl was allegedly threatened with violence, that crucial distribution, advertising and office files were missing, that the IBM typesetting machine, typewriters and other equipment was being removed and that they didn't know what was going on, they called the police. In retrospect this action is regrettable, but at the time understandable. At any event, the police were asked by IT editors not to take any action.

–On Monday night, the editors proposed to solve the dispute by handing over Knullar Ltd., the company which publishes IT, to the occupiers, plus the office and capital equipment. They would ask for at least photocopies of the distribution/subscription lists and other crucial files to be returned and then they would set about to continue IT from somewhere else. Thus there would be two papers serving the community instead of one. An anticipated problem: Both groups would want to call their papers IT.

–This exceedingly generous proposal was put to the occupiers at a meeting in Hyde Park the following Tuesday. It was rejected. No one wanted Knullar Ltd. By Tuesday night the IT staff occupiers had vacated the Endell Street offices, leaving only the London Street Commune, whose members had no loyalty for either side in the dispute, felt they had been used as psychological mercenaries by the IT staff, and were firmly ideologically opposed to the whole concept of IT anyway.

–By the end of the week the editors were back. The London Street Commune vacated Endell Street offices after, it is reported, methodically wrecking it. They are now planning to publish their own paper, called AGGRO.

–Some of the equipment had been retrieved from the IT rebel staff by the editors, but none of it in working conditions. The staff refuse to return the files and distribution lists and at the time of writing, the editors (plus staff allies) are rounding up "Underground intellectual heavies" to persuade them to change their mind – these lists are also important to Transmutation, an independent Underground distribution company, who need them to distribute other Underground magazines.

–While many people do not support some of the tactics of the rebels, there is much sympathy for the need for a second Underground paper. It is also agreed that Ian Dallas, when he worked at Endel Street in his capacity as guest editor, consulted staff members, including long serving packers and 'office boys' who had long felt disgruntled at the "elitest working atmosphere." He is certainly a good editor.

–Rumour: The amazing 'Sack' is planning to bring out their next issue with the IT logo on the cover.

EXPLAINING to OZ readers the gravity of the Government's new drugs legislation is not an easy task. For most of your subscribers, I suspect, have already made the decision to conduct their own lives by their own standards. But meantime, politicians too are 'doing their thing' which will mean higher penalties for all drug offenders, especially pushers, tougher police powers and compulsory treatment for hard drug addicts. To understand how this Government – the party of Life and Soul – arrived at the point of legislating these measures it is necessary to examine the development of political and social institutions in this country since 1966.

When Labour was re-elected with its massive majority the country braced itself for dynamic change; the trendy technocrats had been given a mandate to shore up the contradictions and injustices in our society. The meek were about to inherit the earth.

Apart from the financial conspiracy which seriously inhibited Labour's plans, there was the sudden, inexplicable caution which revealed the Labour Party to be bankrupt of genuine understanding of the masses. There were, however, one or two exceptions. Roy Jenkins became Home Secretary and immediately set in motion inquiries into the state of the prison service. He lent his support to abortion and homosexual reform.

He reconstituted the standing committees on drug dependence and formed the crucial Government sub-committee on LSD and cannabis under the chairmanship of Baroness Wootton. The committee decided cannabis was the more important drug to consider so it launched what was to become one of the most definitive studies a Government has ever undertaken. Membership comprised doctors, social psychiatrists, a police commissioner, magistrates and lawyers. When it reported to the Government in January this year, however, the social atmosphere had considerably changed. Jenkins was trying to run the economy while the previous Chancellor, J. Callaghan, had been despatched to the Home Office. It was a new era of subtle repression: Callaghan had already passed the racialist Commonwealth Immigrants Act and in his talks with his former cronies in the Police Federation he had given the clearest indicators that hippie-bashing was to be a new sport which would earn promotion.

With amazing naievty the cannabis committee handed over its document which concluded that pot-smoking was no more harmful than drinking booze. Three weeks later in Parliament Mr. Callaghan ridiculed the committee and agreed the penalties needed looking at – they would be going up. Now what did the gallant Baroness and her fellow citizens do in the face of this public pillorying? Did they resign? Did they tell Callaghan to elect a tame committee if he was so desperate to get a tame report? Not a bit of it. They are all earnestly slaving away on the LSD report, later they'll join committees looking at peace corps work among the Welsh unemployed. As Trotsky said, bureaucracies once erected take on a life of their own.

Baroness Wootton has what is known as an acute committee mentality. She's served on more committees than any known British subject. And the rules of the committee game are that you never resign when you've been kicked around, you pursue further Good Works in the name of social improvement. Having insulted the committee and received plaudits from the Press, the Pulpit and

Dear Oz,

You give yourselves away at last. The letter you published under my name in your last issue was never written nor signed by me. It is true that I was interviewed about my reactions to your television supplement. I understood from you that this was to be subsequently written up and given back to me for correction. It was only with this clear understanding that I undertook to be interviewed at all.

I was extremely distressed therefore to find myself quoted out of context in the form of a letter. As it stands, the gibberish that you printed bears no relation to what I feel and I would be grateful if you made this clear to your readers.

Yours sincerely,
(Tony Palmer)
BBC

OZ 24
October/November 1968.
OZ is published by
OZ Publications Ink Ltd.
52 Princedale Road, London W11.
Telephone: 229 7541
Printed by OZ Publications Ink Ltd.
Advertising: Contact Felix Dennis at 727 8456.

This issue appears with the help of Richard Neville, Felix Dennis, Jim Anderson, Louise Ferrier, Brigitte Murphy, Martin Sharp, Ken Petty, Garry Brayley, Fytas & Lo.
Cover photograph by David Nutter.

Distribution:
UK: Moore Harness Ltd. 11 Lever St. London EC1. CLE 4882.
Transmutation, Guildford 65694.
California: Rattner Distributors 2428 McGee St. Berkeley, California, 94703.
Holland: Thomas Rap, Regulierswarstraat 91, Amsterdam, Tel: 020-227065.
Danmark: George Streeton, The Underground, Larsbjorn Straede 13, Copenhagen K.
France and Australia: Impossible.

the Politicians, Callaghan is now armed with the forces of reaction to clamp down on people who take drugs. He feels that the Home Secretary's job needs to show a smack of authority. Hitting the blacks is too controversial so hit the hippies. Who'll complain? And what better issue for the party just before the election, "CALLAGHAN STOPS DRUG PERIL". Mr. Callaghan announced today wide-sweeping changes in the law to halt the drugs menace which is imperilling the youth of Britain. He delivered the legislative package to the Commons today to the cheers of both sides of the House. Mr. Callaghan demonstrated the firm hand of Government which will be so helpful in the forthcoming election campaign.

Of special concern is the proposal to compulsorily treat regressive hard drug addicts. Commencing "compulsion" in managing any part of society is fraught with dangers. It is solely invoked at the moment in the treatment of mentally disturbed people — but only after rigorous psychological examination by a panel of doctors. With addicts, however, we have a more sinister and obvious interference with civil liberties if this section of the new Act is passed. Police will have the right to pick up addicts and hand them over to hospitals who can instantly compel the patient to a closed mental institution for so-called treatment. The patient will not have the right to challenge the medical procedure. One can easily foresee circumstances in which the police will arrest so-called troublesome members of the Underground and not have them locked away in Wormwood Scrubs on legal charges, but simply have them incarcerated by the medical profession.

In a year's time the Labour Party will be telling the workers, the middle and upper classes that it is definitely not the permissive party, and it is the party which hammered the hippies, but not will proliferate and so will the number of young people who cannot accept the contradictions and inadequacies of our present society. The Callaghan Bill is due to pass through Parliament at the end of this year; the Tories, if they win office, will probably pass a revised version containing more potent weapons against social outcasts. It is not, however, new laws against hippies which will solve the housing, hospital and education crises in Britain. We look to the answer for these problems in a re-arrangement of our social priorities which neither political party provides today. In helping to get these priorities right, hippies may find it necessary to abandon their Underground lyricism, their pop-cultural side-shows. A real opposition is needed. Maybe after Callaghan has had his way, 'revolution' won't seem such a dirty word.

A. M.

Books received:

Let 'em Roll Kafka, Poems by Peter Brown. Fulcrum Press. Hard back 21/-, paper back 10/-.

Battered poems from a battered cornerstone of the Underground as it was before the flower power days of 1967. The poems are slight, sad, painfully personal, sometimes funny. Here's one "Few":

Alone tired half drunk hopeful
I staggered into the loos
at Green Park Station
and found 30 written on the wall

Appalled I lurched out
onto the windy blaring neon Piccadilly
night
thinking sorely
Surely there must be more of us than
that . . .

Where are the real poets of the Underground? They were not, you probably noticed, at the Isle of Wight — in between sets, poetry was flung to the vast crowd with great energy, but it wasn't the kind of stuff those kids wanted to hear. There were no connections made. Unless you were over 25.

The Marijuana Papers — Edited by David Solomon. Panther Modern Society paperback. 12/-.

Contains no surprises, but it's an exhaustive and definitive book about a subject we all know and love. Buy it and get your facts right for once and for all.

The Pop Process. Richard Mabey. Hutchinson Educational. 20/-.

It seems appropriate that this book should be published by a firm describing themselves as "Educational". It seems destined to go straight to the library shelves for use as a history and reference book, when Pop becomes yet another boring subject for study in comprehensive schools. I prefer Nick Cohn's totally personal approach to Mabey's more analytical study, but the book is interesting nevertheless. Pop is a bottomless barrel of fascination, and Mabey manages to give us a lot of scrapings. Read him for the badness of some of his opinions. For example: "Another Side of Bob Dylan is a failure by any standards" — he didn't even find To Ramona of any value.

Bound for Glory, Woody Guthrie. J. M. Dent & Sons Ltd. 45/-.

This autobiography covers the first thirty years of the life of Woodrow W. Guthrie, up to 1942. It's a moving book, almost too much to take as the searing sixties scorch to a conclusion. It's a book from the golden age of America when the dream was still a dream. The dialogue is idealised, sentimental, like an old John Wayne movie. Guthrie comes across as pacifist, with a narrow masculine range of emotions and so compassionate as to be almost non-human. As a traveller, hobo, man of the road, he has more relevance than Kerouac, and reading the book will show you why and just how much Bob Dylan was under his spell.

Mick Farren's outpourings in the last OZ is from a collection of subversive material to be produced at the end of the year under the title of 'Canned London', a sanitated sardine can of prose, posters, photos, records and other goodies.

EXAMPLE: Alan Aldridge poster pictures by Clive Arrowsmith, a SF comic/novel by Eduardo Paolozzi and Anthony Haden-Guest and a record by The Deviants.

Christopher Robbins has been getting it together over the last few months under the working name of 'Factory'. 'Everything in the can is either about or by the young in London now. That can mean, of course, anything from heads to skinheads, but most of the things and the people we deal with go under the amorphous title of underground.'

Other people involved with the production of the can are Andre Del Amo, promotion, Bob Cotton, graphics, Roger Stowell photos and Larry Pryce street interviews.

Governor Reagan of California captured in a pose from his modelling, pre-Hollywood days.

Groupie, Jenny Fabian and Johnny Byrne. New English Library. 25/-.

The most interesting things about Groupie are its thinly disguised ("only based on" we are assured) portraits of:

Caroline Cook (Liza Donnity)
Anthony Haden-Guest (Reginald Chatterton)
Thom Keyes (Theo)
Jeff Dexter (Lenny)
Jenny Fabian (Katie)
Johnny Byrne (Johnny)
Pink Floyd (Satin Odyssey)
Ben (Sid Barrett)
The Soft Machine (Dream Battery)
The Family (Relation)
Rik Grech (Dir)
Roger Chapman (Spike)
Tony Gourvish (Grant)
The Nice (The Elevation)
The Fugs (The New York Sound and Touch)
Jimi Hendrix Experience (Jacklin H. Event)
Noel Redding (Sam)
Mitch Miller (Sam)
Aynsley Dunbar (Jubal Early Brawback)
Max (Alexander Sigmund Dnochowski)
Spooky Tooth (Shadow Cabinet)
Zoot Money (Zach Franks)
Andrew King (Nigel Bishop)
Dave Hauseman (Jason Wylie)
Dantalian's Chariot (Transfer Project)

J.F.A.

Spike found himself at the Horse of the Year show last weekend — where the upper-middles celebrate their allegiance to the Crown and equestrianism. Earnest young pony-clubbers compete for the big prize — riding through slalom races, with obstacles. One of the games was 'knock the hippies heads off', each team had to ride over a course, dismount, then throw stones at effigies of hippies until their heads fell off, remount and finish the course. Princess Anne loved it — this was the only event that distracted her from non-stop eating and drinking.

THE RADICAL RESEARCH CENTRE is a non-profit organisation formed early in 1969 to index the many publications of the alternative press. The centre operates through a decentralised network of indexers who send reports in for compilation on computers. They need an indexer for OZ. Anyone interested write to Radical Research Centre, Carleton College, Northfield, Minn. 55057, USA.

Solidarity has published a special report on the Ilford Squatters. Price 6d. For copies write to Andy Anderson, c/o Solidarity, 79 Balfour Street, SE 17.

Why did Melody Maker refuse to print the ad from Island Records which appears on our back cover?

HEAVY AUTUMN

THE NEW MOBILISATION COMMITTEE TO END THE WAR IN VIETNAM along with many other groups is planning a series of actions this autumn on an unprecedented scale. The anti-war demonstrations culminate in the US on November 14 with a nation-wide student strike, and November 15 with mass marches in San Francisco and Washington DC, to demand that ALL the Troops be brought home NOW. Co-incidental demonstrations are planned in London.

RONALD REAGAN at the Albert Hall. He will address the Institute of Directors on November 6.
He should be given a big welcome here and anywhere else he goes.
Reagan as killer : His score at Peoples' Park Berkeley, California (see OUTCRY, reprinted in OZ 21) was:
James Rector, student, DEAD, age 25.
Alan Blanchard, artist, BLINDED for life.
Seventy brothers and sisters wounded.
Give him the welcome he deserves.

SOUTH AFRICAN SOLIDARITY COMMITTEE plans a mass demonstration on NOVEMBER 16 to show support for the struggle of the South African people against racial oppression. Inquiries to 211 Ladbroke Grove, London W 10.

BIAFRA WEEK 24th October to 1st November, organised by Biafra '69, a fund-raising committee formed in March this year. Events: Albert Hall Pop Concert — Georgie Fame, Delaney and Bonnie (27th October), Ball — Madame Tussauds (31st October), Film — National Film Theatre (29th October). Information: Peter Hazel-Smith 01-437-6002.

because the boys playing football
        eat out my heart
that is why i protest
because every policeman like a star
        in hollywood detests me
that is why i protest

because the little girl on the fourth
        storey falls like a bomb
that is why i protest
because the grocer is full of knives
        and i am almost dead
that is why i protest

because we are so in love
        and yet are dying
protest protest
because we are men and do what men do
protest

From 21 Songs of the Revolution, by Julian Beck.

COLLECTOR'S DREAM: Two complete sets of OZ 1-21, bound in red leather, embossed in gold. We have only two for sale. They were expensive to bind and will impress your friends. Price: £60 each. Please write to BOUND OZes, 52 Princedale Road, London W.11.

APOLOGY: We were overwhelmed by the response to our Jimi Hendrix poster offer. We had 200 extra printed, but at 5/- a time, we can't afford to run off any more. For those who missed out, sorry.

OZ SUBSCRIPTIONS
42/-, 6 dollars for 12 issues.
52 Princedale Road, London W.11.

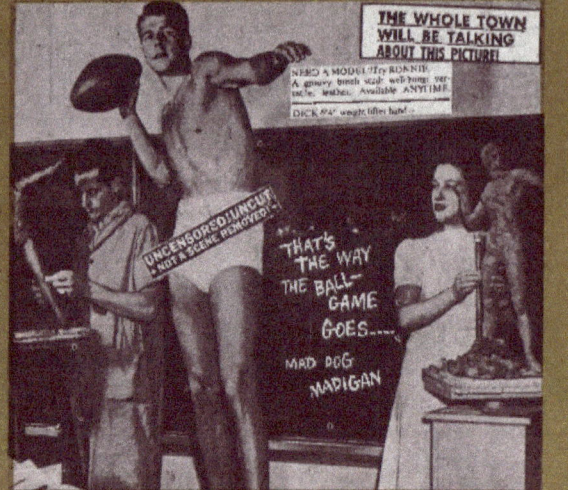

26

Mozic
AND THE REVOLUTION

When Joshua fit the Battle of Jericho the walls came tumbling down. That's revelation. The holy Ghost talking. So it can be done. The way to crack a mirror or shiver a wineglass is to find the right frequency and pound it. Like those strobe lights that picked up the B-rhythms of some kids dancing around in Ealing or somewhere, and threw them into epileptic fits. T.C. knows a cat in Australia who used to make strange music sitting between two huge columns and singing into them and feeding and feeding it back and back. Finally, he burst a blood vessel in his head and now he's crazy. If you sit a man with a bucket on his head and let a water-tap drip onto it, he'll be crazy within hours. The Japanese taught some Australians that. Music hath charms to tame the savage breast, as Shakespeare noticed. Music hath alarums to wild the civil breast, as well, as Tuli Kupferberg pointed out. It is partly a matter of the mode of the music, but then as well something to do with the ears the music exists in. He that has ears to hear, let him hear. The bell tolling in the desert makes no sound.

What then is the mode of revolutionary music in October 1969? And who's it for? Mick Farren is right to agonise over the superficiality of the rock revolution. The underground is falsely complacent, living on an exaggerated notion of its own importance and effectiveness, which Mick Farren tirelessly deflates and derides. He looks back with furious nostalgia at the time when ugly, desperate, grinding songs were million sellers. When shop-girls, mechanics, storemen, packers, gasfitters, wharf labourers and their girls, found dignity, lust and anger in the music of rock. It is painful to hear the skinheads saying as they look over the crowds, past the enclosure where the beautiful people bask in a cloud of Mick Jagger's spittle, "Well, the Stones are one of us, arnay?" Expensive drugs, more expensive butterflies, dead mates, Baby Jane Holzer's dildo, no, baby, the Stones are not one of you. By Marianne Faithfull's sacred Mars bar they are not one of you. They are being protected from you by the Underground's favourite scapegoats, the poor old phoney Hell's Angels. In the official souvenir of that concert there is a photograph of the groupies' enclosures backstage, which features, in filthy yellow

plush trousers, Ibiza vest, chain, and dilly-bag, the underground impresario himself. The expression on his face sums up the whole blind alley of revolutionary music. "Why isn't it working" those hot eyes are saying. "What the fuck happened?"

Why did Mick Jagger not tell those quarter of a million people to take over the city? Why did they behave so well and pick up all their garbage? They were celebrating their togetherness, boasted the underground. They showed the parent-generation how they were gentle and loving and co-operative. Mick Farren knew that that was not how it was. The phenomenon had been contained. No one need be afraid of the Rolling Stones any more. They couldn't

27

change a thing. They didn't want to change a thing. They arrived at the head of the pop wave, expressing the vague discontent of their generation. They were rewarded with money and initiated into the fancy vices of the upper class, drugs, buggery, cruelty and vicarious violence. Home video of the Aberfan disaster with "Yes sir, that's my baby" for a backing. Loving, gentle co-operative my arse. Still, it was genuine. The greasers, the rockers, the mods, the skinheads, the hippies, the yippies, all of your genuine working class youth would have been corrupted in the same way. Only the bourgeo' revolutionary can spurn the insidious rewards this society offers to successful subversion. Only the middle class rebel yearns for the proletariat.

> Someone told me times are changing
> But looking all around it seems the same
> Buying selling running hiding
> Wondering if the world has any shame
> Looking from my window
> Blank faces queue for something new to come
> But nothing ever changes
> And their dreams all wither in the sun
>
> (The Deviants, Transatlantic)

The rock revolution failed because it was corrupted. It was incorporated in the capitalist system which has power to absorb and exploit all tendencies including the tendencies towards its own overthrow. The Rolling Stones have been absorbed, and their music has been corrupted too. *Honky-tonk woman* like the *Salt of the Earth* is merely a new perversion, a kind of self-conscious slumming. It stinks. And yet, even if Frank Zappa has had to throw Mick and Marianne out of his house in Laurel Canyon, Mick Jagger is still a better man than he, because the deficiencies in his revolutionary theory do not matter, because the corruption and faggotisation of his own character are irrelevant. What is only important, is that the Rolling Stones found the frequency, they sounded the chime, they dripped the tap on to the bucket, they cracked the mirror and busted the glass. *Satisfaction* can never be unwritten. It has been heard, for there were ears to hear.

Frank Zappa is more intelligent and a better musician than any of the Stones, and that is probably why he would never risk immolation as a pop hero. For Mick Jagger is a victim, after all, and it makes little difference whether he is aware of the fact. Though, when he chooses to dance in a studded dog collar and his white clown suit, perhaps we may assume that he has an inkling.) Zappa may enjoy his artistic and other sorts of integrity, but he will never make a contribution to the revolution of sensibility which is the pre-requisite of political revolution. The converted seek out Zappa and learn more about their attitudes from him, but the Stones helped thousands of kids to bust out. What pains Mick Farren, and it pains him terribly all of the time, is that the bust out was too trivial in its immediate effects. So his music dashes itself against the horns of a polydilemma, every proposition has its but. Music must reach a mass audience, but it will then become commercial. Music must please those who hear it, but it must not make the unbearable bearable. Music must be violent and exciting, but it must not provide harmless expression for violence and frustration. In such a conflict Mick Farren's Deviants could only use music as a weapon. Tune, harmony, rhythm were a bunch of Uncle Tomisms. The Deviants were offensive. Mick screamed, Russ battered. When the equipment collapsed, or silence ensued for any reason, Mick bawled at his audience, pleading with them to tear the hall down, to fuck, or shit, telling them the home truths about the management, libelling, protesting, complaining, cursing. But the audience remained an audience. They listened. They stood still, patient under barrages of feedback and Mick's incomprehensible yelling. They wanted to have a good time, and there was this wheezing Jeremiah begging them to hate something. They were too good mannered even to hate him. Mick ended up hating nearly all his audiences. He meant to yell at their parents, but he ended up yelling at them.

> We are the people who pervert your children,
> Who lead them astray from the lessons you taught them,
> We are endangering civilisation,
> We are beyond rehabilitation.
>
> (The Deviants, Transatlantic)

But they aren't endangering civilisation. It's all fantasy. The Stones could claim this, they still could, but they never would. Mick Farren is convinced, passionate, sincere and unsparing of himself in his service of the revolution, and that's just what's wrong with him. Electronic music was a glimpse into the possibility of liberation, not expounded but demonstrated on the nerves; kids began to dance, to leap, and their want was born. Mick Farren understood the phenomenon politically, intelligently. He is still the best critic the English Underground has, and like Jeremiah he ought to be heeded. But he cannot sing. He cannot sing because, although he has a freaky throat, he cannot *hear*. And he never did hear what rock music really was, in terms of guts and glory. He is an impresario, but he does not understand exactly what it is that he's peddling, any more than any other Denmark street wheel-and-dealer. The most significant part of the rock revolution, because it did happen, was that kids got into their bodies. Music is a curious medium. Utterly abstract in its construction, but completely sensuous in its apperception. Tunes, rhythms can only be conveyed by exact mimicry. They are not ideas. Mick Farren writes lovely prose, he has good, tough, sharp ideas, but he is not and never will be into his body. He is a victim of one of the meanest tricks that our sick civilisation plays upon the body-soul hookup, chronic asthma. As a result of it, he is addicted to a particularly brutal form of stimulant. This tyrannical dance with death has too much to do with the kind of music he makes, and with the deadly microscopic efficiency of the Pink Fairies' operations in fucking up other people's music. King Crimson are still apologising for the gig they did at the Speakeasy, which is the only regime which the Pink Fairies will ever upheave, because they were put off and harassed by a more than usually drunken and drugged Twink, Steve Tooke and Mick Farren.

But something has happened. The Deviants are no longer Mick Farren's Deviants. Under all the bullshit flummery of the Pink Fairies something was really happening. A leather giant with a deformed arm, and a natural Charles II mane, leans into the mike and says with a maniacal smile, "let's have some fun" before he drives off on deranged lead guitar. That's it. That's the pulse. He has it. The bass player can find it from him, and Russ boxes out the frenzy on drums. The words are inaudible. The band practises these days. They dig it. They are into it. Soon their audiences will fuck without being told. The Deviants have discovered music. They used to be frail and pious. Mick's yelling was still preaching after all. Now Paul Rudolf's "Let's have some fun" could set up a sympathetic vibration in the foundations of the Home Office. Mick has responded to the pressure, which looks these days like bouncing him clean off the stage, with a change in the group's public image. He is no longer il Duce, Russ and Sandy and Paul talk to the papers too. Mick has swapped "The Pink Fairies are organising a musical attack on authority, like the MC5 in Chicago (sic) a strategic, organised and effective attack on the straights" type bullshit for the "If Nat Joseph thinks you're sincere he just lets you get on with it your way" type bullshit.

Factory has yet to publish its deal on the Pink Fairies, with its special record and all that. If it does it really ought to change its name to Fantasy. The basic weapon of the Pink Fairy conspiracy is conservative. The machine gun that will rip open a policeman's chest and furnish Mick Farren with a satisfactory orgasm at last is the weapon of the straights: to kill a man is simply murder; it is revolution to turn him on.

It is not the groups who call themselves Underground who will provide the music that will shake the walls of the city. It is not the polemicists who choose a microphone and electronic backing to continue an argument who will enlighten the straights who continue to be born. It is not the best musicians, and it is not the worst. But it will be done with music.

> Beware a man who is not moved by sound.
> He'll drag you to the ground
> Come dance with me, come dance with me in (Wilson's) land
> Come dance with me, we'll beat that hoary band.
>
> (Tuli Kupferberg)
> Germaine

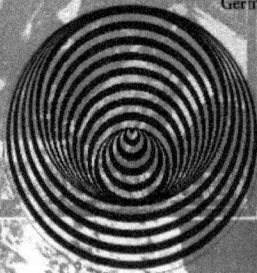

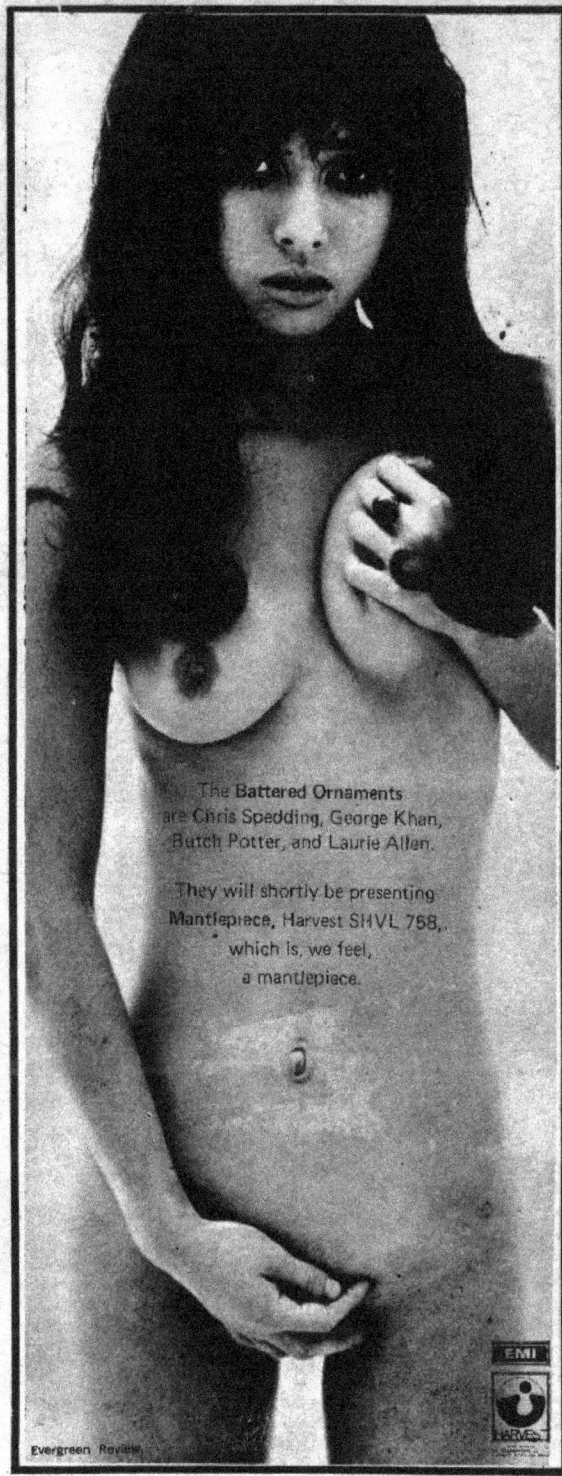

ARTHUR ... OR THE DECLINE AND FALL OF THE BRITISH EMPIRE. The Kinks. Pye NPL 18317.

Ray Davies' appetite for middle-class suburban 'Nowhere Men' seems to be almost as insatiable as it is predictable. From early '66, Davies has been writing and the Kinks have been performing that same old song. Is the distance from YOU REALLY GOT ME to WATERLOO SUNSET really much further than the length of DEAD END STREET? I wonder. But there's no denying that if there is little sign of any change in content on the Kinks specialised menu, Davies is still certainly cooking better than ever. Put it another way, if we hadn't heard it all before, this album would probably be heralded with blaring trumpets and ecstatic acclaim ... but we all know what familiarity breeds.

It's interesting that Davies has always claimed his function in song writing to be that of reporter, rather than preacher. His insistence that he advocates no change in lifestyle for 'Arthur' & friends is fully justified, hearing it amid the strong journalistic overtones of his compositions and the comparatively few lapses into comment. Well, at least his is a more tolerant attitude than say, George Harrison's honking wallowing Piggies in their starched white shirts, whose lives are growing worse, grovelling in the dirt. Davies will have none of this ... dig -

'She's bought a hat like Princess Marina's ... so she don't care.' (what you think of her?) or 'He's bought a hat like Anthony Eden's, he says it makes him feel like a lord'. The M.C.5 would not, perhaps be amongst Mr. Davies' biggest fans?

Instrumentally, 'Arthur' is several steps removed from his predecessors, and Davies always a master of eclectic licence, (nine or is it ten chart single hits is no small feat, whether you care about charts or not), has excelled himself on the arrangements. Ninety per cent of the material is hybrid, it's true, but it's never Xeroxed. I can't ever tell exactly where he steals anything from. Strains of George Martin, Cole Porter, Norman Petty and Benjamin Britten are all in evidence. Weird: Mining Community Brass Bands or B.B.C. Northern Light Dance, Vera Lynn to Beefheart, Ray handles them with the ease that only experience brings. Look, the air-raid siren in 'MR CHURCHILL SAYS' are actually in key! How professional can you get?

But like Townshend's TOMMY, although the music is great fun and an integral part of the whole production, it is specifically designed to serve its purpose, and no more. In fact, no more is required. The music, and even the Kinks themselves, are merely a horse upon which the ever smiling Mr. Davies is firmly mounted.

To give him his full credit, there can be no doubt that Davies lives and breathes his characters. 'Arthur' is his own special anti-heroic creation. You can tell he spies on him, takes notes of him on tubes and buses, collects items on him in newspapers and researches his history with considerable diligence. The album, is, in fact, subtitled OR THE DECLINE AND FALL OF THE BRITISH EMPIRE ... and lines like 'Mr. Beaverbrook says we gotta save our own' cos all the garden gates and empty cans are going to make us win ... have that delicate ring of (authentic) confidence. Twisted phrasing has always been a Davies' specialty too ... 'Pack up your ambition in your old kit bag ...', brilliant!

I do dig this album. It's sometimes sensitive ... 'Some mother's son lies in a field ... somewhere someone is trying to be so brave ...', often heavy handed ... 'Australia no class distinction, Australia no drug addiction ... He's non-progressive and full of Yorkshire Pudding. I can't help feeling, though, that while Ray Davies' lyrical coat is undoubtedly many coloured, surely by now it must be wearing slightly shiny at the elbows and egg-stained round the lapel. After all, he's been wearing it ... for nearly four years. But perhaps he's comfortable in it, like Arthur, in his

FELIX DENNIS

LOOKING BACK John Mayall Decca LK5010 (Mono) SKL 5010 (Stereo)

The cover is presumably symbolic, I mean there's this backwater railway siding Somewhere In The American West, with engine 1273 looking very stagey and antiquated in the background. And there's Mayall, buckskin jacket and all, hitching himself aboard another train in the foreground, glancing away from the camera, over his shoulder, Looking back.

For a long time Mayall has epitomized white English blues and the Mayall group, under its various aliases (The Powerhouse Four, the Blues Syndicate, the Blues-breakers et al) has acted as a watershed, a catchment area for developing musical talents. The list is long and, by now, well known, and most of them are here on Looking Back, naked and unashamed: Jack Bruce, Eric Clapton, Roger Dean, Aynsley Dunbar, Mick Fleetwood, Hughie Flint, Peter Green, Keef Hartley, Dick Heckstall-Smith, Jon Hiseman, John McVie, Mick Taylor. These are all talents which ultimately proved too great for one man to organize and channel. At frequent intervals the watershed has overflowed, the talents coursed away in tributaries until, many times removed from their original source, they have reached the vast sea of their particular public. While Mayall himself remains inland, isolated, accessible only to a few hardy blues pilgrims.

As the title suggests, this is a retrospective album, an historical document rather than a piece of living popular music. It covers a period from April 1964 to December 1967 and demonstrates, with its absence of real musical progression (in the same period, for instance, the Beatles moved from Hard Days Night to Sergeant Pepper) why Mayall has never really made it beyond the record collection of the blues purists, and why so many of those talents found it necessary to split and find their own direction. None of the songs really break new territory. The dominant voice is Mayall's; he explores his own idiom adequately but never attempts to move outside it. This is not to demean Mayall's stature in any way. The musical scene in Britain today owes no man a greater debt than Mayall, but it's sad that the debt will never be paid in the public acclaim the man deserves. Not, that is, while the music remains so insular and the format so rigid.

This then is an album for the pilgrim rather than for the explorers on the frontiers of modern pop. Mayall climbs aboard his train. The train moves off. The rails stretch out ahead, a straight line to the horizon. Occasionally the train makes a halt and passengers alight. They're bored with the journey and this is where they change. New passengers board. The train starts up again. Mayall has to ride it through. He watches the horizon but it never gets any closer.

Graham Charnock

BRAVE NEW WORLD. Steve Miller. Capitol EST 184

Not this time Steve, you didn't try hard enough. You're still beautiful and we luv ya, but you're walking through one track too many, just flashing your credentials. Unfortunately we've got too tough to take the gravy without the potatoes. You taught us to be tough with SAILOR. A battalion of Nicky Hopkins may have helped but then it wouldn't be Stevie Guitar Miller.

I like the cover, it's been out for months in the States you know. Ah yes, that's Steve, all the stuff ... lovely vocals with the drums. Sha la la la la la nice ... a bit of rock and roll, drums good but a bit flashy ... ordinary blues, unnecessary, what's next ... lovely opening lovely, dropping off his consonants like Jagger, and there's Nicky, beaut ... not bad sounds on that side, yeah turn it over for me will you ... some pretty Miller, a celeste or something in the background, yeah it's alright, but playing around a little, maybe the next one will have the right vibes ... God, this is ordinary too a touch of Sailor and Get Back, in fact that's the second bit like Get Back ... bottleneck, sort of early Stones, these parallels are off putting when you notice them, it's poor and there's only one more track ... good good, beautiful bending of guitar strings, nice shuffling beat like Traffic or the band, it's turning heavy, heavier, but it's better than the previous track, the end piece is like the end of side one on Abbey Road which is like the House of the Rising Sun. Well I dunno, it's good but doesn't grab you like Sailor.

It's awfully well produced, thank you Steve and Glyn Johns. The sordid stereo crossovers are delightfully absent. It's a shame you can't produce a one-sided record, then we could salvage a side comparable to Sailor. Not enough of the usual strong tunes, letting the arrangements do too much.

I like it, but, nag, nag, it isn't good enough. You can't save us from drowning and leave us on an island with just a sob, sob, memory of yourself.

Some of it's good to dance to.

T. R. ZELINKA

30
OR THE DECLINE AND FALL OF THE

THE BEATLES Come Together

On initial hearing I thought that the isolated life led by The Beatles had at last begun to show in their work: that they lacked new experience and stimulus and consequently had few new musical or lyrical ideas. Paul at home with Linda and Mary watching the box; John and Yoko watching *Top Of The Pops* on telly in the back of their white Rolls with black glass as it cruises down Saville Row on its way to Ascot; Ringo the happy family man and George strangely upset by his bust, uncertain about his friends but singing *Hare Krishna*. But the more you play *Abbey Road* the better it becomes, this is often the case with Beatles material but this time its more so. The same with their musical activity: To many people very little has happened since *Sgt Pepper*: *Magical Mystery Tour* wasn't is issued as an album here and *The Beatles* seemed disjointed and patchy – but *Sgt Pepper* was a long time ago and in fact SGT PEPPER is DEAD! The Beatles, however, are not and have been doing a stack of things.

John and Yoko released "Two Virgins" (Sapcor 2); "Life With The Lions" (Zapple 01) and formed The Plastic Ono Band, recording "Give Peace A Chance" (Apple 13) in a hotel room in Montreal. John joined with Paul to record "The Ballad Of John and Yoko" (EMI R 5786) without the others.

Paul's working on another album with Mary Hopkin after producing "Postcard" (Sapcor 5) but he's not all in the smaltz bag, if you get out the new Steve Miller Band album "Brave New World" and play the last track "My Dark Hour" you'll hear him very smooth on bass and so tight on drums the sound almost goes up its own ass. He is credited under his nostalgic 1950's Mister Teezi-Weezi style name *Paul Ramon*. Needless to say its the best track on the album.

George has been hard at it with "Wonderwall" (Sapcor 1) and "Electronic Sound" (Zapple 02) and in production he did Jackie Lomax's "Is This What You Want" which he also plays on, along with Paul and Ringo and the more recent Billy Preston album "That's The Way God Planned It" (Sapcor 9). He produced and plays bass on "Hare Krishna Mantra" and is revealed to be *L'Angelo Misterioso* playing rhythm guitar on "The Badge" which he also co-wrote. This little recondite cut is found on "Goodbye Cream" (Atco SD 7002) and is very pretty.

Ringo's been into films and has been recording plans which I'm told I can't reveal, but he has been getting interested in country and Western music of late – check out his tracks on *The Beatles* and *Abbey Road*.

They made the "Get Back" film and album (now scheduled for January release) but got so fed up with it that they couldn't finish it. Some of the numbers: "Maxwell's Silver Hammer", "Oh Darling!" and "She Came In Through The Bathroom Window" were taken from the Twickenham sound track and re-recorded for the "Abbey Road" album. I heard an early take of "She Came In Through The Bathroom Window" back in May. It was on reel 97 of the Nagra recordings of "Get Back". The amount of Beatle material is staggering, if they ever

issue a variorum edition of out-takes such as the one done with Charlie Parker material, it will take up several hundred albums. The Beatles have moved on again: from the fab four moptops to psychedelia and musical complexity and now a paring down to a more simple music, not a return but a progression.

ABBEY ROAD:

The sleeve photographs by Iain Macmillan, who did their first album sleeve, represent this album perfectly. The picture shows the Beatles happily back at the EMI Abbey Road studios, after a brief flirtation with Kingsway and Trident studios they've gone home to where "Rubber Soul" and "Sgt Pepper" were made on old 4-track equipment. Now EMI has 8 tracks and The Beatles usual engineer, one of the world's best, Geoff Emerick is there and so is (Big) George Martin and all . . . Its like a British *Carry On* film, Abbey Road itself with gentile trees and late Victorian mansions, the studios Battle of Britain modern. All under a blue sky.

Its good British Rock, The Beatles at their worst being better than anything that ever came out of San Francisco and this being much better than that. They combine East Coast Rock with British Umpah music. They reach undreamt, of highs and a few lows but not many and they're still good. You can even dance to it like you did when Beatle-jackets were all the rage (remember them?). I imagine you have this album by now so we won't describe each track, just some of them . . .

The album opens with John's rocker "Come Together". The title is the slogan of Tim Leary's campaign but as John says: "Obviously this isn't a good campaign song, so I'll write him another one. This one just turned out to be a funky bit of rock!" Its simple and good and may be the backside of "Something" when its issued in The States as a single, so John can listen to it without having to hear the whole album. "Something" is by George. It represents the full maturity of George as a song writer (no-matter what Tony Palmer says). Its a pretty song and will last a long time, its also not underground (fortunately, as most underground music sucks). Paul includes "Maxwell's Silver Hammer", a complex little piece, locked firmly into his particular style and often with references (both musical and lyrical) to previous 'hits'. The references to 'pataphysics concerns Alfred Jarry's science of the exceptional. Paul's interest dates back three or four years but he isn't a member. The only British pop group holding any pataphysical honours are The Soft Machine who hold the *Ordre de la grande Gidouille*. This track is a perfect example of Paul's combination of American Rock with British brass band music (he produced The Black Dyke Mills Band if you remember). Ringo's track "Octopus's Garden" shares the same brass band influences, this time combining them with country and with Beatle high harmony backings. Look out for these as they are absolutely perfect! The two heavy numbers on side one are "Oh Darling" and "I Want You" which show the Beatles can do it better than everyone else and that they like it; so do I and I'm sure that you will as

well! "I Want You" in fact shows up most heavy blues albums as a pile of shit as nothing could be heavier and yet they don't resort to distortion and feedback, in fact they include some really subtle and delicate passages . . .

Side two *Abbey Road* consists largely of the medley Paul assembled but includes fragments of mid-period Lennon Rock like "Mean Mister Mustard" and "Polythene Pam", the latter of which has lovely English lyrics, "She's the kind of Girl that makes the News Of The World" etc . . . The whole side is an exercise in harmony, colour and texture ("Because" and "The Sun King"), very complex in tone and mood change, meaningless words throughout most as the language of music and musical images are what counts on this album (and on future ones). Some pieces are extrovert *'Beatlemusic'* such as "The End" but others are very personal such as Paul's "You Never Give Me Your Money" which is surely dedicated to Allen Klein . . . "You just give me your funny papers". The Beatles are evolving a whole new musical language again, the words don't matter, they arrive from here and there, often from schooldays: "1234567, all good children go to heaven" or the traditional words to "Golden Slumbers" which are sung (with a very different tune) in junior school. The music with these two pieces is some of the most beautiful on record, particularly behind the "1234 . . ." section where the mixing is done with extreme care and sensitivity.

Throughout the side there are flashbacks to previous tracks, "You Never Give me Your Money" and also references to previous Beatle records "Monday's On The Phone To Tuesday . . ." The Beatles are wrapping it up, progressing to a new simplicity (lyrically) but a new complexity (musically) and between them creating a new high in British pop: "You Never Give Me . . ." is more complex in its editing (actual tape splicing and overlay) than anything on "Sgt Pepper". It makes me happy because when The Stones brought out "Honky Tonk Women" I thought that we only had two top groups anymore (Stones and Who) now the Beatles have soared ahead again and its very nice!

Things have changed: John and Paul haven't written together for two years and the musical identity of each member of the group is becoming more and more obvious in the group albums. I asked John about some of these points:

ON WRITING:
John: We haven't written together for two years except to help if someone needs a line or two.
Miles: *Has this effected your playing together?*
John: It doesn't make any odds who writes 'em. Its when The Beatles perform that makes it into Beatle music. Its a long time since we've sat down and written together for many reasons. We used to write together mainly on tour and then there's a valid reason for it, but it got false: sort of, "Come round to our house and we'll write some songs" you know, just didn't work anymore.

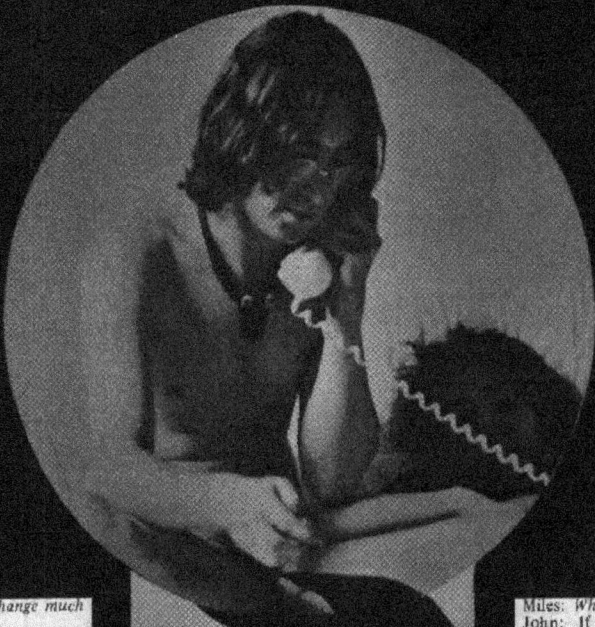

Miles: *Do you find the songs change much when you record them?*

John: Oh Yeah. I mean they can change completely unless you've got a specific idea of exactly how you want the song to go. The whole thing can change completely at the session, just a speed change can alter it. "Come Together" changed at the session: you know you sort of do it the way you wrote it, embarrassedly, because you know that that isn't the answer. Then we thought: "Let's slow it down, lets do this to it, lets do that to it . . . " and it ends up however it comes out.

Miles: *So you still go to a studio without much idea of how it will finally sound?*

John: Yeah . . . you have a . . . like for "Come Together" I just said to 'em, "Look I've got no arrangements for you, but you know how I want it!, you know: mmmmmmmm, yeahhhhhh, and like that" and they play like that. I think that's partly because we've played together a long time so I can say, "Give me this. Give me something funky" and I set a beat maybe and they all just join in.

Whoever sings a Beatles song is the one who wrote it. If they all sing as on "Octopus's Garden" where the lead voice is Ringo and the rest provide harmony then Ringo wrote it and they helped with the arrangements. There is, however, the unifying factor which seems to be a mysterious quality known as *Beatlemusic*.

BEATLEMUSIC:

Miles: *You all seem to play in different areas on this album, there's a very wide range of music.*

John: Well . . . I do what I like and Paul does what he likes and George etc . . . we just divide the album time up between ourselves. Its more apparant on the double album, but its always been that really. The combination music is what we call pure Beatles, maybe like "Its Getting Better" and things like that, where we've all written it and we've all turned it into sort of pure Beatle.

Miles: *The number of new things you've been doing don't seem to have given rise to many new subjects for songs.*

John: Well, what's there to sing about? On the album I sing about Mean Mister Mustard and Polythene Pam, but those are unfinished bits of crap I wrote in India. When I get down to it I'm only interested in Yoko and Peace so if I can sing about them again and again, its only like I'm going through my blue period as a painter. That he's going to paint this cup for a year, go into it, get into that cup. Maybe I'm doing that, and I'll do that till I get tired. I can always write "Mr. Kite" any time of day and those songs . . . But when I get down to it I like funky music. I like Rock or Blues or whatever you call it, so what I say is in that given area. On '24 Hours' they sardonically read "I Want You" lyrics "I Want You. She's So Heavy" that's all it says, you know, but to me thats a damn sight better than "Walrus" or "Eleanor Rigby" lyricwise because its progression to me. If I want to write songs with no words or one word, then maybe that's Yoko's influence. But when it gets down to it, Bop-Bop-a-lula Ba-lrn-bam-bam's great!— That's what I'm getting round to. I remember in the early meetings with Dylan. Dylan was always saying "Listen to the words, man," and I'd say, "I can't be bothered." I listen to the sound of it, the sound of the overall thing. Then I reversed that and started to be a words man. I naturally play with words anyway. I made a conscious effort to be wordy a-la-Dylan or whatever it is. Now I've relieved myself of that burden and I'm only interested in pure sound.

Miles: *What's your concept of pure Beatle?*

John: If I want to sound like "Come Together" and "I Want You" all the time, which I do, always did. You know, "Dizzie Miss Lizzie", whatever it is, I wanted to be THAT GUY. And Paul wanted to be whoever it is he wants to be . . . whenever we all combine and do it, that's what we term Beatle music.

Miles: *You no longer have a group direction?*

John: But we never did! It was just whoever was pushing the limits of the bag at the time. I mean, we often all pushed at the same point, but it was never "This is the way we're going!" As far as we're concerned this album is more Beatley than the Beatles double album, because that was just us saying "This is my song and we do it this way, and this is your song and do it that way."

Miles: *How do you conceive of an album? Do you have a great backlog of material to release?*

John: We've got a lot of songs. The three of us write the most of it. Trying to fit the three guys' music onto one album, its pretty hard, thats why we did a double album, we have so much stuff. But its hard to bring out double albums all the time, it takes us a long time, so we'll probably outlet them on other things like Plastic Ono. We'll split 'em off like that because its like being constipated with all the material. We don't have conceptions of albums. I think Paul has conceptions of albums or attempts it. Like he conceived the medley thing. I'm not interested in conceptions of albums or making it into a show. I like it to be whatever happens. For me I'd just put fourteen Rock songs on.

MILES

SMALLS

OZ SMALL ADS — New Rates. 1/6 per word. 7/6 Box Number Send copy to OZ SMALLS, 52 Princedale Rd. London W.11.

GREEN STAMPS FOR RELEASE
Honestly. Release, which needs a fair amount of money to keep in proper working order, can, as a social help organization, get back 12s. instead of 8s. per book of stamps. They can also make use of British picture stamps and foreign stamps, and hope soon to get extra money in Pink stamps and cigarettes coupons. Send stamps, or any other help to: RELEASE, 50a Princedale Road, W.11.

LONELY! JOIN THE PATRA CORRESPONDENCE CLUB.
Friendly, private and confidential. Share your hobbies, find new friends, both sexes, all ages, world wild. Send stamp for details to Mrs P. Gill, 66 Laburnum Road, Redcar, Teeside, England.

KEEP IN TOUCH
Letters held or forwarded, telephone answering service. Full Details 01-788 5570.

33⅓% DISCOUNT PROTECTIVES.
Durex Featherlite   13/4d. doz.
Durex Nuform   13/4d. doz.
Durex Gossamer   10/- doz.
Only from: DIRECT DISCOUNT SALES. BOX NO. 24 1)

FLEET STREET PRODUCERS REQUIRE YOUNG GOOD LOOKING GIRLS WITH VERY GOOD FIGURES FOR GLAMOUR, NUDE, SEMI-NUDE, BIKINI ETC. MODELLING. WORLD WIDE MAGAZINE, NEWSPAPER, ADVERTISING AND THE OFF FILM PROMOTION. PAYMENT FROM 5 TO 15 gns DAILY ACCDG TO AMOUNT OF WORKING HOURS. ON ACCEPTANCE COMPOSITE FREE OF CHARGE. ALL WORK ACCDG TO EXISTING LAWS. PHONE BETWEEN 10.30 a.m. AND 5 p.m. 583-0912.

'CONFIDENTIAL' B/W.
Developing printing service. Send sample negative. Lists. S.A.E. Prince, 94 Ewhurst Road, London, S.E.4.

DAYS PERSONAL MONTHLY ADVERTISER for the swinging permissive society and the sexually aware. Over 100 personal ads. Send 2/6 to: MAGAZINE, 5 Country Road, Staffs,

WORLD CALL! Swedish liberty in sex. Send 10/- (no postal Order) or, $1 for rich illustrated brochures of magazines and photos. Write to:- HERMES — OZ Box 6001, S-20011, Malmo 6, Sweden.

Bird Fanciers, Physique Fanciers Photos to please. Let us know and we will show S.A.E. for details. Box No. 24 (2).

Talented, uninhibited attractive singers and dancers for West End musical. Tel: 493-1464.

Practical and positive help is now available to men with sexual defects or deficiencies. S.A.E. for free details. Box No. 24 (5).

The BIG—EAR device hears through walls, ceilings, across the street. Easily made. Instructions 10/-. Also for See Through from Behind Mirror 10/-. Latest edition United Kingdom Homosexual Meeting Place Directory. Box No. 24 (6).

FORUM

Contraception
VD
Drugs
Homosexuality
Abortion
Erotica & Pornography
Masturbation
Nudism
Yoga
Corporal Punishment
Prostitution
Racism & Sex
These are some of the topics dealt with in FORUM MAGAZINE.
No other periodical in the world gives a more forthright and comprehensive coverage of the ever changing panorama of socio-sexual behaviour.
NEWSAGENTS PRICE — 7/6 per copy. Save 30/- by Subscribing — £3 for one year (12 issues).
FORUM, Dept. U, 2, Bramber Road, London, W.14. Send 7/6 for sample copy.

GAY YOUNG MEN WITH STYLE & POSE & LACK OF CLOTHES
16 SUPERB, BRAND NEW PHOTOS OF GAY YOUNG MEN. This frank, startling & intimate set of 16, exciting, different & new photographs is yours for only 25/- or a sample set of 8 for only 16/- Sent by 5d post in plain sealed envelope with 7 DAY REFUND GUARANTEE.
Send cheque, P.O. or Giro. ORDER NOW from:
Studio 16, Dept Z, 52, Earls Court Rd., London, W.8.

PUSSYCATS — A BRAND NEW SET OF FIVE SUPERB FEMALE PHOTOS IN INTERESTING POSES — YOURS FOR ONLY 10/-.
'LES-BITCHES' — A SET OF FIVE SUPERB FEMALE PHOTOS FOR ADULTS – ONLY 10/-
'DANDY JIM' — A SET OF THREE SUPERB MALE PHOTOS FOR ADULTS – ONLY 7/-.
SPECIAL OFFER – PUSSYCATS AND LES-BITCHES FOR ONLY 16/- OR ALL THREE SETS FOR £1. ALL SENT WITH A SEVEN DAY REFUND GUARANTEE BY 5d POST IN A PLAIN ENVELOPE. SEND CHEQUE OR P O ORDER NOW FROM.... MANNERS ART, Department ZO, 38 CRAWFORD ST, LONDON W1.

PORNO SWEDEN
Yes, you still have to send to Sweden for your Porno. For £1. we will send you our Glossy samples. Richly coloured catalogues on Films, Colour-Slides, Photos, Magazines and Books. We accept I.R.C.s International Reply coupons which you can buy at any Post Office. Cash Postal Orders and cheques are also acceptable, but leave all payee columns blank. MAYFAIR DESIGN, BOX 9077, 12109 JOHANNESHOV 9, SWEDEN.

IRON

GAY MEN
are invited to send £3 for our new Magazine IRON BOYS. This uncensored Magazine from Sweden shows scenes never published before, covering every angle of love. Should you desire catalogues only, then send £1. Delivery by registered Air Mail from a country with a reputation to protect. International Reply coupons IRPs available from all Post offices do not contravene the currency regulations. We also accept cash, Cheques and Postal Orders with payee column left bland.
SEND NOW TO: H. Gerens Esq., Box 523, ALVSJO, SWEDEN.

BOYS

EIGHT FIRST CLASS PHOTOS OF YOUNG MEN AT PLAY, and in a relaxed, 'informal' mood for only 16/- or a sample of 4 for 10/-.
FIVE SUPERB FEMALE MODELS in 'interesting' poses for only 10/- or 8m and 5f photos at a reduced price of only 22/-
ALL THESE PHOTOS WILL COME UP TO YOUR EXPECTATIONS, OR YOUR MONEY REFUNDED, sent by first class post in plain sealed envelope. Cheque or P O to: G B PUBLICATIONS, DEPARTMENT
ZO, 1. Sherwood St., London, W.1.
Sorry no lists.

INTERZONE A VILLAGE VOICE
News — Poetry — Articles — Reviews.
Works by   Roger Mcgough
                Glen Sweeney
                Dave Tomlin and others.
Out now at 1/- from London Bookstalls or from Gart Butler, 50a Princedale Road, London W.11. Add 6d Postage and Packing. Other enquiries 01-229 7753.

STUDIES OF THE YOUNG MALE
Artistic lighting & studio photography. Unretouched frontal nudes. Relaxed, natural poses. Don't hesitate — these sets of 5 photos are superb at 20/- for postcard size and 30/- for large 8" × 5". Don Busby, 103A, Friern Barnet Road, New Southgate, London, N.11.

I have a massage cream. Would like female to rub it in. Preferable if you have flat. Write to:
C. Giles, 32, Dale Gardens, Woodford Green, Essex.

WORLDWIDE PEN PALS. Illustrated brochure free. Hermes, Berlin 11, Box 17/29, Germany.

Meet Sexy Birds, Gay Men, Kinky Couples, through a monthly magazine. Nationwide Contacts. Send 10/-. Lewis. G.P.O. Box 16, Blackpool, Lancs. FY1 5RD.

Attractive chicks who like swing along in Italy and France for the next months write with photo to:
Alfred C. Rive, Photo Studio, Via Odeschalchi, 30, Como, Italy.

AX LE TRANSPORT ORGANISATION
Axle has no agro-free service, for all types of scenes:- 15 seater buses, goods vehicle cars, trailers, road managers and drivers. (Breakdown towing a speciality). Can we provoke YOU into using us.
5B, Turners Hill, Cheshunt, Herts. Phone: 97/31046.

TENSION RELIEVED — portable, battery operated vibrator Scientifically designed for either sex, massages any part of the body. Send £3. 3s. 0d. to CASANOVA ASSOCIATES, 5 Gerrard Street, London, W.1.

MOBILE DISCOTHEQUE: parties, any music. Phone CUN 3414.

TATTOO PHOTOS S.A.E. LIST 5/- SAMPLES BILL SKUSE TATTOO ARTIST 15 HIGH STREET, ALDERSHOT HANTS.

Gay Guys Rendezvous Guide 10/-, Gay Paperback 10/-. John: BM/FBGH, W.C.1.

THE KEYS (incorporating "Offbeat" and "Meeting Point"). We proudly present, under one fantastic cover: the latest and greatest adult advertiser on the market today. Full of GENUINE personal ads to suite all tastes. Send 5/- for your introductory copy now. Strictly adults only. P. Bayley Ent., 12, Eccles New Road, Salfords, Lancs.

R.P.I. — sexually-compatible partnerships. Bisexual trios £1. Heterosexual or homosexual duos 30/-. Complete discretion. No lists. Every introduction discretion. OZ 3, 23 Arcadian Gardens, London N.22.

Just arrived in London, Colin. Model seeks engagements photographic. Box No. 24 (3).

Young men will pose for fashion or nude photography will travel anywhere. Anything considered. Very genuine Box No. 24 (4).

34

The People

No. 4577   Sunday, September 7, 1969   7d.   ★ L

AND TIME TO GIVE A WARNING TO EVERY PARENT...

Can YOUR kid buy this?

YOUR KID may pick up a magazine in a discotheque or record shop.

It will look way-out, switched-on and hippy.

And it will contain precise details of sexual practices that make Fanny Hill seem as depraved as Goldilocks.

It is in such journals that advertisements of the three-in-a-bed type appear.

That's the sort of literary freedom that the proprietors of the so-called "underground" magazines, Oz and It, are getting.

Now another hippy journal, called SUCK, is about to be launched. Available under plain cover from Amsterdam. Just what it will contain is not certain.

Bearded Jim Haynes, who runs London's hippy centre, the Arts Lab in Drury Lane, where the magazine will be sold, said: "If you think that pictures of people making love is pornography you're wrong. Pictures of bombs dropping on people is pornography. Love is beautiful."

It is. But not the way Oz and It portray it. I hope that the new journal does not follow their example.

Filth can be swept under the carpet, out of sight. But then nobody bothers to get rid of it.

So, for the benefit of square old parents, I will reveal something of the contents of these journals, distributed all over the country from boutiques, discotheques, record bars, and a few newsagents.

Issue Number 19 of Oz (price 3s.), for example, contains a purported interview with a "groupie"—a girl who hangs around pop groups, offering herself to them. "All the men who get inside me are stars," she boasts.

Evocative reading for your pop-fan daughter....

Lady Chatterley's four-letter words are sprinkled happily about the pages—Oz never keeps its printers very long because they are afraid of prosecution.

Some issues have contained an "advice column" in which a Doctor Schoenfeld, of California, gives advice on grotesque sexual problems.

One reader (presumably female) asks about the physical effects of having four men in one afternoon. And adds (understandably): "And what are the signs of nymphomania?"

But another correspondent is not so comical. He describes in detail a horrific amateur surgical experiment to heighten sexual pleasure and asks: "Is it dangerous?"

LEFT: The kind of advertisement that Oz has ... "increase your pleasure."

RIGHT: The kind of front page that Oz has ... a kinky embrace.

The kind of editor that Oz has ... Mr. Richard Neville.

"Yes," says the doctor. But how many youngsters will experiment just the same?

Perhaps more dangerous still is an article on how to take the drug L.S.D., or acid as the hippies know it.

For that, more than any reason, this sort of stuff should not be freely distributed around the country.

A page headed "John Willcock's Other Scenes" reports the sexual revolution and declares that "high school chicks" these days are having sexual intercourse (they use the four-letter word) when they are 12 years old.

The advertisements set the tone of Oz. One offers a "stimulant personal massager" for £4 (post free).

This instrument, "uniquely shaped to body contours," is said to be "absolutely safe to use on any part of the body."

Another promises a sound and successful method of increasing size and virility.

Richard Neville, proprietor and editor of Oz, estimates they sell about 30,000.

His company, with three directors, has London offices in Princedale Road, Holland Park. "We have approached W. H. Smith three times to distribute Oz," he said, "but each time we have been turned down without a reason given.

"There is, theoretically, a profit being made, but we have a lot of printing difficulties."

Both Oz and It, so far as I can understand them, contain political and social comment in a zany kind of way.

Maybe they are published for ideological reasons.

But there's no ideology in teaching kids to take drugs and mutilate their sex organs, as Oz does.

I implore shop and discotheque owners: Don't help to spread this muck.

"HONEY BUNCH" KAMINSKI, 13 OF L.A.
WHAT A LITTLE YUMMY!

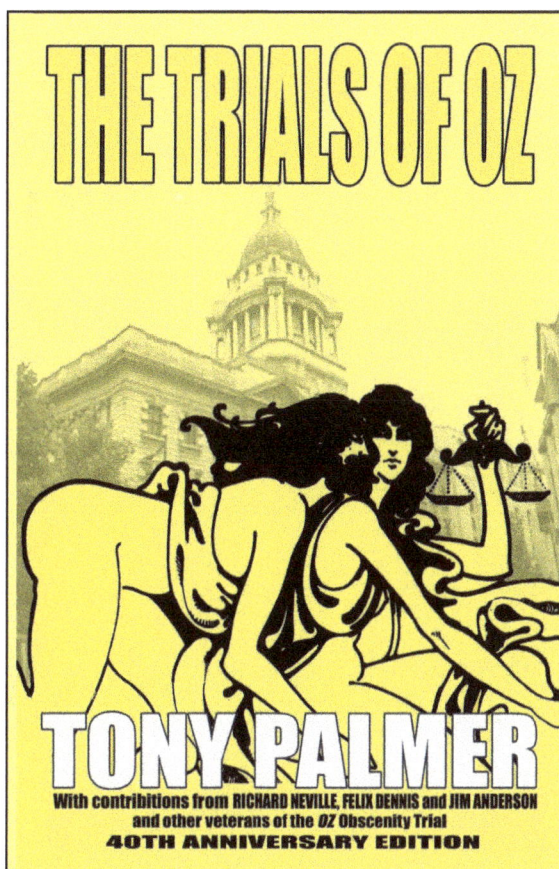

THE TRIALS OF OZ

TONY PALMER

With contributions from RICHARD NEVILLE, FELIX DENNIS and JIM ANDERSON and other veterans of the *OZ* Obscenity Trial

40TH ANNIVERSARY EDITION

The *OZ* trial was the longest obscenity trial in history. It was also one of the worst reported. With minor exceptions, the Press chose to rewrite what had occurred, presumably to fit in with what seemed to them the acceptable prejudices of the times. Perhaps this was inevitable.

The proceedings dragged on for nearly six weeks in the hot summer of 1971 when there were, no doubt, a great many other events more worthy of attention. Against the background of murder in Ulster, for example, the *OZ* affair probably fades into its proper insignificance. Even so, after the trial, when some newspapers realised that maybe something important had happened, it became more and more apparent that what was essential was for anyone who wished to be able to read what had actually been said. Trial and judgment by a badly informed press became the order of the day. This 40th Anniversary edition includes new material by all three of the original defendants, the prosecuting barrister, one of the *OZ* schoolkids, and even the daughters of the judge. There are also many illustrations including unseen material from Felix Dennis' own collection...

ALSO AVAILABLE FROM GONZO MULTIMEDIA

Gonzo
Books

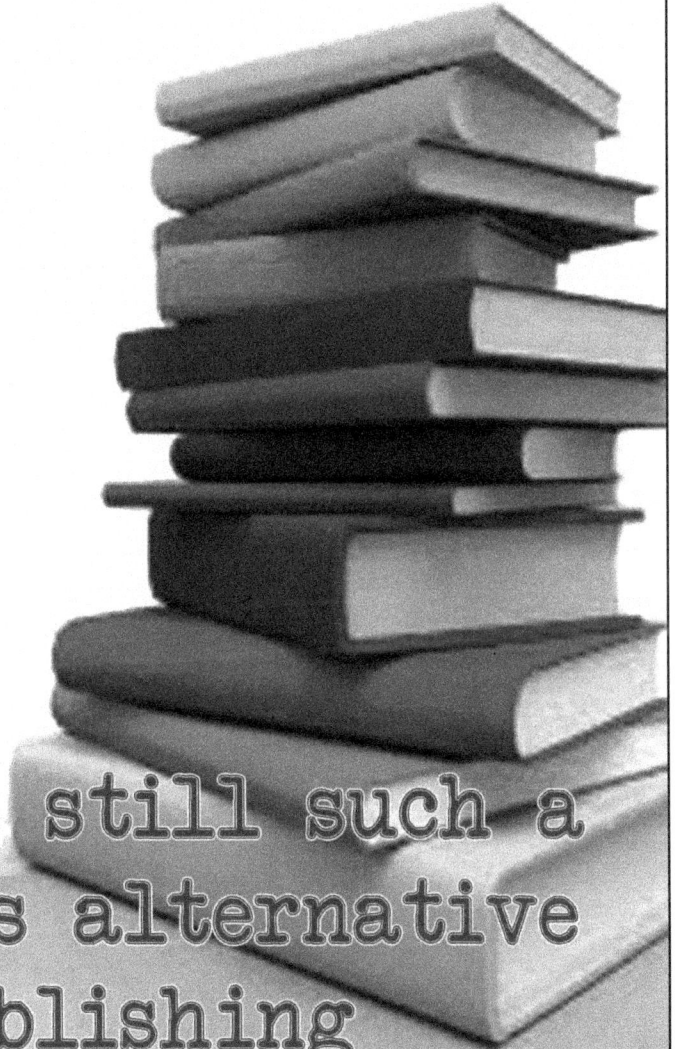

There is still such a
thing as alternative
Publishing

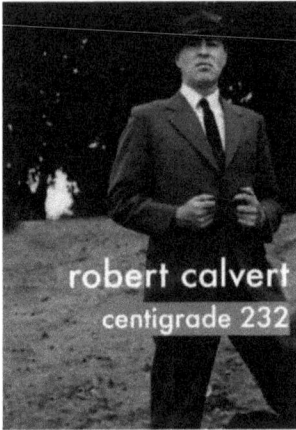

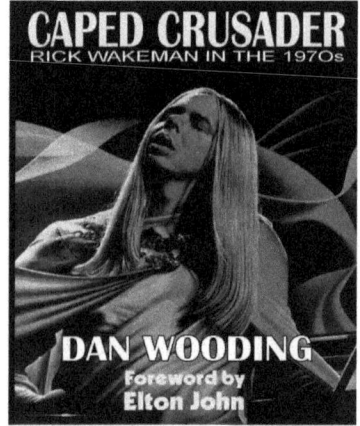

Robert Newton Calvert: Born 9 March 1945, Died 14 August 1988 after suffering a heart attack. Contributed poetry, lyrics and vocals to legendary space rock band Hawkwind intermittently on five of their most critically acclaimed albums, including Space Ritual (1973), Quark, Strangeness & Charm (1977) and Hawklords (1978). He also recorded a number of solo albums in the mid 1970s. CENTIGRADE 232 was Robert Calvert's first collection of poems.

Hype   'And now, for all you speed ing street smarties out there, the one you've all been waiting for, the one that'll pierce your laid back ears, decoke your sinuses, cut clean thru the schlock rock, MOR/crossover, techno flash mind mush. It's the new Number One with a bullet … with a bullet … It's Tom, Supernova, Mahler with a pan galac tic biggie …' And the Hype goes on. And on. Hype, an amphetamine hit of a story by Hawkwind collaborator Robert Calvert. Who's been there and made it back again. The debriefing session starts here.

Rick Wakeman is the world's most unusual rock star, a genius who has pushed back the barriers of electronic rock. He has had some of the world's top orchestras perform his music, has owned eight Rolls Royces at one time, and has broken all the rules of com posing and horrified his tutors at the Royal College of Music. Yet he has delighted his millions of fans. This frank book, authorised by Wakeman himself, tells the moving tale of his larger than life career.

"So many books, so little time."
Frank Zappa

THE NINE HENRYS
By Peter McAdam

TERRY DENE: BRITAIN'S FIRST ROCK & ROLL REBEL

DAN WOODING

King Squealer

MAURICE O'MAHONEY
WITH DAN WOODING

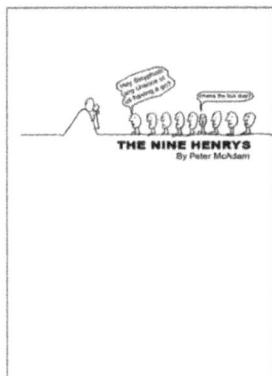

There are nine Henrys, pur
ported to be the world's
first cloned cartoon charac
ter. They live in a strange
lo fi domestic surrealist
world peopled by talking
rock buns and elephants on
wobbly stilts.

They mooch around in their
minimalist universe suffer
ing from an existential
crisis with some genetically
modified humour thrown in.

Marty Wilde on Terry Dene: "Whatever
happened to Terry becomes a great deal
more comprehensible as you read of the
callous way in which he was treated by
people who should have known better
many of whom, frankly, will never know
better of the sad little shadows of
the past who eased themselves into
Terry's life, took everything they
could get and, when it seemed that all
was lost, quietly left him ... Dan Wood
ing's book tells it all."

Rick Wakeman: "There have
always been certain 'careers'
that have fascinated the
public, newspapers, and the
media in general. Such
include musicians, actors,
sportsmen, police, and not
surprisingly, the people who
give the police their employ
ment: The criminal. For the
man in the street, all these
careers have one thing in
common: they are seemingly
beyond both his reach and,
in many cases, understanding
and as such, his only associ
ation can be through the
media of newspapers or tele
vision. The police, however,
will always require the ser
vices of the grass, the
squealer, the snitch, (call
him what you will), in order
to assist in their investiga
tions and arrests; and amaz
ingly, this is the area that
seldom gets written about."

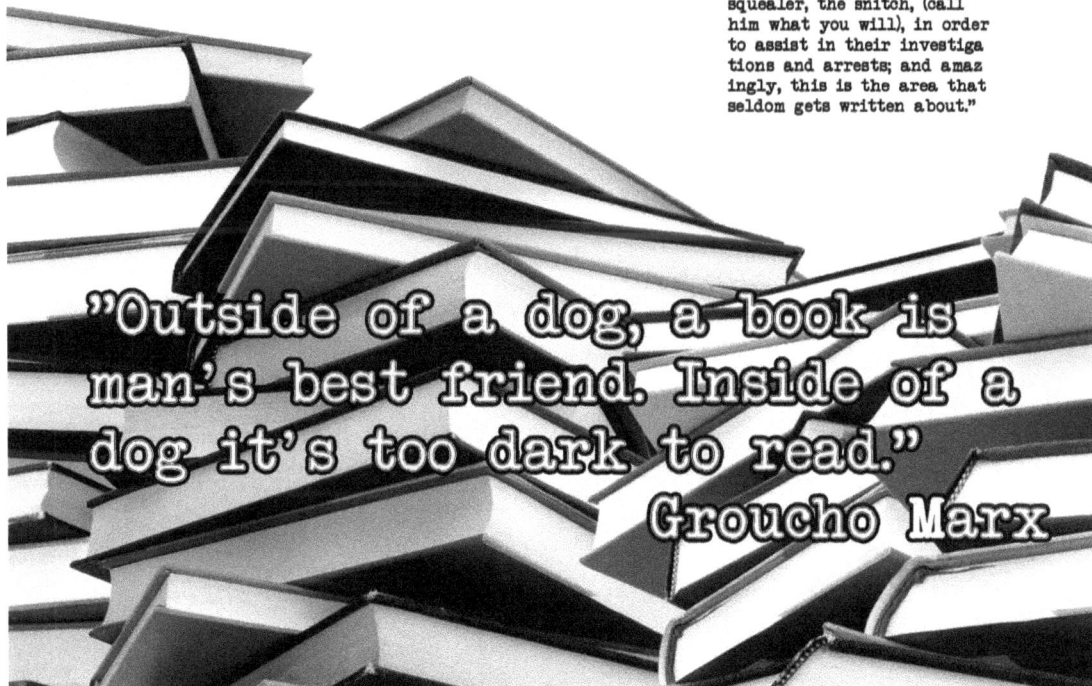

"Outside of a dog, a book is
man's best friend. Inside of a
dog it's too dark to read."
Groucho Marx

LUNAR NOTES
ZOOT HORN ROLLO'S CAPTAIN BEEFHEART EXPERIENCE
BILL HARKLEROAD with BILLY JAMES

THE EMPIRE OF THINGS
SELECTED WRITINGS 2003 - 2013
CJ STONE

The Time of Feasting
mick farren

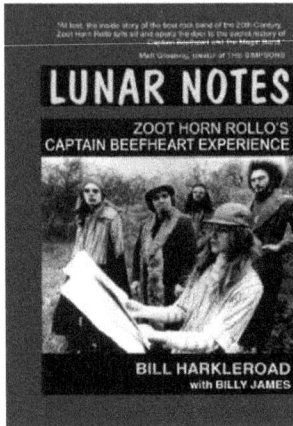

Bill Harkleroad joined Captain Beef heart's Magic Band at a time when they were changing from a straight ahead blues band into something completely dif ferent. Through the vision of Don Van Vliet (Captain Beefheart) they created a new form of music which many at the time considered atonal and difficult, but which over the years has continued to exert a powerful influence. Beefheart re christened Harkleroad as Zoot Horn Rollo, and they embarked on recording one of the classic rock albums of all time Trout Mask Replica - a work of unequalled daring and inventiveness.

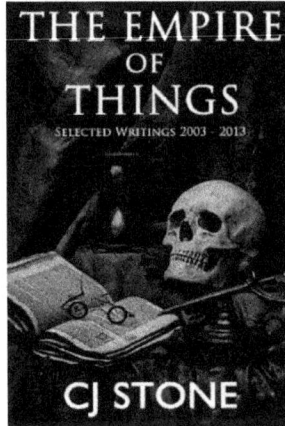

Politics, paganism and …. Vlad the Impaler. Selected stories from CJ Stone from 2003 to the present. Meet Ivor Coles, a British Tommy killed in action in September 1915, lost, and then found again. Visit Mothers Club in Erdington, the best psyche delic music club in the UK in the '60s. Celebrate Robin Hood's Day and find out what a huckle duckle is. Travel to Stonehenge at the Summer Solstice and carouse with the hippies. Find out what a Ranter is, and why CJ Stone thinks that he's one. Take LSD with Dr Lilly, the psychedelic scientist. Meet a headless soldier or the ghost of Elvis Presley in Gabalfa, Cardiff. Journey to Whitstable, to New York, to Malta and to Transylvania, and to many other places, real and imagined, polit ical and spiritual, transcendent and mundane. As The Independent says, Chris is "The best guide to the underground since Charon ferried dead souls across the Styx."

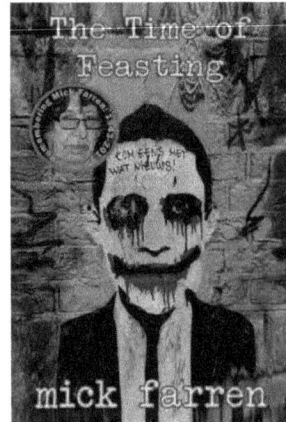

This is is the first in the highly acclaimed vampire novels of the late Mick Farren. Victor Renquist, a surprisingly urbane and likable leader of a colony of vampires which has existed for centuries in New York is faced with both admin istrative and emotional prob lems. And when you are a vampire, administration is not a thing which one takes lightly.

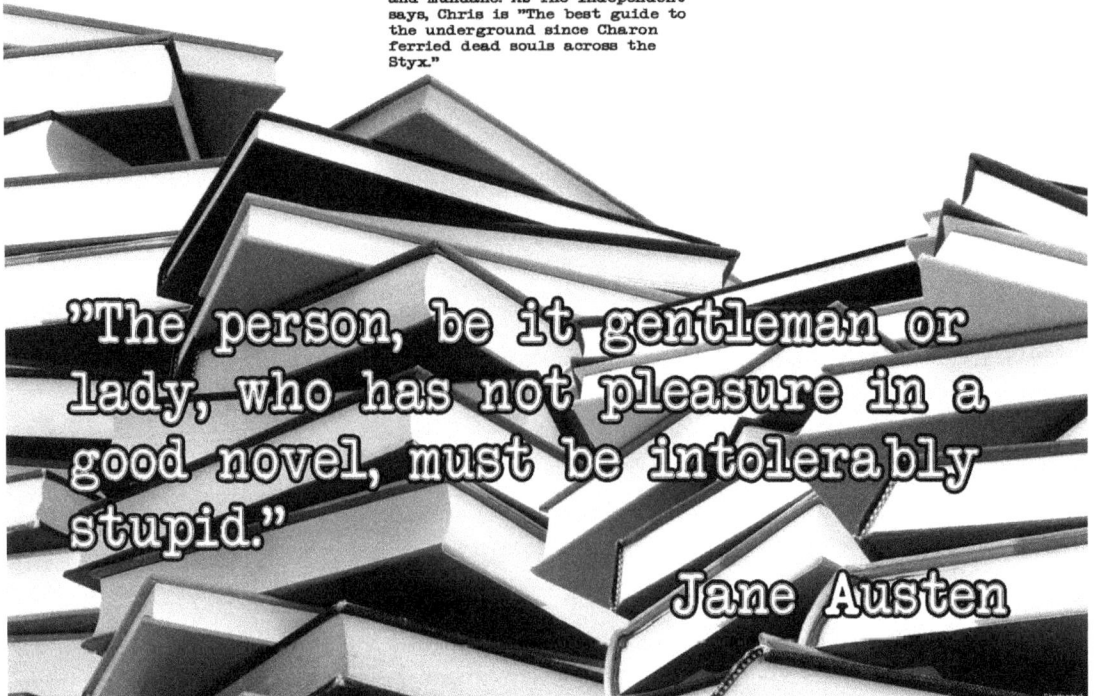

"The person, be it gentleman or lady, who has not pleasure in a good novel, must be intolerably stupid."

Jane Austen

Darklost
mick farren

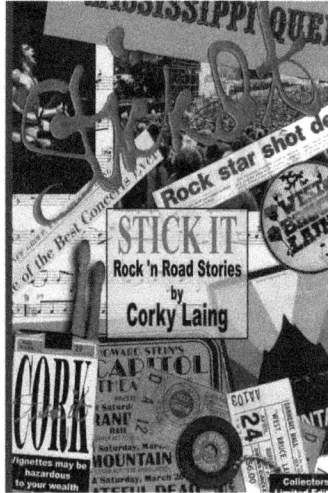

MISSISSIPPI QUE
Rock star shot de
STICK IT
Rock 'n Road Stories
by
Corky Laing

STRANGE BOAT
MIKE SCOTT AND THE WATERBOYS
IAN ABRAHAMS

Los Angeles City of Angels, city of dreams. But sometimes the dreams become nightmares. Having fled New York, Victor Renquist and his small group of Nosferatu are striving to re establish their colony. They have become a deeper, darker part of the city's nightlife. And Hollywood's glitterati are hot on the scent of a new thrill, one that outshines all others immortality. But someone, somewhere, is med dling with even darker powers, powers that even the Nosferatu fear. Someone is attempting to summon the entity of ancient evil known as Cthulhu. And Ren quist must overcome dissent in his own colony, solve the riddle of the Darklost (a being brought part way along the Nosferatu path and then abandoned) and combat powerful enemies to save the world of humans!

Canadian born Corky Laing is probably best known as the drummer with Mountain. Corky joined the band shortly after Mountain played at the famous Woodstock Festival, although he did receive a gold disc for sales of the soundtrack album after over dubbing drums on Ten Years After's performance. Whilst with Mountain Corky Laing recorded three studio albums with them before the band split. Follow ing the split Corky, along with Mountain gui tarist Leslie West, formed a rock three piece with former Cream bassist Jack Bruce. West, Bruce and Laing recorded two studio albums and a live album before West and Laing re formed Mountain, along with Felix Pappalardi. Since 1974 Corky and Leslie have led Mountain through various line ups and recordings, and continue to record and perform today at numer ous concerts across the world. In addition to his work with Mountain, Corky Laing has recorded one solo album and formed the band Cork with former Spin Doctors guitarist Eric Shenkman, and recorded a further two studio albums with the band, which has also featured former Jimi Hendrix bassist Noel Redding. The stories are told in an incredibly frank, engaging and amusing manner, and will appeal also to those people who may not necessarily be fans of

To me there's no difference between Mike Scott and The Waterboys; they both mean the same thing. They mean myself and whoever are my current travel ling musical companions." Mike Scott Strange Boat charts the twisting and meandering journey of Mike Scott, describing the literary and spiritual references that inform his songwriting and explor ing the multitude of locations and cultures in which The Waterboys have assembled and reflected in their recordings. From his early forays into the music scene in Scotland at the end of the 1970s, to his creation of a 'Big Music' that peaked with the hit single 'The Whole of the Moon' and onto the Irish adventure which spawned the classic Fisher man's Blues, his constantly restless creativity has led him through a myriad of changes. With his revolving cast of troubadours at his side, he's created some of the most era defining records of the 1980s, reeled and jigged across the Celtic heartlands, reinvented himself as an electric rocker in New York, and sought out personal renewal in the spiritual calm of Findhorn's Scot tish highland retreat. Mike Scott's life has been a tale of continual musical exploration entwined with an ever evolving spirituality. "An intriguing portrait of a modern musician" (Record Collector)

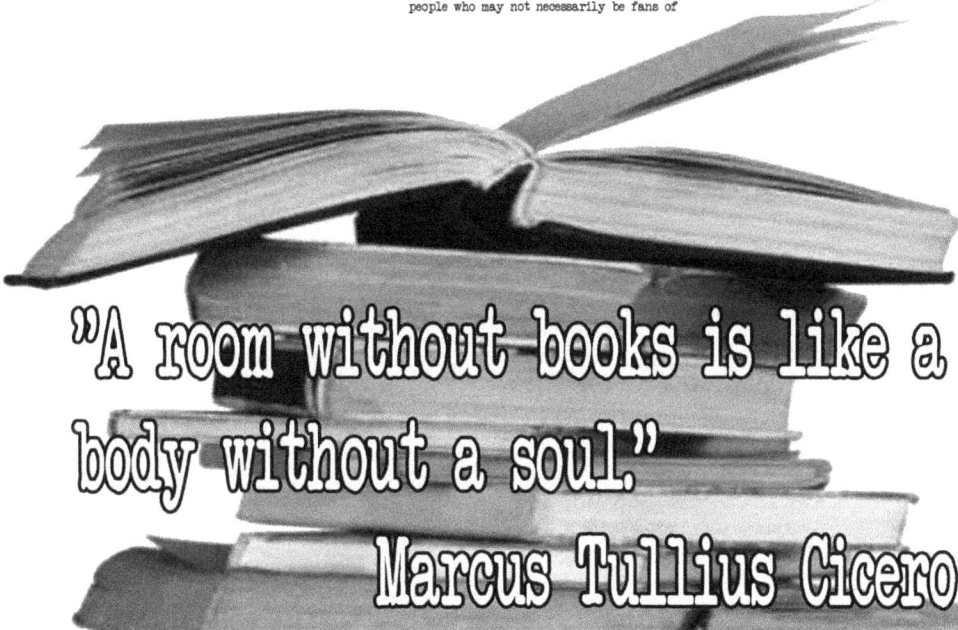

"A room without books is like a body without a soul."
Marcus Tullius Cicero

THE TRIALS OF OZ

TONY PALMER

With contributions from RICHARD NEVILLE, FELIX DENNIS and JIM ANDERSON
and other veterans of the OZ Obscenity Trial

40TH ANNIVERSARY EDITION

CALLING FROM A STAR

THE
Merrell Fankhauser
STORY

THE REAL PORN WARS

EXPLICIT CONTENT

RECORD LABELING
HEARING
COMMITTEE ON COMMERCE,
SCIENCE, AND TRANSPORTATION
UNITED STATES SENATE

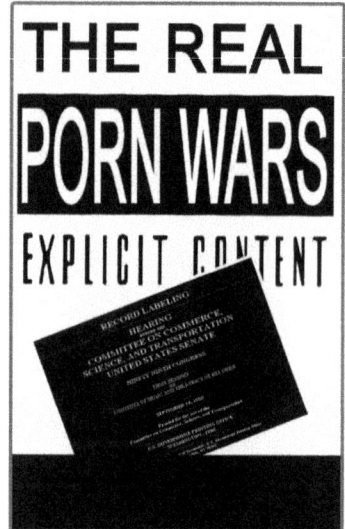

The OZ trial was the longest obscenity trial in history. It was also one of the worst reported. With minor exceptions, the Press chose to rewrite what had occurred, presumably to fit in with what seemed to them the acceptable prejudices of the times. Perhaps this was inevitable. The proceedings dragged on for nearly six weeks in the hot summer of 1971 when there were, no doubt, a great many other events more worthy of attention. Against the background of murder in Ulster, for example, the OZ affair probably fades into its proper insignifi cance. Even so, after the trial, when some newspapers realised that maybe something important had hap pened, it became more and more apparent that what was essential was for anyone who wished to be able to read what had actually been said. Trial and judgment by a badly informed press became the order of the day. This 40th Anniversary edition includes new material by all three of the original defendants, the prosecuting barrister, one of the OZ schoolkids, and even the daughters of the judge. There are also many illustrations including unseen material from Felix Dennis' own collection...

Merrell Fankhauser has led one of the most diverse and interesting careers in music. He was born in Louisville, Kentucky, and moved to California when he was 13 years old. Merrell went on to become one of the innovators of surf music and psychedelic folk rock. His travels from Hollywood to his 15 year jungle experience on the island of Maui have been documented in numerous music books and magazines in the United States and Europe. Merrell has gained legendary international status throughout the field of rock music; his credits include over 250 songs published and released. He is a multi talented singer/songwriter and unique guitar player whose sound has delighted listeners for over 35 years. This extraordi nary book tells a unique story of one of the founding fathers of surf rock, who went on to play in a succession of progressive and psychedelic bands and to meet some of the greatest names in the business, including Captain Beefheart, Randy California, The Beach Boys, Jan and Dean... and there is even a run in with the notorious Manson family.

On September 19, 1985, Frank Zappa testified before the United States Senate Commerce, Technology, and Transportation committee, attacking the Parents Music Resource Center or PMRC, a music organization co founded by Tipper Gore, wife of then senator Al Gore. The PMRC consisted of many wives of politi cians, including the wives of five members of the committee, and was founded to address the issue of song lyrics with sexual or satanic content. Zappa saw their activities as on a path towards censor ship,and called their proposal for voluntary labelling of records with explicit content "extor tion" of the music industry. This is what happened.

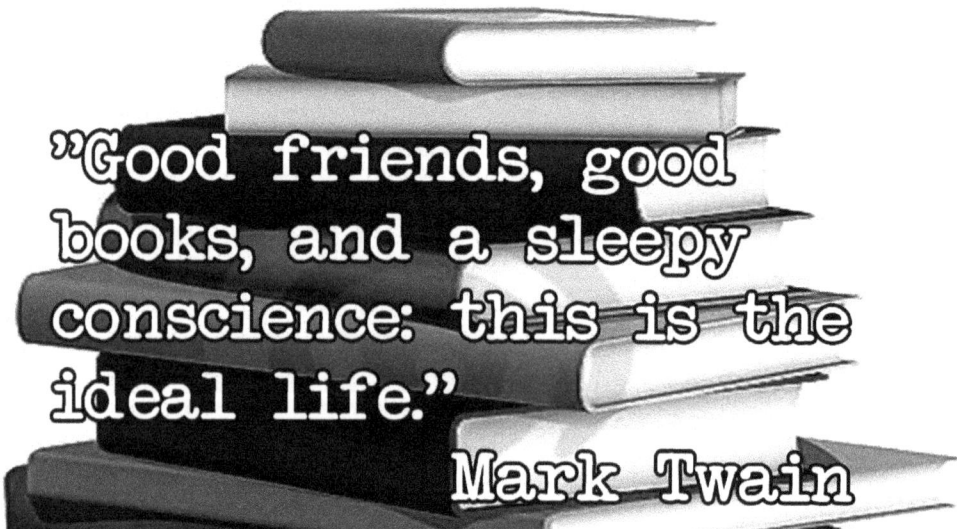

"Good friends, good books, and a sleepy conscience: this is the ideal life."
Mark Twain